Arthur Preuss

New German-American Studies
Neue Deutsch-Amerikanische Studien

Don Heinrich Tolzmann
General Editor

Vol. 16

PETER LANG
New York · Washington, D.C./Baltimore · Boston
Bern · Frankfurt am Main · Berlin · Vienna · Paris

Rory T. Conley

Arthur Preuss

Journalist and Voice of German and Conservative Catholics in America, 1871–1934

PETER LANG
New York · Washington, D.C./Baltimore · Boston
Bern · Frankfurt am Main · Berlin · Vienna · Paris

Library of Congress Cataloging-in-Publication Data

Conley, Rory T.
Arthur Preuss, journalist and voice of German and conservative Catholics
in America, 1871–1934 / Rory T. Conley.
p. cm. — (New German-American studies; vol. 16 =
Neue deutsch-amerikanische Studien)
Includes bibliographical references.
1. Preuss, Arthur, 1871–1934. 2. German-Americans—Biography. 3. Catholics—
United States—Biography. 4. Journalists—United States—Biography.
5. Press, Catholic—United States—History—20th century. I. Title. II. Series:
New German-American studies; vol. 16.
BX4705.P6919C66   282'.092—dc21   [B]   97-48962
ISBN 0-8204-4002-7
ISSN 1043-5808

Die Deutsche Bibliothek-CIP-Einheitsaufnahme

Conley, Rory T.:
Arthur Preuss, journalist and voice of German and conservative catholics
in America, 1871–1934 / Rory T. Conley. –New York; Washington, D.C./Baltimore;
Boston; Bern; Frankfurt am Main; Berlin; Vienna; Paris: Lang.
(New German American studies; Vol. 16)
ISBN 0-8204-4002-7

The paper in this book meets the guidelines for permanence and durability
of the Committee on Production Guidelines for Book Longevity
of the Council of Library Resources.

© 1998 Peter Lang Publishing, Inc., New York

Printed in the United States of America.

To my uncle,
the Reverend Monsignor Raymond J. Conley.
To the Reverend Monsignor Robert O. McMain,
Historian of the Archdiocese of Washington,
And to Brother Randal Reide, C.F.X.,
former Librarian of the North American College,
I owe much more than words of gratitude can convey.

Acknowledgements

The author owes a debt of gratitude to numerous individuals who have made this book possible. To my ordinary, James Cardinal Hickey, Archbishop of Washington, I extend my heartfelt thanks for supporting my pursuit of studies in the field of American Catholic church history. I am indebted to Monsignor Robert Trisco, of the Catholic University of America and editor of the *Catholic Historical Review,* for his careful and patient attention to the draft of this manuscript. Dr. Christopher Kauffman is to be thanked for having first introduced me to Arthur Preuss and his importance in American Catholic history. I also wish to thank the Dr. Michael Warner for his thoughtful suggestions concerning the final form of the text.

Numerous favors were extended to me as I conducted my research on the life of Arthur Preuss. First and foremost I wish to thank Arthur Preuss's children, Alma Preuss Dilschneider, Charles Arthur Preuss, and Austin Preuss, for sharing with me their memories of their father. I wish to thank Cletus Preuss for making available to me photographs of his grandfather and his family. I also wish to thank the Rev. John C. Miller and his staff at the Archives of the Central Bureau of the Catholic Central Union for making Arthur Preuss's correspondence available to me and for granting permission for the reproduction of photographs of Frederick Kenkel and Rev. John Rothensteiner. Several archivists blessed me with their cooperation including the Rev. Victor Kingery, O.F.M., Director of the Library of Quincy College, Quincy, Illinois; the staff of the Archives of the University of Notre Dame; Dr. Timothy J. Meagher and the staff of the Archives of the Catholic University of America who provided me with photographs of Rev. Joseph Pohle and Rev Msgr. Joseph Schroeder; the Rev. Robert Myers, S.V.D., archivist of the Society of the Divine Word Provincialate at Techny, Illinois; the Rev. Vincent Tegeder, O.S.B., archivist of St. John's Abbey, Collegeville, Minnesota; Amy Inskeep for providing a photograph of Patrick H. Callahan and Brother Anthony Marecki, O.S.B., archivist of St. Leo's Abbey in St. Leo, Florida. My thanks is also due to Mrs. Urusla Rhodes and the Rev. Edward Evans for their assistance in translating from the German some of the handwritten letters among Arthur Preuss's correspondence. Finally, I wish to thank Dr. Don Heinrich Tolzmann, General Editor of the New German-American Studies and Dr. Heidi Burns and the staff of Peter Lang Publishing, Inc. for their assistance in preparing the manuscript for publication.

Contents

Preface

American Catholic historians have consistently regarded the decades surrounding the turn of the twentieth century as a pivotal era in the development of the Roman Catholic Church in America. For it was in this period that the Church in the United States experienced an intense internal struggle concerning the "Americanization" of Catholics and the Church's relationship with the modern world. This struggle reached a high point in the Americanist controversy of the late 1890s and appeared to have come to its conclusion following the publication of Pope Leo XIII's brief, *Testem Benevolentiae* in 1899. However, the issues which had brought about "the great crisis in American Catholic history," were not resolved and the controversy over Americanism continued, albeit in more subdued tones.

While their own changing historical contexts have provided recent commentators on this era with new perspectives, the documentation itself seems reasonably complete. However, there is a gap in the record that remains to be filled. To date, very little research into the crisis of Americanism and the decades that followed has concerned itself with the activities of the anti-Americanists, or more properly, the conservative Catholics within the Church in the United States. In fact the very identity of these individuals has been obscured from view. Although any number of reasons could be proposed to explain the rather one-sided treatment the Americanist controversy has received, we have in part been subjected to "victor's history." The wide currency given to the notion that the Americanists were the prophetic forerunners of the Second Vatican Council's reconciliation with modernity has relegated the anti-Americanists to the dustbin of history with similarly unpopular causes.

One of these forgotten conservative Catholics was Arthur Preuss (1871-1934), who, as the lay editor of the *Fortnightly Review*, played an important role in the Americanist crisis. It was Preuss's participation in the controversy surrounding Americanism that established his reputation and it is what he is primarily remembered for today. However, just as the fractious issues of the Americanist controversy continued well beyond the official resolution of the crisis in 1899, so too the influence of Arthur

Preuss on the history of the Church in America extended beyond this date and at least until his death some thirty years later.

This biography is predicated on the belief that American Catholic historians are correct in seeing the era of the Americanist crisis as a sort of prism through which the many "colors" of the Catholic Church's history in this country are displayed in a unique way. The purpose of this study is to assist in the completion of the historiographical "prism of Americanism" so that the full spectrum of views present at that pivotal juncture in American Catholic history, and not just those most commonly regarded as the "brightest," may shed their light on our understanding of our past, our perspective of the present, and our vision of the future.

As a biography of Arthur Preuss, this work chronicles his life, examining both how he was formed by the issues and events of his day and, in turn, how he attempted to shape them. Arthur Preuss is depicted within the context of his age through an analysis of the sources pertinent to his life and times. These sources include forty-one volumes of Preuss's *Fortnightly Review* as well as his numerous editorial contributions to *Die Amerika* and the *Echo*. In addition, some five thousand pieces of Preuss's professional and private correspondence which are extant are studied. These data are compared and contrasted with information available in other sources in order to provide a sketch of the German and conservative Catholic perspective on the controverted issues of the day. Specific issues which are studied include the controversy surrounding German Catholic ethnicity and "Americanization," the foundation of the Catholic University of America, the crisis over "Americanism," the "social question," the German Catholic experience of World War I, the establishment of the National Catholic Welfare Conference, the presidential campaign of 1928, the Great Depression, and the first years of the Roosevelt Administration.

Introduction

In this age of electronic media it is difficult to appreciate just how important the print medium was a hundred years ago. At that time, newspapers and journals had an influence on society analogous to that which television exerts today. There were thousands of papers and magazines being published in America for all types of audiences. One important audience was the German immigrant population. For the German immigrants, newspapers and periodicals in their mother tongue performed an essential task in preserving their cultural heritage while they struggled to accomplish their integration into American society. Among the German-speaking immigrants, the need for these instruments of cultural cohesion was especially pronounced for German-American Catholics. German American Catholics had a communal self-awareness based on a double-edged experience of alienation. The historian Philip Gleason has described the German Catholic predicament in America at the end of the nineteenth century as the experience of becoming "aware of who they were by becoming aware of who they were not."

> ...they were not just Americans, pure and simple, because they differed too much in language, religion and culture from the native American majority to be able to consider themselves Americans without further qualification. [Secondly] ...they could not identify themselves unreservedly with the whole body of German speaking immigrants in the United States, because of differences of religion and weltanschauung.[1]

Great attention has been paid to the alienation German American Catholics experienced vis-à-vis their fellow Catholics and other Americans because of their German identity.[2] American Catholic historians have dutifully recorded the role that the Kulturkampf in Germany, 1871–1887, played in stimulating the emigration of German Catholics to America, noting in particular the number of priests and vowed religious who were forced into exile. However, they have given surprisingly little attention to the experience of German Catholics in Germany prior to their emigration and how that experience formed their world view. Yet, the formative character of the differences in "religion and weltanschauung" between the immigrant German Catholics and non-Catholics, German or otherwise, were rooted in their pre-immigrant experience. In fact, the alienation that German Catholics experienced first in the Fatherland did more to form the consciousness of being an "embattled" minority than did the "immigrant experience" itself.[3]

Historical studies done on the status of German Catholics during the period of German unification and the Kulturkampf disclose that as a group German Catholics had already formed much of their conservative outlook on modern society before reaching America.[4] The perception of being a "harassed" minority struggling to retain their religious identity had been formed among German Catholics by 1850 in conflicts with the Prussian state over parochial schools and other matters. Likewise, the political conservatism of German Catholics in the United States and their hostility toward the developing bureaucratic modern state have their roots in their resistance to the overbearing Prussian government of the mid-nineteenth century. Similarly, the flowering of the religious associations, processions, and other manifestations of "public Catholicism" German Catholics brought with them to America, had begun against the backdrop of cultural conflict with the liberal Protestant and increasingly secular German society in the period from 1850 to 1870. Following the political turmoil throughout Europe in the years 1848–49, Catholic spokesmen regularly made a connection between religious laxity, moral failings, and liberal sympathies. Also, during these decades Catholic leaders in Germany began voicing their criticism of the materialistic tendencies of advancing industrial capitalism.[5]

A critical element in the German Catholic struggle to maintain their religious identity before, during, and after the Kulturkampf was their loyalty to the Holy See. Devotion to the papacy in the person of Pope Pius IX was a powerful stimulus to, and consequence of the revival of Catholicism in Germany in the middle decades of the nineteenth century. Pius IX became a strong symbol of unity among German Catholics, even among those who had misgivings about the Ultramontanist stand for the definition of papal infallibility. The pope was not only a sympathetic leader when the German government lost its credibility as a legitimate authority, but Pius IX, after the fall of the Papal States in 1870, was a fellow sufferer of unjust persecution. The "prisoner of the Vatican" became a "symbol of the struggle between the forces of atheism and subversion and those of order."[6] This German Catholic loyalty to the papacy was only intensified by the persecutions of the Kulturkampf and was a symbol of their identity that they took with them to America. Just as the "liberalism" which inspired the Kulturkampf became the label for all the forces arrayed against the Catholic Church, Ultramontanism was the standard under which was mounted her defense.

Ironically, the supra-national loyalties of German Catholics which led to the Prussian government's decision to launch a severe persecution of the Church, were, much to the dismay of Bismarck, strengthened by the Kulturkampf. The Kulturkampf, by forcing Catholics in Germany to choose between patriotism and their religious convictions, only increased their alienation from the national government and from non-Catholic Germans. The Kulturkampf deepened the animosities between denominations and increased Catholic defensiveness. At the same time, it strengthened the bonds of the German Catholic people, priests, and hierarchy and forced them "to live in the limited circumstances for which history had destined them."[7]

Given the large number of Catholics who emigrated from Germany to America during the Kulturkampf, particularly priests and members of religious orders, it is not surprising that the experience of being pushed into a cultural ghetto would dominate the German Catholic community's outlook on America. For many of them, American society, the offspring of the Enlightenment as was the French Revolution, was a fertile seedbed for the "militant liberalism" that had launched the Kulturkampf in the fatherland. Emigration had distanced German American Catholics from overt, state-sponsored persecution, but the change in venue had not brought an end to the cultural struggle. They were still a despised minority within a hostile larger culture. Thus, the Kulturkampf was not simply an isolated event in German history, but a battle within the larger struggle being waged between orthodox Catholicism and "godless liberalism" which made its way in the world under the banner of modernity. This Kulturkampf, whether waged in Europe or America, was much more important in defining the distinctive *weltanschauung* of German Catholics in America than the vicissitudes of the "immigrant experience." And it was German Catholicism's experience of the Kulturkampf that dominated the contribution of German American Catholics to the life of the Catholic Church in the United States.

German Catholic Kulturkampf in late nineteenth-century America, as in the Fatherland, was sustained by and manifested itself through three social institutions. These were the parish church with its school, various devotional, benevolent, and professional societies, and the German-language press. Although each of these institutions had a vital part in maintaining German Catholic culture, by its nature, the German-language press assumed the most aggressive role.

The Catholic German-language press in America was inaugurated by Father John Martin Henni in 1837 when he established *Der Wahrheitsfreund* in Cincinnati.[8] The Catholic German-language press had an enormous potential audience as some 1.2 million German Catholics emigrated to America between 1840 and 1900.[9] In this time period more than sixty other Catholic German-language publications were established. Although many of them were of brief duration, in 1900 there were still thirty-eight such periodicals being published.[10] The height of the Catholic German-language press's influence was reached in the 1880s and '90s that were also the peak years of German Catholic immigration and the accompanying tensions within the Church over "Americanization." Of the dozens of German Catholic editors at work at this time, ten were still remembered fifty years later as the leading lights of the German Catholic press.[11] Among these men were Rev. Joseph Jessing, who established the *Ohio Waisenfreund* in 1873; Wilhelm Kielmann, editor of the *Tägliche Volksfreund* of Buffalo; Johann Baptist Mueller of *Die Stimme der Wahrheit* of Detroit; Rev. Johann N.

Enzelberger of *Der Herold des Glaubens* of St. Louis; Rev. Anton Heiter, editor of the *Christliche Woche* of Buffalo; Nicholas Gonner, Sr., editor of the *Luxemburger Gazette* of Dubuque; Hugo Klapproth of *Der Wanderer* and Edward Preuss, editor of *Die Amerika* of St. Louis.[12] In addition to these daily and weekly Catholic papers, the German Catholic community in America also prided itself in the monthly journal *Pastoralblatt* of St. Louis, which enjoyed wide popularity among German-speaking priests for over fifty years.[13]

Of all of these accomplished German Catholic editors perhaps the most influential voice of the German American Catholic experience at the turn of the century belonged to Arthur Preuss. Preuss's influence, and his contribution to the history of the Catholic Church in the United States, rested in part on his role as a combatant in the universal Kulturkampf. However, this was a "duty" he shared with a great number of other German-American Catholics. What makes Arthur Preuss stand out as a notable figure in the Catholic Church of this era was that the particular gifts that he brought to "the struggle" were those of a layman who had taken up the apostolate of Catholic journalism. By consciously following in the tradition of independent Catholic journalism as established in France by Louis Veuillot (1813–1883), and in the United States by Orestes Brownson (1803–1876) and James McMaster (1820–1886), Arthur Preuss established himself as a leading figure in the American Catholic Church of his times. Groomed for a career in writing and editing for the German language Catholic press, Preuss transcended the confines of his ethnic background and established one of the most influential English-language Catholic publications in the country.[14] Through his *Fortnightly Review*, and his contributions to other publications, Preuss became not only a representative voice for German-American Catholics, but also for his conservative co-religionists who shared with him the view that life for the Church in the modern world would be an unrelenting Kulturkampf. Preuss's labor in the field of Catholic journalism from 1894 until his death in 1934, is significant in what it discloses regarding the world view of German-American and conservative Catholic elements within the Church in America on the questions of ethnicity, Americanism, social reform, the First World War and on other issues of the day. Arthur Preuss's historical importance is heightened by the fact that while the circulation of his *Fortnightly Review* was never more than about two thousand copies, his readership was composed almost entirely of priests and lay intellectuals. Thus, his journal was written by and for the leaders of the Church in America and reflected their views. The life of Arthur Preuss is also of interest for what it reveals about the vision and experiences of a dedicated layman as he pursued his apostolate in Catholic journalism.

The vision of the world which Arthur Preuss presented in the pages of the *Fortnightly Review* was that of a world, and at times a Church, at war over the meaning of culture, morality and faith itself. It pitted his conservative conception of society against the ever more influential liberal world view of the modern era. As Preuss was a journalist, not a philosopher, he never attempted to present a systematic "plan" for society. Yet, by studying his commentary on the issues of the day Preuss's positive conception of how the world ought to be emerges. Preuss's response to the increasing secularization of society that accompanied the rapid industrialization of America at the turn of the century indicates a longing for a simpler, and, in some ways, idealized past. In defending the Catholic Church against perceived threats Preuss was endeavoring to instill in his fellow Catholics a theocentric or, more specifically, an ecclesiocentric view of life which he regarded as the proper Catholic world view. The Catholic world view that Preuss promoted was, according to him, founded on divine revelation as mediated by the Roman Catholic Church. Preuss's world view placed a high premium on hierarchically structured authority and so, quite naturally, Preuss was an ardent Ultramontanist. He believed that a powerful papacy was essential to preserving the Church's fidelity to its apostolic mission. And just as Pope Pius IX had been the rallying point when the Catholics of Germany were menaced by the Kulturkampf, his successors were to play a similar role in leading the universal Church in the general struggle to preserve an ecclesiocentric Catholic world view.

Preuss's world view in part reflects his deep personal religiosity and conservative temperament. But it also indicates that his thinking had been profoundly influenced by the nineteenth-century romantic movement which was so much a part of his German heritage. For a Catholic romantic like Arthur Preuss, the Church and the family formed the core of community life. Therefore, social developments of the modern era such as rationalism, individualism, the growing power of the state and nationalism, which seemingly undermined allegiance to these institutions, were to be vigorously resisted. Similarly, Preuss also wrote in opposition to the two dominant economic philosophies, capitalism and socialism, as forces that were working against the stability of both the family and the Catholic community.

Readers will have to decide for themselves whether Arthur Preuss's jeremiads concerning the Church and the world of his time were overwrought or genuinely prescient. Whatever judgment they arrive at concerning the significance of the life and work of Arthur Preuss, it will help them to remember that Preuss sincerely believed that as a Catholic journalist, he had received a prophetic vocation. His calling was not that of presenting grand visions of humanity's future but rather that of keeping alive the remembrance of the ways in which God had always kept His promises to His faithful people in the past.

I Beginnings

"My Beloved Saintly Father"

In studying the work of Arthur Preuss one need not look far to discover the greatest influence upon his life. Arthur Preuss was preeminently, and proudly, his father's son. Arthur Preuss's father, Edward Friederick Reinhold Preuss (1834–1904) has been given comparatively little notice in the pages of American Catholic historiography. As he was the editor of the most important German Catholic newspaper in the country, *Amerika*, from 1877 to 1902, when the nationality struggle within the American Church was at its height, his contribution to our history is worthy of notice in itself, without reference to his son.

Edward Preuss was born in 1834 in Königsberg, East Prussia. Raised as a devout Lutheran, he earned a doctoral degree in philosophy from the University of Königsberg in 1853, and a doctoral degree in theology from the University of Berlin four years later. He then spent the next ten years as a tutor at the University of Berlin, numbering among his students some members of the Prussian royal family. He was also well acquainted with some of the most prominent men in Berlin, including Otto von Bismarck and the historians Theodor Mommsen and Leopold von Ranke.[1]

Despite his tremendous intellectual gifts and access to important circles in Berlin, life was not without its cares for the young theologian. At that time orthodox Lutherans were not only engaged in the age-old controversies with Catholics, but the Lutheran community itself was deeply divided theologically. Coming out of the Enlightenment period, liberal and rationalistic theology had divided the evangelical churches between those who held fast to the authoritative character of Scripture, and those who embraced the new rationalism which effectively denied the reality of divine revelation. In the midst of this tension, as he would later write, Edward Preuss believed that "the conversion of liberal Protestants to the genuine and original Lutheranism could be brought about solely by a thorough-going renewal of the literary fight with Rome."[2] Edward Preuss's point of attack on the Catholic Church would be the recently proclaimed dogma of the Immaculate Conception of the Blessed Virgin Mary. He spent several years researching the topics, and in 1865 his book was published in Germany.[3]

However, not only was "the proud, joyous and hopeful author" disappointed that his "brilliant apologetics" was largely ignored by Catholics, but he was stunned by the hostile reaction to his book from the rationalists who attacked him for his assertions regarding the Incarnation of Christ. Things got worse for the young scholar as his vehement defense of Lutheran orthodoxy on the question of justification alienated him from his colleagues at the University of Berlin.

By December 1868 he felt compelled to resign his position at the university. Shortly after, with funds anonymously donated, Edward Preuss took passage on a ship bound for America. On this voyage, the series of decisive events which began with his attack on the dogma of the Immaculate Conception, climaxed in a spiritual "storm" that led to his conversion to Catholicism. Edward Preuss wrote a third-person account of this event which rivals the conversion of Saul of Tarsus and Martin Luther's "tower experience" for drama. Halfway across the Atlantic the ship on which Preuss was sailing was caught in a violent storm,

> the hurricane waxed so terrible that the destruction of the ship appeared inevitable…the tempest blew us as though all the furies of hell were unchained. On his knees our Professor [Edward Preuss] reached his cabin. He was no longer able to pray for help. He began to prepare himself for death amidst the howling of the hurricane, the deafening roar of the breakers on deck, and the still more tremendous peals of thunder. With all his might he clung to the 'bloody passion of Christ.' This and this alone he held up to God… But to all his ardent prayers, to the crys (sic) of his poor heart…he heard only one reply, which though spoken by no human lips, out-thundered the revolution of the elements: 'And their works follow them'…his soul cried out, 'have I not publicly professed Thy Name before all men? Have I not suffered persecution for Thy sake?' And a voice answered: 'I have never known thee. Depart from me, you malefactor. For I was hungry, and you gave me not to eat…' And from that moment the abyss of hell had thus begun to open beneath him, his fear of death increased tenfold…[4]

Edward Preuss was not asked to forfeit his life that night, but he arrived in America in January, 1869, with his faith in Lutheran orthodoxy badly shaken. Nonetheless, with letters of introduction from von Ranke and others, Preuss took a teaching position at the theologically conservative Concordia Lutheran Seminary in St. Louis. A man of Preuss's talents was well received at the seminary. He was quickly assigned to teach courses in exegesis, church history, and Hebrew. Within a year of his arrival in St. Louis, Edward Preuss married a young woman from a prominent and staunch Lutheran family, Concordia P. Schuricht. On March 22, 1871 their first child, Arthur, was born, and the young family seemed firmly established on the campus of Concordia Seminary.

However, as much as he tried, Edward Preuss could not suppress his misgivings about the credibility of Lutheranism. He began to see the history of Lutheranism as "either a tissue of the most irrational occurrences" or simply as a "transition stage" between Catholicism and the outright apostasy of the rationalists.[5] After an intense personal struggle, Edward Preuss found that he could no longer teach the theology of Martin Luther. On the first of December 1871 he resigned his position at Concordia Seminary, and seven days later, noting the irony that it was the Feast of the Immaculate Conception, he left behind the Lutheran fold forever.

> All exited and unstrung, he arrived in his new home, far away on the outskirts of the city. 'The Mother of God, whom thou hast publicly accused of sin,' an inner voice said to him, 'is mightier than thou. Three years after the publication of thy pamphlet against her Immaculate Conception, she destroyed thy house in Berlin, which by no means was built on a rock. Today, three years later, on the Feast of the Immaculate Conception, she robs thee of thy new home and a treasure which was a thousand times dearer to thy soul —thy faith'.[6]

Not long after this, Edward Preuss called on Archbishop Peter R. Kenrick. Preuss was put under the tutelage of the German vicar general of the Archdiocese of St. Louis, Rev. Henry Mühlsiepen, for six weeks and then baptized into the Roman Catholic Church on January 26, 1872. Father Muhlsiepen, a native of Cologne, and pastor of St. Mary's Church in St. Louis, was so prominent in German Catholic affairs that he came to be known as "the apostle to the Germans in Missouri."[7] Also at this time, Preuss's infant son Arthur, who, unlike his father, was judged to have been validly baptized, was received into the Church. Edward Preuss noted that through "natural circumstances" the church of his baptism was under the patronage of "St. Mary of the Victories." Twelve months later, on the Feast of the Immaculate Conception, Dr. Edward Preuss had a shrine erected in this church in honor of the Blessed Virgin Mary under the titles of the Immaculate Conception and Our Lady of Victory. Below the image of Our Lady of Perpetual Help there is an unsigned Latin inscription which reads, "This memorial is dedicated to the Virgin Mary of Victory as a sign of her victory over one in the past who did not shrink from defaming her, who, however, now with a most grateful heart is serving her, Mother most meek, conceived without original sin."

This account of the conversion of Edward Preuss is of crucial importance in understanding the religious outlook of his son. Arthur Preuss learned well that his father's conversion had come about because the latter had come to believe Lutheranism an untenable position between the rock of Catholicism and the de facto apostasy of liberal Protestantism. Second, Edward Preuss's conversion had been an affair of the mind, more so than of the heart, as it had come in a collision with the superior intellectual claims of Catholicism. Third, it had been precisely a Catholic dogma that Protestants have difficulty in accepting, the Immaculate Conception, that had broken the hold of "erroneous" opinion on his father. Fourth, Edward Preuss attributed his conversion to the direct intercession of the Blessed Virgin Mary. Finally, Arthur Preuss knew that when his father came face to face with the truth, "he heroically sacrificed a fine position as a seminary professor, and a brilliant future within the denomination," because he had to be faithful to that truth.[8]

Fidelity to the truth of Catholicism exacted an even higher price. For not only did Edward Preuss renounce the Lutheran faith, but he created division in his own family as his wife, Concordia, could not follow him into the Catholic Church. Though four of her sons dedicated their lives to the service of the Catholic Church (three of Arthur's brothers became priests), Concordia Preuss remained a devout Lutheran until the day of her death.[9] From the example of his father, Arthur Preuss had inherited the convictions that one's life must be lived in accordance with divinely revealed truth, no matter what the personal cost, and that the Roman Catholic Church was Christ's appointed mediator and protector of this truth. Fidelity to these two principles would guide the course of his life.

There is little detailed information available about Arthur Preuss's formative years. He received his elementary education at the parish school of Ss. Peter and Paul and it was through his affiliation at the parish that he began his life-long friendship with Father John Rothensteiner who would later share prominence with Preuss in St. Louis' German-Catholic community. After a brief stay at Canisius College in Buffalo, New York, Arthur Preuss obtained most of his secondary education at Quincy College in Quincy, Illinois, where he received an M.A. degree in philosophy in 1890. Quincy College, founded in 1860 by Franciscans from Saxony, Germany, was a boarding school modeled after the German gymnasium. Originally named for St. Francis Solanus, the college offered courses in liberal arts, theology, and practical business training. The catalogue for the years in which Preuss attended the college in the late eighteen-eighties indicates that nearly thirty years after its founding, the faculty and student body of Quincy College remained overwhelmingly German in their origins. Transcripts of Arthur Preuss's years there state that he attained the highest marks and an "exemplary" rating in academics, conduct, and "general diligence."[10]

While Arthur Preuss certainly made an impression on his teachers, it is clear that the greatest influence on his life remained his father,

Edward. References that Arthur Preuss made to his father in the *Review*, and from the letters from father to son which Arthur published in the newspaper *Amerika* upon his father's death, indicate that their relationship was a strong one. Edward and Concordia Preuss had eight children but Arthur, it would seem, was a source of special pride to his father. He had inherited his father's convert's zeal for the Faith, his intellectual gifts, and the desire to be a Catholic journalist. In his memorial to Arthur Preuss, John Rothensteiner offered another perspective on the elder Preuss's relationship with his son.

> The elder Preuss had something of a mystic in his spiritual make up. As he was about forty years old when his son was born, Arthur never became very intimate with his father, who was rather stern and exacting in regard to the education of his children; as philosphy and theology were uppermost in the mind of the old professor, Arthur's mind was naturally turned into this same channel. There was but little room for poetry and romance, and none at all for frivolity.[11]

However, Edward's affection for his son is evident in the letters he wrote to Arthur during the latter's years at the College of St. Francis in Quincy, Illinois.

13 September 1887

My dear Son!
Your letter of the 10th brought me joy. It pleased me to read that you arrived in Quincy safely...I miss you very much. But it is best this way. Only remain loyal dear son and unite your prayers daily in the litany and the rosary with mine. We both need this very much...

22 January 1889

My dear Son,
Your letter of the 19th has pleased me very much...You have five difficult months ahead of you. Do work hard to get through. Your superiors are taking cordial interest in your character development. Trust them and try to please them. This will be important for your future. I think of you daily and will offer my holy Communion which I intend to receive this week for you.

Edward took a "warm interest" in his son's studies and encouraged him to persevere in the study of Latin and Greek. The elder Preuss also insisted that Arthur write every other one of his letters home in the English language as "you may need this skill later on."[12] His son's philosophical training was also a concern for Edward Preuss.

> 25 September 1888
> ...I am so happy that you have the opportunity to study healthy philosophy. I did not have that chance during my gymnasium and first year at the university...The classical studies together with the philosophy of Aristotle and St. Thomas give you a good basis for judging all earthly things...

Much to his father's pleasure, Arthur excelled in his studies and confessing his "bibliomania," noted proudly that his schoolmates considered him a "bookworm."[13] While Arthur's academic training was a great joy to his father, Edward's letters to his son indicate that it was a struggle for Edward, with seven other children, to meet the expenses.[14] Indeed, it appears that the initial expense of Arthur's college education was met in part by their pastor, and another leader in the German-Catholic community, Father Francis Goller.[15] In November of 1888, Edward Preuss suggested to his son that he should write a letter in Latin to Father Goller in order to express his gratitude and diligence. Edward even provided to Arthur the text for the letter which is revealing as it encapsulates the ideas which motivated Arthur's years as journalist.

> Most honored Father !
> It is due to your kindness that the way I had desired to follow for my life's profession was opened. I will now try to show my gratitude first by living the life of a good Catholic and also by using my pen to promote and defend the doctrine of the Catholic Church; furthermore, by remaining faithful to the German language and the German spirit. So, as at the time of the reign of Christ and His Saints in the Middle Ages, the German nation was the main support of the Catholic faith and the Holy See, it shall be that way again. Already we can see the beginning in the splendid position of the Centre Party in Germany as well as in the beginning organization of the German Catholics in

America. I want to help in this with all my strength...[16]

In addition to fidelity to the Church and the "German Spirit," Edward Preuss instilled in his son a strong devotion to the Blessed Virgin Mary.

> My beloved Son,
> Many thanks for your letter...You have made me especially happy by renewing your vow. Yes! Be a child of the dear Mother of God! Consecrate your life to Her as I have consecrated mine to Her. Let us together work for Her honor and according to Her will...

As Arthur neared the completion of his studies for a master's degree in philosophy, his father Edward wrote to him of the days ahead.

> You will finish your studies at the end of July. If we were suffering from hunger or would no longer be living you would have to find bread winning work right away. But God's providence grants us better. You can rest when you return home. Our quiet house, with trees in the garden still has a place for you. Even more than that —a big room. I am going to clear off one of the bookshelves to make room for your library. So rest yourself well here. The 'Kindly Light' which guided us will help us to find the future.[17]

The "Kindly Light" that Edward Preuss referred to comes from the famous hymn "Lead Kindly Light" based on John Henry Cardinal Newman's poem "The Pillar and the Cloud." Both father and son claimed this hymn as their favorite.

> Your favorite poem is also my favorite...Often on the way home at night, in my soul too resounds the last line,
> 'So long Thy power has blessed me
> -sure it will still lead me on;
> O'er moor and fen and crag and torrent,
> till the night is gone;
> and with the morn those angel faces smile
> which I have loved long since
> and lost a while
> Lead kindly Light, amid the encircling gloom
> Lead thou me on!

The night is dark and I am far from home—
Lead thou me on!'[18]

Newman's poem, "written at sea" in 1833, resonated with the shared vision of both the elder and younger Preuss that the Christian life was a matter of being led by the *"Kindly Light"* through the "encircling gloom" of an increasingly faithless world. Still, they were not content to simply curse the darkness but sought to testify to the Light by their witness to the truth of the Catholic faith. For both father and son, this testimony would be given through their dedication to Catholic journalism.

Weltanschauung

As the son of a convert to Catholicism and a devout Lutheran mother, the family religious environment that Arthur Preuss grew up in was much different from that of other German American Catholics. The type of Catholic devotional life which prevailed in other immigrant homes would not have been part of his childhood experience. In fact, out of sensitivity to his Lutheran mother, those practices of Catholic piety that Protestants found disturbing never became part of his home life.[19] Thus, unlike other members of the "immigrant church" for whom he was often a spokesman, he did not have a long Catholic heritage from which to draw. On the other hand, while Preuss grew up in a family which had to be religiously tolerant in order to survive, he had little use for Protestantism as an institution. Like his father, Arthur believed that the "so called reformers," with their religious subjectivism, had initiated the movement that led inevitably to the indifferentism and the practical atheism of the modern world. So not for him the benevolent "fraternizing" with non-Catholics that the "Americanists" engaged in. His father's conversion to Catholicism had been too much of a definitive break with Protestantism for his son Arthur to now temporize with "sectarians." This family background explains Arthur's seemingly contradictory behavior of objecting to the use of Protestant hymns in Catholic churches while dutifully seeing to it that the local Lutheran pastor would come to his home to care for the spiritual needs of his mother.[20]

If Arthur Preuss's familial religious inheritance was unusual, he did share with his fellow German American Catholics their alienation from American society because of their religion and their detachment from their fellow Catholics on account of their language. Although Arthur Preuss's father, as a convert, could not directly mediate to him the experience behind the German American Catholic sense of alienation, certainly the people, priests and vowed religious of the German Catholic community of St. Louis and at Quincy College would have had firsthand knowledge of that experience.

As mentioned earlier, the German Catholic response to the societal alienation imposed on them by the Kulturkampf was a fervent embrace of Ultramontanism. The German Catholics in America brought this loyalty to the papacy with them and for many, including Arthur Preuss, Ultramontanism became synonymous with Catholicism. Writing in 1902, Preuss defined what it meant to be an Ultramontane, and clearly his definition was formed not only by his own experience, but also by that of the German Catholic people.

> There are in the pale of the Church millions who profess their religious faith fearlessly, love it sincerely, and live according to its dictates. They venerate in the person of the Roman Pontiff the vicegerent of Jesus Christ on earth and the successor of St. Peter, whom they owe obedience in all things pertaining to salvation. They feel and resent every insult offered to him as a grievous wrong and protest against it. They behold in the bishops the successors of the Apostles and adhere to them with unshakable loyalty. They honor their priests, obey them and do not allow them to be maligned or persecuted. They deny the State the right of ruling the Church and are not afraid to so declare themselves. They strenuously oppose the suppression of religion in the schools and public life. They receive the sacraments often, devoutly and conscientiously, keeping not only the commandments of God, but those of the Church as well. They do not read irreligious or immoral newspapers and refuse to vote for any candidate for public office whom they know to be hostile to their religious conviction. In short, they dispose their daily life, private and public, according to the

commandments of God, the dictates of their conscience, and the directions of their divinely appointed religious authorities, without much regard to the spirit of the times or the ruling fashion.[21]

When issues of cultural identity, similar to those previously faced by Catholics in Germany, came to the fore in America during the years of Arthur Preuss's early adulthood and his founding of the *Review*, the intellectual and emotional basis of his response had a strong foundation in the historical experience of German Catholicism. Arthur Preuss's experience of being "embattled" which he articulates in his definition of Ultramontanism cited above must have been particularly acute as he had come of age in the 1880s and '90s, when the wounds inflicted on the Church by the Kulturkampf in Germany were still fresh and when the ethnic struggles within the American church were at their worst. For Preuss, the alienation that accompanied these cultural identity struggles was an integral part of his life experience and world view.

Before moving on to consider Arthur Preuss's public career, two other aspects of his personal life, which undoubtedly contributed to the formation of his character, must be noted. The first is his physical health. Throughout his sixty-four years Arthur Preuss was plagued by physical illness, much of it brought on by overwork. The first recorded intimation of this came as early as 1887, when he was only sixteen years old. Arthur wrote to his father of pain in his hands from writing, signs of the rheumatoid arthritis that would make an invalid of his father four years prior to his death in the Alexian Brothers hospital in St. Louis in 1904. Arthur Preuss fought an annual winter battle with this intensely painful arthritis from about age thirty on. Often his hands and feet, gnarled from arthritis, were effectively paralyzed for days and weeks at a time. In an age lacking the medicinal pain relievers that are now taken for granted, such physical suffering simply had to be endured. Overworking himself at his literary endeavors aggravated matters. The first public acknowledgment of his poor health came in 1897, when at the age of twenty-six he had to suspend publication of the *Review* for a few weeks to recover from nervous exhaustion. Often his doctor would demand that Arthur restrict his working hours or cease working altogether.[22] The spirit with which Arthur Preuss carried his daily cross is captured in the following meditations that he wrote in the *Review*.

> Oh, do not pray for easy lives. Pray to be strong men. Do not pray for tasks equal to your powers. Pray for powers equal to your tasks. Then the doing of your work shall be no miracle. But you shall be a miracle. Every day you shall wonder at yourself, at the richness of life which has come to you by the grace of God.

> An intolerable headache that would otherwise wreck reason is softened into Christian resignation by the reflection that God surely gave His most precious gift to her He called Mother and that gift was a diadem of thorns.[23]

Also, in considering Arthur Preuss's personal life it is necessary to note his experience of death. While it is true that generations previous to our own lived with a greater familiarity with death, that did not make its reality any less sharp or painful. Apart from the death of his father at the comparatively "old" age of seventy, Arthur Preuss had to endure the death of his first wife after only seven years of marriage, and at least four of the children he fathered did not survive infancy. Given the times, these events may not seem particularly remarkable from a historical perspective. But for the individuals who had to endure such sadness each death of a loved one was a personal sorrow not alleviated by the statistical realities of life expectancy. In light of these experiences, and his own habitual suffering, it is not surprising that when Arthur Preuss referred to Jesus Christ the title he used in preference to all others was "Saviour."

A Vocation

Fortunately for Edward Preuss and his family, shortly after his conversion, his talents were put to use by the German Catholics in St. Louis on their daily newspaper *Die Amerika*. In October, 1871, just four months before Edward Preuss was received into the Church, two prominent laymen, Henry J. Spaunhorst and Anthony Roeslein, met with Father Henry Muhlsiepen to discuss the need for a German Catholic daily paper in St. Louis. Joseph Gummersbach, who had been sent from Germany to St. Louis by the Herder book company to establish a plant for the publisher in the United States, played an instrumental role in the founding and funding of *Die Amerika*.[24] Father Francis Goller, pastor, friend, and benefactor of Edward Preuss, also played an advisory role in the operations of *Amerika*. These men recruited several hundred supporters of the project and formed an organization called the "German Literary Society of St. Louis." The German Literary Society was then the owner and publisher of *Amerika*.

The paper made its first appearance on October 17, 1872. For the first six years of *Amerika*'s existence a former school teacher, Anton Hellmich, was the editor and Edward Preuss his assistant. Edward Preuss did not formally take over the job of editor until January 17, 1878. However, he had been "the real editor from the start."[25] Under Edward Preuss's editorship, *Amerika* became "the largest and most successful German Catholic daily" in the United States.[26] Approximate circulation figures indicate that *Amerika* started with three thousand subscribers, and had reached a circulation of 13,000 subscribers by 1895.[27] Edward Preuss made *Amerika* the best paper of its kind with his "short and pregnant articles" and "his noble attitude" toward his adversaries. Joseph Matt, publisher of *Der Wanderer*, called Edward Preuss "the prince among German American journalists."[28] In recognition of his contribution to Catholicism in America, Edward Preuss was chosen by the University of Notre Dame to be the recipient of its Laetare Medal in 1887. However, in keeping with a repentant vow he had made never to profit personally from his conversion to Catholicism, Edward Preuss respectfully declined this honor and his medal remains at the University.[29]

Die Amerika stated that it was not to be a religious or church paper. "Theological disputations and fruitless polemics we will always exclude from our columns." But *Amerika* declared, "we will be ever ready and

prepared fearlessly to meet every attack upon the rights of Catholics...."
Arthur Preuss adopted the same editorial style and tone when he
launched his *Review*. Recognized as the central organ of the German
Catholics in the United States, *Amerika* was actively involved in the
controversies of the eighteen eighties and nineties surrounding the
continued use of the German language in the Church. Given this
background, Arthur Preuss would have been quite familiar with the
conflicts over the Abbelen Memorial and the Cahensly affair. He came
of age when the leaders of the German Catholic community in St. Louis
were disenchanted with the apparent Irish domination of the American
hierarchy, and it was a grievance which he would share.[30]

While Edward Preuss's entry into the field of Catholic journalism was
no doubt necessitated by his conversion, Arthur's choice of a career in
this field was deliberate. At the age of sixteen, when less serious boys
dream of other things, Arthur was already laying the groundwork for his
future in the field of Catholic journalism. Shortly after his arrival at St.
Francis College, Arthur asked his father to send him copies not only of
Amerika, but of other leading Catholic papers and journals as well.
Arthur was soon receiving the *Catholic Columbian* from Ohio, the *New
York Freeman's Journal*, the Boston *Pilot*, and *Church Progress*, from
St. Louis and the Paulist's magazine, the *Catholic World*. In addition,
Arthur began to read the German Jesuit journal, *Stimmen aus Maria
Laach*, from which, when he had his own journal, he would often
republish articles.[31]

According to one of Arthur's friends, Joseph Matt, Edward Preuss had
initially tried to perusade his son to enter a "practical profession."[32] But,
having resigned himself to accepting his son's vocational choice, Edward
Preuss's letters to Arthur often imparted advice to the aspiring Catholic
journalist. During the fall of 1887, at the height of the battle in the
Catholic press over the Abbelen Memorial, Edward delayed sending
Arthur some papers in the English language because "many of these
papers were exceedingly unpleasant." Edward Preuss warned his son
against getting caught up in the newspaper wars.

The offensive position of certain weeklies is regrettable. Let us learn from it thus: the profession of faith without keeping God's commandments is not pleasing to God; causes damage, and carries with it noticeable punishment.... The intensity of polemic blossoms especially in the Protestant sects, and so Catholics sometimes allow themselves to be misled. But believe me, and I am speaking from bitter experience, polemics only causes damage, threefold damage at that. Firstly, it causes the author to be disliked everywhere. Secondly, religion, on account of which there is this discord, this badmouthing, is then despised by reasonable people. Thirdly, it causes so many deadly sins that in time God's wrath is provoked. Therefore, be on guard against it as you would the plague![33]

In the spring of 1889, father and son prepared for Arthur's summer internship on the staff of *Amerika*. But Edward let his son know that the placement was not automatic since "...it will take the good will of the other workers in order not to transgress on account of my son."[34] Later, Arthur wrote of his apprenticeship.

My father was editor of the German Catholic *Amerika* when I grew up, and I was initiated into daily newspaper work at a very youthful age. Before I had graduated from college I had acted as a police reporter, telegraph editor, Sunday editor, —in fact had filled practically every position on the editorial staff. The experience thus gained inspired me to become a Catholic editor. My college and university courses were shaped with that end in view.[35]

From the counsel that Edward Preuss gave his son, it is clear that for both men a career in Catholic journalism was not simply a profession, but was in fact a God-given vocation. In light of the contemporary attitude toward the role of the laity in the Church, Arthur Preuss's view of his work as a vocation was rather progressive.

[The motivation] for a Catholic editor, [is] the consciousness of serving his ideals in championing a cause which is the noblest that can appeal to any man's fealty and devotion —the cause of Catholic truth and justice to which this *Review* has been consecrated for twenty six years.[36]

I seek no honor, and I take none. What I do, I do for God and His glory. As a vowed religious surely you understand me.[37]

These expressions were not mere sentiments. Arthur Preuss truly believed that his work as a journalist was an apostolate, and he spoke of "consecrating" his *Review* to the glory of God just as he had consecrated his children to Him.[38]

Following the completion of his studies for a master's degree in philosophy in June 1890, Arthur Preuss returned home to St. Louis to begin working on the staff of *Amerika* with his father. In addition to his various assignments for *Amerika*, Arthur also wrote a few pieces in English for the *Church Progress*. These essays included topics such as "the language question" and a literary review of the works of Thomas Carlyle.[39] Some eighteen months after Arthur Preuss returned to St. Louis, he received and accepted the offer of William Kuhlmann to become the editor of his *Katholisches Sontagsblatt*. Kuhlmann offered Preuss a salary of twenty-five dollars a week for the first year. Undoubtedly, this offer, coming a week before his twenty-first birthday, was welcomed as a golden opportunity by the younger Preuss. However, it did require that he leave home again, this time for Chicago, where the *Katholisches Sonntagsblatt* was based.

Established by William Kuhlmann in 1891, the *Katholisches Sonntagsblatt*, was a weekly German Catholic paper. It advertised itself as a "Familien Blatt fuer Wahrheit und Recht." Preuss took over the editorship of the *Katholisches Sonntagsblatt* in June 1892 and his first two years with the paper coincided with the acrimonious debate surrounding Archbishop John Ireland's "Faribault-Stillwater" school plan, the Parliament of Religions at the World's Columbian Exhibition of 1893, and the establishment of the Apostolic Delegation.[40] It appears that the young editor's comments regarding these events may have been a bit too caustic as both his father and Bishop Otto Zardetti of St. Cloud, a friend of the family, admonished him to be less aggressive in his criticism of the American hierarchy.[41] Still, Arthur Preuss established his credentials as an editor in these years and during his tenure at the helm of the paper, the *Katholisches Sonntagsblatt* increased its circulation from five to eight thousand subscribers.[42]

Concurrent with his duties as editor of the *Katholisches Sonntagsblatt*, Arthur Preuss began a doctoral-level reading course at an institution called Lake Forest University. Preuss enrolled in a "course of study in Psychology, Logic, Metaphysics and Aesthetics." The course of study was designed to last three years with periodic examinations. Preuss never completed the course, but in the two semesters that he was in the program the works studied included, in addition to Plato and Aristotle, those of Descartes, Locke, Hume, Kant, and Hegel. There was nothing Thomistic about the program.[43]

Though Arthur Preuss demonstrated a knowledge of modern philosophy in his writings, there is no record of him discussing publicly his work at "Lake Forest University." Nor is there any explanation extant for his decision not to complete the course. Perhaps the demands of being a family man ended his studies early for, less than a year after becoming a Catholic editor, Arthur Preuss also took up the vocation of being a husband and father. In May 1893 Arthur Preuss married the twenty-year old, Mary Dohle, also of St. Louis. It is unclear how long their courtship lasted, but the earliest letters in Preuss's correspondence date from October 1892. The newlyweds returned to Chicago following the nuptuals, and in March 1894, Arthur's wife gave birth to their daughter, Isabelle Marie.

The birth of Preuss's daughter, Isabelle, preceded by a month the birth of his *Review*. Although the period in which the latter was conceived is uncertain, letters from his father indicate that in early 1894 Arthur was reevaluating his future with the *Katholisches Sonntagsblatt*.

During the last weeks I have thought much about you and your well being. Through the distress of the past and things which might arise from it, the formerly so promising prospects of a Sunday paper for the German Catholics in Chicago have diminished. These thoughts coincided with the visit of the publisher of the *Pittsburger Beobachter* who came to make connections with our plate business. In the course of the conversation he mentioned that some time ago he had contacted you about joining his editorial staff. I spoke to him of all the good things I know about you and asked if he already had a chief editor. He said no. What would you think if I wrote to him and told him he should offer to you a position comparable to the one you now hold? Such an offer might keep us from great difficulties.[44]

By way of responding to his father's inquiry, Arthur must have told him for the first time about his plans for publishing his own journal, for on March 15, 1894 Edward wrote to Arthur,

I read of your plan to publish an English monthly with mixed feelings because however much I am pleased with the progress you are making with your life, I hoped that you would avoid the troubles and dangers of the present situation and move to Pittsburgh. Even now Mr. Jaegle would come to Chicago to make arrangements with you if you would let me know right away that you are interested. But I cannot wait any later than the end of March.[45]

What the "troubles and dangers" Edward Preuss referred to were is uncertain. They may have been the financial risks in such a venture, but then William Kuhlmann would be the publisher of the *Review* at its inception. Perhaps Edward Preuss was simply concerned that his son was becoming too involved in the ongoing conflicts between the German Catholics in America and their co-religionists. In any case, despite his father's apprehensions, Arthur Preuss launched his *Review* on April 1, 1894 and thus embarked on his remarkable forty-year career as an important commentator on American Catholic life.

II The Birth of the *Review* and Americanism

The inauguration of the *Review* coincided with the development of "the great crisis in American Catholic history," the controversy over Americanism.[1] As Preuss's *Review* was just that, he regularly published excerpts from other publications, most of which he agreed with, some of which he opposed. Much of the significance of the *Review* during the controversy over Americanism was that it gave international circulation to the opinions of conservative Catholics. For this reason, it is perhaps best to consider Preuss's part as that of the "conductor" of the conservative symphony that sounded from the pages of the *Review* rather than as the composer of every note.

The years covered in this chapter, 1894–1901, have been divided, albeit superficially, into four periods that reflect in a general way Arthur Preuss's changing editorial focus. During the first period, from April 1894 until August 1896, the *Review* was primarily concerned with speaking to and for the German-Catholic community. The second period, from September 1896 until April 1898, marks the emergence of the *Review* as a cross-cultural conservative voice during the controversies surrounding the removal first of Bishop John Keane and then, of Msgr. Joseph Schroeder, from the faculty of the Catholic University of America. The third period, May 1898 through February 1899, covers the Americanist controversy proper, until the issuance of *Testem Benevolentiae*. The final phase, from March 1899 until July 1901, involved the struggle over the interpretation of the papal condemnation of Americanism.

"A German Paper in English Dress" April 1894–August 1896

"A German paper in English dress" with these words Arthur Preuss defined the purpose of the *Review* on the first page of the first issue, published on April 1, 1894.[2] Preuss's *Review* began as a sixteen-page publication, with three columns per page. Its appearance was more like that of a newspaper than a magazine or journal. For the first six months of its forty-year existence, the *Review* was a monthly publication, and the subscription cost was a dollar a year.[3] In September 1894 it began publishing on a weekly basis, which was an ambitious undertaking as Preuss was still the editor of the *Katholisches Sonntagsblatt* and would remain at that post until the summer of 1896. The stated purpose of the *Review* was "to be an organ of that large portion of our people which is German born or of German descent." However, what made the *Review* different from hundreds of other publications across the nation that had the same stated purpose was that the twenty-two-year old editor of the *Review* had the foresight to publish in English. Preuss stated that it was a dream of his youth to found a journal "in my English mother-tongue" for the propagation of "the grand ideas for which the German press of this country has for so many years been fighting." Preuss recognized that "the German language as a popular tongue is doomed in this country." By publishing in English, the *Review* hoped to see that the "best part of our Deuschtum will live in our descendants long after the German idiom will have died out among the American people." It was the defense of "our Deuschtum," or the German-Catholic heritage, that would be the focus of the *Review* for its first few years.[4]

As the son of the editor of *Amerika*, growing up in the strong German community of St. Louis, Preuss would have been long familiar with the efforts of German Catholics in America to preserve their heritage. He came into adulthood at the height of the conflict between German and Irish Catholics over what it meant to be Catholic and American. The conflicts over the Abbelen memorial, the School controversy, and the Cahensly affair had all taken place between 1886 and 1892 and the animosities they engendered between German-speaking and English-speaking Catholics were still quite strong when the *Review* appeared in 1894.[5]

Preuss leapt right into the fray. The front page of his second issue carried the deliberately provocative essay, "Are We A Nation?"[6] Since for Preuss the answer was negative, no "racial" [ethnic] group had the right to decide what qualified as being either "American" or "foreign." Until the natural process of Americanization was completed, and America became a "nation," which could take decades, "there are no foreign tongues." So when English-speaking Catholics criticized their German brethren for keeping German in their schools, they were not only unjust, but were aiding the anti-Catholic bigots of the American Protective Association.[7] In this essay, and in many others like it, Preuss indicated that the defense of the German-Catholic heritage was, of necessity, a war on two fronts. On the one hand, the *Review* voiced to the general public the loyalty of German Catholics to America, "with frank sincerity" and "cheerful acquiescence." And on the other, the *Review* would do battle with the "Irish bigots," "Americanizers," and the "hide-bound clodhoppers who consider it their heaven appointed mission to wage a deadly war of extermination against foreignism and all its trappings."[8]

Topping the list of "clodhoppers," not surprisingly, was Archbishop John Ireland of St. Paul, "notoriously a bitter enemy of the Germans" and "father of that unfortunate bastard, the Faribault School Plan." Commenting on a speech Ireland gave in Washington in the spring of 1894 criticizing those who resisted assimilation into American culture as "poisonous," Preuss responded that "the true apostles of the faith concerned themselves with Christianizing not nationalizing."[9] Preuss held Ireland responsible for creating the myth of "Cahenslyism" to discredit German Catholics both in Rome and in the eyes of their fellow Americans.[10] In reality "'Cahenslyism' was a bugaboo" that had originated "in the fertile but morbid brain of a certain chauvinistic prelate who demeaned himself as if he and his followers had an exclusive patent on American patriotism."[11]

R. Laurence Moore's recent study, *Religious Outsiders and the Making of Americans*, affirms the German-Catholic view that the dispute was not about Americanization, for the process was inevitable. The real argument was over what it mean to be an American. Moore makes this point within his larger argument that while religious "outsiders," including immigrant Catholics, were quite critical of American society, their criticism was based on a latent hopefulness about the way America could be. Further, by maintaining their religious and ethnic distinctiveness, German Catholics and other outsiders, were not only establishing their own identity but they also manifested a greater understanding of America as a pluralistic society than did the Americanizers. Moore also asserts that the position that Preuss and others took was far more realistic than that of the Americanizing party led by John Ireland. "The so-called non-Americanizers recognized that immigrants did not have the option of becoming quite anything they wanted. They also recognized better than their opponents that certain ways of becoming American were not compatible with remaining Catholic."[12]

In addition to challenging Archbishop Ireland's prescriptions for the successful Americanization of Catholic immigrants, the *Review* took delight in reproving the hero of the liberals for the comic excesses of his public foibles. Preuss joined the general criticism of the Archbishop's partisan political activities on behalf of the Republican party, and his hobnobbing with wealthy businessmen. On June 4, 1896, the *Review*, with apparent amusement, quoted Ireland as commending war as "the great instigator of patriotism." Preuss respected Ireland's sincerity in his views; "no one has ever doubted his faith or his devotion to his Church, because he has never given any reason for such doubt."[13] It was just that Ireland, in his "hyper-patriotism" and naivete, did not seem to grasp the import of the views he promoted.[14]

While Archbishop Ireland was generally portrayed in the first issues of the *Review* as simply foolish, the other publicly recognized promoter of Americanism, Bishop John Keane, rector of the Catholic University of America, was seen as the embodiment of "liberalism" in the Church.[15] Keane's prominent involvement in efforts such as the 1893 Parliament of Religions promoting interdenominational cooperation marked him as a man who was, at best, injudicious in his relations with non-Catholics. The *Review*'s first notice of Keane and the Catholic University was in issue one, on page one, where Preuss remarked on the financial difficulties of the university.

> The Church is invincible only so long as she remains orthodox. Liberalism is a deadly blight...There is already too much Liberalism in the Catholic University at Washington. An unhealthy baneful spirit pervades the institution. This is the cause for the lack of financial support.[16]

As long as Keane was rector of the Catholic University, the notices in the *Review* never got any better. Under the liberal Keane, the University was "spreading liberalism over the land and liberalism is uncatholic." With a proper house cleaning, the University would become what Pope Leo had intended it to be when he gave it its charter. "Let us have a good old-fashioned, thoroughly Catholic, ultra-montane university, with no Bouquillonism and no O'Gormonism about it..."[17] In addition to the University's perceived liberalism under the rectorship of Keane, Preuss was also critical of the "un-American and unchristian spirit of national prejudice" that existed there as evidenced by the hostility exhibited by the liberal majority among the faculty against its only conservative members, Monsignor Joseph Schroeder, the Reverend Joseph Pohle, and the Reverend Georges Périès.[18]

The *Review*'s most pointed attack against Bishop Keane and the Catholic University came in March 1896 with the publication of a letter to the editor by a correspondent identified simply as "S.W." The unnamed correspondent, exhibiting a detailed knowledge of the affairs of the University, accused Keane of deceiving the American bishops on the status of the university by inflating enrollment figures, and misleading American Catholics by hiring Protestant professors. The author reasoned that if the university was going to entrust courses to Protestant instructors, "why bother spending money on Catholic University instead of sending students to Protestant universities that are assuredly superior to ours?" The writer concluded his letter by predicting accurately, "the rectorship of Bishop Keane will end before the present year has run its course."

Arthur Preuss's extant papers do not contain this letter from "S.W.," so conjecture as to the identity of its author can only remain that. However, in his book, *German Americans and the Catholic Church,* written some forty years ago, Colman Barry noted that in "the Arthur Preuss papers there are numerous letters from Msgr. Joseph Schroeder to 'Dear Arthur' in which the former discussed his articles and his visits with the Apostolic Delegate in which he presented the German Catholic position in the United States."[19]

Still, while highly critical of Keane, in May and June of 1896, the *Review* would stand virtually alone among German-Catholic publications in supporting Msgr. Schroeder's promotion of a "German" chair at the University, while the rest of the German press continued to keep the "liberal" institution at arms length "because they cannot and will not support 'Keaneism'."[20] While Schroeder, a professor of theology at the Catholic University, had long been a champion of German Catholics in America, he apparently was not an immediate favorite with Preuss. "For a while we did not like Monsignor's attitude and bearing, but we gladly note the change of heart that has come over him."[21] It is difficult to know who had a change of heart, but by January 1895 Preuss would write of Schroeder, "his productions ever exhale the true spirit of the Church."[22] In the spring of 1896, Schroeder conducted his defense of Salvatore Brandi's critique of the neo-Pelagian tendencies of the American church from the pages of the *Review.*[23]

Preuss also had second thoughts about the Apostolic Delegation in the United States, and the first Delegate, Archbishop Francesco Satolli. Critical of Satolli's handling of the "McGlynn affair" and his involvement in the "school question," Preuss alleged that Satolli was the instrument by which the liberals were cleverly manipulating both Rome and American Catholics. Additionally, his public "blunders" had only strengthened the A.P.A. and his "incompetence" was such that "we shall breathe a sigh of relief when Mgr. Satolli is recalled."[24] Even Pope Leo's Apostolic Letter, *Longinqua Oceani,* issued in January 1895 in part to bolster the position of Satolli in America, could not dispel the suspicion with which the *Review* regarded him, and Preuss wondered whether German editors might be the first to feel the newly strengthened Delegate's "mailed fist."[25] Satolli's stature in the pages of the *Review* rose considerably after his speech praising German-American Catholics at Pottsville, Pennsylvania in April 1895.[26] But Satolli never did receive an unqualified endorsement from Preuss even after the former turned against the Americanists. As for the Apostolic Delegation itself, with Satolli's gradual reconciliation with the German-speaking community, it too came to be looked upon favorably.

At the basis of these and other controversies that the *Review* engaged in was, as has been mentioned, the dilemma as to how to be both Catholic and American. For the German Catholics that Preuss spoke for, many of whom were refugees from the anti-Catholic Kulturkampf in Germany, life in modern society, even in America, was an endless struggle over culture. And the most important component of their culture was their Catholic faith. According to this view, the United States, as a predominantly Protestant country founded on the principles of the eighteenth century "enlightenment," was inherently antithetical to Catholicism. However, with its liberties, America also offered Catholics the opportunity to practice their faith freely, and to preserve their heritage, provided that they were not beguiled into compromises with the prevailing liberal culture. Put simply, since American society was not Catholic, it was, in Preuss's view, by definition anti-Catholic. Therefore, to preserve their integrity, Catholics could not acquiesce to an uncritical acceptance of American ways and institutions. Spiritual corruption, as represented by the "national selfishness" and moral laxity, must be vigorously resisted.[27] Likewise, the religious "indifferentism" promoted by the "godless" public school system was also a great threat to the integrity of the Catholic faith, and an obvious cause for much of the "leakage" in Church membership among immigrants. While conceding that the public school system "serves well the ends for which it was founded," its institutions were not "supplemented and permeated by religion" and so could not be an acceptable, long-term option for

Catholics. In the conservative understanding, the ultimate goal of education was to raise the mind to the reality of the divine. From this perspective, an "education" that is professedly secular is an absurdity. Since the true purpose of education went unrecognized in such institutions, the reading of Bible passages in public schools in an attempt to instill morality would not make them any less godless. Worse still were measures like Archbishop Ireland's Faribault school plan, that would surrender schools "permeated by religion" to the forces of secularism. All such measures that would give the secular state entree into the Catholic schools, including tax support, must be opposed.[28]

When the *Review* began publication, the issues of Americanization, the Catholic University, the Apostolic Delegate, and the schools were all considered from a self-consciously German-Catholic perspective. With the inevitable assimilation of the German-speaking community, and the forming of alliances with others who shared his outlook, Preuss's journal would no longer be simply a "German paper in English dress" and would become an organ of conservative Catholic opinion.

"Aggressive Vigor With Charity" September 1896–April 1898

In July, 1896, so that he might assist his ailing father in the editing of *Amerika*, Preuss moved the *Review* to his hometown of St. Louis. The move to St. Louis of course necessitated his resignation as editor of the *Katholisches Sonntagsblatt*. On returning to St. Louis, Preuss deemed it wise to call on the ordinary of the Archdiocese, Archbishop John J. Kain, to inform him that the *Review* would be beginning publication within the latter's jurisdiction. Though Preuss had enjoyed cordial relations with Archbishop Patrick Feehan in Chicago, the response from Kain was outright hostility as Preuss recounted in a letter written two years later, in 1898.

> [Archbishop Kain] has never been friendly to me. When I moved to St. Louis from Chicago two years and a half ago, and presented myself

before him, to inform him of the fact, he treated me like a dog. He said
that he had heard of the *Review*, that it was a very bad paper, that he
wouldn't have such a sheet in the house, and that, if I wasn't careful, he
would issue a circular against my paper. This incident taught me to be
very cautious and prudent, so as not to give him occasion to forbid my
journal.[29]

By the time that Preuss moved the *Review* to St. Louis many
original features of the journal aimed at a German audience had been
dropped.[30] Gone were the columns carrying the latest news from the old
country, German literature, and cultural events. It was not that the *Review*
ceased trying to represent German Catholics. But the battle had become
one over the defense of orthodoxy rather than ethnicity. Almost a year
before, Preuss had established a cooperative relationship with the editor
of *La Vérité* of Quebec, Jules Tardivel, through their mutual interest in
supporting the non-English speaking Catholics in North America and in
resisting the Americanizing efforts of the liberals.

The conflagration that was ignited in the press following the
resignation of John Keane as rector of the Catholic University in
September 1896, also consumed much of what was left of the *Review*'s
German particularity. The *Review*'s first comment on Keane's resignation
appeared in the October 15, 1896, issue under the title, "The Death
Throes of Liberalism."[31] Reporting that "the Holy Father has at last got
to the bottom of Church affairs in America," Preuss rejoiced that "The
cause of the 'Liberals' is hopelessly lost." As happened in the earlier
case of the *"tolerari potest"* given to Ireland's Faribault school plan, and
would occur again with the publication of *Testem Benevolentiae,* a
ferocious struggle took place in the American Catholic press over just
how to interpret Keane's resignation.[32] Influenced by the praises being
accorded Keane by Roman officialdom, including his elevation to a
titular archbishopric as well as by cables being anonymously generated
from Rome, much of the press reported that Keane had received some
sort of promotion. While admitting that "Bishop Keane is a good and

pious and well meaning man," Preuss maintained that Keane had been removed as rector by the pope because of his numerous "mistakes" that had alienated many Catholics in America. These mistakes included his involvement in the agitation over "Cahenslyism," the Parliament of Religions, and his hostility toward the German professors at the Catholic University. Because of these involvements, Keane "had no reason to complain if he was looked upon and denounced as one of the chief representatives of the liberal school."[33] Preuss quoted approvingly the *Catholic Journal* of Rochester that stated that Keane's removal as rector was not a personal matter, but rather a "deadly blow at Liberalism...there will be no more 'liberal Catholics' in America after this; nor are we likely to hear of the American Church again." [34]

Soon however, the optimism over Keane's resignation gave way to concern as "leaders of the liberal movement" tried "to make the American public believe that it is all the fault of Msgr. Schroeder."[35] Through the winter and early spring of 1897, the controversy over Keane's resignation continued in the press. The struggle between liberals and conservatives in the Church reached new intensity in late March when the *Review* published Msgr. Schroeder's broadside, "Can A Liberal Catholic Be A Good Catholic?."[36] Ten days later, Archbishop Ireland delivered a sermon at St. Patrick's church in Washington entitled "The New Age" in which he labelled his conservative opponents as "réfractaires" and implied that they were disloyal to the Pope.[37] On April 8, the *Review* reprinted Ireland's speech and Arthur Preuss made a point-by-point response. He noted that German Catholics had consistently supported papal claims to temporal power while Ireland and the liberals remained silent. German Catholics had resisted attempts "from certain quarters" to secularize the parochial schools. Also, German Catholics had opposed the Parliament of Religions, "where the robes of Catholic prelates brushed the tunics of heathenism" in a spectacle "which made the angels weep and the children of the one true Church hide their faces in anguish of soul." Preuss closed his essay in dismay that Ireland would have used the occasion of a Lenten sermon to question the loyalty of

Catholics who differed from him.[38]

Preuss was not alone in being offended by Ireland's speech and the German-Catholic press as a whole took up its cudgels in response. The *Review* itself ran essays on "Fin de Siecle Catholicism," "On Liberalism," and "The Church and Modern Progress."[39] These three articles, the first and last written under pseudonyms and the second translated from the French, criticized the liberals who "would put the Church in sympathy with all the movements with which humanity palpitates," accommodating her to the "zeitgeist" and the "imaginary progress" of the modern age. That one of these essays was originally published in France was a harbinger of the role the *Review* would shortly assume as an international voice of conservative Catholicism. As what Archbishop Ireland called "the War of '97" unfolded, Preuss's *Review* would form a lasting alliance with European conservatives in the struggle against the liberals.

Ireland's "War of '97" was the struggle of the liberals to exact revenge on the Germans and the conservatives for Keane's removal as rector of the Catholic University.[40] The point of attack was Monsignor Joseph Schroeder, whom they both opposed ideologically and despised personally. Their antipathy to Schroeder was particularly intense as they held him to be personally responsible, along with Cardinal Satolli, for Keane's ouster. The process of removing Schroeder was long and sordid. One of the charges levelled at Schroeder by the University's new rector, Rev. Thomas J. Conaty, was that he had made "frequent contributions to papers of recognized hostility to the University which engages him as a professor, notably the *Review*, whose editor Preuss. [sic]"[41] The campaign against Schroeder culminated in accusations of excessive drinking and the suggestion of moral improprieties. However, when it became known that Schroeder's opponents, Ireland, Keane, and O'Connell, as well as faculty members at the Catholic University, had stooped to having their quarry followed by private detectives, German Catholics in America were incensed. The *Review* carried a series of articles on Monsignor Schroeder and his enemies, and Preuss wondered at the use of detectives to follow Schroeder ("All that the spies were able to ferret out was that the Professor occasionally entered a restaurant and there —*horrible dictu* —publicly drank beer!"). Preuss castigated those involved, especially Archbishop Keane for such "unpriestly and un-Christian conduct."[42]

In the eyes of the *Review* at least, the "persecution" of Schroeder only endeared him as a conservative champion and "right minded people all over the land" were "indignant and disgusted" about the way he had been treated.[43] The Schroeder affair added a personal element to the conflict with the liberals that had not been evident before. The *Review* would be less willing to concede the personal virtue of its opponents Keane and Ireland in the future. Also, the fight over Schroeder's resignation brought to prominence in the pages of the *Review* the Reverend John F. Meifuss, a German-born priest of the Diocese of Belleville who had been educated in Belgium. There he had been a onetime student of Schroeder's and in the "War of '97" he came to his former mentor's defense. In the coming year Meifuss would play a major role in the *Review*'s attack on Americanism.[44]

"Rome Is With Us..." May 1898–February 1899

During the first months of 1898, as the polemical firestorm surrounding the Schroeder case played itself out, the *Review* attempted to be a salve against the war fever that was consuming the nation. Preuss responded to the destruction of the *U.S.S. Maine* in February 1898 by suggesting that the cause was accidental, or perhaps even a cynical ploy by the Cuban insurgents to obtain American intervention in their rebellion by provoking a war with Spain.[45] A month later Preuss condemned the lust for war of some Protestant preachers who were whipping up hatred against Catholic Spain. Part of the *Review*'s resistance against war with Spain included countering the "hyper-patriotism" of Americanists like Archbishop John Ireland. On April 7, 1898, as hostilities against Spain were about to be officially proclaimed, the *Review* reprinted an editorial from the *Catholic Journal of the South* that criticized recent remarks by Archbishop Ireland.

> There is no need for Archbishop Ireland or any other prelate or priest
> to inform American Catholics what their duty is. They know their duty
> full well and have amply demonstrated this in the past. Only a bigoted
> hypocrite or errant knave would question the loyalty of the Catholic
> citizens of America. (There is) ...no more need for Archbishop Ireland
> to explain than for Methodist or Baptist prelates...[46]

Preuss was also critical of the Vatican's use of Ireland in an attempt to
avert the war.

> To us American Catholics, who know public sentiment...it appears
> ridiculous to suppose that the personal or political influence of any one
> or a group of prelates on the President of the United States can have
> any weight.[As for rumors that successful negotiations might lead to a
> red hat for Ireland, Preuss remarked]...we would prefer peace even
> with Cardinal Ireland.[47]

The *Review* continued its opposition to the war, albeit more subtly, even
after hostilities had commenced. The May 12th issue, coming a month
after the war began, carried an essay entitled "Can War Be Justified?"
that had originally appeared in the *Humane Journal*. While Preuss
differed with the author of the article, "Don Quixote," by upholding
Catholic teaching that some wars are justified, the inferred application to
America's current war of the author's condemnation, calling war a
"collective and contagious insanity," was obvious.[48]

In the calm before the storm that was soon to break over
"Heckerism," Preuss found occasion to express his views on the internal
structure of the Church and its relations with contemporary forms of
government. His essay of March 31, 1898, "The Church —Monarchy,
Aristocracy, and Democracy," articulated the view that through the
papacy, the episcopacy, and the universal gathering of believers, the
Roman Catholic Church embodied the best aspects of these three forms
of government. Further, by embracing these three forms of government,

none of which possessed any intrinsic moral superiority, the Church strengthens her universal appeal and was "capable of receiving into her arms all nations, no matter how diversified their languages or customs or needs...."[49] Absent from the pages of the *Review* is any agreement with the Americanist myth that democracy and the republican form of government are indications of divine favor or the spiritual maturity of Americans.[50]

The topic of Americanism was first treated in the *Review* in October 1897, at the height of the battle over Monsignor Schroeder. At that time, in an article entitled simply, "Americanism," Preuss reported that "much ado has been made in Liberal organs" over the speech of Denis O'Connell, "A New Idea in the Life of Father Hecker," that he had given at the International Catholic Scientific Congress in Fribourg on August 20, 1897. Preuss reprinted O'Connell's description of "religious Americanism" and then dismissed it by saying that the liberal errors it contained were "nothing new at all" so "we save ourselves the trouble of commenting at length."[51] Also in October of 1897, Preuss published an essay by the Reverend A. H. Walburg on "True vs. False Americanism." Walburg described "true Americanism" as those aspects of American life that promoted virtue and morality. False Americanism is manifested by the "hunger and thirst for money" and the "spirit of pride and self-conceit."[52] The following week, Preuss noted the accolades that Walter Elliot's *Life of Father Hecker* was receiving in France. He attached to this notice a review of the "La Vie du Père Hecker" written in the French Jesuit journal, *Etudes*, by A. de la Barre, S.J. De la Barre's warning as to the possible consequences of distorting Hecker's life for propaganda purposes was very soon to be proven true.

> ...let us not express in absolute and in comprehensive theses the character of a man and the tendencies of his teaching when the man is multiple and his doctrine not precise; otherwise we will, while trying to establish theses bring out antinomies...Let us beware above all of school abstractions and the shibboleths of coteries.[53]

Other criticisms of Americanism came in the spring of 1898 when John F. Meifuss wrote three articles criticizing Archbishop John Keane's essay in the *Catholic World*, "America As Seen From Abroad."[54]

However, the *Review*'s fired its first real salvo in the campaign against Americanism on the front page of the May 19, 1898 issue in an article by Monsignor Schroeder's former protege, Father Meifuss, entitled "Bishop Neumann and Father Hecker."[55] Meifuss began what was to be the first in an eight-part series comparing John Neumann, C.SS.R., who was subsequently canonized, with Isaac Hecker, by recounting the publication of Father Walter Elliott's *The Life of Father Hecker*. Meifuss noted that in his introduction to the book, Archbishop Ireland had proclaimed Hecker as "the typical American priest," the "ornament" and "flower" of the priesthood in America. Meifuss, while quoting extensively from Denis O'Connell's Fribourg speech, also stated that "another reason for bringing the life of Father Hecker prominently before the public is found in the necessity of having someone to father the new 'American ideas and aspirations' or what is understood by 'Americanism.'" Meifuss then announced that he would make a comparison between Neumann and Hecker, using John Boerger's biography of the Bohemian missionary and Elliott's *Life of Hecker*, to determine which of the two men was truly a "typical American priest" and a "model" for priests of the future.

In the June 2, 1898, issue of the *Review* Meifuss began his detailed comparison of the two men. Under the heading "Father Hecker —Typical American Priest?" Meifuss recounted Hecker's youthful enthusiasm for the works of the "subjectivistic" and "pantheistic" philosophers Kant, Hegel, and Schilling. Continuing to quote from Elliott's life, he notes that in contrast to Hecker's diligent studies as a youth, during his preparation for the priesthood, by his own admission, he studied hardly at all. Meifuss remarks, "His special training for the ministry, as we have seen, was not much more than zero." If under these circumstances Hecker's superior, as Elliott related, decided that grace supplied for the defects of Hecker's training, then "good for them both." However, by no means could Hecker's preparation for the priesthood "serve as a model for ordinary mortals." The June 9 issue of the *Review* provided details on Hecker's "restless" youth. The "nervous temperament" described by Elliott was seen by Meifuss as the cause of Hecker's visions, which he and his biographer "want to make out as supernatural." On June 23, 1898, Meifuss related Hecker's dutiful but unexceptional career as a missionary priest.[56] The fourth and fifth installments of the series described Hecker's expulsion from the Redemptorists and the founding of the Paulists. Again Meifuss asked the question, can Hecker be called a "typical" or "model" priest? The final comparative article covered the period of Hecker's illness.[57] While conceding the evident suffering that Hecker endured, Meifuss expressed shock at Elliott's report that for the last three or four years of his life, Hecker not only did not celebrate or "hear" Mass, he went for months at a time without receiving Holy Communion. This "strange behavior" cannot serve as a model for the American priesthood and certainly is not characteristic of a saint.

The cumulative effect of Meifuss's focus on Hecker is to undermine the claims of Ireland, O'Connell, and others establishing him as a "type" and "model" of the priesthood. But when these details of his life are compared with the recognized heroic sanctity of John Neumann, the critique is devastating. Meifuss acknowledged that his comparison of Hecker and Neumann had drawn criticism, and the *Review* reprinted what it regarded as the most virulent attack on the series. But Meifuss countered that he had not altered Elliott's descriptions,

> ...neither have we dilated upon the weaknesses and defects of Father Hecker; we simply showed up the 'hero' of the Liberals in Father Elliott's colors...What we found and brought out were such traits as stamp the 'hero' an ordinary mortal and deprive him of those qualities essential in 'heroes' and 'saints' as understood by the Church. We doubt not that Father Hecker is in Heaven and hope to meet him there ourselves; but we do not doubt, either, that from Heaven he looks down with pity upon his overzealous friends and admirers, who make such desperate efforts to make him something he never was: 'a hero,'

'a saint,' 'a typical American priest,' a 'flower' and 'ornament of the American priesthood,'etc.[58]

Having used his Neumann "razor" on the liberal icon of Hecker, Meifuss next applied the same blade to its devotees, Gibbons, Ireland, and Keane.

We want more John N. Neumanns; our heart's desire is to see a venerable Neumann with his love for the Catholic press in the see of Baltimore, rather than a prelate who subsidizes the Liberal papers, such as the defunct *Moniteur de Rome*; we would prefer in the see of St. Paul 'a humble Bohemian mountain boy' with a vow of poverty, rather than a prelate whose landgrubbing propensities have brought him into collision with the courts of the country; the titular see of Damascus [Keane's titular archbishopric] would be more properly filled by a religious who modestly refuses the episcopal dignity but obeys at the command of the Sovereign Pontiff, than by one whom when the same Pontiff commands, goes sulking about the country...[59]

The *Review*'s renewed assault on liberalism in the Church was not limited to Father Meifuss's articles. On June 9, 1898, Preuss reprinted George Tyrrell's "True and False Liberalism." At this point in his career the future Modernist could be approvingly quoted for saying that the Church and society have their own understanding of the ideal civilization "which in every age and country" are "to some greater or lesser extent" incompatible.[60] In the June 30, 1898, issue readers of the *Review* were brought into direct contact with the European controversy over "Heckerism." The front page of this issue carried Father Meifuss's review of Father Charles Maignen's *Le Père Hecker, est-il un saint?* [61] Meifuss began his review by recounting the public controversy over the French translation and orchestrated promotion of Walter Elliott's *Life of Father Hecker*. He noted the involvement of Archbishop Ireland, Abbe Félix Klein, and recently Cardinal Gibbons with this literary enterprise and its "complete success."[62] Meifuss then recounted for his readers that Maignen's book had first appeared in March and April 1898 as a series of articles in *La Vérité* of Paris and that the "infuriated" liberals had "worked on" the Cardinal Archbishop of Paris, "who, no doubt to please

Cardinal Gibbons, refused his 'Imprimatur.'"[63] However, despite these efforts, Maignen's book attained an imprimatur and publication on Rome.

Summarizing Maignen's book, Meifuss notes that its most important section is part III, which "deals with the machinations of 'Americanism.'" He states that in this section Maignen "has given us a complete history of our Liberalism, called with preference by its adepts 'Americanism.'" The work is "free from exaggeration" and "rather mild in its criticism of persons, especially Father Hecker." As for his criticism, Meifuss remarks that Maignen does not mention Hecker's hopes for the inclusion of women in the work of the Paulists and his dream for an "androgynous" congregation. Meifuss speculates that this section of Elliott's book was left out of the French translation. Meifuss also criticizes Maignen's depiction of tensions within the Church in America. "To call the fight between Liberals and Conservatives in the U.S. a war between races, is wrong." According to Meifuss, the struggle within the Church in America transcended ethnic identities.

A week after the review of Maignen's book was published, the *Review* began to follow the controversy as it was being carried on in the Catholic press. The *Review* quoted the Rome corespondent for the Boston *Pilot* as saying that Maignen's book was an "unreasoning attack" on "what the author terms Americanism." Preuss appended to this report a piece from *La Croix* of Paris dated June 14 contending that before Father Albert Lepidi, O.P. had granted an imprimatur to Maignen's book, he had submitted the case to the highest Vatican authorities, including Pope Leo. Preuss added to this article his own note, "Liberalism has felt the weight of a mighty blow and is staggering to its doom."[64]

The July 7, 1898, issue of the *Review* also carried a "Roman Letter" from "Synchronos" that detailed the response that Maignen's book was receiving in Rome.[65] Synchronos wrote that "the battle between 'Liberals' and 'Ultramontanes' is on anew, more fiercely than ever." Synchronos confirmed the report of *La Croix* that approval for Maignen's critique of the *Life of Father Hecker* came from the highest levels. He also noted that a former associate of Monsignor Eugene Boeglin's, the Americanists' press "agent" in Europe, was busy in the Italian press trying to undermine the importance of the Vatican imprimatur.[66] Meanwhile, "the Liberal movement is spreading." The French papers were filled with "the escapades of apostate liberal abbes," and in Germany "Kraus and Schell are spreading the new gospel."[67] However, soon the "great surgeon will unsheathe his scalpel, and we'll have an operation, very painful but salutary..."

On July 14, 1898, Preuss reprinted an article from the *Freeman's Journal* reporting that both the *Life of Father Hecker* and "the movement comprehensively known as 'Americanism'" were being subjected to "exhaustive" and "unimpassioned scrutiny" in Rome. This article also noted the publication of A. J. DeLattre's "important book on Hecker and Americanism entitled *Un Catholicisme Américain.*"[68] For the next three weeks the *Review* published numerous articles on the controversy including French and Italian notices. The article from France in the August 4 issue was penned by George Périès, alias "St. Clement" and "Don Abbondio," under his own name and was a reprint of an article that had first appeared in the *Revue Canonique*. Périès' article is of special interest for its depiction of Americanism.

> Love for the new, the unpublished, joined to the audacity of noisy personalities, served by a syndicate of dissimulated interests...has pushed the leaders of the new school to excesses which at various times set Catholic opinion in commotion. The school question in the United States, the not less burning issue of secret societies, the nature of biblical inspiration, the too much vaunted separation of Church and State, the exaggerated spirit of independence, the Socialism of Henry George and McGlynn, are as many phases of these 'progressive ideas' dubbed by their upholders with the big name of 'Americanism.'[69]

Commenting on Périès' essay, Father Meifuss remarked that "we agree fully with the ideas here expressed." Further, the "Liberals made their biggest blunder" when they promoted Isaac Hecker as depicted in Elliott's biography as a "typical personage" and the book itself as a "resume" of Americanism.

The "Italian View" of Americanism that the *Review* printed on August 11 was taken from an anonymously published pamphlet that began circulating in Rome during July 1898.[70] This essay called the Americanists the "new Gnostics" and rebuked Hecker as the man "who felt himself called to convert Protestants to a Catholicism that is not Catholic!" While not naming names, Preuss stated that "we have a strong suspicion as to the identity of the pamphlet's author." He mischievously opined, "the fun is only just beginning in sunny Italy. Wait till the promised Italian edition of the 'Life of Father Hecker' appears and you'll hear all sorts of music on the Tiber's bank."

On August 18, the *Review* published two pieces of private correspondence relating to the controversy. The first was Preuss's own letter of July 7 to Charles Maignen, that had been published in the July 19 edition of *La Vérité*. Preuss's letter was in response to Maignen's request for articles the *Review* had published "relatifs au Père Hecker." Preuss took the occasion to thank Maignen for his writings, "au nom de milliers de prêtes et de laiques américains qui abominent 'l'américanisme' parce que c'est doctrine fausse et dangereuse." Commenting on his letter, Preuss remarks that while it was not intended for publication "we are ready to stand by every sentence it contains."[71]

Preuss was not the only one surprised to find his private correspondence printed on the pages of *La Vérité*. Three letters that Denis O'Connell had written to Lepidi in July were printed by *La Vérité* on August 15 and by the *Review* on August 18. In one of these letters O'Connell is quoted as saying "what is called Heckerism or religious Americanism, not only do I have nothing to do with it, but I despise it." Preuss commended "Msgr. O'Connell's disavowal of Americanism."[72]

The August 25 issue of the *Review* carried three articles relevant to the Americanist controversy. The first was the complete text of Cardinal Satolli's August 4 commendation of the English version of Maignen's book. Satolli wished Maignen divine assistance in "arresting this most dangerous pest." However, he also remarks on his pleasure that

Maignen's book has been "happily modified" in its English edition so that the discussion "will proceed more serenely and efficaciously." The second article on the controversy in this issue was Preuss's defense of Georges Périès, "our good friend," against charges that he had been dismissed from the Catholic University for being "extremely obnoxious" to his fellow faculty members. In the same issue of the *Review*, Father Meifuss took Monsignor Boeglin, alias "Innominato," to task for blaming the "the continental defenders of Americanism" for the controversy, saying that they had claimed no more for Hecker than the American Americanists had asserted.[73]

The influential review of Maignen's book written by Father Hippolytè Martìn, originally published in the French journal *Etudes* on July 20, was reprinted in the *Review* on September 1, 1898.[74] As a critique of Americanism, Martìn's review noted the boastfulness of the "Americanizers" for whom "modesty counts for nothing." He also condemned the "low estimate adherents of Americanism put on the supernatural" and the movement's "pretensions to 'modernism' of which it alone claims to hold the secret." Martìn ridiculed the Americanists who "have invented the 'modern soul,' as if man had been changed and grace and truth had to follow new paths to get at a new being." As for Hecker himself, he was "a virtuous priest" but "little equibalanced, passably nervous, no theologian at all and very conceited about his personal ideas."

Martìn's essay was the last major European exposition of Americanism to appear in the *Review* prior to the papal condemnation. Perhaps this fact reflected the "silence" Leo had imposed on the issue in Rome. This silence carried across the Atlantic as Walter Elliott reported in October 1898 to his French collaborator, Felix Klein. Elliott wrote "America is mute on the whole controversy" with "the exception of the *Review* edited by Arthur Preuss..."[75] The *Review* continued to publish articles on the controversy through the fall and winter of 1898. With a few exceptions, most of the stories the *Review* carried were speculation as to just what action Pope Leo was going to take on the controversy. One of the exceptions to these speculations was a short essay entitled "The Elements of Americanism," that was published in the November 3 issue under the pseudonym "Tilly." This is clearly an American critique of Americanism. According to the author, Americanism is comprised of three elements. The first is "'hyper-patriotism' growing out of a superficial comparison of the liberty of the Church in this country with her servitude in Europe." In making this comparison, the separation of Church and state "is readily imagined to be an ideal condition." While this separation "may be acknowledged as necessary and useful" in America, "it is by no means an ideal for Catholic nations." Material progress and the wealth of America have also fostered this "exaggerated patriotism." The second element of Americanism was "a mania for Americanizing foreign nationalities and foreign languages." The third element of Americanism was "an inordinate desire to please the Protestants and to make the Catholic Church palatable to them." This tendency led to "the Catholic total abstinence agitation and fondling the irreligious American school system, losing sight of the fact that these endeavors were condemned in the Syllabus and other official documents." Although America is a new nation, "it nevertheless can not arrogate to itself a new religion" but must "affiliate itself as a faithful and obedient member of the ancient universal Church."[76]

Another bit of original work that the *Review* engaged in during this period was the promotion of the English version of Maignen's book in America. The September 29 issue carried a brief report that Benzinger Brothers of New York had withdrawn their sponsorship of Maignen's book. The notice quoted Maignen's assertion that the publishers, "intimidé sans doute par les libéraux," had withdrawn their consent to distribute the book in the United States. Preuss admonished Benzinger to provide the public an explanation.[77] Three weeks later, in the October 20 edition of the *Review*, Preuss returned to this subject. He noted that "the influential and otherwise sober *Ave Maria*" had joined the campaign against Maignen by supporting Benziger's refusal of his book in an editorial. After intimating that *Ave Maria,* published at the University of Notre Dame had been influenced in this position by the new Holy Cross provincial, Father John Zahm, Preuss recounted with knowledgeable detail how Benzinger's had reneged on an agreement with Maignen. He stated that Benzinger Brothers had accepted "the agency of the book in the United States" in a letter to Dr. Maignen of July 12. However, on August 16, after the book had already been printed in Rome, and "shortly after Archbishop Keane landed in New York" Maignen received a cable from Benzinger Brothers cancelling their agreement and requesting that Maignen remove their name from the title page.[78] Subsequently, Benzinger Brothers also wrote to the superior of the Paulist Fathers to deny that they had ever consented to distribute the book, and promised not to sell the copies in their possession. Preuss adds that a Baltimore publisher had also refused to handle the book, and suggests that these publishers had been threatened with a boycott if they had agreed to distribute Maignen's book. However, Preuss was not going to be outdone by this sinister plot.

> We do not mean to leave this conspiracy to accomplish its purpose. The *Review* has cabled a large order to the publishers in Rome and expects to have them in St. Louis in a few weeks....The Liberals have been rubbing it into us 'old fogies,' that this is a free country, in which liberty of speech and press cannot be gagged. Their attempt to suppress a book that comes to us from the Eternal City with the Imprimatur of the Vatican and the recommendation of Cardinal Satolli, brimful of sacred and timely truths,...this dastardly attempt shall not succeed![79]

A month later Preuss carried Maignen's own comments on the attempt of the liberals to suppress the English version of his book, saying "the time for monologues is past." Preuss seconded the "doughty champion of conservatism" and noted that he had sold two full "orders" of Maignen's book. Preuss evidently regarded the distribution of *Father Hecker—Is He a Saint?* as a personal mission. "We are not making a penny on this transaction; all we want to do is to counteract the Benzinger-Murphy boycott and to spread Maignen's work in America."

Preuss adds that he is sorry "for those numbskulls who imagine they can scare the *Review* into silence by threatening letters" or by "stopping the paper." He vowed that "no power on earth" would force him to back down.[80]

Arthur Preuss evidently had some real concerns that an attempt would be made to stop the publication of the *Review*. In a letter to his canonical advisor, Father Peter Baart, dated December 17, 1898, Preuss wrote that "Maignen's book has made [Archbishop Kain] exceedingly angry, especially against me..." Preuss told Baart that "I have spoken to Bishop Janssen [of the Diocese of Belleville] who has no objection whatever to my moving the *Review* over the river to East St. Louis...in case I should get into trouble here." Preuss also asked Baart if he would present Preuss's case before the Apostolic Delegate should the need arise. Archbishop Kain never did attempt to silence the young lay editor but clearly Preuss's war against Americanism was making him enemies among powerful members of the American hierarchy.[81]

For the next four months, until Pope Leo's Apostolic letter was actually made public, Preuss and the *Review* were left to speculate as to just what action Rome would take on the Americanism controversy. Numerous dispatches from Rome were published and Preuss's unnamed correspondents were well informed. In fact, their dispatches were much more accurate than those circulating in the liberal camp, particularly those sent by Denis O'Connell.[82] The reports that Arthur Preuss was receiving enabled him to offer on November 17, 1898, a fairly accurate prediction of the measures that Leo XIII would take to settle the affair.

> Our own idea is that it will not take the subtle Leo long to find a way of condemning the false doctrines in Elliott's *Life of Hecker* without administering a direct public rebuke to the author and his friends and the champions of Americanism, so called, in general.[83]

The *Review*'s reporters, unlike O'Connell, never had any doubts about whether the errors associated with Americanism were to be condemned. In a letter published in the *Review* on December 8, 1898, "Synchronos" had reported "Rome is with us" in "our fight against Liberalism." The only unsettled question concerned the severity of the condemnation and whether Elliott's *Life of Father Hecker* would be placed on the Index.[84] In an article that appeared on December 29, 1898, entitled "Americanism in Agony," the *Review* accurately predicted the general content of the Pope's forthcoming letter to Cardinal Gibbons. Readers were also told "Msgr. Keane is sick. Has he seen the first proofs of the Holy Father's letter?" Father Meifuss added that Keane, now *persona non grata* at the Canadian College, had taken refuge with his friend the Sulpician procurator, who would doubtless feel the "reverberations" when "the stroke of lightning comes down on the head of the hero who proclaimed the World's Parliament of Religions as the non plus ultra of the century." Meifuss revelled in the change of fortunes.

> How things have changed within a year; a twelve month ago the Liberals gloried over the removal of their arch-enemy, Msgr. Schroeder, from the Catholic University; the year 1898 ends with the triumph of the Conservative cause. Msgr. Schroeder, we may add, will soon have his vindication too.[85]

A week later. January 5, 1899, Meifuss would defend the *Review*'s allies, "the French critics of Americanism." Rather than blaming them like so much of the Catholic press in America, "we thank them for their strong help they have given us in our struggle against these pernicious ideas." The essay was titled "The Reason Why," and provided the conservative justification for the agitation against Americanism.

> The German Catholics and the Jesuits have stood up manfully for the Catholic principles against all Liberal pretensions. In the first place to defend the truth in all its purity, and, secondly, to avert from our country the decadence which is the necessary result of Liberalism. Many of them have seen, some of them have been the victims of the Kulturkampf in France, Belgium and Germany, that was made possible only by the Liberalism of Catholics.[86]

Father Meifuss's defense of the French conservatives was necessitated by the increased support that the liberal apology for Americanism was garnering in the American Catholic press and foreshadowed the debates that would follow the publication of *Testem Benevolentiae*. To the claims that the controversy over Americanism was simply the result of a mistranslation into French of Elliott's *Life of Father Hecker* and the misrepresentations perpetrated by Charles Maignen, Preuss pointed to the series of articles Meifuss had written based on the English edition that turned up the same errors "long before Dr. Maignen's book saw the light in Rome."[87] As for whether Americanism existed in America in practice, the *Review* continued to refer to the Parliament of Religions, support of non-sectarian schools, and the lax attitude toward secret societies, as examples. The men who had set Isaac Hecker up as a "saint" and "the type of the modern priest—Archbishop Ireland, Msgr O'Connell, the Abbes Klein and Dufresne, et al.—committed a faux pas and it was the duty of orthodox theologians to protest and set matters right."[88]

Finally, on March 2, a week after its publication in Rome, the *Review* was able to print Pope Leo's response to the Americanism controversy, *Testem Benevolentiae*. The headline of the *Review* read, "Americanism Condemned" and the Pope's letter was greeted as a vindication, not only for the *Review*'s position over the preceding year, but from the journal's inception.

> We need not emphasize that we look upon this letter as a great victory for the true Catholic principles which were in such imminent danger in the United States and for which the *Review* has battled so tenaciously, against heavy odds, for several years. Archbishop Ireland needless to say, has fully submitted...[89]

"The Americanism Which Pope Leo Condemned"
March 1899–July 1901

As reported in the pages of the *Review*, the publication of *Testem Benevolentiae* with its papal condemnation of Americanism actually had little apparent effect on the life of the Church in America. Although the Pope's letter was proclaimed a "great victory," the war against liberalism was far from over. In fact, much to Preuss's apparent annoyance, the vanquished Americanists and their journalistic allies did not even have the courtesy to admit their defeat.

The first indications that the Americanism condemned by Pope Leo might elude its destruction came in the general press reaction to the Pope's letter. While the maneuverings of Cardinal Gibbons succeeded in limiting coverage of the condemnation in the secular press, reaction in the Catholic press tended to follow pre-ordained patterns. The German-American, French-Canadian, and conservative allies of the *Review* shared its praises of the "great victory." The majority of the English-speaking press, following the line of the Americanists themselves, maintained that the tendencies condemned existed only in France, and there only in the fevered imaginations of anti-American reactionaries.[90]

For months following the issuance of *Testem Benevolentiae*, Preuss skirmished with the editors of other Catholic journals over whether the condemned principles were held in the United States or only in France; whether a faulty translation of Elliott's *Life* was to blame or whether the English version was also errant; and on the personal motives of some of the anti-Americanists, especially Georges Périès.[91] The *Review*'s response to these attempts to de-Americanize the Americanism condemned by Leo was to point out that the Pope's letter was addressed to America, not France, and that well-known Americanists like Archbishop Ireland, Denis O'Connell, and the Paulist Fathers had seen the necessity for submitting unsolicited disavowals. Further, at least six archbishops had thanked the Holy Father for his letter, and two full provinces were on record as stating that Americanism did exist in the United States.[92] In addition, there was Bishop Bernard McQuaid's sermon of June 25, 1899, refuting the assertions of the liberals by citing four major indications of Americanism in the United States.[93]

The *Review* also kept its eye on the activities of Americanist scholars. It reported on the submission of Félix Klein, the "Indexing" of Herman Schell's writings, and the withdrawal of both Elliott's *Life of Father Hecker* and Zahm's *Evolution and Dogma*.[94] Preuss incurred a rebuke from his own bishop, Archbishop John Kain, that he published, when he reprinted charges by Victor Charbonnel, an apostate priest and self-proclaimed Americanist, linking Cardinal Gibbons with the views condemned in *Testem Benevolentiae*.[95] In a letter to the Sulpician Alphonse Magnien, Gibbon's friend and advisor, Archbishop Kain lamented the fact that he could not take stronger action against Preuss for publishing the article, "Charbonnel and Cardinal Gibbons." Kain wrote, "there would be no use in my using extreme measures with a man who, year after year, received from Cardinal Satolli such high commendation for his services to religion."[96]

Apart from its general defense of the applicability of the papal brief to America, the *Review* was directly involved in a major controversy that followed in the wake of the condemnation of Americanism. The controversy concerned the comparison made between the apologists of Americanism, who accepted *Testem Benevolentiae* while denying the existence of the errors it condemned, and the Jansenists who had taken a similar stance when a papal bull had condemned doctrinal errors that it asserted existed in the writings of Cornelius Jansen.[97] This comparison was first made on the front page of the *Review* on April 6, 1899, when Preuss reprinted Salvatore Brandi's essay from *La Civiltà Cattolica* of March 18, "Leone XIII e l'Americanismo."[98] On May 11, 1899, the *Review* lampooned the *Catholic Citizen* of Milwaukee "which pretends to be scandalized by a remark of the German daily *Amerika* to the effect that 'more than half the Catholic papers of the United States were not Catholic in their responses to the papal letter; they were Jansenistic.'"[99] Not mentioned here by the *Review* is that Arthur Preuss himself was the effective editor of *Amerika*, having taken over for his ailing father. Also noteworthy is the fact that the letter sent to Pope Leo by the bishops of the Milwaukee province in May 1899 lamented the "many especially among the Catholic newspaper editors" who do "not hesitate to proclaim again and again, in Jansenistic fashion" that the condemned errors did not exist in America.[100]

The Milwaukee bishops' letter and the issue of the Jansenist-like response to *Testem Benevolentiae* came up again in the September 14, 1899, issue of the *Review*. There Father Meifuss wrote in response to a letter by one "H.M." criticizing the Milwaukee bishops that had appeared August 25 in the *Northwestern Chronicle*. "H.M." was a pen name used by Archbishop Ireland.[101] Part of "H.M."'s rebuke to the bishops was based on the contention that *Testem Benevolentiae* was not an infallible "ex cathedra" statement. The *Review* reprinted "H.M."'s letter with Meifuss's response attached that Charles Maignen had demonstrated that the papal brief was infallible in his "Little Syllabus" published on April 6 by the *Review*.[102] On October 5 Meifuss reported that the *Northwestern Chronicle* of September 22 carried an article, "apparently by the same author," ridiculing Charles Maignen as "an obscure pamphleteer" and calling Meifuss "an immature heresy hunter."[103] While there is no indication that Preuss and Meifuss knew that they had been shadowboxing with Ireland himself, this "Jansenism" episode demonstrates the capability of the *Review* for providing polemics for some bishops and for provoking them in others.

Arthur Preuss continued to cover the controversy over Americanism throughout 1899, but as the first anniversary of the publication of *Testem Benevolentiae* passed his thoughts most certainly were closer to home. For throughout January, 1900, his wife Marie, "for seven years my visible guardian angel," was in the throes of "severe suffering." Marie Preuss died on February 8, and Preuss confessed that her death "has so completely unnerved me that I must take a week or two off."

> I crave my friends' and subscribers' pardon and patience and beg them most earnestly, especially those of the reverend clergy, to pray for me, but above all for her who was such a faithful, devoted and untiring helpmate.[104]

His grieving over the death of his wife was evidently also a time of grace that brought out in Arthur Preuss an even greater faith.

> For I have experienced that our only consolation in bereavement and suffering, is not philosophy, but religion; not science, but faith; not self-redemption and proud consciousness of our strength, but divine grace, humble submission to the will of God and loving immersion in our Saviour's passion.[105]

In October 1900, Arthur Preuss, a twenty-nine-year old widower with a six-year-old daughter, was married again, this time to Pauline Beuchmann of East St. Louis, Illinois, who was four years his junior. They were happily married for almost thirty-five years and had ten children.[106]

On the death of his wife Marie, Preuss received many cards and letters of sympathy from his friends and readers. Among these were letters from Joseph Schroeder, Charles Maignen, and Georges Périès.[107] In addition to these letters from old friends, Preuss also received letters of condolence from some new ones. Principal among these was one from Abbot Charles Mohr, of St. Leo's Abbey in Florida. Abbot Charles' letter to Arthur Preuss initiated a close friendship between the two men and Preuss became a frequent guest of the Abbey of St. Leo. Additionally, Abbot Charles would often assist Preuss with his translations of German theological works.[108]

Another important letter that Preuss received upon the death of his wife was from Archbishop Michael A. Corrigan, of New York. Dated February 24, 1900, and marked "Private & Confidential," Corrigan's letter runs as follows.

> Dear Sir,
>   A good priest friend, one of our German rectors, has sent me a clipping from the *Review* regarding Mr. Martin Griffin and the late Rev. Dr. McGlynn. In the same enclosure I learned of the death of your excellent wife. Permit me to offer my respectful sympathy and add that I will offer the Holy Sacrifice...
>   Regarding Dr McGlynn, both Card. Satolli and Mgr Martinelli most strongly advised that he should not receive any city parish in New York.
>   I am dear sir very faithfully yours, M. Corrigan, Abp.[109]

Archbishop Corrigan's letter and Preuss's response of March 1, 1900, is the earliest extant exchange between the two men.[110] Corrigan's references to an article in the *Review* were by way of correcting a report from another journal that Preuss published that stated that Corrigan had been uncharitable in not giving McGlynn his old parish back.[111] On March 5, 1900, Corrigan wrote back to Preuss that he could not accept a "gratis" subscription to the *Review* but that he would be happy to pay for it. Corrigan also elaborated on the reasons why McGlynn was not allowed to return to his former parish by stating that shortly after being restored to ministry he "had relapsed into his old ways."

Arthur Preuss had already been supportive of Archbishop Corrigan. But from the time of this exchange of letters, Preuss became an ardent admirer of Corrigan, ever grateful for the confidences that the Archbishop had shared with him. When Corrigan died in May, 1902, Preuss noted that the Archbishop's death was a special loss to him as Corrigan had supported the *Review* with "warm and unstinted sympathy" and because he was "the only one of his exalted rank who was ever ready to furnish inside information on ecclesiastical questions and subjects."[112] In the months following Corrigan's death, the *Review*, relying on information Preuss received from the late Archbishop's brother, carried the story that Corrigan could have been a cardinal but asked Rome to bestow the honor on James Gibbons instead. James Corrigan also told Preuss that his brother had been approached about being the Apostolic Delegate in the United States prior to the appointment of Archbishop Satolli.[113] However, apart from this information from the Archbishop's brother, and the letters regarding McGlynn previously mentioned, there is no extant correspondance between Corrigan and Preuss regarding the other controversies of the day.

If, even after their initial contact in February, 1900, Archbishop Corrigan supplied Preuss little material, the activities of the prelate's opponents John Ireland and John Keane frequently provided Preuss sufficient grist for his mill. In the period after the condemnation of

Americanism Ireland continued to be portrayed in the pages of the *Review* as part fool and part fanatic. The fool came out in reports on Ireland's political boosterism and hyper-patriotism. The fanatic was depicted in his "pettifogging" on his Americanist views, and whenever rumors of a red hat for Ireland surfaced in the press.[114] On Archbishop Keane, the *Review* was at first incredulous at reports in the spring of 1900 that he was to be made ordinary of the Archdiocese of Dubuque. "We think we can safely predict that the name of the next occupant of the see of Dubuque will not be John J. Keane." Once Keane's appointment became certain however, Preuss voiced no dissent.[115] In the October 11, 1900, issue of the *Review* Preuss reprinted a story from the secular press carrying Keane's statements about his enemies who had called him a heretic. The reprinted story also quoted Keane as being "very sarcastic" and calling Preuss "a poor creature" and that "some one ought to take him in hand and teach him his catechism." Preuss rejoined that it was the *Western Watchman* that had called Keane a heretic and a semi-Pelagian, and Preuss offered to send Keane the editor's address.[116]

In addition to jousting with other journals over the interpretation of *Testem Benevolentiae* and following the doings of the Americanists, there was an Americanism "watch" kept up by the *Review*. A regular column began to appear in the fall of 1899 called "Outcroppings of Americanism" and it covered manifestations of the "Americanist spirit." These included everything from the criticism of Scholastic theology in the Catholic press, to a women's minstrel show at a church fair, and "half-dressed clericals disporting themselves" at a YMCA.[117]

But the *Review*'s continued war on Americanism was not only one of journalistic repartee and skewering clergy for "compromising" the dignity of their office. There remained a serious commitment to educating the public about the gravity of the errors condemned by Pope Leo. In the period under discussion, the three most important articles that the *Review* published on the theological aspects of Americanism were all written by Europeans. The first of these, written by the Belgian Jesuit, A. J. DeLattre, entitled, "Is Heckerism Really Condemned?" appeared in the *Review* on May 18, 1899. In this article DeLattre took the statements in *Testem Benevolentiae* relating to specific condemned errors and matched them up with passages in the English version of Elliott's *Life of Father Hecker*. DeLattre concluded his article by noting that no one was even attempting to defend the theological opinions that the Pope had condemned.[118]

The second important essay on "religious Americanism" was "The End of Americanism in France" by Monsignor P. L. Péchenard, Rector of the Catholic Institute of Paris. First published in the *North American Review*, Preuss carried this essay as a three-part series shortly after its initial publication.[119] In this article, Péchenard asserted that, contrary to the claims of the defenders of Americanism, that not only did the condemned errors exist, but they were most certainly American in their origin. According to Péchenard, "opinions and doctrines" known as Americanism, "after a long incubation in America," "burst forth" in Europe through the *Life of Father Hecker* "as a complete system, where were found altogether dogma, discipline, Christian and religious life, and democratic and social doctrines." Americanism was "upsetting" and had "aroused much passion in France," but it dissipated quickly after the issuance of *Testem Benevolentiae*. Though Americanism presented "real dangers," it disappeared quickly in France because it was only supported by an "imperceptible minority." As a body of thought, Americanism "implied a certain bending in the matter of dogmatic affirmation, a separatist tendency with respect to central ecclesiastical authority, a claim to a larger individual independence, and a minimizing in the practices of the Christian, and especially the religious life." For Péchenard, what really doomed Americanism was that after the papal letter, "the chief American supporters of these novelties were seen vying with each other in the reprobation of them and declaring with the greatest non-challance that they never had anything in common with them." Consequently, Americanism in France, "in its religious, dogmatic, disciplinary and mystic sense is dead." Even that "illustrious prelate," Archbishop Ireland, on his recent visit to France, "understood himself that he must say no more about it."[120]

Actually, if the suppositions of numerous historians are correct, John Ireland had a lot more to say about "it," and did so in direct response to Péchenard's article in an essay called "The Genesis of Americanism" that was published by the *North American Review* in May 1900 under the pseudonym, "J. St. Clair Etheridge." The Etheridge article upheld the standard Americanist endorsement of the separation of Church and state, co-operation with non-Catholics and the adaptation of "the external methods of the Church to the needs of the times."[121]

The *Review* had no immediate comment on the "Etheridge" article. In fact, its response came a full year later in Charles Maignen's essay, "The Americanism Which Pope Leo XIII Has Condemned."[122] Here Maignen refers to the Etheridge piece as "the most daring effort" by the adherents of Americanism "to mislead public opinion regarding the true sense of the teachings of Leo XIII." The purpose of his essay, Maignen says, is "to establish here that the 'Americanism' condemned by Leo XIII, is really that of Father Hecker and his followers, and not a phantom heresy, as St. Clair Etheridge makes bold to assert." Maignen begins by arguing that to say that Americanism as condemned by Leo does not exist, or does not exist in America, is to insult the Pope's teaching office as well as his intelligence. Also, Maignen demurs at the importance that his opponents gave to his criticism of Americanism as the cause of the controversy, saying that they pay him too much honor.

After these initial parries, Maignen launches his own thrusts by asserting that the errors condemned by the Pope are found in the original English as well as the French translation of Elliott's *Life of Father Hecker*. Second, while the Americanists have tried to distance themselves from this book subsequent to the crisis, in the year before "we began our campaign against Americanism," Ireland, Keane, and O'Connell had already loudly endorsed it. Third, Maignen states that the foundation of all the errors comprised by the term Americanism "is the adaptation of the Church to the age" or, in Keane's words, "'the synthesis of progress and pure Catholicity.'" According to Maignen, these are the very principles of liberalism, that were condemned in the Syllabus of Errors by Pius IX. Maignen notes that some admitted Americanists, like Victor Charbonnel, even want to apply this principle of adaptation to the dogma of the Church. Fourth, while Maignen recognizes that Leo allows for "the utility of change in the Church's discipline" he is critical of the attempts to universalize "those American reforms that Father Hecker envisioned" without due regard for the judgment of Church authorities in such matters. Maignen goes on to match specific points condemned by Leo to passages in Elliott's *Life of Father Hecker*. Thus, having tied the leading Americanists to Elliott's book, and having demonstrated that the errors condemned by Leo were taken from this book, including Ireland's introduction, Maignen closed his case for the existence of the condemned Americanism in the United States by noting that many American bishops, and American Catholics, "like the editor of the *Review*," supported the papal condemnation. Finally, Maignen notes, as the *Review* had done before him, that *Testem Benevolentiae* was just one part of the general struggle against liberalism, that included the encyclical that Leo had sent to the French clergy in September 1899, and the pastoral letter of the bishops of England on liberal Catholicism issued in January 1901.[123]

"Is This A Christian Country?"

For the anti-Americanists that Arthur Preuss and the *Review* spoke for, Americanism was only an "outcropping" of the much larger evil of liberalism. In fact, it was the conciliation and even the endorsement of liberalism represented by the Americanist movement that fueled the conservative opposition to Americanism. Therefore, it is only by recognizing what men like Arthur Preuss meant by liberalism, that one can understand their vehement opposition to it.

In addition to the official statements, the *Review* published numerous essays on liberalism and its consequences for Catholicism in the years surrounding the Americanist controversy. The most definitive of these was an essay by Preuss himself called simply "Liberalism." Printed on November 9, 1899, this piece warmly endorsed a book recently published entitled *What is Liberalism?* This book had been written by a Spanish theologian, Don Félix Sarda y Salvary, in 1886.[124] Its appearance thirteen years later in the United States was the work of Dr. Condé B. Pallen, a lay theologian and writer. Pallen shared with Preuss a German background and conservative Catholicism. Moreover, until shortly before the appearance of *What Is Liberalism?*, which Pallen had "Englished and adapted," he had been editor of the other conservative Catholic journal in St. Louis, *Church Progress*. Pallen, as the title page indicates, did more than simply translate Sarda's book. He adapted it to the American situation and even added a chapter on liberalism in America. From Pallen's hands, *What Is Liberalism?* came forth as a conservative Catholic apologia for America. Though coming five years after Preuss had started his journal, it provides a systematic presentation of the visceral conservative reaction to liberalism that had filled the pages of the *Review* from its beginning. It is no wonder that Preuss greeted the publication of *What Is Liberalism?* with unbounded enthusiasm. Preuss wrote of this book,

> ...we would scatter a million copies broadcast over all the land if only we had the means...It is a vade mecum for every conservative Catholic and a most powerful antidote for the heresy which Pope Leo has but a short while ago warningly raised his pontifical boast...It has often been alleged that 'Liberalism,'especially in America, is...undefinable and intangible. Don Sarda shows clearly and victoriously that it is Rationalism, or the doctrine of the absolute sovereignty of human reason, and that it exists and operates everywhere where absolute freedom of worship, the supremacy of the state, secular education, civil marriage—in one word secularisation holds sway. And where are these pernicious principles glorified more enthusiastically than right here in the United States?

Preuss then went on to quote Pallen at length on liberalism in America. In the United States liberalism manifests itself primarily as "non-sectarianism." Non-sectarianism holds as a "fundamental truth" that one religion is as good as another because all creeds are "after all but differences in forms of expression," that "one has the right to believe what he pleases," and that "religion is a thing entirely apart from our civic and social life." In practice, the fallacies of non-sectarianism in our civic and social life work to the detriment of religion and morality.

> Civil marriage and divorce, mixed marriage, and the consequent degradation of family life, business standards, morality in general pitched on a low key, a vicious literature, a materialistic journalism, catering to lax thinking, and lax living, religion publicly mocked and scoffed, denied or held indifferently...[125]

This conservative indictment of American society, when read by the *Review*'s faithful subscribers, must have been as immediately recognizable to them as Preuss's editorial viewpoint as it was to Preuss himself. In subsequent issues he continued to articulate this line of thought by giving prominent place to essays of his own like "Is This a Christian Country?" and "Paganism In Our Christian Country."[126]

A century after the fact, within a social milieu that has enshrined "non-sectarianism" in public life, it is difficult to appreciate why this manifestation of liberalism was so hated by men like Preuss and Pallen. Quite simply, in liberalism, with its foundation in "the absolute sovereignty of human reason" and manifested in secularization or non-sectarianism, they saw the denial of God. To these conservative Catholics the call and the claims of the Catholic faith were radical and absolute. Non-sectarianism and its consequences, the separation of Church and state, civil marriage, compulsory public education, etc., were "pernicious" and ultimately corrosive to the one true faith. All of these activities reduced the truths of Catholicism to mere "expressions." That is why for Catholic prelates to congregate with representatives of other religious bodies was not only manifesting tacit approval of them and the errors they propounded; it was in effect stating that Catholicism had no stronger claims to true teaching than these other bodies of belief. As for the separation of Church and state, it could, of necessity be tolerated but it contributed to the practical atheism of American public life. In non-sectarian America, the godless state became the witness to holy

64

matrimony and the purveyor of divorce. Godless public education was an oxymoron. How could children be educated if their "education" taught them nothing about the Truth? In such institutions children were explicitly taught that all views of the truth must be tolerated, and implicitly, that no one view is absolutely true. The result of this indoctrination in religious indifferentism was that American public education was a primary cause of "leakage" of Catholics from the faith.

As for the consequences of the practical atheism that pervaded American society, they were there for all the world to see. A case in point was the war on Spain, a needless war, bringing "atrocities" by American soldiers against civilians, the occupation of the Philippines, and the desecration of Catholic churches. Preuss noted with sad irony that as U.S. soldiers returned home they sold as booty the sacred vessels of a Catholic society in American junk shops.[127] Of course, where Preuss saw the war on Spain as a symptom of American corruption, the Americanists Denis O'Connell and John Ireland gloried in the conquests as manifestations of America's providential destiny.[128] Reflecting on the treatment of the Filipinos and the nationalism of the Americanists, the *Review* paraphrased one of Archbishop Ireland's paeans to America as a chosen nation. "The matron prudently stepping, with the ethereal breezes caressing her tresses has turned out to be a patron rudely shooting them into the land of liberty."[129]

Another manifestation of the anti-Christian animus of American society was the social acceptability of racism and "our national disgrace" of lynchings, condoned in the communities in which they occurred. Preuss remarked that if these events occurred in any other country but the United States, "there would be the utmost indignation throughout this land." On December 13, 1900, he urged that Catholic organizations speak out for "fair play for the black man whenever necessary."[130]

In addition to these violations of justice, there was the general spiritual decline of American society as indicated by lax attitudes to public morals, marriage, and divorce, and the decline of religious practice among the population as a whole.[131] And of course, on top of the decadence, there was the widespread anti-Catholic bigotry manifested in the American Protective Association, the hatred toward Spain, government discrimination against Catholic Indian schools and the effective bar to Catholics holding high government office.

Viewed from this perspective, the compromises with liberalism and the national chauvinism of Americanists such as John Ireland and John Keane, were naive and dangerous. Conservatives saw "modernity," the paramour of the Americanists, as the offspring of liberal rationalism, that needed to be resisted in the Church without equivocation. The only way that Catholics could preserve their faith within such a "poisonous" environment, was through a strong ultramontanism within the Church and with militancy toward her external adversaries.[132]

Preuss maintained the social perspective of the Christian "exile." His comments in an essay entitled "The Apostle of Patriotism," written as a reaction to the speech Archbishop Ireland gave at John Keane's investiture as Archbishop of Dubuque in 1901, provide a sort of summary of their conflicting world views. These quotations also indicate how little either had changed in the seven years since Preuss had first printed a critique of John Ireland's Americanism. First Preuss quoted Ireland in his addressing the Catholics of America,

Be you in the truest and best meaning of the word, Americans, loving America, its institutions, devoted to its interests, chary in blaming it, ardent in defending it....There is among some of us...a disposition to criticize every moment...to exaggerate faults, to minimize virtues, to pile up grievances, to grumble perpetually. Such a disposition is unpatriotic and does most serious harm to the Catholic faith in the eyes of earnest, intelligent Americans. Surely the time has come to leave off the old spirit which the days of real persecution beget, to live for the present and future... Let us be just to America and know and proclaim, that nowhere, all things duly considered, is the Church freer than in America...

To Ireland's admonition Preuss responded,

> Is it really necessary for the Catholics of these United States to be
> continually reminded that they must be Americans?... When we read
> of the suppression of our Catholic Indian schools, the maltreatment of
> our brethren in the Philippines, the growth of gambling and divorce,
> the many bills aimed at our schools, the flaying and burning of
> defenseless men in Texas and Louisiana, the constant and alarming
> increase in greed and selfishness and the decay of the spirit of Christian
> charity, the multiplying indications of national unbelief and dishonor,
> some of us feel...that perhaps after all the venerable old fashioned
> Pontiff... was not entirely wrong when he warned us that the condition
> of the Church in this country is hardly ideal and the Catholicity of
> some of us not absolutely sterling and unalloyed...While we love our
> country dearly, though not undiscriminatingly, we must never forget
> that our real patria is beyond the bourne, and whatever is apt to
> sidetrack us...even be it stamped with the magic brand 'American,'
> must be to us anathema...Msgr. Ireland's admirers love to compare
> him with St. Paul, who is the patron of his episcopal city. But whatever
> virtues he may have in common with the Apostle of the Gentiles, we
> nowhere learn that the latter made love of country the keynote of his
> exhortations...we should prefer to hail him [Ireland] as a real latter day
> St. Paul, preaching not America and her glories, but Christ and Him
> crucified.[133]

In evaluating the role that Arthur Preuss played in the Americanist
controversy there are two principal questions to be considered. The first
concerns the position that he supported and the second, the degree to
which Preuss's view was shared in the Church in America. Taking the
second question first, the standard works on the Americanist controversy
indicate that neither the Americanists nor their most ardent opponents
enjoyed wide support. The membership of either group was comprised
almost entirely by the leadership "elite" of clerics and lay intellectuals.
Within this subgroup of the American church it seems reasonable to
assume that only a minority would have been active as either liberal or
conservative partisans.

Seen in this light, the views of Arthur Preuss, as those of the
Americanists, were those of a minority. While Walter Elliott told Félix

Klein in October of 1898 that the *Review* was the only paper working against the Americanists, "with a very limited subscription of mostly German priests," there were no nationally distributed liberal papers in America that gave the Americanists unequivocal support. Since the *Review* did not carry advertisements Preuss did not regularly publish circulation figures. However, in March 1899 he did have occasion to mention that he had just over a thousand subscribers.[134] It also needs to be remembered that the positions of the *Review* were being cited in numerous other papers, in America and in Europe, in both those with which Preuss had friendly "exchanges" and those who opposed his views. That Preuss's *Review* was also noticed by the leading Americanists, Ireland, Keane, O'Connell, and Elliott is another indication that his minority views were reaching a broad audience.[135]

As for the position that Preuss articulated in regard to the relationship between the Church and American society, it can be seen as his attempt to be faithful to Christ's admonition that His followers must be "in the world" but "not of it" (John 17:14-16). Fidelity to Christ necessarily demands of the Church and the individual believer that they too must be "signs of contradiction." The consequent social alienation of true Christian discipleship opposes the natural desire for assimilation and acceptance. The alienation inherent in being a Catholic in a non-Catholic society also resists the facile intellectual synthesis of fundamentally different world views. Emmett Curran refers to this tension among conservative Catholics in his book on Archbishop Corrigan. Curran remarks on the process of "bifurcation" and "compartmentalization" that took place among Catholic conservatives because "they in effect had abandoned any attempt to find an equation between Catholicity and Americanism." "What the American Catholic was as a Catholic had little to do with what he was as an American."[136]

This interpretation, at least in so far as it applies to Arthur Preuss and the views that he represented, is inaccurate. True conservatives could not "abandon" an attempt they had never made. Nor need the philosophical and theological incompatibility of Catholicism and the liberalism that formed the basis of American society, fracture the conservative Catholic's world view. While the terms "Catholic" and "American" are both designations that refer to one's character, as delimitations, they operate on completely different levels. Catholicity is first and foremost a statement about one's relationship with God and His Church. It is a divine calling and a grace. By contrast, ethnic or national distinctions, while they effect the context within which one encounters the divine, they are strictly of this world and have little bearing on one's actual relationship with God. For Arthur Preuss, a self-taught Scholastic theologian, Catholicism was of the "substance" of his identity, and "Americanism," or "Germanism" a mere "accident." This being the case, the affinity that Preuss expressed for "our brethren in the Philippines" was not hyperbole. He sincerely believed that the communion of the faithful was infinitely more important than the ties of nationality. Hence his impatience with the providential pretensions and jingoistic perorations of the "apostles of patriotism."

III Militant Catholicism for the Twentieth Century

With the publication of Charles Maignen's essay, "The Americanism Which Leo XIII Has Condemned," on July 11, 1901, the personalities involved in the Americanist controversy and their specific activities ceased to be the a main topic of interest in the pages of the *Review*. After all, Rome had spoken, and so the urgency of the battle waned particularly as the proponents of Americanism had assumed a prudent silence on the matter. Subsequently, the *Review* broadened its scope from Preuss's first preoccupation with ethnic and inter-Catholic struggles. The columns of the *Review* were opened to more discussion of other contemporary issues. There was much to discuss.

The first two decades in which Preuss's *Review* was published were characterized by social ferment on an international scale resulting from the process of rapid industrialization. In the United States, the most important development of the late nineteenth century was the transformation of the country from an agricultural society into an industrial power within a generation's time. Virtually all of the other developments during this period, the increase in national wealth, the flood of immigration, widespread urbanization, the birth of the labor movement and the changing views of the role of government in society, were consequences of the process of rapid industrialization. The social tensions in the United States produced by industrialization led to the "Progressive Era," that began with the presidency of Theodore Roosevelt and concluded with American entry into World War I. The "Progressive Era" has been called "a golden period in American development," characterized by prosperity and a general improvement in living conditions. It was also a time of great optimism manifested by a "virtual crusade" to revitalize democracy and to end the "twin evils of special privilege and poverty."[1]

This crusade took many forms. There was a movement among workers and their advocates for higher wages, reduced hours, and improved working conditions. Political reformers sought to end corruption in government by reforming election procedures. Government involvement in the promotion of social welfare began to be widely promoted as well. In addition to a wide range of interests, the reform movements of the Progressive Era had a broad base of support in American society. And significantly, in explaining the success of these simultaneous movements for social justice and economic reform, they were primarily middle-class movements led by small businessmen, bankers, farmers, clergymen, and editors, in short, men like Arthur Preuss. Of course, while other social commentators had their own views of the reforms that society needed, Arthur Preuss answered this question from his own perspective, the perspective of a Catholic in America.

A survey of the articles published by Arthur Preuss in the years from 1902 through 1914 disclosed that the subjects receiving the most frequent notice were the "social question," education, and a cluster of issues related to Catholic assimilation or inculturation in America. Preuss's traditional view of education, that it must by definition be directed toward the elucidation of the faith, has already been discussed. His observations on the "social question" will be covered subsequently. For now the category of articles related to Catholic assimilation will be reviewed.

Preuss's handling of this cluster of issues was a type of apologetics on behalf of Catholicism in its encounter with American modernity. However, these apologetics took on a more general character than the earlier articles aimed at Americanism and were published only periodically as opposed to the fusillades issued at the height of the controversy. Father Charles Maignen, Preuss's "doughty grenadier," made another appearance in the *Review* with his observations on the Church in America. Under the title, "A French View of Religion in America," Preuss published a book review by Maignen on May 14, 1903 which renewed the old charges but added a new twist. The book under review, "La Religion dans la Societe aux Etats-Unis," by Henry Bargy, actually praised all the characteristics of religion in America that

Maignen and Preuss condemned. Bargy had also included the Catholics in America within his positive appraisal of "the American religion." Maignen for his part began his review of the book by distancing the majority of American Catholics from the "religion" that Bargy extolled. "The majority of the American episcopate, the bulk of the clergy and especially of the laity, do not hold or practice a Catholicity different from that held or practiced by the Catholics of any other country." However, said Maignen, "the most noisy portion" of American Catholics, "the party who call themselves 'Americanists,'" have fully embraced "the American religion." Maignen then quotes Bargy as saying,

> The American religion has two characteristics...it is social and it is positive; social in as much as it devotes more attention and care to society than to the individual; positive, so far forth as it is solicitous for that which is human rather than for that which is supernatural.

According to Bargy, and Maignen agreed, the "positivism" of American religion made American denominations more similar to each other than they were to their mother churches. This positivism was also the secret of American religious toleration. Bargy noted approvingly that American religion, as a "civic and moral religion," was continually being modified by scientific "facts" in a way that dogmatic religion could not be. Maignen agreed with Bargy when the latter stated that the "American religion" cannot even be identified as Protestantism.

> It does not protest anything, because it is sprung from a soil where nothing grew before it. The name 'Protestant' recalls controversy too strongly to fit it. It needs a title which the polemics of Europe have not staled....American Liberalism has its roots in American history rather than in the reform of Luther; it is the religion of colonization; it has flourished in Catholic Maryland and Anglican Virginia no less than in the Puritan settlements; it is as much at home among the Jews and in the Catholic Church as in the reformed sects; it is a product of the soil. The American religion is alive and fruitful because it is a national religion. It is born of three centuries of common effort for the organization of a society and the creation of a civilization on a barren

soil. It has for its aim the progress of humankind, because its origin is in human labor. It is a religion of humanity grafted on to Christianity.

Maignen concluded his review by reiterating that while Bargy mistakenly includes the majority of American Catholics within the grasp of "the American religion," his description of it is "entirely well founded."[2]

In addition to intellectual arguments about "the American religion," the *Review*'s apologetics also continued in a very practical vein. Sometimes the articles would be directed at the way that Catholics conducted themselves within the Church community. Examples of this can be seen when Preuss challenged his co-religionists on the level of their financial support of the Church in comparison to their enjoyment of luxuries, their "needless multiplication of Catholic societies," their treatment of Negro Catholics, or the disreputable character of so many "prominent Catholics."[3]

While these obvious vices were occasionally pointed out, some presumed virtues, particularly popular devotions, were under constant scrutiny. As previously noted, because of the strong Lutheran influences in Preuss's family life and the fact that he was the child of what became a mixed marriage, he was not raised in the sometimes overly rich devotional practices of nineteenth century Catholicism. It is no surprise then that he was not always comfortable with certain forms of Catholic popular piety. Further, with his deep conviction that the Church stood only to gain by fearless dissemination of the truth, Preuss had no use for the pious legends that were such a staple of Catholic devotional life in this period.

Consequently, the *Review* carried numerous articles calling into question various devotions and challenging the hagiography that surrounded many saints. The legend of the "Holy House of Loretto" which held that Jesus' home in Nazareth was carried to Italy by angels, was often criticized as an example of piety unbounded by the minimum of common sense.[4] There were many other "objectionable devotions" that came in for criticism like the swallowing of little pictures of the Blessed Virgin Mary, or the cult which surrounded that "curious relic," the "Praeputium Domini," which at one time was preserved at the Lateran.[5] Preuss found these devotions objectionable for the obvious reasons that they distracted from the essential truths of the Catholic faith and because their absurdity was often used as a "weapon" against the Church. Always concerned that Catholic piety not be distorted by popular enthusiasms, Preuss also took a critical stance regarding the miracles reported at Lourdes, and the "alleged secrets" of La Salette. Preuss summarized his attitude to such phenomena by saying, "Let us, after the example of Rome, also be cautious and critical in all such matters, lest in endeavoring to advance the cause of piety, we draw ridicule upon our holy Church!"[6]

Though he was chastised by lay and clerical readers alike for opening the pages of his *Review* to the "critical discussion" of such topics as "the legend of St. Dominic and the Rosary," the Holy House of Loretto, and other pious devotions, Preuss believed that such discussion was "profitable" for the education of Catholics. It made them better apologists for the Faith because they would understand the basis for Catholic devotions and the difference between historical events and pious legends. For these reasons Preuss frequently published articles by European Jesuits such as Herbert Thurston, Hippolyte Delehaye, and Hartmann Grisar because these scholars applied historical criticism to hagiography and popular devotions.[7]

On the positive side, Preuss used his *Review* to promote the spirituality centered on the Eucharist that had accompanied the nineteenth-century "devotional revival" in Catholicism. Initially, this renewal of Eucharistic piety focused on adoration and processions with the sacrament where "the idea of religious reparation was coupled with something like a silent protest."[8] However, with the beginning of the pontificate of Pius X in 1903, greater emphasis was now put on frequent reception of Holy Communion. While pontifical promotion of any movement was a strong influence on Preuss's response, the *Review* had held up frequent

74

reception of the Eucharist as the ideal of orthodoxy even before this date.[9]

As for his own attitude toward frequent Communion, in an article published in January 1906, Preuss recalled that in his college days while the students attended Mass every day, they had been required to receive the Holy Communion once a month. He thought that this was fine as a minimum requirement but he believed that college students should be exhorted to receive the sacrament more often. As an adult, Preuss himself frequented daily Communion, although as his friend Father Francis Markert recorded, he had to give up this practice as his precarious health was aggravated by the stringent rules of fasting then in force.[10] It is also of note that Father Bede Maler, O.S.B., promoter of the Priests' Eucharistic League and founding editor of *Emmanuel* magazine, which was dedicated to Eucharistic devotion, was a friend of Arthur Preuss.[11] With these experiences and influences, it was to be expected that when Pius X put the power of the papacy behind the promotion of more frequent reception of the Eucharist, Preuss enlisted the pages of the *Review* in support of the cause.

The first task in promoting more frequent reception of Communion among Catholics was to overcome Jansenistic viewpoints that discouraged reception in order to protect "the due reverence owed to our Lord." The Eucharist was not to be portrayed as a reward for virtue in this life, but as its guarantee. Taking his cue from Pius X's teaching on the matter, which in turn referred back to the decrees of the Council of Trent, Preuss published an article by an anonymous contributor in 1909 stating that for the reception of the Eucharist "the primary purpose of reception was remedial."

> The Eucharist must be viewed in the light of a heavenly tonic, a universal remedy for all our spiritual ailments. It was the Jansenists that used to be scandalized at the frequent approach of the faithful to the sacred banquet. A remnant of that Jansenistic poison may still be found in many, priests as well as lay people....When there are grave disorders in a congregation the pastor must blame himself if he fails to

urge daily or frequent communion…An awful responsibility he takes on himself, if, contrary to the unmistakable law of the Church, the holy Eucharist be reserved for the few but withheld from the many.[12]

Consonant with this position, the *Review* carried articles emphasizing that sacramental confession should not be an obstacle to frequent Communion for those unburdened by mortal sin.[13]

Questions also began to be raised about the utility of the fasting regulations then in force. For those who wished to promote more frequent reception of Communion, the Eucharistic fast was unnecessarily severe and counterproductive. The rules not only hindered lay reception of the sacrament, they seriously taxed the energies of priests. In an editorial published on January 1, 1913, Preuss declared his "cordial sympathy" for the movement then gathering strength which sought to have the clergy appeal to Rome for a modification of the fasting regulations. He also offered to facilitate the petition drive.[14] Although the advocates for a change in the fasting regulations were disappointed that such a change was not included in the Code of Canon Law of 1917, they continued to promote this change in the pages of the *Review* into the 1920s.

In addition to the issue of the Eucharistic fast, the movement promoting more frequent Communion also raised the question as to what age children should make their first Communion. The decree of the Sacred Congregation of the Sacraments, *Quam Singulari* issued in 1910, suggested that first Communion for children not be delayed after they had reached the age of discretion. The general practice had been for children to make their first Communion at about age fourteen, which coincided with their departure from the parochial schools. For the next few years the *Review* carried articles urging that the age of discretion be interpreted as broadly as possible. Some articles criticized the apparent financial motivations of pastors who refused to implement the papal decree for fear that children's Communion at an earlier age would mean an earlier departure from school and a loss of revenue for the parish schools.[15]

In these various articles promoting more frequent reception of Communion, the Eucharist is habitually depicted as having a protective or even a medicinal effect. Frequent reception of Communion was the best preventive medicine against sin. Children should be permitted to receive Communion as soon as possible before their innocent souls were allowed to be corrupted by sin. Perhaps this was the result of having to counter the Jansenistic teaching on the relationship between the Eucharist and sin. In any case, it was not until the liturgical movement gained ground that the Eucharist began to be described as something more than an inoculation.

Additionally, even the frequent reception of the Eucharist remained largely an individual affair. With the reception of the sacrament occurring usually before the Mass itself, it remained isolated from the liturgical action. Further, the individual communicants, all equally isolated from the liturgy itself, "saw only the union of the individual soul with Christ but not the community of those communicating." The "Communion movement" promoted by Pius X had successfully restored the primacy of reception of the sacrament over mere adoration and had "relaxed that only too close connection between Confession and Communion." However, the reintegration of the Eucharist with the Mass and the individual communicant with the community celebration would come only with the liturgical movement of the nineteen-twenties.[16]

Just as Preuss supported Pius X's "Communion movement" he also supported the Pope's efforts to reform Church music. Actually, Preuss's enthusiasm for Church music reform predated Pius X's *motu proprio* on the subject, *Tra le sollecitudini,* which was promulgated on November 22, 1903. Nine years before the papal decree Preuss had observed that "appropriate and strictly liturgical music Church music is found solely in German kirks in this country. In our Irish churches you hear the melodies of the opera and the concert hall." Preuss published a translation of the *motu proprio* in full "because of its great importance and because it confirms views often expressed and defended in the

Review and as often criticized and impugned by well-meaning but 'liberally' inclined friends."[17] Seven years earlier, Joseph Otten, then organist and choir director at St. Francis Xavier Church in St. Louis and later choir director of St. Paul's Cathedral in Pittsburgh for twenty-six years, became a regular contributor to the *Review*. Otten usually wrote several articles and book reviews for Preuss each year until his death in November 1926. Under Otten's guidance, the *Review* regularly promoted Gregorian Chant and called for the purging of "operatic" and "music hall melodies" from the Mass. The *Review* also promoted lay recitation of the responses at Mass and congregational singing of the chant. The reform of Church music, according to Preuss, should also include the exclusion of Protestant hymns from Catholic churches. Their continued use only promoted religious indifferentism and suggested "our own poverty" when in fact Catholics had sacred hymns at least as "equally stirring as 'Onward Christian Soldiers', etc."[18] In retrospect such fears may seem inordinate, but for Arthur Preuss and his readers such matters were always a question of how Catholics should maintain their identity in the diaspora.

Far more inimical to the faith of American Catholics was the problem of mixed marriages. For the period under study in this chapter, 1902 to 1912, Preuss published twenty articles on the subject of mixed marriages. While some of these articles were no more than a paragraph in length, their message was consistent and pointed —mixed marriages were evil. They were evil because they almost inevitably led to religious indifferentism and the loss to the Faith of the Catholic party and the children of the marriage. Preuss was encouraged that as time wore on, fewer bishops were willing to grant dispensations for mixed marriages as they "proved a terrible engine for ruining the faith of Catholics." And he evidently supported the policy of only granting dispensations in those cases where the non-Catholic party agreed to receive instructions in the Catholic faith.[19] Preuss's hardline on this matter is somewhat surprising considering that his mother remained a devout Lutheran even after his father's conversion to Catholicism. Arthur Preuss and his three priest brothers were themselves a strong argument against the notion that religious indifference was promoted by the "mixed marriage evil." But as Preuss would record some years later, he was never really at peace with the religious division in his family.

> We have often wished that every Catholic could have had the opportunity we had in our young days to observe the inevitable results of a state of mixed religion in the family circle. There had been no mixed marriage, but the father had become a Catholic two years after the wedding, while the mother remained a Protestant. Both were intensely religious and though the children never witnessed a clash or heard harsh words, they instinctively felt that there was something wrong somewhere, and as they grew older and realized what it was, the tragedy of the thing fairly overwhelmed them. None of the eight children ever dreamed of contracting a mixed marriage because all had imbibed an instinctive horror of such unnatural unions.[20]

Because of his experience of a family life founded on a mixed marriage, Arthur Preuss's views on the matter were unwavering, even when they brought him into apparent conflict with the Holy See. That he should find himself correcting bishops for "adding dignity and seeming sanctity to such unions" by participating in mixed marriage ceremonies would have come as no surprise to Preuss.[21] But he was clearly pained to report in July 1911 that Pope Pius X himself had apparently given his blessing to the marriage of a wealthy Catholic woman from Denver to a Protestant New Yorker while two bishops were in attendance. Preuss confessed, "[W]e have been vainly hoping for some sort of official or at least semi-official explanation to remove the public scandal" caused when the bestowal of the Pope's blessing was widely publicized in both the Catholic and secular press. "As for the congratulatory telegram from Rome, we may safely assume that His Holiness knew nothing about it. The Pope is not in the habit of blessing mixed marriages." Though he tried to differentiate between the actions of the Pope and the role of his subordinates in creating the scandal, it is clear that Preuss perceived a dangerous double standard at work in this affair.

We do not presume to criticize any priest or bishop; we merely state a notorious fact, and at the same time voice the painful conviction of many loyal Catholics ...[that] the honors showered upon rich or socially prominent couples on such occasions, which ought to be occasions of sadness for their parents and sincere friends, lead many Catholic young men and women to contemn the wholesome principles instilled by the Catechism and to aspire to matrimonial alliances with wealthy or socially distinguished Protestants as something really desirable and distingue, whereas every means ought to be employed to deter them from mixed marriages as a calamity and an evil 'which' in the words of Leo XIII, 'the Church has ever detested' (quae semper Ecclesia detestata).[22]

There were other evils in American marriage practices which were related to the Catholic apologetic vis-à-vis the general culture. These evils were the rising incidence of divorce and the practice of contraception, or as it was called in the parlance of the day, "race suicide." The frequency of divorce in the United States had already drawn the notice of Leo XIII, and he had included a caution against this "deadly pest" in his encyclical *Longinqua Oceani* addressed to the American hierarchy on January 6, 1895.[23] But the "divorce evil" continued to spread. In 1908 the *Review* reported that 1.2 million divorces had been granted in the United States in the previous twenty years and that "nearly two million innocent children were worse than orphaned with the full approval of their parents and the State." Further, some three hundred thousand men and women were "living in legalized adultery," bringing "shame and ruin upon their offspring, and upon the society of which they are members."[24] According to the *Review,* the root of the divorce evil was to be found in the Reformation, which had "reduced the Sacrament of Matrimony to the level of an ordinary contract" and which had given "the guardianship over the marriage bond from the Church to the State." In addition, "the liberal ideas in religion," which were furthered by the intellectual heirs of Rousseau, were eliminating "the bounds of reason and revelation" and reducing man to "his polygamous nature."[25]

Equally pernicious, but not yet as overt, was the practice of contraception. This practice would be a greater concern in the nineteen twenties and thirties but already in the first decade of the century Preuss was foretelling its destructive effects on American family and social life.

> Everything is endangered in a society where people egoistically throw off the duty of rearing children. The very presence of children safeguards man against himself; it stimulates those habits of order, work and saving which go to make up the real power of a nation. Where children are missing, one may justly fear that the husband has no character, the wife no dignity and both no morals.[26]

The growing scourge of abortion was also decried in the pages of the *Review* in these years.[27]

Divorce and race suicide were just two of the more virulent plagues spread by "the decadence of Protestantism."[28] As part of his apologetic for Catholicism, Preuss frequently published statements by Protestants commenting on the failure of the Reform churches "to dam in the utilitarian and eudaemonistic materialism of the masses."[29] While the masses were succumbing to the allure of materialism, Protestant theologians, by denying the normative character of Scriptural revelation, were rendering the rule of faith of Protestantism "utterly and hopelessly bankrupt."[30] Observing these developments Preuss remarked that "Christianity is indeed in a bad way so far as American Protestants— even 'orthodox' Protestants are concerned." That Protestantism as a system of belief was disintegrating was inevitable.

> It is the eternal curse resting upon Protestantism that it must slowly drift into rationalism and utter infidelity....The principle of free interpretation of the Bible has gradually emptied that sacred volume of its divine element, and Protestantism, even orthodox Protestantism, is today little more than undisguised rationalism or thinly veiled infidelity. And thus it comes to pass that the ancient Catholic Church is again the sole custodian of the 'depositum fidei' without which Christianity and all true religion is but a sham and a snare. While Protestant preachers are daily heralding in a more or less unblushing manner their final apostasy from the dogmatic teaching of the Master, the high priest of

the old Church proclaims amid the acclamations of Catholic Christendom the necessity of 'restoring all things in Christ.'[31]

Within the triumphalism, there remained a certain sadness in Preuss's commentary on the failure of Protestantism. Unlike Isaac Hecker and John Ireland, Preuss did not see any "Catholic moment" in America arising from the demise of Protestant orthodoxy, only mass infidelity to the teachings of Christ. Preuss read a number of Protestant publications; the *Independent* of New York seems to have been a particular favorite. When Preuss encountered statements by Protestant leaders in these journals which he found consistent with Christian orthodoxy he would publish them.[32] Additionally, in his personal life his practical estimation of Protestantism was much more positive than his printed polemics would suggest. His solicitude that his mother would regularly receive the ministrations of her Lutheran pastor is indicative of this.

Preuss appears to have viewed Protestantism as a household of faith built on the sands of subjective interpretation of revealed truth. For some, their individual interpretations still retained a sufficient amount of Christian dogma to keep their "house" standing. But for the vast majority of Christians under the sway of Protestantism, their faith, buffeted by the temptations of this world and corroded by rationalism, was in imminent danger of collapse into outright apostasy.[33] Preuss's judgment that Protestantism was engaged in a massive retreat from traditional Christian dogma and morality was accurate.

> From the 1880s to World War I, the mainline Protestants saw much of their intellectual leadership adopt various versions of the new theology and much of their reformist passion shaped into a new social gospel. Biblical criticism, evolutionary thought and modern secular philosophy were absorbed into the liberal Protestant patterns of progressivist thought.[34]

While "the spirit of error" was dividing Protestants, for Catholics, the "duty of the hour" was to resist "the advancing secular spirit."

In the spirit of error we are all of us swimming as in a boundless ocean; every mother's son of us off and on gulps a mouthful of salty brine, and many of us alas! are no longer able to distinguish it from clear spring water. This spirit seeks for the cause of the world in the movement of material atoms, the supreme good in finer or coarser sensual indulgence, and reason's point of support in the autonomous human spirit.... It strives in dead earnest to establish science, religion, art, morality, the State, right and family on a Darwinistic or evolutionistic basis...it is high time to make a strong fight against the modern secular spirit, which controls not only most institutions of higher learning, but extends its suctorial organs deep down into our common schools.[35]

The American Federation of Catholic Societies

That it was "high time to make a strong fight against the modern secular spirit" was a sentiment shared by other American Catholics. Now that many of them had attained secure social positions as members of the middle-class, and, having "proven" their loyalty during the war on Catholic Spain, some American Catholics were expressing themselves more forcefully on issues of concern to them. This new aggressiveness was based on their conviction that "Catholic rights and interests were being violated to such an extent" by the predominantly Protestant, though increasingly secular culture, that "united and aggressive action" was now justified.[36] There were three main areas of concern for these Catholics: the "schools question," the administration of the territories acquired in the war with Spain, and the discrimination against Catholics in the distribution of public offices.

Then, as now, the "schools question" centered on whether Catholic schools should receive funding of any sort from the government. At the turn of the century this question was further aggravated by the fact that schools for Indian children sponsored by Catholics, which the federal government initially encouraged and funded, were denied funding by Congress. The debate was particularly acrimonious as the attack on the Catholic Indian schools was led by Protestant missionaries, who at one time had their own Indian schools before government schools, which promoted the "Protestant outlook and ideals" were established. This controversy dragged on for two decades and was colored by the outbreak of strong anti-Catholic bigotry that occurred in the 1890s.[37] Appropriations for the Catholic Indian schools were debated in Congress each year between 1894 and 1899 before they were finally ended on June 30, 1900. Once the government appropriations were cut off, Catholic advocates labored to keep the schools open and continued to seek redress for policies that they regarded as discriminatory against the Catholic Indians. Between 1900 and 1912 there were conflicts over whether funds that the Indians received from the government under treaty agreements might be used for the schools at the request of the Indians and whether women religious could wear their habits while teaching in the schools that had been taken over by the government. These conflicts quite naturally aggravated the already skeptical attitude that many Catholics had regarding the sensitivity of the American government toward their interests in education. The *Review* reported regularly on these conflicts and Arthur Preuss became an active supporter of Father Ganss, the leading advocate of the Catholic Indian schools.[38]

Another matter of concern to Catholics was the resolution of Church-and-state conflicts in those lands seized by the United States following the war with Spain. Once again the government's promotion of secular education for Catholic children was an issue. Also of concern, especially in the Philippines, was the compensation of religious orders for lands that were taken from them.[39] In addition to these specific concerns, the general program of "Americanizing" these Catholic cultures was opposed by some American Catholics. Not surprisingly, Arthur Preuss was an outspoken opponent of this trend, and in the years 1899 through 1902 he published some seventy-five separate notices on the situation in the Philippines. Though he remained circumspect while Spain and the United States were engaged in hostilities, once the war was over, Preuss was unsparing in his criticism of American policy. The war was "unjust" and "preventable." As for the American administration of the acquired territories, especially the Philippines, again, Preuss was vehement in his criticism. Preuss railed against what he and many others regarded as the corruption of a Catholic culture and the despoiling of the Church.[40]

The fact that few Catholics were involved officially in the formulation of American colonial policies, or in their administration, was another complaint added to the list of grievances. Catholic influence on the colonial level reflected the national scene where Catholic influence "was almost negligible" and "hardly representative of one sixth of the country's total population."[41]

Manifesting their growing assertiveness based on their stronger social position, lay Catholics began to speak about organizing themselves nationally in order to overcome their political impotence. Precipitated by a call issued by the Knights of St. John in June 1899 for the many existing Catholic societies to unite, the "federation movement" gathered momentum rather quickly. Within a year of the first invitation, twenty-two other Catholic societies had responded favorably to the idea of federating in a national organization. Also, by early 1900, the federation movement had gained the enthusiastic support of Bishop James McFaul of Trenton, who in turn enlisted the support of his friend, Bishop Sebastian Messmer of Green Bay.[42]

Arthur Preuss's reaction to the federation movement was also quite favorable. To a self-described "Vox Clamantis," preaching Catholic opposition to the evils of American society, the sudden growth of the federation movement must have seemed to Preuss like a mass conversion to his way of thinking. As early as November 1898 the *Review* had seconded Condè Pallen's call for a Catholic Centre Party in the United States in order to "protect Catholic interests" and "to bring about reforms."

> Our politicians, small and great, fear nothing more than a solid phalanx of voters; we have the votes, let us form the phalanx. Who knows but what a 'Kulturkampf' is in store for us; if the early foundation of a Centre will not nip it in the bud, it will surely enable us to defend our rights more promptly and vigorously.[43]

Five months later, Preuss criticized an editorial in *Ave Maria* which questioned the wisdom of an American Catholic Centre Party. Preuss stated that since Cardinal Gibbons had been unable to persuade Congress to reconsider funding the Catholic Indian Schools, it was clear that the politicians were not concerned about Catholic interests. While acknowledging the reluctance of American Catholics to organize themselves politically, "a Centre Party with a Windthorst at its head is fast becoming necessary." In the same issue of the *Review* Preuss published excerpts of a letter which suggested that a Centre party could never exist in America because it would have to be conducted by laymen and "such laymen would soon be hampered by priests and bishops." The unnamed letter writer correctly predicted the demise of the federation movement before it had even begun.[44]

Another prescient on the nature of the federation movement was published in the *Review* of February 1, 1900. There Preuss quoted his French-Canadian collaborator, Jules Tardivel, editor of *La Vérité* of Quebec, as saying that if American Catholics refused to form their own political organization "rather than provoke the popular fury by trying to protect themselves" that was their prerogative but they should at least "cease their incessant bluster about the liberty Catholics enjoy in the United States."[45]

When in fact the predominantly German-American Knights of St. John issued the call for a federation of Catholic societies it was precisely the earlier history of the German-Catholic Centre Party which inspired them. Founded in 1870 to protect the interests of the Catholic minority against Prussian state authoritarianism, the Centre Party and its leaders, Bishop Wilhelm von Ketteler and Ludwig Windthorst, had attained legendary status among German-American Catholics.[46] Given his own previous interest in promoting an American Centre Party, when the groups in favor of a Catholic federation began to coalesce in the spring of 1900 Preuss could justifiably say that he had been advocating such a movement for some time.

Surprisingly, though, Arthur Preuss did not immediately recognize the possible correlation between the nascent federation movement and his hoped-for Centre Party. In his first article on the proposed union of Catholic societies Preuss stated that, despite the support for the movement in the press and among ethnic groups he saw "Neither need nor possibility of such a union, at least under present conditions."[47] Three weeks later Preuss reprinted an article translated from *Der Wanderer* which expressed doubts that the federation movement would ever come to anything because most of the Catholic societies which were to comprise the federation were no more than mutual insurance groups. These societies "had forgotten their real duty to battle for something sublime, something holy: the culture of the inner life, without which external rights and goals are valueless." For his part, Preuss was now conceding that the movement might be "useful" in improving relations between the different ethnic groups in the Catholic Church.[48]

In his study of the American Federation of Catholic Societies, Alfred Ede ventured to say that Bishop James McFaul played a "highly significant role in the history of the federation movement." McFaul's role would be more aptly described as indispensable. Certainly McFaul's enthusiastic endorsement of the movement improved Arthur Preuss's estimation of the federation's potential. Having remained silent on the topic for two full months, the *Review* boldly proclaimed on page one of its May 31 issue, "Bishop McFaul in Favor of a Catholic Centre Party For the U.S." Never mind that the text of the article carried McFaul's explicit disavowal of the intention to form a political party. Preuss reported McFaul as saying that if Catholics were organized their grievances regarding the Philippines, Indian schools, and public offices for Catholics would not be ignored. Commenting on McFaul's plan for federation, Preuss stated,

> It is the same plan that has been outlined and advocated in the *Review* from time to time during the last four or five years. It is exactly what we meant when we said repeatedly, in season and out of season, that what we American Catholics need most is a Centre Party. If this name is obnoxious we are willing to drop it; but the movement is opportune and necessary, and we hope to see some more of our wide awake

bishops express themselves as emphatically in its favor as Msgr. McFaul, or better still, take the matter actively in hand and bring it to successful realization. Whatever aid the *Review* can lend will be cheerfully given.[49]

Preuss's endorsement of the federation movement discloses a number of things about his thinking on the matter. First of all, Bishop McFaul's involvement seems to have helped change Preuss estimation of the movement from skepticism to enthusiasm. Second, while willing to forego the name of "Centre Party," Preuss clearly envisioned the federation as having political purposes. Finally, as Preuss called for greater episcopal involvement in the movement, he, unlike many others, was not concerned that clerical participation would cause controversy among non-Catholics or be an intrusion on the rightful preserve of the laity.

Preuss continued to portray the objectives of the federation movement as inherently political. On June 21, 1900, the *Review* published an article written under the pen name of "Bezimie" which asked, "How Are We To Make Our Rights Respected?" One of the means to this end proposed by the author was concerted political action by Catholics akin to what was done by the German-Catholic "Centrum." It was suggested that such action could put "twenty men in Congress like Fitzgerald of Massachusetts" and "would make things look different."[50] The same issue of the *Review* carried a notice indicating that the secular press, at least in Preuss's hometown, was aware of his agitation on behalf of Catholic federation and suggested that it be stopped. Preuss quoted the St. Louis *Mirror* as saying "the new movement of Bishop McFaul of Trenton and Editor Preuss of St. Louis should be squelched" by "higher ups" in the Church.[51]

That Catholics were being discriminated against in the allocation of public offices was a view shared by others in the Catholic press. In July Preuss reprinted an editorial from the *Providence Visitor* which answered in the affirmative its own question, "Is Catholicity a Bar to Public Office?"[52] Preuss's view that the federation should become a vehicle for

Catholic political power was also given a boost with the public endorsement of this view by Bishop Sebastian Messmer in August 1900. Speaking before the German-Catholic Convention in Fond du Lac, Wisconsin, on the "The Duty of Catholic Laymen In Our Age," Messmer outlined a plan that laymen must pursue if they were to fulfill their duties as Catholics. Messmer observed that society was embroiled in several struggles, between rich and poor, the free and the oppressed, and between the Church and the State. He also stated that "there is no country where the Catholic Church is not obliged to fight for her rights." This being the case, Messmer called on Catholic laymen both to be faithful to the Church's teachings on morality and the "social question" and to diffuse those teachings throughout society. This was their duty and since at present they had little influence on American society, unified political action by Catholics was now a necessity. This political action was necessary not only to protect their rights from "assaults," but also to promote social reform that was in keeping with Catholic teaching.

Within his speech Messmer commended "Arthur Preuss and his excellent St. Louis *Review*" for supporting Bishop McFaul and the federation movement. Messmer stated: "We need a Catholic Centrum…[not a political party] but a centre of action for our Catholic people, a general organization for the purpose of united public action socially, religiously and, if necessary, also politically." Messmer went on to urge the various ethnic groups to end all "un-Catholic and pernicious self-conceit" for "we are neither Germans or Yankees, nor Irish, nor French, nor Polish, nor Bohemians, only Catholic…with that all embracing charity in our hearts that teaches us that non-Catholics are also children of God and brethren of Jesus Christ." Finally, Bishop Messmer dismissed

the pusillanimity and false witness of so many of our own people. Priests and laymen will say with trembling lips: 'For God's sake! no Catholic politics, no Catholic agitation. That would arouse the non-Catholics against us'…The battle is here —we are not making it…it was ever thus, persecution, vituperation…should never prevent the faithful son of the Church from taking part, fearlessly and courageously, under the protection and guidance of his spiritual mother, in the battle for the interests and blessings of the human race.[53]

Judging from Messmer's remarks, it seems that he and Arthur Preuss shared the same vision for the federation. It could be the collective voice, and if need be, the collective vote of Catholics in America on the issues of the day. Both men were also equally certain that the battle for the interests of the Church was also "the battle for the interests and blessings of the human race."

Of course, as Messmer noted, not all American Catholics were in favor of the federation movement. Liberal Catholic newspapers like the *Northwestern Chronicle*, of Minneapolis, and the *Catholic Citizen,* of Milwaukee, both published by Humphrey Desmond, denied the existence of anti-Catholic prejudice on the part of governmental officials and attacked the political aspirations of the federation movement. These criticisms were ameliorated when Bishop Messmer released a program for the federation in November 1900 which stated that the organization would be non-political and that it would cooperate with non-Catholics.[54]

Behind the scenes Preuss's Americanist adversaries, Archbishop John Ireland and Cardinal James Gibbons, were very concerned that the political aspirations of the movement would hinder the acceptance of Catholics in American society that they had worked so hard for.[55] Preuss too saw connections between the Americanist agenda and the movement for federation, but from a much different perspective. In Preuss's view, by suppressing the tendency to "whittle down doctrine," *Testem Benevolentiae* had strengthened Catholic identity and could be the "providential basis of energetic practical Catholic action in this country." However, the false accommodationism of Americanism was still being promoted in some quarters and "until Americanism is eradicated we may not hope for better things."[56]

As previously noted, Arthur Preuss strongly hoped that the federation movement would do much to foster unity among the various ethnic groups within the Catholic Church. To that end, he called on the leaders of the federation movement to make a special effort to invite French Canadians, Poles, Bohemians, and Catholic Negroes to the upcoming convention of the movement as they had not been present at the preliminary meetings of the federation. Noting that his *Review* was on the exchange lists with four of the leading French Canadian papers published in the United States, Preuss appealed to the French Canadians to see beyond their present grievances with English-speaking Catholics and to participate in the federation movement. "Being Catholics first and above all, our French-Canadian brethren will most assuredly not refuse to cooperate in a movement designed to foster our sacred common cause."[57]

As the federation movement progressed, Preuss frequently reported on its activities and the various responses it was eliciting from observers. In fact, a side-bar headed "The Catholic Federation" became a regular feature in the *Review*. Most of the articles published in 1901 were taken up with the continued discussion of the federation's potential political role and preparations for its first national convention to be held in Cincinnati. As Bishop McFaul and others sought to distance the movement from the aggressive and political tones of their previous statements, Preuss continued to promote a confrontational stance for the federation. Writing in February 1901, Preuss stated that the federation was needed to "preserve Christian principles of right and liberty" as all vestiges of Christianity were disappearing among Protestants.[58]

Even as Preuss was beating the drum for the federation as the embodiment of Catholic political power, Bishop McFaul was being advised by Archbishop Ireland in March of 1901 to delay the proposed May convention in order to undermine such aspirations.[59] The following month the postponement of the convention was announced ostensibly so that the constitution for the federation could be completed and submitted to the "hierarchy for criticism and approbation." In response to this announcement, Preuss asked what the committee on the constitution "has been doing the last six months?"[60]

In June the *Review* carried another of McFaul's now routine disavowals of a political purpose for the federation. It was to be a laymen's movement "in defense of citizen's rights," bearing "no resemblance to a political party on a religious foundation." Preuss gave no voice to what he thought of McFaul's hedging on the issue but he was pleased with the advice offered to the federation by the newly consecrated bishop of Portland, William H. O'Connell:

> We have passed the days, and passed forever, when we quietly stole unnoticed to our humble little chapel, and were grateful for being ignored. The Church has grown to immense proportions...its cathedral spires tower above our great cities...our men are a power in the nation...the voice of our best, most influential laymen, must be heard and felt in public life, indicating and proclaiming to all the highest Catholic public sentiment.[61]

Preuss continued to maintain that, to attain its goals, the federation must fight its battles on political grounds. This was so because those who opposed Catholic interests did so through the exercise of their political power. Therefore, the only way that Catholics would gain respect, would be if they earned that respect through unified involvement in the political arena. "That is why the *Review* has from the start said that a Catholic federation disavowing politics in its program, and eschewing it in its activity, would be stillborn. If the federation is not to be the groundwork for a Catholic Centre Party it will do more harm than good and deserves to die aborning."[62]

In addition to seeing the federation as a means of defending Catholic interests, Preuss stood with those who, inspired by Leo XIII, saw a role for the movement in promoting social reform. "A twentieth-century Catholic federation that would ignore the social question would not be up to the times nor in full accord with the views and directions of the Pontiff gloriously reigning."[63]

As the date of the convention drew near, articles began to appear in the *Review* offering different opinions from within the German-Catholic community on just how their societies should be represented within the federation. A debate was carried on between the national officers of the German-Catholic Central Verein and the local leaders of their member societies. Preuss sympathized with the concern of Nicholas Gonner, President of the Central Verein, that the unity of the Verein would be threatened if each of its member societies sent its own delegates to the convention. However, Preuss shared the view of those who believed that the individual German societies should be represented with delegates on a state-by-state basis in order to give German-Catholic societies a role in the deliberations of the convention commensurate with their importance.[64] This was just what Archbishop Ireland feared. In the letter he wrote to Bishop McFaul in March of 1901, Ireland stated that because of the strength of the German societies "before very long the Celt would be beaten out of sight and the whole federation would be a one-sided affair, wearing a most foreign aspect and a most ungracious one to the eye of the American."[65]

Preuss believed that whatever concessions were necessary to gain the support of the various Catholic societies for the federation should be made. The important thing was that the federation, and hence the Catholic Church in America, should be strong. For, as Preuss continued to say to the French-Canadians, "no loyal Catholic who puts the welfare of the whole body above that of any group or section would desire to limit the strength of the Federation."[66]

Concurrent with his involvement in inter-German debates regarding the formation of the Federation, Preuss was busy countering those who, on the eve of the Federation's first convention, still questioned the need for its existence. On November 21, 1901, the *Review* cited an article in the Paulist Fathers' *Catholic World* which questioned the supposition of a strong anti-Catholicism in America that necessitated the formation of a federation. However, while the *Catholic World* differed with Preuss as to the need for a Catholic federation, it shared his view, "It is created in order to secure political rights. It must of necessity go into politics." For this reason the *Catholic World* opposed the formation of the Federation: "A huge political factor in the hands of men who, though worthy in themselves, yet are responsible to no one, is a most dangerous element."[67] Preuss's response to the *Catholic World* illustrates his own view of militant Catholicism: "Si vis pacem, para bellum."[68]

While the *Catholic World* and other journals were publicly opposing the formation of a federation, Preuss suspected that Archbishop Ireland was also involved in opposing the movement. His view that Ireland was behind the public opposition to the Federation was shared by other editors, one of whom wrote that "those Catholic journals supposed under his [Ireland's] influence have strenuously thrown cold water on the federation idea." Ireland's apparent inconsistency was also noted as he had promoted such lay involvement in a speech before the English Catholic Union in 1899 while now he was hindering the federation movement in America.[69]

After the Cincinnati convention was finally held in December 1901, Preuss had many positive things to say and a few criticisms to make regarding the proceedings. On the positive side, he was pleased with the level of participation with three hundred delegates representing some 600,000 Catholics present. He also saw the participation of the German Catholics as "beneficial to them and the common cause." That he would make such a remark indicates that the German Catholics still felt themselves to be out of the mainstream to some degree. In any case, Preuss hoped that the example of the Germans would encourage those national groups that still stood aloof "to join forces with their brethren."

On the negative side, Preuss sided with the German-Catholic delegates who disapproved of the Federation's including women's organizations. While Preuss never articulated why he held this position, it is probable that it was based on his opposition to the involvement of women in politics. Preuss also faulted the convention for not choosing the plan of organization advocated by the German societies. The plan that the convention approved called for the "meshing of all societies together in local and state subunits of the Federation." Wishing to maintain the ethnic identity of their societies, the German Catholics proposed that the societies of the different ethnic groups should form their own separate federations. These in turn would then be affiliated with the national body "which would serve as a sort of parliament of ethnic organizations."[70]

But Preuss's biggest disappointment was that the convention as a body renounced political involvement. Citing this renunciation, Preuss asked in reference to Catholic grievances regarding schools,

> How is this injustice to be righted except by the judicious use of the ballot? And what value can the Federation prove if it shuts itself off from political debates and the endorsement of candidates for office?...it is well that partisan politics as such be rigidly excluded, but when the rights of the Church and of Catholic citizens are attacked by iniquitous laws, is the Federation to stand idly by on the plea that it is non-political?

Despite these criticisms, Preuss remained enthusiastic about the future of the Federation even if "for the present" it abstained from practical politics, and he pledged "our sincere good will and best wishes."[71]

However, the dissatisfaction among German-Catholic societies regarding the plan of organization of the Federation continued to grow. They feared both that individual societies would lose their independence in the centralization of authority in the national body and that their German societies would lose their ethnic identity. The *Review* voiced these concerns and also the warning that the Federation had to move beyond general statements and address specific issues at its next convention.

> [If the Federation does not] take a decided stand in regard to questions just now agitating Catholic public opinion such as the education of our Catholic Indians, the treatment of the Philippine friars, the school question...it will have missed its purpose and have no longer a raison d'etre. [72]

The same issue of the *Review* reprinted a notice from the *Catholic Columbian* of Columbus, Ohio which announced that the recently elected president of the Federation, Thomas B. Minahan, had agreed to speak in a Protestant church on the subject of temperance.[73] A week later, the

Review reiterated the German complaints about the present constitution of the Federation and opined that unless the Chicago convention reorganized the Federation movement, and issued a strong public platform, "the whole movement, so auspiciously inaugurated and so pregnant with good promises, will we fear, turn out a fizzle."[74] Preuss, no stranger to criticism, was stunned by the response that these articles provoked.

On April 3, 1902, Preuss published a long article entitled "The President of the Catholic Federation and the Review." The substance of the article was a letter by Thomas Minahan sent to Preuss concerning the *Review*'s notice on Minahan's speech in a Protestant church. Referring to Preuss's implied criticism of his action as "the black vomit," Minahan also castigated the German-Catholic press in general for its "carping criticism" and "pernicious influence" in regard to the organization of the Federation. As Minhan had sent copies of his letter to Preuss to a number of other papers, the incident became a major controversy in the Catholic press.

Obviously stung by the ferocity of Minahan's attack, Preuss responded in kind. He noted first of all that he had simply reprinted the article from the *Catholic Columbian* on Minahan's address in a Protestant church "without a syllable of unfavorable comment." Second, Preuss rejected Minahan's defense that his address was a private matter. "For while as an individual Mr. Minahan, at least outside of the city of Columbus, is a nobody," as President of the Federation, "he is a representative Catholic whose utterances and acts are subject to public criticism." As for Minahan's attacks on the German-Catholic press, it was not only "criminally unjust," but also

> ...highly temerarious and impolitic on the part of the President of an organization professing such tender love and profound respect for all nationalities. The French Canadians have roundly refused the cold, clammy, dead fish like hand of fellowship proffered by the Honorable Mr. Minahan. Can he expect the Germans to do otherwise after his

unprovoked and vicious assault upon their representative newspaper organs?

Preuss concluded his rejoinder to Minahan by stating that, in addition to its other tasks, the Chicago convention of the Federation now needed to replace "this raw and thin skinned Columbus epistler."[75]

The removal of Minahan as President was now added to the German demands for the reorganization of the Federation. On May 1, 1902 Preuss reported that the German-Catholic press was "practically unanimous" in these views and that the Federation would not receive the support of the German societies "unless it shakes off the incubus of the utterly incompetent Mr. Minahan." Two weeks later, Preuss published an editorial from *Der Wanderer* which once again called for Minahan's ouster. It went on to add that if competent laymen could not be found to lead the Federation, "then we must not be afraid to choose priests, for priests and bishops too are citizens and as such are free to champion the civil rights of Catholics." As Preuss gave *Der Wanderer*'s position his "unqualified approbation," it is clear that, accomplishing the objectives of the Federation as Preuss envisioned them, took precedence over other concerns such as, in this case, the role of the laity in the movement.[76]

The reorganization of the Federation that German Catholics insisted on was largely accomplished at the second convention of the Federation held in Chicago during the first week of August 1902. Under the constitution of the Federation adopted by the convention provisions were made so that the Germans and other ethnic groups were able to select their own delegates to represent them in the Federation. In addition, the ethnically based societies, as well as state and county federations of societies, were guaranteed their autonomy. As for political involvement, "partisan politics were not to be discussed at any meetings national or local; nor were candidates to be endorsed for public office." This ban on partisan politics did not inhibit the convention from adopting resolutions on the Philippine situation and the Catholic Indian schools. However, these resolutions were general in nature and were expressed in "moderate tones."[77]

The *Review* had no direct comment on the convention itself. Some months later Preuss did note that after the new constitution was adopted "a large number of German organizations at once lent their support" to the movement.[78] But immediately after the Federation's convention Preuss was more taken up with refuting its most important opponent and his old adversary, Archbishop John Ireland.

At the time Ireland was under pressure from President Theodore Roosevelt to counter American Catholic opposition to U.S. policies in the Philippines. Roosevelt was particularly upset by Catholic opposition to the Taft Commission's efforts to negotiate a settlement on the friars' land question with the Holy See. Roosevelt believed that the "most extraordinary agitation among Catholics in the United States" against the government's policies in the Philippines was "organized by the Anti-Ireland people to get even with him." These "Anti-Ireland people seemed to control the larger part of the organized Catholic societies, lay and clerical, and papers which give expression to distinctly Catholic opinion."[79]

Apparently embarrassed by attacks on Roosevelt's policies emanating from supporters of the Federation, Ireland defended the impartiality of the administration and dismissed the charges of anti-Catholicism within the operation of Filipino schools. Ireland also challenged the authority of the government's Catholic critics for protesting against these policies, as no ecclesiastics officially involved in Philippine matters voiced similar complaints.[80] Ireland's implicit rebuke to the Federation and denial of the laity's right to promote the cause of the Church brought a sharp rejoinder from the *Review*.

On September 4, 1902, Preuss sought to hoist Ireland by his own petard in an article entitled, "Archbishop Ireland *vs* Archbishop Ireland." The article simply quoted a fiery speech on the right and responsibility for lay initiative within the Church that Ireland had delivered in 1889.[81] Two weeks later Preuss published an essay by Condè Pallen which asserted that the successful formation of the Federation had destroyed "the cult of Irelandism."

> Irelandism seized upon a trait in the American character which is its
> shabbiest and weakest side, braggadocio. Irelandism boasts itself
> peculiarly and solely American...[but] it never accomplished a jot or
> tittle, and when American Catholics, outraged in their faith and their
> patriotism by the calumnious and unjustifiable policy of the dominant
> political party in regard to the Friars in the Philippines, united in
> earnest protest against the contemplated expulsion of the religious
> orders, Irelandism sought to stifle that utterance, that it might shield an
> administration which had committed not merely a blunder, but a
> crime...It sought to smother the expression of Catholic sentiment and
> thought through the recent utterance of the Federation, and it was
> ignored...It achieved nothing through all its unfortunate domination
> though it pretended much. It was a continuous fiasco, and it is now
> dead....[82]

Pallen went on to describe the formation of the Federation as the
beginning of "Catholic Emancipation in America," as the Federation
would actively pursue religious equality and freedom.

After the publication of this essay, the *Review* concerned itself less and
less with the development of the Federation. Preuss conceded in an
article published in February 1903 that "our original enthusiasm for the
Federation was dampened by certain grievous mistakes on the part of its
leaders." These mistakes included Minahan's attack on the
German-Catholic press, his "foolish open letter" to Preuss, and his later
reelection as president of the Federation. Still, despite these "blunders,"
Preuss praised "the necessity and opportuneness of the movement" and
the "indubitable good will and commendable zeal of the leaders, from
Mr. Minahan down." In the same article Preuss tacitly acknowledged
that his vision of the role of the Federation had been rejected. However,
he conceded the point only for the present.

> If, as we sincerely hope, the Federation has 'come to stay,' it will
> surely some day, despite the present views and intentions of its
> officers, 'mix in politics,' because as a Catholic body it can not stand

idly by when Catholic principles are attacked or the rights of Catholic citizens trodden under foot, which is bound to happen sooner or later where godless State schools are raising up a generation of infidels who despise and hate the Church.[83]

Preuss's promotion of the American Federation of Catholic Societies as the foundation of a Catholic Centre party in the United States is, in one way, rather surprising. His aspirations for a political role for the Federation suggest a confidence in the American electoral system that Preuss really did not have. As a conservative Catholic whose worldview had been shaped by the Kulturkampf, Arthur Preuss distrusted the modern secular state. In theory, Preuss upheld "the Catholic ideal," which, "as every one knows, spells out not separation [of Church and state] but union and harmonious cooperation between the two divinely constituted powers." However, in practice, Preuss was willing to live with the less than ideal separation of Church and state though he warned, "let us beware of exalting it as 'ideal.'"

Accepting the separation of Church and state did have its positive side. Since the modern state no longer conducted its affairs in a manner befitting "a divinely constituted power" but rather, "acted in a godless manner," Catholics could justifiably use lawful means to resist its ever increasing incursions on their rights. Within this general view of the modern state Preuss does not seem to have had a preference for any particular form of government. He did however believe that democracy in America was not quite the blessing that its promoters claimed it to be. To begin with, it was based on the atheistic rationalism of the Enlightenment which refused to recognize the sovereignty of God and instead made man the measure of all things. Second, it promoted a false notion of universal equality. "All men are equal before God but on the natural plane men are quite evidently unequal. There are clear differences between them physically, intellectually, and morally. Therefore, to try and make them equal and to give them equal political rights is to subvert the order of nature and to court disaster." The system of government based on universal political equality was unjust to all. Unjust to "the better sort" because it infringes on their right as persons to have an influence in the community commensurate to their contribution to the common good. Strict political equality was also "unjust to the masses for it infringes on their right to the guidance of men of vision and learning, and subjects them to the base oligarchy of political adventurers." Finally, the American system made good government nearly impossible by degrading politics to the level of "ceaseless struggle between competing selfish interests."[84]

Preuss continued to support the agenda of the Federation until its demise. A few more times he would push for the Federation to engage in political action.[85] In 1907 he opposed the brief efforts of the Federation to obtain from the government a share in the public school fund for parochial schools. Preuss opposed these efforts for fear of government interference with Catholic institutions. He also restated his opposition in principle to the government's regulation of education.[86] For the most part, he simply reported on the various campaigns for "public morals" promoted by the Federation.[87] His hopes that the Federation would become an American Centre Party gradually died. Though he never said so, perhaps the idea of a Catholic political party in America had become quixotic even for him. In its absence, he would pursue other means for promoting the Catholic vision of society.

IV The Fallacy of Socialism and Masonic Tomfoolery

"The Fundamental Fallacy of Socialism"

Although the goals of the American Federation of Catholic Societies would have been regarded as largely sectarian by the rest of American society, its formation at the turn of the century is indicative of the major role that organized religion, most especially Protestantism, played in the Progressive movement. Seemingly in reaction to the "gospel of wealth" based on Social Darwinism, that characterized the last decades of the nineteenth century, American Protestantism placed a new emphasis on the social mission of the church. In a sense, the Progressive Era marked the triumph of social Christianity over Calvinism through "the awakening of the social consciousness of Protestantism."[1] Interestingly, "the social gospel" had also been influenced by Darwinism. However, its advocates interpreted the theory of evolution in a direction away from the doctrines of the "survival of the fittest" and "laissez faire" government. Instead the promoters of the social gospel saw in evolution theory confirmation of their notions of the universal brotherhood of man and that God worked through human institutions to effect progress in the human condition. The mainline Protestant denominations became increasingly less other-worldly in outlook "and began to view the extension of the kingdom in social and ethical, as well as theological terms."[2]

While simple altruism, and even Christian charity were motivating factors behind middle-class involvement in the Progressive movement, their activism was not all disinterested. The agitation for electoral reform sought to bring to the middle class a proportionate share in political power that was perceived as being dominated by the privileged few. The social justice campaign on behalf of the poor and downtrodden entailed an element of self-protection. As the labor movement tried to win for its members a share in the nation's prosperity, unrest among the working class was widespread. The national leadership of the trade union movement under Samuel Gompers and the American Federation of Labor was pragmatic and accepted the capitalistic economic system in principle. Other labor leaders, however, proposed radical and even violent solutions to the social question. Europe and America witnessed a series of terrorist acts in this period perpetrated by anarchists and revolutionaries. A potential path for organized labor in America at this time was an alliance with the Socialist Party, which in the 1890s was dominated by doctrinaire Marxists. Later, in the first decade of this century, the "moderates," Eugene Debs and Morris Hillquit, gained control of the party, though Marxists remained in its ranks even as the party sought power through the ballot box. Even more threatening to middle-class sensibilities was the Industrial Workers of the World organization formed in 1905. The "Wobblies" as they were called, sought to establish a "proletarian commonwealth" and would not disavow the use of violence.[3]

In retrospect the potential of the radical movements gaining large-scale support among the working class was limited. Nevertheless, in the context of the period, with numerous and often violent strikes and an enormous influx of poor and powerless immigrants, the rhetoric of the revolutionaries could be frightening. Thus, to some degree the strong support for social reform found among the middle class was motivated by fear of the consequences if the conditions of the working class were not alleviated.

Opposition to socialism certainly was a strong impulse propelling American Catholic interest in the social question and motivated Arthur Preuss's initial interest in the matter. A series of articles that he wrote against the socialistic ideas of Henry George led to the publication of Preuss's first book.[4] An "agrarian radical" who was supported by some socialists, Henry George did not proclaim himself to be a socialist as such. However, Preuss and others asserted that George's "Single Tax" proposals in effect denied the right to own property and therefore considered George a socialist. In his "brilliantly written" *Progress and Poverty* (1879), George advocated that the government should confiscate through a single tax on land, the "unearned increment" that normally accrued to the owners. He maintained that the rents paid to landowners, that increased without any effort on their part, unfairly burdened all the other participants in the economic system. While George's economic theories were difficult to fathom, his proposed curtailment on the rights of landownership as a quick remedy for poverty struck a responsive chord among the working classes throughout the English-speaking world. More importantly, through his promotion of the idea that society could be reconstructed through collective political action, George became "the leading democratic philosopher of the Gilded Age" and "the chief link between the reform movement of the ante-bellum period and the Progressive movement of the twentieth century."[5]

Preuss's involvement in the discussion of George's political ideas came about through the *Review*'s coverage of the conflict between the Archbishop of New York, Michael A. Corrigan, and one of his priests, Father Edward McGlynn. Doctor McGlynn, as he was known, was an ardent supporter of Henry George and engaged in political activities on his behalf.[6] While McGlynn had been excommunicated for a time because of his refusal to go to Rome to explain these activities, he had been officially reconciled to the Church in 1892 by the Papal Delegate, Archbishop Satolli, before Preuss began publishing the *Review*. Still, though officially reconciled, McGlynn continued a public feud with Archbishop Corrigan.

In the first issues of the *Review* Preuss criticized Satolli's acceptance of McGlynn's apologia, contending that in supporting the theories of George, McGlynn contradicted Church teaching regarding the right to own property.[7] Preuss also supported the disciplinary measures that Corrigan had taken against McGlynn. As conservative Catholics, Preuss and Corrigan held similar positions on the other issues that polarized the Church in America during the 1890s. But it was Preuss's support of Corrigan in his ordeal with McGlynn that endeared the young editor to the Archbishop as evidenced by the letters he and his brother sent to Preuss. While the Single Tax movement lost momentum with the death of Henry George in 1897, it continued to have supporters into the next century.[8]

As for the Corrigan-McGlynn battle, it continued to excite passions even after both men had died, McGlynn in 1900 and the Archbishop two years later. In the spring of 1904, the *New York Freeman's Journal* reopened the case by sponsoring a discussion as to whether George's Single Tax theory was compatible with Church teaching. This renewal of the debate inspired Preuss to write seventeen articles between April, 1904 and June, 1905 on the issue. In these articles Preuss compared the positions of Henry George with Leo XIII's encyclical *Rerum Novarum* to prove that the former contradicted the Church's teaching on private property. The next step was to show that McGlynn endorsed George's positions. This done, Preuss then asserted that although McGlynn had been reconciled to the Church, his statements in support of George could not be. In fact, Preuss insisted, Satolli "had been deceived by his advisors" who were supposed to evaluate McGlynn's positions, and so Satolli's restoration of McGlynn was itself an error.[9] Three years after he ran this series of articles, Preuss had them republished as a book, *The Fundamental Fallacy of Socialism: An Exposition of the Question of Landownership*, that was published by the Herder Book Company of St. Louis where he had established himself as the literary advisor some years before. The subtitle of the book, *"Comprising An Authentic Account of the Famous McGlynn Case,"* discloses that Preuss was not only concerned with refuting Georgian economics. Preuss wanted to vindicate Archbishop Corrigan in regard to the disciplinary actions he had taken against McGlynn. This inference is born out by the remarks that Preuss made on page 154 of his book that were not carried in the original series of articles.

> Dr. McGlynn's absolution from ecclesiastical censures was, under the circumstances, a great humiliation for Archbishop Corrigan: for it made the steps which had been taken against the Doctor by his immediate ecclesiastical superior appear before the whole world as arbitrary and unjust. Yet the saintly Archbishop never uttered a word of protest but preferred to be silent after the example of his Divine

Master. The generosity of Msgr. Corrigan's conduct throughout 'the McGlynn case' can be fully appreciated only by those who, like myself, have had access to the documents left behind by the saintly Archbishop. Some day, no doubt, these documents, authentic copies of which I had the privilege of examining in the winter of 1904-5, will be published, and only then will the McGlynn case, in all its details, appear to the public in its true light.[10]

Preuss's interest in the social question extended beyond simply reacting to perceived attacks on Catholic positions, but there was a certain defensiveness, or more properly, a "conservative cast" to his approach to social reform. As Philip Gleason pointed out in his book on the promotion of social reform by German American Catholics, *The Conservative Reformers*, "the same partial non-acceptance of American ways that had animated German Catholics in the battles over Cahenslyism and Americanism" also governed their approach to social reform. German American Catholics collectively promoted social reform through the Central Verein. While Arthur Preuss was not prominent in the Central Verein, the leadership of the organization, men like Nicholas Gonner, Joseph Matt, and Joseph Frey, were friends of his, and they shared a common outlook on the questions of the day. Additionally, Preuss was instrumental in bringing to the Central Verein its great leader and social theorist, Frederick Kenkel. It was Preuss who persuaded Kenkel to leave Chicago and come to St. Louis in May 1905 to take over from Preuss the editorship of the German Catholic daily newspaper, *Die Amerika*.[11] From his position as the editor of "the most influential German Catholic newspaper in the United States" Kenkel became a prominent figure in the German Catholic community and in the councils of the Central Verein.

The relationship between Arthur Preuss and Frederick Kenkel was a curious one. The two men were contemporaries, endowed with comparable intellectual gifts and held equally conservative principles. Additionally, their personal lives held several congruencies. Preuss was the son of a convert, while Kenkel underwent an adult "conversion" to the faith of his baptism. Both men experienced the death of their first wives at a young age. Both began their careers in Catholic journalism at the helm of William Kuhlman's German-language papers in Chicago. Finally, both men were on intimate terms with the Franciscan friars at Quincy, Illinois, where Preuss was educated and where Kenkel spent eight months following the death of his wife in 1891 discerning his vocation.[12] With such backgrounds, Preuss and Kenkel might have been fast friends. However, their relationship was not close in these years. Perhaps because Preuss had hired him, and even sold him the Preuss's family home in St. Louis, Kenkel might have felt beholden to Preuss.[13] Maybe it was Kenkel's abrasive manner, or Preuss's quiet one.[14] In any case, their relationship while always polite, was not close at this time. Only in the twenties, when Preuss and Kenkel were no longer bound to each other professionally in the publication of *Die Amerika*, would their friendship really flower.

Still, the formality that characterized their relationship did not prevent Preuss from recognizing Kenkel's gifts both as a journalist and a social theorist. After 1909, when Kenkel had involved the Central Bureau of the Central Verein in promoting his own vision of social reform, Preuss was a faithful supporter. Preuss concurred with Kenkel in reacting against "the general quality of life in the modern world" and in his belief that the solution to the social question required "a fundamental restructuring of society and a concomitant reordering of attitudes and values."[15] Preuss also agreed with Kenkel's program of emphasizing the education of Catholics, especially workingmen, in the principles of the Church's social teaching as the first step toward the much-needed social reconstruction of American society. While Preuss had not been as heavily influenced as Kenkel by the German romantic writers of the early nineteenth century, both men promoted a vision of the social order based on idealized notions of medieval Christendom.[16]

Of course, Arthur Preuss had been a social commentator for some years before becoming acquainted with Frederick Kenkel. From the first issue of the *Review* Preuss had challenged some of the practices of the capitalistic economic system on which American society was based. The capitalist system was seen by Preuss as the inevitable outcome of the individualism and moral relativism set loose by the "so called reformers" and accentuated by the Enlightenment. Capitalism oriented Americans toward the single-minded pursuit of mammon. It fostered the materialism that blinded Americans to spiritual realities and their duties toward God and neighbor.[17] Further, it was the capitalists' pursuit of profits based on the exploitation of labor that led to the disgraceful living and working conditions for the urban poor. Given their plight, workers became susceptible to the atheistic materialism of socialist propaganda and were led away from God and His Church.[18] Capitalism and socialism were for Preuss just two sides of the same materialist coin. However, as the socialist movement was more openly inimical to the Christian faith, Preuss, like many other Catholic commentators at this time, was preoccupied with socialism.

Of immediate concern at the turn of the century was providing Catholic alternatives to the potential socialist domination of the labor movement. As organized labor was met with a concerted attack on unionism in 1900 through the aggressive promotion of the "open shop" by groups such as the National Association of Manufacturers, Catholic leaders feared that the union rank and file would go over to the radicals in the labor movement.[19] Faced with this situation, Preuss took a position favorable to Catholic participation in non-Catholic unions. He still saw Catholic trade unions as "the only means" to make "a leaven fit to regenerate the working classes and effectively ward off socialism." But in their absence Catholics could participate in non-Catholic unions in order to both promote their own welfare and to prevent the socialists from taking over the unions.[20] Well read in the development of labor relations in western Europe, Preuss advocated for America a "strong Catholic social movement" based on the principles of *Rerum Novarum*. For "if we do not in a measure anticipate the social movement that is steadily developing, and guide it in right channels, there is no telling what havoc it may cause when it breaches the dikes."[21]

Preuss sought to guide the social movement by combatting the errors of socialism, promoting Catholic alternatives, raising awareness of the evils of capitalism, and by giving notice to developments that furthered better labor relations. Thus, in the period 1902 to 1912 the *Review* carried numerous articles on the social question that took as their focus one of these four perspectives.[22] Preuss's concern with the rise of socialism clearly predominated, and he was particularly alarmed by efforts such as that of the famous advocate of the "social gospel," Walter Rauschenbusch, to show the compatibility of socialism and Christianity.[23]

Preuss always tried to do "battle against Socialism on the one hand and Capitalism on the other" using "calm, fair, and constructive criticism by men who have studied the subject thoroughly."[24] One of Preuss's favorite constructive critics in this period was Father John A. Ryan. From 1907 until 1915 Preuss published more than two dozen articles and book reviews on the social question by Ryan. While Ryan's critique of American society was never as radical as Preuss's, the former's balanced evaluation of both capitalism and socialism from the perspective of Catholic moral theology was very pleasing to Preuss.[25] In the pre-World War I years Ryan was a rising star in Catholic intellectual circles and having his essays printed in the *Review* was of benefit to both men. Following the war, Ryan's liberal critique of the American economic system and his support for increased state interventionism led to a philosophical parting of ways between Ryan and Preuss. The increased alienation from American society experienced by German Catholics during the war years made Ryan's critique appear too mild and his promotion of "bigger" government a mistake. In the post-war years Preuss would give greater attention to the more radical corporatist views of Frederick Kenkel and other commentators associated with the Central Verein. Additionally, Preuss's opposition to the National Catholic Welfare Conference in the twenties was a contributing factor to the end of their association although Preuss would always speak well of John Ryan.

"Masonic Tomfoolery"

As has been noted, Preuss's interest in the social question was largely motivated by his concern that unless the Church offered assistance to workers in gaining redress for their grievances the working class might be lost to the Faith through the alluring propaganda of socialism. However, laborers were not the only ones being enticed away from the Church by anti-Christian creeds. The loyalty of the middle class to Christianity was also at risk to the pernicious power of Freemasonry and similar secret societies.

In order to understand the apparent preoccupation with Masonry that led Preuss to write dozens of articles and two books on the subject, it is necessary to recognize how strong secret fraternal societies like the Masons were at the turn of the century. An awareness of Church teaching on the subject of Masonry is also helpful to understanding Arthur Preuss's perspective on the subject.

Originating in London during the early 1700s as "a club for tradesman, merchants and a few much celebrated noblemen," by 1896 Masonry's American branch and similar secret societies had an estimated five and a half million members out of a total adult male population of nineteen million.[26] Almost exclusively a white, native, Protestant, urban, middle-class movement, Masonry had overcome earlier bad press to become the epitome of respectability in American society. Masons were public figures, politicians, and noted businessmen. They even numbered American presidents among their members. Protestant ministers were also prominent in their orders, and they maintained good relations with the major denominations. The charitable works of the Masons and similar societies were well publicized, and to the public at large they presented an image of good character and strict probity. As Preuss himself remarked, they played an important role "in shaping American ideas and molding American life."[27]

Yet for the leadership of the Catholic Church, and Arthur Preuss, the benevolent faces of individual Masons and members of other fraternal orders simply masked the real evil at work in these secret societies. A characteristic Catholic condemnation of Masonry and like secret societies was issued by Pope Leo XIII in 1884 in the encyclical *Humanum Genus*.[28] This encyclical reiterated the indictments made against Masonry in previous papal condemnations including the first one, *In Eminenti*, issued in 1738.[29] Leo XIII's encyclical stated that the Church's opposition to Masonry was due to the latter's promotion of "Naturalism" which teaches "that human nature and human reason ought in all things to be mistress and guide." This "Naturalism" undermines belief in Divine Revelation and promotes "the great error of the age," religious indifferentism, by discounting any "dogma of religion or religious truth which cannot be understood by human intelligence." As the purveyor of naturalism, the ultimate purpose of Masonry according to the encyclical is "the utter overthrow of that whole religious and political order of the world which Christian teaching had produced." To attain its goals Masonry was working to counteract Christianity's influence on society by subordinating the rights of the Church to the claims of the State in areas such as education. Should Masonry have its way, it would "destroy the religion and the Church which God Himself had established" and would "bring back the manners and the customs of the pagans." In his encyclical Leo called on his brother bishops to join his efforts "to strive for the extirpation of this foul plague which is creeping through the veins of the state."[30]

Leo's depiction of the Masonic order was obviously colored by the Church's encounter with the European branches of Masonry. From their early days Masonic orders in the supposedly Catholic countries like France, Italy, and Spain were powerful opponents of the Church. As proponents of the Enlightenment, European Masonic societies had promoted among other things, the subordination of the Church to the State, the establishment of State education, and the secularization of marriage laws.[31] For these reasons, Masonry and the Catholic Church had been bitter enemies in Europe.

In the United States the relationship between the Catholic Church and the Masonic orders was far less acrimonious. Because Church-and-State issues had been to a large measure defined by the "disestablishment clause" in the American Constitution, Catholicism and American Freemasonry had few occasions to do battle. In fact, American Masons always maintained that they were different from the European orders and had no animosity toward the Catholic Church. Even some Catholics in America subscribed to this notion. Arthur Preuss, however, was not one of them.

Preuss whole-heartedly agreed with Leo XIII's assertion that the ultimate goal of Masonry was the destruction of the bastion of Christian orthodoxy, the Catholic Church. But he also recognized that the threat that American Freemasonry posed to the Church was less political and must be opposed primarily on religious grounds. Thus, when Preuss set out to explain why Catholicism was opposed to Masonry his arguments centered on the religious antagonism between the two and were not based on a defense of the social prerogatives of the Church. It should also be noted that while Preuss was an ardent opponent of Masonry, he was not given to credulity regarding purported Masonic plots. Throughout 1896, while many Catholics, including some of Preuss's future French allies, were duped by the spurious revelations by "Diane Vaughn" regarding a violent Satanic cult connected with Masonry, Preuss refused to believe the tale. When the fraud was finally exposed, the Boston *Pilot* gave the *Review* credit for being the first American paper to explode the swindle. Another Catholic editor wrote, "thanks to Mr. Preuss's *Review* we were saved from swallowing the gudgeon."[32]

Preuss had reported on the controversy regarding Catholic involvement in various secret societies from the time of the *Review*'s inception.[33] This coverage was intensified beginning May, 1903 in when Preuss began a series of articles entitled, "Studies in American Freemasonry." These articles, thirty-six in all, ran through June 1904. Later, as in the case of his treatment of Henry George and the Single Tax movement, Preuss had his articles on Masonry published in expanded form as a book, *Studies in American Freemasonry* (B. Herder: St.Louis, 1908).[34] In his essays on Masonry Preuss followed the same methodology that he used in writing his articles on the Single Tax movement. He began by presenting the teachings of Masonry and then set out to demonstrate how these teachings were in conflict with the tenets of Christianity. For his study on Masonry he used six of the order's basic texts describing its rituals. Five of these books were written by Dr. Albert Mackey, who was regarded by Masons as a "learned" scholar of their order. The sixth text, *Morals and Dogma of the Ancient and Accepted Scottish Rite of Freemasonry* (New York, 1881) was written by the controversial Confederate general, and "foremost nineteenth-century Masonic ritualist, Albert Pike."[35]

Preuss's analysis of Masonry concentrated on that element of the fraternal movement that was distinctively its own, the rites of initiation. Preuss's focus on the rites of the Masonic orders was well placed for, as Professor Mark Carnes, author of one of the most recent studies of American Freemasonry has documented, the "founders of the fraternal groups emphasized rituals from the outset and added other activities almost by chance." Rather than the rituals being a prerequisite to participating in the other activities of Masons, they were the principal activity of the orders.[36]

In addition to taking the rituals of the Masons seriously as indicators of their belief system, Preuss also followed the distinction Mackey candidly made between merely "exoteric Masonry," and the order's secret tenets, or "esoteric Masonry." Preuss quoted Mackey as saying that like the ancient Greek philosophical schools, Masonry was divided into two classes of "disciples." There are those who receive instruction in the ways of the order "which ordinary intelligence could grasp and against which the prejudices of ordinary minds would not revolt." And then there are those for whom "the more abstruse tenets" are reserved, the "chosen few" who received "lessons too strange to be acknowledged" and "too pure to be appreciated by the vulgar crowd."[37]

It was Preuss's contention that "esoteric Masonry" as disclosed in the rites of the various orders belied the benign impression that most people had of these societies. According to Preuss, the rites of Masonry revealed that it was not the "handmaid of religion" that its proponents claimed it to be and that its support of Christianity was mere pretense. In fact, Masonry itself was a religion akin to the ancient pagan cults. Not only did Masonry manipulate Christian symbols and distort the meaning of the Bible to suit its own ends, at a fundamental level it rejected Jesus Christ.[38] In summing up his report Preuss asserted that Masonry, by virtue of its paganism, was anti-Catholic and therefore must be actively resisted by the Church.

> ...Masonry is and clearly asserts that it is a religion. It asserts more: that it alone imparts to its votaries the true knowledge of the nature and essence of God and the human soul, ...hence every Christian and Catholic, who is not a Mason, is wandering in ignorance, darkness, helplessness and pollution, devoid of the first elements of morality...
> I have shown that Masonry is essentially paganism in its origin, its ceremonies, its affections, its symbolism, its doctrines...that it remits its students to the doctrines of the pagan mysteries for the true explanation of its own; that its considers the differences between such mysteries and itself to be one of mere external form, since the spirit and the life blood are the same.
> Lastly, I have shown that the religion of Masonry is practically the phallic worship of the ancients, the prominent feature, nay the very groundwork, of all the pagan mysteries. It is the worship of the procreative powers of nature...a worship whose symbols are found in every well constituted lodge and of which every lodge itself and its principal officers are the permanent of symbols.[39]

Preuss's indictment of Masonry in its supposedly innocuous American form, is severe. However, his charges cannot simply be dismissed as editorial exaggeration. Mark Carnes, in his more dispassionate study of Masonry, published some eighty years after Preuss's work, remarked on the same anti-Christian aspects of Masonic rituals. Carnes upholds Preuss's distinction between the external manifestation of Masonry and the esoteric meanings of its rites. Carnes notes that the authors of Masonic rituals "repeatedly insisted" that Masonic symbols "simultaneously afford concealment and revelation as some mysteries were explained while others were newly propounded."[40] Carnes also upholds Preuss's point that Masonry misappropriated traditional Christian symbols for its own ends.

> ....the cross itself figured prominently in many fraternal rituals, but initiates gradually learned that it did not refer to Christ. The cross, Pike wrote, was a sacred symbol among the Druids, Indians, Egyptians, and Arabians 'thousands of years before the coming of Christ.' The obvious Christian meaning of these symbols merely concealed a deeper association with ancient —and pagan —religions.[41]

According to Carnes, by the mid-nineteenth century, "Christ ceased to have a place in the ritual of the order." And in the rituals devised by Albert Mackey, Masonry implied the "insufficiency of Christian worship." In fact [the rituals] "served as a means of personal transformation in which the rites of the lodge supplanted the mediation of Christ."[42] Carnes also validates Preuss's conclusion that, in the highest degree of Masonry, in which the "royal secret" is disclosed, the Masonic rites are inextricably connected to "the worship of the procreative powers of nature." The royal secret of Masonry, says Carnes, is "God's bisexual character" which explains "the cosmic opposition of heaven and earth, spirituality and sensuality, male and female" and man's "double nature." Carnes goes on to venture a psychological explanation for the attraction of these rites for so many American men that goes well beyond the analysis that Preuss offered. However, Carnes explanation corroborates Preuss's assertion that Masonry was advancing its own radical view of human nature.

Arthur Preuss's concern that the popularity of Freemasonry posed a threat to Christianity continued throughout his life. As an ongoing project he collected information on the hundreds of fraternal organizations that existed in America. This work culminated in 1924 with the publication of *A Dictionary of Secret and Other Societies* (St. Louis: B. Herder). It is only in the context of Preuss's well-founded concerns regarding the true nature of Masonry that one can understand his hostility to the Knights of Columbus. Critical articles on the Knights appeared in the *Review* almost as frequently as those on the Masons. The principal point of Preuss's complaint against Columbianism was that as a secret society, "aping Masonic tomfoolery," the Knights served as a stepping stone for Catholic men to enter the Masonic orders.[43] Preuss first incensed the Knights by publishing an extract of their ritual and referring to them derisively as "the Catholic Elks."[44] The *Review* would provide a "forum" for anti-Knight criticism for years to come.[45]

V The Modernist Crisis

Given the passion with which Arthur Preuss had involved himself in the controversy over Americanism, as well as his concern for defending Catholic orthodoxy, it is rather startling at first to discover just how little coverage the *Review* gave to the Modernist crisis. During 1907, the year the papal decrees on Modernism were issued, the *Review* carried only three articles on the subject. There were nine such articles in 1908, but just two in 1909. This was considerably less by comparison than the newsprint Preuss had expended on Pius X's other initiatives such as the *motu proprio* on the reform of church music, *"Inter pastoralis officii"* (1903), or the decree promoting frequent communion, *"De quotidiana S.S. Eucharistiae"* (1905).[1]

In another American Catholic journal with a different editor, this seeming lack of interest in the Modernist crisis might be explained away as indifference to what was perceived as essentially a European problem. However, Arthur Preuss could never be accused of provincialism. He regularly read German, French, and Italian Catholic journals and frequently translated and published excerpts from them in his *Review*. So, some other explanation as to why the Modernist crisis did not dominate the pages of the *Review* must be found. It appears that Preuss did not concentrate a lot of energy on the discussion of Modernism because from his point of view, the issue was not new. For Arthur Preuss, Americanism and Modernism sprang from the same source. Both fell under the rubric of liberalism in the Church with Americanism being its practical application and Modernism being its theological manifestation. Preuss's conflation of the two movements under the general heading of "Liberalism" is manifested very clearly in his 1902 essay, "Conservative vs. Liberal Catholics."

> 'Americanism' is the modern form of Liberalism. It is not easy to define Liberalism, because it is a very peculiar heresy, in as much as it does not deny or distort any well-defined Catholic truth or any order of truths, but rests upon an utterly false conception of the entire system of Catholic doctrine and practice. The 'Liberal Catholic'(really a

contradictio in terminis) denies no particular dogma, and is therefore armed against criticisms of what he is pleased to call a 'supersensitive Conservatism;' but he dilutes and weakens them all...Besides, as a 'Liberal Catholic,' he does not champion absolute Liberalism, but only a modern form thereof –the 'true' and 'genuine' Liberalism. He admits the plenary powers of the highest ecclesiastical authority, but at the same time does his level best to limit the exercise thereof and to weaken the import of its pronouncements and decisions, whenever his notion of the necessary 'reconciliation' of the Church and the age requires it. He is 'Catholic,' genuinely Catholic, even more Catholic than the Pope upon occasions, and solemnly professes that he considers the Catholic religion the only true faith; all of which does not, however, prevent him from advocating enthusiastically the 'reform' or 'evolution' of Catholicism demanded by the Zeitgeist...Thus the error is practical rather than theoretical; elusive as a doctrine but all the more dangerous in practice.[2]

As for the practice of liberal Catholics Preuss wrote,

They are not interested in the fate of the Holy See, and care little for how the hierarchy or the clergy fares. They hold that religion ought to be confined as closely as possible to four walls of the churches. Too rigid teachings ought to be softened and their acceptance or non-acceptance on the part of the individual Christian be made dependent on the degree of his scientific accomplishments....Any definite and firm statement of Catholic principles and their defense in public life is eschewed by them as a sign of 'retrogression' which they abhor. Toleration is their great watchword, and this toleration they carry so far that they do not hesitate to join liberal clubs or Socialistic groups, nor to keep and read newspapers inculcating the most pernicious heresies and errors.[3]

These essays describe liberalism and its adherents in much the same way that Pius X's encyclical, *Pascendi dominici gregis* (1907) would depict Modernism. This similarity is perhaps owed to the influence the pastoral letter of the English bishops condemning liberalism had on Preuss's thinking. Preuss published this pastoral in the *Review* in February 1901. David Schultenover, S.J., in his *A View From Rome,* has recently documented the influence that Raphael Merry del Val, then an advisor to Leo XIII, had on the composition of both the English bishops' condemnation of liberalism and on *Pascendi*.[4] Thus, by taking his cues from the English bishops' pastoral letter, Preuss's own essays on liberalism appeared as harbingers of the condemnation of Modernism.

Apart from these long essays written in 1902, however, even "Liberalism" does not appear that often as a separate topic in the pages of the *Review*. Rather, Preuss's war on liberalism, and hence Modernism, is encountered within the context of articles dealing with the controversial issues of the day such as the theory of evolution, higher biblical criticism, and the discussion of the development of doctrine. Articles on the works of European liberal Catholics and their American counterparts appeared frequently in the *Review* before the condemnation of Modernism in 1907.

Following the flow of contemporary debate, the *Review* carried numerous articles on the question of "theistic evolution."[5] A direct connection between the evolution debate and Modernism is made by R. Scott Appleby in his recent study, *Church and Age Unite! The Modernist Impulse in American Catholicism*.

> For it was in the ongoing and bitter debate over evolution, and Darwin's theory thereof, that many American Catholics first encountered a scientific worldview buttressed by historical consciousness and developmentalist thought.[6]

In his chapter on John Zahm, C.S.C. as a Catholic proponent of theistic evolution, and thus a Modernist, Appleby rightly numbers Preuss among Zahm's American critics as the *Review* carried several articles criticizing Zahm's positions. Preuss also published translations of *La Civilta Cattolica*'s critiques of Zahm's works, thus making them known to Preuss's American readers.[7] However, it should be noted that Preuss's criticism of Zahm's theories, and those of his British forerunner, St. George Mivart, was not a blanket condemnation of evolutionism. Preuss acknowledged that there "are many phenomena in nature which make it probable that a limited evolution must be admitted." However, he argued that since according to its own promoters, evolutionary theory had yet to be proven scientifically, it remained only a hypothesis. When the theory is established by scientific proof "religious truth will have nothing to fear." However, he did not believe that "the derivative origin of man" could ever be proven because in such a version of humanity's beginnings it is "impossible to account for the spirituality of the human soul."[8] Additionally, the fervor with which evolutionists supported materialistic philosophy and agnosticism could only cause the Christian believer to question the true motivations driving the unproven theories of evolution.

Evolution, and in particular, "the descent of the human body by descent from the brute," remained a topic of discussion in the pages of the *Review* for years to come. The articles that Preuss wrote himself and those of his contributors were consistent in accepting the plausibility of evolution theory while rejecting its corollaries, natural selection and the derivative origin of man. The articles opposed natural selection and human evolution as having no proven scientific basis, and as contrary to the testimony of Scripture regarding the God-given dignity of man. Preuss and his contributors were concerned that the unsubstantiated theory of physical evolution was being utilized by "the enemies of religion" to undermine Christian metaphysics and "belief in a supernatural revelation."[9] Among Christian believers Preuss's position on evolution was a moderate one that still has reputable supporters today.[10]

Right from the start the debate over "theistic evolution" has been entwined with issues relating to modern biblical criticism. At the turn of the century the connection between the two was perhaps even greater as the proponents of these two new "sciences" seemingly travelled in the same intellectual circles. This was certainly the case with the Americanists. Before the condemnation of Americanism, John Ireland, John Keane, and Denis O'Connell actively cultivated friendships with European and American scholars who took liberal positions on evolution and "higher" biblical criticism.[11]

As for Arthur Preuss, a self-proclaimed "Ultramontane," his published comments on biblical criticism took their tone from Roman pronouncements on the subject. Thus, through the duration of Leo XIII's pontificate, the *Review*'s articles on contemporary biblical scholarship reflected the diversity of positions that existed even in Rome on these matters.[12] Therefore, while the *Review* was critical of the American Sulpician scholar John Hogan for undermining Leo XIII's teaching on inspiration, it was also moderate enough to assert that "there is no official injunction requiring Catholics to believe in verbal inspiration or the entirely supernatural character of the Scriptures."[13]

Writing in 1903, Preuss praised the Jesuit scholar and member of the Pontifical Biblical Commission, Ernest Pratt, for his moderate views regarding the relationship between Scripture and science.[14] In reviewing an article published in the *Kölnische Volkszeitung* in 1905, Preuss noted approvingly the Pratt's conclusion that "historical science is not limited by the Bible, and vice versa, the Bible suffers no injury if the progress of our historical knowledge compels us to change traditional ideas and theories."[15] Later that year, Preuss published articles adapted from the work of the German scholar Norbert Peters, which, while firmly grounded in the encyclical *Providentissimus Deus*, effusively praised the findings of contemporary biblical scholarship.

> For a long time, in the past century, Biblical science among Catholics was characterized by conservative traditionalism. Its professors were content in handing down the old material in the usual form according to the current methods. There was no scientific research in the strict sense, and therefore, no progress...During the past ten years there has been a vast improvement. Biblical science, especially of the Old Testament, is pulsating with new life...Scientific progress aims at progress, and progress invariably calls forth opposition from those who adhere fixedly to tradition and its antiquated forms. Therefore the increasing study of the Biblical sciences and the progress made by our younger exegetists, is accompanied by an exaggerated skepticism, an insulting distrust, directed not, it is true, against scientific research as such, but against the personal orthodoxy of the champions of the new

school, culminating in some instances even in persecution, at least in secret, of our best scholars. For there are those among us who, still under the ban of the old school with its stereotyped conception of revelation and the Bible...consider that real scientific Biblical research is incompatible with the true Catholic spirit.[16]

Preuss published two more articles in 1905 based on Peters' book.[17] While these articles were rather moderate in their application of the "higher criticism," like the passage quoted above, they were remarkable in their tone. Such criticism of "antiquated forms of biblical teachings," the "insulting distrust" directed at the personal orthodoxy of the champions of the new school," and the "secret persecution of our best scholars," was unique in the pages of the *Review*. That Arthur Preuss went to the trouble to translate and publish these remarks indicates that while he was cautious in regard to the new biblical criticism, he was not a reactionary.

Another example of Preuss's receptiveness to the new biblical scholarship is found in the remarks of "an esteemed colleague" that Preuss published upon the appointment of the Dutch scholar, Henry Poels, to the faculty of the Catholic University of America. The article noted that Poels was "a protagonist of the progressive tendency in the Catholic school of Biblical criticism," and that "his advanced views...were displeasing to some ultra-conservative seminary professors." However, Preuss's unnamed colleague went on to say that Poels's "progressiveness" was "strictly orthodox." Poels was "a profound and brilliant Bible critic," whose selection as a professor "is a happy one and a real gain to the University."[18] Ironically, while Arthur Preuss took no part in the post- *Pascendi* attacks on Poels, the "liberal clique" administering the Catholic University of America, specifically, Cardinal Gibbons, and two of its rectors, Denis O'Connell and Thomas Shahan, proceeded against the Dutch scholar in such underhanded fashion as to justify claims of an anti-Modernist "witch hunt."[19]

It seems that, like many of the liberal Catholic intellectuals of the period, Preuss also struggled to balance his enthusiasm for contemporary scholarship with the teachings of the Magisterium. One difference, of course, was that Arthur Preuss, as a self-professed Ultramontane, more readily adjusted to the constriction of the field of Catholic biblical studies that occurred during the pontificate of Pope Pius X.

Still, even while the range of accepted biblical scholarship was gradually being narrowed, Preuss was willing to explore the limits of official pronouncements. For example, while "deploring" the publication by the Modernists Charles Briggs and Friedrich von Hügel of their correspondence critical of the Pontifical Biblical Commission's 1906 decision regarding the Mosaic authorship of the Pentateuch, Preuss asserted that "the decision is in no sense an 'ex cathedra' definition of faith."

> Furthermore, the Commission, in its decision, or more correctly its opinion, nowhere asserts that the Mosaic authorship is proved. It simply declares that it has not been disproved. Should science and scholarship at any time in the future adduce new arguments against the Mosaic authorship, there is nothing that would prevent the Commission from accepting them, provided they are conclusive.[20]

Preuss's conservatism, it is clear, did not prevent him from being receptive to the findings of genuine biblical scholarship. Preuss's conservatism also did not blind him to the deficiencies of current Catholic philosophical studies. In 1905 Preuss commended a book review by Ernest Hull, S.J. that Preuss had entitled, "Ultra-Conservatism in Our Textbooks of Scholastic Philosophy." Perhaps recalling his own endeavor to study of modern philosophy during his years in Chicago, Preuss quoted Hull on the need for Catholic courses in philosophy to take cognizance of modern philosophy and science.

> The fact is, no man can really understand the philosophy of other systems without studying them for himself, from the point of view of their own exponents; nor can a student be competent in philosophical

questions bearing on science without a grasp of the scientific position from the point of view of science itself.[21]

A year later, in an article promoting the Neo-Scholastic movement at Louvain under Desire Mercier, Preuss recounted his own experiences as a student of philosophy in a Catholic college. His ruminations once again demonstrate that his conservative views did not result from a want of critical thinking.

> We in this country...scarcely know what Neo-Scholasticism means. Our students are taught from antiquated, dry-as-dust Italian textbooks a 'Philosophy' which, if they think at all, they find inadequate and uninteresting, and utterly out of joint and unconnected with contemporary thought. In consequence most of us either have no philosophy at all, or become easy victims to the nebulous vagaries — they do not deserve the name of a 'system' — put forth by certain native and foreign writers who are either steeped in Positivism or impregnated with the errors of Kant, Hegel or Schopenhauer...Had it not been for Kleutgen's *Philosophie der Vorzeit*,...the present writer, after a two years' course of philosophy in which he was fed the dry husks of unutterably tedious and indigestible Italian manuals, which in his private readings he cast aside to study with keen appetite John Stuart Mill's *Logic* and the essays of Herbert Spencer, would, probably have turned from Neo-Scholasticism with disgust never to be overcome...[22]

Arthur Preuss was an intellectual with a brilliant mind. And as he was quite capable of discerning intellectual competence in the work of others, he gave other scholars their due, even when he disagreed with them. This point can be illustrated by his ambivalent attitude toward John Hogan's book, *Clerical Studies*. As Hogan "endorsed much of the Modernist enterprise" and gave his "support to the Americanist cause," he came in for criticism in the pages of the *Review*. As has been mentioned previously, Preuss also found fault with Hogan's views on Scripture that the latter published in his book *Clerical Studies*. Yet, when Preuss published his own adaptation of Joseph Pohle's series on dogmatic theology Preuss included Hogan's book in his bibliography.[23]

Another case in point is the *Review*'s treatment of the German priest-professor Herman Schell. A proponent of "reform Catholicism" in Germany, Schell is recognized today as "an outstanding intellectual" and a "sincere and original philosopher and theologian."[24] In a pamphlet published in 1897 entitled, "Katholizimus als Prinzip des Fortschritts," Schell declared that "the Church had to ally itself to progress in whatever form, requesting that Catholics not be forced to behave like 'mental eunuchs.'" A second pamphlet, "Die neue Zeit und der alte Glaube," with similar sensational declarations landed Schell on the Index. At the time, Preuss called Schell as "the chief exponent of Americanism in Germany," which was an accurate description considering the affinity between Schell and the Americanists, Ireland, O'Connell and Zahm.[25] After Shell's death in 1906, Preuss asserted that Schell's "collision with the Index served to ennoble Dr. Schell's character and to enhance his reputation as a true and loyal son of the Holy Catholic Church." Preuss even praised Schell's last work, *Apologie des Christentums*.[26] Within a year of Schell's death and in the midst of the Modernist crisis, a vigorous debate regarding Schell's orthodoxy developed in Germany. Commenting on this debate, Preuss wrote that Schell was "brilliant and well meaning" and dismissed the notion that Schell was a Modernist as, contrary to the Modernists, Schell exaggerated the human ability to comprehend the divine. However, Preuss also condemned the fact that Schell "has been looked upon by Modernists and 'reform Catholics' in Germany and elsewhere, as a leader and a sort of patron saint."[27]

Even the notorious Modernists, Alfred Loisy and George Tyrrell, at least initially, received a studied evaluation in the pages of the *Review*. In 1903, speaking of Loisy, several of whose books had already been placed on the Index, Preuss described him as "foremost among modern Bible critics." As for Loisy's heterodoxy, Preuss noted rather mildly that Loisy had "strayed from the Catholic way of interpreting the Bible."[28] When Loisy's conflicts with Church authorities intensified, the *Review* would depict him in more negative shades. In 1906, an article reprinted from the *Freeman's Journal*, "Loisyism" had become "the great apostasy today."[29] By 1909, after the condemnation of Modernism and Loisy's excommunication, a contributor to the *Review* asserted that Loisy's conclusions in regard to Scripture and the Church would not survive another twenty years of "scientific research." However, in the meantime it was necessary for the Church to condemn his works in order to protect the faith of individual Catholics.[30]

The *Review*'s treatment of the English Modernist, George Tyrrell, follows a pattern similar to its references to Loisy, going from mild criticism to condemnation. In the case of Tyrrell however, Preuss appears to have been personally familiar with his work and Preuss's first mention of George Tyrrell was a favorable one. In an essay published on June 9, 1898, Preuss paraphrased an article of Tyrrell's on liberalism that had originally appeared in the English Jesuit journal, the *Month*.[31] Tyrrell's name reappeared in the *Review* eight years later in an article quoting the French Jesuit journal, *Etudes*, criticizing Tyrrell's book, *Lex Orandi*. At this time, Preuss also published Tyrrell's letter to the press concerning his separation from the Society of Jesus.[32] Preuss referred once again to Tyrrell's "unfortunate case" in February 1907, when publishing an account of Tyrrell's apologia "A Much Abused Letter." An article appearing in the *Review* two months later attributed the errors of Tyrrell, "the brilliant priest" to hubris. In May 1907, while regretting that "we cannot recommend unreservedly" Tyrrell's book, *Lex Orandi*, Preuss quoted this work of Tyrrell's against Friedrich Nietzsche's concept of the "übermensch." As late as July 1907, Preuss questioned press reports that all of Tyrrell's works had been placed on the Index.[33] Following the publication of the decree, *Lamentabili* by the Holy Office on July 4, 1907, and Pope Pius X's encyclical, *Pascendi Dominici Gregis* on September 8, 1907, Preuss made few references to Tyrrell's work and these were wholly negative.

Arthur Preuss's first comments on the decree *Lamentabili*, in the September 1, issue of the *Review* made a direct connection between Americanism and Modernism.

Leo XIII stamped out, at least in theory, 'Americanism' in this country; it remains for his gloriously reigning successor Pius X to extirpate what is essentially the same amalgam of errors, only, if possible, more radical and more highly developed, in Italy, Germany and France.[34]

The evidence indicates that Preuss was the first to state this connection. David Schultenover contends that "the connection was first made in print by the French Jesuit, Maurice de la Taille," in the journal *Etudes* published on September 26, 1907.[35] As Preuss's remarks were published almost four weeks prior to those of de la Taille (and a week before *Pascendi* was signed), it is reasonable to conclude Father Schultenover's contention is incorrect. Seeing as *Etudes* was on the *Review*'s exchange list, it is even possible that the French Jesuit's remarks were derived from Preuss's comments. In any case, the connection between Americanism and Modernism was officially stated in *Pascendi*.

An essay Preuss published in the October 15 issue of the *Review* reiterated the connection between Modernism and Americanism "which may, we think, in several aspects be justly classed as 'modernistic.'" This essay went on to state that "the heretical exegesis of the Abbe Loisy and the symbolism of Father Tyrrell, at both which the encyclical "De Doctrina Modernistarum"(*Pascendi*) is particularly aimed, have obtained a foothold among American Catholics." As an example of Modernism in America, Preuss cited the case of "the apostate Father Slattery," who had declared publicly that "'his priesthood had fallen from him'" as a consequence of reading "the books of Loisy and others of that stripe."[36] This same issue of the *Review* carried an article on the juridical import of *Lamentabili,* stating that while the decree must be obeyed "under pain of sin," it was not infallible or "unalterable." Preuss also stated that it was incorrect to assert, "as at least one American Catholic journal has done, that the propositions condemned in the decree *Lamentabili* are all heretical."[37]

Perhaps as a result of the *Review*'s comparatively moderate stance, Preuss himself was subject to accusations regarding his loyalty. In July,

1909, the Wichita *Catholic Advance* pronounced Preuss "guilty of Modernism of the worst sort" for printing a "heretical sermon" by Billy Sunday.[38] A few months later, the *Review* confronted reactionaries when one of Preuss's friends and contributors, Father Frederick G. Holweck, a priest from St. Louis and editor of the *Pastoralblatt*, was accused of being a Modernist on the basis of his article in the *Catholic Encyclopedia* on the Feast of the Assumption. Preuss gave Holweck four pages in the *Review* in which to refute the charges.[39]

That Arthur Preuss took a moderate position on the controverted questions of the day, even after the condemnation of Modernism, is not often credited. Emile Poulat, in his study of "Integralism," lists Arthur Preuss as the sole American collaborator with Monsignor Umberto Benigni's secretive "Sodalitium Pianum" organization which sought to ferret out Modernists in the Church.[40] However, there are no letters from Benigni in Preuss's personal papers and careful study of the *Review* yielded just three minor references to Benigni's publication, *Correspondance de Rome*. These references to the *Correspondance de Rome* were all carried in the *Review* in 1911. In the first notice, the *Review* reported on a story in the *Correspondance* regarding the "leakage" from the Church of Catholic immigrants in America. When Preuss ran this notice, he described the *Correspondance* as a "semi-official" publication.[41] Perhaps as a result of these few references to the integralist's journal, Preuss received two letters from his "doughty grenadier" of the Americanist struggle, Father Charles Maignen who was an active member of Benigni's Sodalitium Pianum. The second of these two letters indicates that Preuss did write to Maignen regarding the character of the American clergy and that his remarks were critical. However, Maignen's response to Preuss's letter suggests that Preuss also had some concern regarding the reputation of the *Correspondance de Rome* and its methods.

> Vous me parlez de gagner la Corr. de Rome a cette cause. Vous pouvez etre assure que c'est chose faite, et si elle n'est entree

publiquement en campagne, c'est qu'elle n'est pas libre de le faire.[42]

Whether Arthur Preuss was "assured" by Maignen's letter or not, it was the last letter from Maignen in Preuss's files. Judging from this material, Preuss's own interest in modern scholarship, his printed statements regarding the limitations of the anti-Modernist decrees, his own experience of responding to anti-Modernist accusations, and his personal character, it is both inaccurate and unfair to suggest that he had any significant "relations" with Umberto Benigni's anti-Modernist vigilantes.

If Preuss gave only scant attention to the European Modernists, Loisy and Tyrrell, he paid even less notice to their fellow travellers in America. In his book on the Modernist impulse in American Catholicism, Scott Appleby identifies nine priests in America as being under the influence of this "impulse."[43] Of the nine, six were specifically mentioned in the *Review* for either their Americanist, "progressive," or Modernist affiliations. As previously mentioned, John Zahm and John Hogan were included in the *Review*'s attack on Americanism, and John Slattery's apostasy and Modernist tendencies were noted in the fall of 1907. Also noted, was the *Review*'s praise for the "progressive" biblical scholar Henry Poels's appointment to the Catholic University of America.[44] Edward Hanna, later Archbishop of San Francisco, made the pages of the *Review* in February 1908 when allegations of his Modernist tendencies prevented his appointment as coadjutor to Archbishop Michael Riordan of San Francisco.[45] Noting that Hanna "has been formally charged with Modernism" on the basis of his articles in the *Catholic Encyclopedia* and the *New York Review*, Preuss expressed doubts regarding the accusations.

> It is almost incredible that the Rochester Seminary, founded and ruled by that eminent champion of simon-pure orthodoxy, the veteran Bishop McQuaid, should produce the first victim of the encyclical Pascendi, and that the *Catholic Encyclopedia*, which has on its board of editors such a lynx-eyed custodian of the Church's traditions as Father Wynne, S.J., should have made itself the vehicle of Modernistic errors.[46]

The removal of James Driscoll as rector of St. Joseph's Seminary in Dunwoodie, New York, and the controversy surrounding the *New York Review*, "a primer of the modernist worldview,"[47] published there, were covered in two articles published in the *Review* in the fall of 1909. The first of these articles, run on September 1, 1909, attributed the "displacement" of Driscoll as rector of Dunwoodie to a recent Roman decree barring ex-members of religious orders from acting as teachers in seminaries. This article depicted Driscoll's dismissal as the result of Sulpician complaints regarding the employment of some of their ex-members as professors at the seminary after the Society itself had been asked to leave by the Archdiocese of New York.[48] In the October 15 issue of the *Review* Preuss responded to criticism of his earlier statements regarding the Dunwoodie affair that had been issued "in rather magisterial fashion" by *America*, the new Jesuit journal. *America* depicted Driscoll's resignation as a routine matter and criticized Preuss's conjectures regarding the affair. In response to this criticism, Preuss noted that the New York secular press had already indicated that Driscoll left under a cloud. Preuss also observed that Driscoll's resignation was connected to "the demise of the unfortunate *New York Review*" which "drew upon itself a great deal of criticism both in this country and in Rome owing to the character of the views expressed by some of its contributors."[49] Apart from these references however, it would appear that Preuss knew little about the exact nature of the Dunwoodie controversy. Nor does he give any indication that he had actually ever read a copy of the *New York Review*.

As for William Sullivan, whom Appleby describes as the embodiment of the Americanist-Modernist synthesis, he appeared in the pages of the *Review* in 1910, but only as the anonymous author of *Letters to His Holiness Pope Pius X* (Chicago, 1910). Arthur Preuss mentioned Sullivan's book as an example of the direct connection between Americanism and Modernism.

We had no 'Americanism' in America; nor, of course, have we any Modernism. We are as innocent of heresy as new born babes. We are 'too busy' to indulge in such luxuries. Such at least was and is the contention of a portion of the American Catholic press. But what about such disquieting publications as the *Letters to His Holiness Pope Pius X 'by a Modernist'*, who claims to be an American ecclesiastic in good standing? (We understand that he is a former member of the Paulist community.) Of course Americanism and Modernism, as systems of thought, have fewer adherents in these United States than they have in Europe, for the simple reason that there are few among us comparatively, who have the ability and the leisure to engage in theological and philosophical speculations. But isn't there enough *practical* Americanism and Modernism in evidence around us to give pause to the optimist?[50]

The quotation above provides an adequate summation of Arthur Preuss's response to the Modernist crisis. Clearly, for Preuss there was a connection between Americanism and the "modernist impulse in American Catholicism." In this regard, Preuss's position, which was rejected at the time by American church leaders and then later by the "old Americanist historiography," has now been affirmed by the "new Americanist historiography" as represented by Mary M. Reher, Christopher Kauffman, and Scott Appleby.[51] These contemporary historians describe the connection between the Americanists and the Modernists as their shared desire to "appropriate" modernity into the life of the Church.[52] Preuss saw that John Ireland's call "Church and Age unite!" was very much the rallying cry for both Americanism and Modernism. Taking the Americanists at their words, Preuss also saw then what Appleby sees now –that if the ideas of the Americanists followed their logical "trajectory," they would propel their adherents right out of the Church, as they did in the cases of John Slattery and William Sullivan.

Because Arthur Preuss could see clearly the potential path of liberal Catholics, he resisted their call for the "reform" of the Catholic Church along lines "demanded by the Zeitgeist." Preuss did not reject modernity outright. He was simply wary of binding the eternal verities of

Catholicism to passing intellectual fashions. One last note should be made in regard to Arthur Preuss's treatment of Americanism and Modernism. While he would certainly feel vindicated that the "new Americanist historiography" shares his view of the interrelationship of these two movements, he would not have much use for the inference of the new historiography that if the Church had only been less defensive, men like Loisy and Tyrrell, Slattery and Sullivan could have been accommodated. Arthur Preuss recognized that the "trajectory" of their ideas could never be contained within the professions of the Creed.

VI Lay Theologian
and Catholic Journalist

"My Lay Nose"

As Arthur Preuss entered his second decade as editor of the *Review* he began to show signs of slowing down. The restless energy that had enabled him to run two newspapers at one time (the *Katholisches Sonntagsblatt* and the *Review* from 1894 to 1896, the *Review* and *Amerika* from 1896 to 1905) had dissipated. The demands of raising a family and the increasingly more severe bouts with rheumatoid arthritis took their toll as well. At least one of his readers, writing in 1906, was concerned that Preuss appeared to be losing his edge. This reader complained that Preuss "was entirely too positive" and that he feared that the *Review* was "degenerating into an organ of compromise." Preuss responded,

> ...advancing years, —though I am only thirty-five, I am thirteen years older now than when I founded this journal, —teach the need of compromise and bring a tolerant sense of the infinite complexity of human motives. One learns too, that the paradoxes are very old and that stranded good and evil have always been the very tissue of life.[1]

After resigning as editor of *Amerika*, Preuss devoted more of his time to his duties as the literary editor of the B. Herder Company of St. Louis. Under the direction of the venerable Joseph Gummersbach, B. Herder had employed Arthur Preuss since his return to St. Louis in 1896. In this capacity Preuss advised the company on the acquisition of manuscripts and acted as a translator and proof reader. It was from this position that Arthur Preuss began writing theology books.

Preuss's contribution to the field of theology was somewhat akin to the role he served as editor of the *Review*. When launching the *Review* Preuss described his role as that of mediating the beliefs and traditions of German Catholicism to an English-speaking audience. His work in theology was also one of mediation. Rather than producing original theological works, Arthur Preuss utilized his facility with both English and German, as well as the talents he developed as a book editor, in order to adapt German theological texts into the English language.

The first, and most successful, of these projects was the adaptation of Joseph Pohle's three-volume, *Lehrbuch der Dogmatik*. Joseph Pohle (1852–1922), like his friend Joseph Schroeder, was a native German who had been exiled during the Kulturkampf. In his exile he had taught in Switzerland and in England. After his return to Germany, he was on the faculty of the seminary at Fulda, and it was there that Bishop John Keane recruited him for the original faculty of the Catholic University of America in 1888. Keane brought Pohle to Washington in order to teach Thomistic philosophy.[2] In 1894 Pohle left the Catholic University to accept "an imperial appointment" to teach dogma at the University of Breslau. On his departure from the Catholic University, Pohle had protested the treatment he and Schroeder had received from the other faculty members because of their support for German causes within the Catholic Church in America. In a private letter to the chairman of the Board of Trustees, Archbishop Patrick Ryan, Pohle admitted that both he and Schroeder had become publicly involved in the Cahensly affair and the school question. But, he protested, it was only after other members of the faculty had involved themselves against Cahensly and in support of Archbishop Ireland's school plan. Then, unjustly, Pohle and Schroeder alone were castigated for their partisanship.[3]

Arthur Preuss had printed Pohle's letter when it became public in December 1897 at the height of the "Schroeder case." However, Preuss would not mention Pohle again until six years later when he gave an enthusiastic review of Pohle's *Lehrbuch der Dogmatik*. At that time Preuss said of the work that it was "thoroughly orthodox and up to date and we must say that of all the theological handbooks we have perused, it is the most interestingly written."[4]

As for Arthur Preuss's qualifications for evaluating theological texts, formally, he had none. Preuss's undergraduate and graduate work had been in philosophy. However, he took a keen interest in theology both professionally, in his work for the B. Herder Company, and as an avocation.[5] So it was as a self-taught theologian that Preuss entered the field. While it is unclear whose initiative it was that led to his collaboration with Joseph Pohle, his willingness to do so reflected his genuine enthusiasm for the clarity and popularity of Pohle's *Lehrbuch* in the German original that reached four editions in eight years.[6]

The earliest extant correspondence between Pohle and Arthur Preuss is dated February 21, 1908. In this letter, Pohle mentioned that there had been a previous unsuccessful attempt to produce an English version of the *Lehrbuch* that the prospective publisher scuttled as too great a financial risk. For his part, Pohle was unconcerned about making any money on the project. His main objective was to see an English version of his work produced and Pohle voiced his confidence in its success if "you, who are theologically educated and, as my friend Mgr. Schroeder used to say,'Catholic to the bone,' take this matter in hand." Pohle also concurred with Preuss's suggestion that an English-language bibliography be compiled for the work.[7]

To produce an English version of Pohle's work, Arthur Preuss first divided the three volumes into ten separate books. He then began with the translation of the first book, *God: His Essence and Attributes*, appending an English-language bibliography as he went along. With the Pohle series, Preuss relied on his friends, Abbot Charles Mohr and Rev. A. J. Wolfgarten, to act as proof readers.[8] The draft translations were then sent to Pohle for his comments. When he saw the drafts of the first volume, Pohle critiqued Preuss's word-for-word translation and encouraged him to be "less slavish" to the original text. Reflecting on his experience of teaching at the Catholic University of America, Pohle asked Preuss to use "common sense language" to "sweeten the bitter pills."[9] Pohle also suggested to Preuss that he read some of the reviews that the *Lehrbuch* received in order to incorporate any helpful suggestions into the English version.

The adaptation of Pohle's *Lehrbuch* for an English-speaking audience proved an enormous undertaking, as Preuss attested in a letter to Francis

Markert, S.V.D. in October, 1910, as the first volume neared publication.

> For nearly two years I have spent nearly all of my free time in this
> beautiful and interesting work and I will have to do the same for the next
> five years if this project is to be completed in the foreseeable future.
> Hopefully, it will please you, glorify God and edify souls![10]

The first volume of the Pohle-Preuss dogmatic series appeared in December, 1910. Preuss promoted the work in the *Review* and the book met with immediate success. Once the first volume had been in circulation for a while, Preuss began to reprint some of the glowing reviews that it received. Preuss was commended for his "excellent translation" of "perhaps the greatest German dogmatic treatise extant."[11] The evaluation of the work carried in the *Ecclesiastical Review* emphasized the fact that Pohle's *Dogmatic* "appeals to the modern mind" and that "he neither ignores nor belittles the services done to critical science by such philosophers as Kant, and points out the advantage of an unbiased viewpoint as the start of every inquiry into objective truth." This is rather unusual praise considering the "repressive" atmosphere that is supposed to have existed in years following the promulgation of *Pascendi*. As for Preuss's adaptation of Pohle's work, the reviewer stated that while

> a translation from the German of a work of this kind is a most hazardous
> undertaking...Dr. Preuss has shown good judgement in accommodating
> himself to those to whom he proposes to make Dr. Pohle's work
> accessible. We have no doubt that this edition of Dr. Pohle's *Dogmatic
> Theology* when completed will become a standard of reference for
> Catholic apologists in English speaking countries.[12]

Preuss worked on the adaptation of Pohle's *Lehrbuch* from 1908 until 1916. When completed it comprised twelve volumes. With their systematic, neo-Thomistic presentation, the Pohle-Preuss dogmatic studies "became standard seminary fare" as these volumes offered American seminarians an English-language equivalent of their Latin theological texts.[13] The enduring popularity of the Pohle-Preuss Dogmatic Studies series is indicated by the fact that some volumes in the series went to fifteen editions. As late as January, 1959, more than forty years after the series first appeared, the B. Herder Company was still sending royalty checks to Preuss's widow. The royalties that Arthur Preuss collected on the Pohle-Preuss series, "10% of the price of the book for the first edition of 1000 copies and a royalty of 15% for the second and all following editions," became an important source of income for him.[14] In fact, as the *Review* barely paid for itself, Preuss came to depend on the additional income he earned from the adaptation of German theological texts for the support of his wife and ten children. Even so, the royalties he earned hardly made him a rich man. Writing to Frederick Kenkel in 1926, Preuss stated that the royalties "have amounted, all told, to about $500. per anum for last the last 12 or 15 years. And as for the *F.R.,* you know what a wonderfully profitable business that is!"[15]

The Pohle-Preuss series was followed by his five-volume adaptation of Anton Koch's *Moral Theologie* published in English as Koch-Preuss between 1918 and 1921. This was followed by his adaptation of Johann Brunsmann's *Lehrbuch der Apologetik*, which was published as Brunsmann-Preuss between 1928 and 1932. On the Pohle series, Preuss did all the translations himself. However, on the later works his other duties and declining health led him to employ others to do much of the translation work. The two men that helped Preuss most in this area were Father Harry Heck, a young classics professor at the Josephinum seminary in Ohio, and Horace Frommelt, an engineering professor at Marquette who had been in the Jesuit scholasticate with Preuss's younger brother, James. Preuss became a mentor to the two younger men and Frommelt became a regular contributor to the *Review.*[16] Arthur Preuss reported to his friend Father Francis Markert, S.V.D., that not every one was enamored with his entrance into the field of theology. "That I should not stick my lay nose into Theology has been sung to me in all kinds of tones for twenty years."[17]

While Preuss's theological publications provided him with much-needed income, his work on them, as on the *Review*, was sincerely offered for the greater glory of God. With his health seriously impaired in his last years, he labored to complete the Brunsmann series. And when it was completed he regarded the fact that he was able to finish what he had started as a gift from God. These types of theological books fell into disuse after the Second Vatican Council. However, when they were written, and for many years after they were widely praised for their accessibility and their relevance. That he aided in the theological formation of generations of American priests was a legacy that Arthur Preuss would rightfully be proud of.

"An Eminent Journalist"

As the *Review* approached its twentieth anniversary, Arthur Preuss was confronted for the first time with the real possibility that he might have to cease its publication. For between 1911 and 1914 a series of events called into question the continued viability of Preuss's *Review* as an independent Catholic publication. However, before relating these events, it would be well to consider how Preuss's years of experience in Catholic journalism had shaped his boyhood vision of his vocation.

Arthur Preuss, like his father, belived that a Catholic journalist ought to be a type of crusader for the truth. Fidelity to Catholicism would invariably entail standing against the popularly embraced errors of a non-, and frequently anti-Catholic society. The vocation of a Catholic journalist had a certain prophetic charism. And like true prophets of all ages, the faithful Catholic journalist could expect misunderstanding and hostility even from those he had been commissioned to serve.

In addition to fulfilling his unique role within the Catholic community, the Catholic journalist must also come to terms with the practices employed in professional journalism. At the turn of the century, in precisely the years that Arthur Preuss was establishing his reputation as an editor, the field of journalism was being "re-created." Newspaper publishers like Joseph Pulitzer in St. Louis and William Randolph Hearst in New York transformed American journalism. Prior to the last decades of the nineteenth century, newspapers and magazines had catered almost exclusively to the educated upper and middle classes. Through the utilization of modern production techniques and lowering the intellectual content of their publications, men like Pulitzer and Hearst made the "penny newspaper" a vital force in the lives of the masses.[18] By 1900, metropolitan dailies, with their enormous circulations and advertising revenues, had become big business. The wealthier publishers developed chains of newspapers across the country, giving them a voice in most of America's major cities. Newspapers were employed to galvanize public opinion around certain issues of the day. Positively, the print media energized the populace behind the reforms of the Progressive movement. Negatively, the sensationalism of the "yellow" press could propel popular opinion into supporting questionable causes such as the American war with Spain.

Concurrent with the growth in power and influence of the "mass media," older literary journals, such as the *North American Review* and *Harper*'s were losing subscribers. Even the most popular journals of opinion had to rely on generous subsidies in order to survive. More and more Americans were turning to publications that satisfied their craving for excitement and ready explanations of the political and economic developments of their time.[19]

There has yet to be any comprehensive study on the Catholic press of this era. But based on the remarks of Catholic journalists like Arthur Preuss, it appears that the Catholic press was also losing ground to the popular mass organs. Their sense of integrity as specifically Catholic newspapers placed obvious restrictions on the methods they could employ in their competition with the secular press for the attention of the reading public. The Catholic press was also limited by financial considerations. While diocesan papers were funded by the bishops who maintained them as "official" organs of communication, independent Catholic publications like Preuss's *Review* clung to a precarious existence. This was especially true as the Americanization of the second and third generations of

Catholic immigrants diminished the desire for ethnically oriented papers.

The endurance of some independent Catholic newspapers was further undermined by local bishops who resented their autonomy and the competition they gave to the bishops' own "house" organs. Arthur Preuss was well aware of the desire of some bishops to monopolize their local Catholic newspaper market. For a number of years Preuss was in charge of compiling the information on Catholic publications that was printed in Joseph H. Meier's *Catholic Directory*.[20] Even after Meier had been bought out by the P.J. Kenedy Company of New York, he continued to work on the *Catholic Directory*. It was in this capacity that Meier wrote to Preuss "confidentially" in the fall of 1911 regarding the efforts of the bishops of New England to "weed out" from the *Directory* all publications that were not "officially" sponsored. As many of these newspapers were published by French-Canadians, they maintained that their removal from the *Catholic Directory* was linked to the campaign to "Americanize" the French-Canadian Catholics of New England. Preuss had "exchanges" with some of these papers and he gave credence to their complaint.[21]

The lack of a strong Catholic press in America was one of Preuss's most frequent laments. He was particularly interested in the establishment of a Catholic daily paper that would be the English-language equivalent of *Amerika*. Such a paper, while not a "religious" paper,

> should be Catholic in thought and tone, just and fair in its presentation of the news of the day, rigorous in its exclusion of those morbid or filthy details of scandals or crimes which occupy so much space in the average modern newspaper, as well as of all advertising [of a questionable character]…No less important than the proper presentation

> of the news of the day, is the expression of editorial opinion which should find place in such a journal and which ought to be philosophically sound, historically accurate and, of course, orthodox according to the teachings of the Church upon all questions…[22]

For the successful establishment of a Catholic daily paper Preuss believed that four basic requirements must be met. First, such a paper would have to be established in a city with a large enough Catholic population to sustain it. Second, it would require the "unstinted and steady support of the ordinary of the diocese. We make bold to add that such a bishop in learning and character would have to be somewhat above the present average of the American hierarchy." Third, it would require "a scholarly, experienced and self-sacrificing editor." Finally, a successful Catholic daily would require a moderate amount of capital to begin with and the support of the clergy in promoting subscriptions.[23]

The establishment of such a paper would not only help protect the Catholic sensibilities of Church members, it could also influence American society in general. Preuss even ventured to dream that a successfully established Catholic daily could become "the forerunner of a mighty chain of Catholic dailies extending from the Atlantic to the Pacific, and working wonders for God and country."[24] Unfortunately, the right combination of episcopal support, editorial competence, and financial resources never coincided. The *Review* chronicled the birth and death of a number of such projects over the years. Always, some necessary element was lacking. Most often the missing elements were episcopal support and adequate capital. Preuss himself was several times importuned to head up such a project. However, he too was unable to garner sufficient financial backing or episcopal support to begin such an undertaking.[25]

Arthur Preuss's frustration in his attempts to promote Catholic journalism in the United States, particularly in the form of a Catholic daily paper, intensified over the years. In the end, he ascribed most of the blame to the American bishops who lacked the perception to see the importance of such a project, and the leadership abilities to see it through. Preuss's frustration would give way to bitterness when some of the American bishops attempted to stifle one of the few quality Catholic publications in the United States, Preuss's own *Review*.

Between 1912 and 1916, Arthur Preuss was involved in three separate controversies with three different American prelates, that threatened the survival of the *Review*. Prior to this time, Preuss had enjoyed the support of conservative bishops, and he maintained friendships with a number of ordinaries of German extraction. His episcopal friends, however, were not the most prominent or powerful bishops among the American hierarchy.[26] As for his liberal episcopal opponents, Preuss's unpleasant encounter with Archbishop Kain has already been recounted. Still, even when the controversy over Americanism was at its height, there is no indication that the various targets of Preuss's barbs ever attempted to stifle his pen. Unfortunately for Arthur Preuss, and perhaps Catholic journalism in general, the generation of bishops that succeeded John Ireland, Michael Corrigan, et al., were neither as thick-skinned nor as self-effacing as their predecessors.

The trouble began for Arthur Preuss in the fall of 1911 and, as in the controversies that followed, centered around the question of what makes a paper "Catholic." In the September 15 issue of the *Review* Preuss published a report by the Rev. F. M. Lynck, S.V.D. on the Catholic Press Convention that had been held on August 23, 1911, in Columbus, Ohio.[27] Father Lynck gave particular notice to an address delivered at the Congress by the young editor of the Boston *Pilot*, Rev. David J. Toomey.[28] According to Lynck, Toomey "went out of his way" in his address, "A Real Catholic Press," to "cast slurs on the entire Catholic press of this country so far as it does not consist of 'official organs.'" Toomey maintained that only the newspapers owned and operated by the bishops could be truly considered "Catholic." As the editor of an independent Catholic journal, Preuss was greatly insulted by Toomey's remarks and wrote an editorial to accompany Father Lynck's piece. Preuss noted that none of the most renowned Catholic papers in Europe or America met Toomey's criteria. Taking a shot at the sycophantic character of so many of the official organs, Preuss charged that "their chief occupation seems to be to glorify their owners." He also vowed that "the real Catholic editors of the land...will refuse to be 'Toomeyized.'"[29]

Toomey responded to the *Review*'s criticism by writing to the superior at the Divine Word provincialate in Techny, Illinois, complaining about Lynck's article. Toomey apparently told Lynck's superior that the *Review* "could scarcely be considered a Catholic paper."[30] Privately Preuss regretted that Toomey had not also written to him, thus depriving him the opportunity of telling Toomey off personally. Preuss noted that the *Review*'s coverage of the affair had been favorably noted by the non-Catholic *Independent* of New York. He also reflected on the decimation of the independent Catholic press.

> There are only a few of us free lancers still left who can freely state the truth so this loudmouth is seeking a way to stop us...I will go on barking as long as I can, and then pack it in and take up another vocation if it comes to that. I will feed myself and my family by writing books.[31]

The matter soon passed and Preuss quit speaking about shutting down the *Review*. However, that he would even mention such a possibility was a reflection of his growing concern about the continued financial viability of his journal.[32] The number of subscribers to the *Review* was declining as many of Preuss's original readers were dying off. At the same time, new subscribers were hard to come by. Preuss believed that the main obstacle to increasing the *Review*'s circulation, which in 1905 stood at about 1800 copies, apart from the growing indifference of his American co-religionists to things Catholic, was the journal's slow publication process. Since 1905, when Preuss gave up printing the *Review* himself and renamed it the *Catholic Fortnightly Review,* the journal had been published bi-monthly in Techny, Illinois, by the Society of the Divine Word.[33] While this arrangement freed Preuss from the burden of the technical production of the *Review* and reduced his printing costs, it had its drawbacks. First of all, since the *Review* was not actually published in St. Louis it diminished its appeal to potential local advertisers. Preuss did not like having advertisements in his journal, but he eventually decided to carry a few "ads" on the last two pages of the *Review* to defray some of his costs.[34] A more important draw-back to publishing the

Review at Techny was that it slowed down the production process. Preuss had to send his "copy" to his collaborator at Techny, (at first this was Father Lynck; beginning in 1910 it was Father Francis Markert) who supervised the printing of the first proofs. These were then sent back to Preuss by mail for corrections and then subsequently returned to Techny. The issue was then printed and placed in the mails from Techny. The process could be further delayed by disruption of the railroads or mail.

After several years of publishing the *Review* in this fashion as a bi-monthly, Preuss came to believe that his journal was losing the "freshness" that had been part of its earlier appeal. Preuss considered returning to weekly publication of the *Review*. His other literary obligations and his precarious health, however, convinced Preuss that this would be "extremely difficult." Another possibility he entertained was moving his family to Chicago so that he could be closer to the production of the *Review* at Techny. Discussing the matter with Father Markert, Preuss asked the priest, "Do you think Archbishop Quigley would let me have a free hand?"[35] Eventually, Preuss decided to remain in St. Louis while trying to shorten the *Review*'s publication process. It was a fortunate decision as before too long Preuss would discover just how little freedom Archbishop Quigley was willing to let him have.

Considering the many criticisms Arthur Preuss had directed at members of the American hierarchy over the years, the cause of his first official censure by a bishop was really quite trivial. However, it is illustrative of the change that was occurring in the relationship between the Catholic press and the episcopate. The new leaders of the Church in America were much less tolerant of criticism, real or imagined. Ironically, the article that landed Preuss in hot water was entitled, "A Hopeful Sign of the Times."

Published on page one of the March 15, 1912, issue of the *Review*, this very short article by Preuss described a recent appeal made by Cardinals Gibbons and Farley for greater support for "the negro and Indian missions." The Cardinals' appeal included their own critical assessment of "the far too prevailing heedlessness of religion" in contemporary American society. Commenting on their evaluation, Preuss wrote:

> This statement describes the situation to a 't' and to see it in an official document addressed to the whole body of the faithful throughout the United States is a real relief after the buncombe with which a large portion of the Catholic press whelmed us on the occasion of the elevation of one of the august signatories of this circular to the cardinalate.[36]

To the objective reader, Preuss was clearly taking a poke at his colleagues in the Catholic press for ignoring the real problems facing the Church in the America while exaggerating its successes, as they did on the occasion of the elevation of the Archbishop of New York, John Farley,to the College of Cardinals. Unfortunately, Cardinal Farley was not an objective reader. His attention having been brought to Preuss's remarks, Farley immediately sent a letter to Archbishop Glennon of St. Louis citing the above passage and stating

> I hereby beg respectfully to request your Grace to demand from the editor, supposedly a Catholic, an apology for the insulting remarks contained on said page referring to myself...It is rather singular that the only contemptuous references in the press of the United States to the recent creation of the American Cardinals should be made in this so called Catholic publication...Permit me to add for his better instruction that, if this apology is not forthcoming, I shall consider it my duty to lay the matter before his Eminence the Cardinal Secretary of State of His Holiness.[37]

Perhaps suspecting that Archbishop Glennon would not appreciate the full gravity of this matter, Farley also wrote to Archbishop Bonaventura Cerretti, Regent of the Apostolic Delegation. Farley enclosed a copy of the "insulting remarks referring to myself" and added

> The editor is supposed to be a Catholic; and therefore it is that I call the attention of the Apostolic Delegation to the matter and respectfully request that you demand of the editor of this publication a full apology

to be made as public as the insult. Things have appeared hitherto, from time to time, in the same publication, treating most insultingly the highest church dignitaries, have passed unnoticed. I refer to remarks made of several Archbishops and bishops. But, in the present instance, my position as a member of the Sacred College of Cardinals will not permit me to overlook what is, indirectly an act of contempt of His Holiness.[38]

Both Glennon and Cerretti wrote to Preuss demanding that he make an apology to Cardinal Farley. When Glennon's letter arrived, Preuss was incredulous. He did not understand how his words could be construed as an insult to Cardinal Farley. Preuss immediately prepared an explanation of his remarks and sent it along with Glennon's letter to Father Markert, telling Markert to publish them in the April 1 issue of the *Review* "otherwise I will be in for it." Preuss also wrote to his friend Markert that "Farley's demands are only further proof that this prelate suffers from megalomania and abnormal sensitivity, as they all do. Lord have mercy on our American episcopate."[39]

As Markert was arranging for the publication of Preuss's explanation, Cerretti's letter arrived. Stunned by the lengths that Farley had gone to force his apology, Preuss sent Cerretti a four-page, sentence-by-sentence explanation of the offending article. Preuss also sent a copy of this letter to Archbishop Glennon. After explaining his article, Preuss added:

...next to committing a mortal sin, or offending our Holy Father the Pope, there are few things I would regret more keenly than to have insulted a member of the Sacred College...[Besides] in this case I cannot persuade myself that the incriminated article really 'contains an insult or at least a lack of respect toward a member of the Sacred College'...In case this explanation should not prove satisfactory to His Eminence Cardinal Farley, will you please request him to point out to me precisely which one of the seven statements contained in my article he desires me to retract? [40]

While awaiting Cerretti's reply, Preuss cancelled his original plan to publicize the controversy as "without a doubt the anti-Catholic; especially the Socialist press would exploit the matter." However, he was irate over the tone that Cerretti had taken with him. One might even say that Cerretti brought out the American in Arthur Preuss who in his anger gave vent to some of his more closely held opinions:

> One does not wish to publicize an example of the press being gagged and free speech being violated when it comes to prelates.[It would be especially damaging to publicize] the outrageous letter of that little Italian pretender in Washington who, while presenting himself as the regular Apostolic Delegate, behaves like an angry czar. He calls himself the Holy Father's representative in this land and then tramples on the constitutionally guaranteed rights of American citizens.
>
> However, if the Cardinal drives me to extremes, then all such considerations must fade before my duty to defend my own honor and independence as well as that of the Catholic press in general. If this tyrant succeeds in humiliating the *Catholic Fortnightly Review* you can imagine what fate lies in store for other, less popular and less determined Catholic newspapers. You see, I was not wrong in my pessimistic remarks over the speech that the Rev. Toomey gave...By the way, have you read the latest speech by Cardinal O'Connell on the *Pilot*? ...It reflects the same mentality as that of Farley in his demands on the *CFR*. Both of these men suffer from delusions of grandeur which is only to be expected given their character. It is too bad that the Holy Father, who has the best intentions, goes around with his head in the clouds. He could hardly have made worse choices [for the cardinalate] than Farley and O'Connell.

Preuss closed his remarks to Markert by relating that he had been approached by the editor of the New York *Independent* to "write an article about the tyrant of Boston," but had refused. "I am too loyal to provide information to our common enemies. It would have been base and dishonorable and a violation of my German conscience."[41]

Arthur Preuss was further antagonized by Cerretti's response to his explanation conveyed to him through Archbishop Glennon. Cerretti wrote that while he personally "did not doubt for an instant that Mr. Preuss in making the statements alluded to, had not the slightest intention of offering insult to anyone," Preuss must still publish an apology, the text of which Cerretti provided. Otherwise, Cerretti informed Glennon and Preuss, "the superior ecclesiastical authority will find itself obliged to consider whether or not Mr. Preuss should be allowed to continue publishing a Catholic periodical, with the title 'Catholic,' and this in virtue of the legislation of Leo XIII and Pius X."[42]

Having been advised by his closest friends not to be publicly "caustic" about the matter,[43] Preuss published the required apology in the April 15 issue of the *Review*. While expressing his regret over the affair, Preuss asserted that "our remark has been misconstrued," and that we "formally disavow the false interpretation put upon it."[44] Privately, Preuss was still fuming over the whole incident. He grumbled to his friend Markert about the hypocritical pretensions of bishops like Farley whose vanity fabricated imagined slights that then must be atoned for. "From us laity he asks a positive heroism in the virtues of patience, obedience, self-denial, etc. But what does he ask of himself?"[45]

Since both Farley and Cerretti had based their right to censure Preuss on his use of the word "Catholic" in the title of his *Review*, Preuss dropped this designation from its masthead. From May 15, 1912 onward, Preuss's journal was known simply as the *Fortnightly Review*. Preuss's friend, Abbot Charles Mohr tried to console him by suggesting that having "Catholic" in the title suggested "a wishy washy" official organ anyway.[46] Despite Mohr's assurances, Preuss had had a bitter experience of the episcopate's attempts to define the character of the "Catholic" press. When Preuss was asked later to explain the name change, he wrote that "it was done to save certain super-sensitive prelates a lot of useless worry and ourselves unnecessary letter writing."[47] Unfortunately for Arthur Preuss and his *Review* there were more such conflicts with "super-sensitive prelates" to come.

Preuss's second sad experience of episcopal displeasure came two years later, in early 1914. The previous December, Father F.M. Lynck, the Society of the Divine Word priest whose earlier criticism of the Rev. Toomey had caused a stir, contributed an article to the *Review* on the

"Mission Congress" recently held in Boston. This article, which did not disclose Lynck's authorship, contained a number of critical remarks concerning the Congress and its coverage in the Catholic press. Lynck criticized the fact that little of the program was given over to actual missionaries to relate their experiences in the field. Instead, much time and notice was given to "the altogether unimportant utterances of prominent delegates." Father Lynck was also skeptical of a proposal to create a "Supreme Bureau" in America to coordinate support for overseas missionary activities. He speculated that, like the Church Extension Society to which the proposed "Bureau" was being compared, such a body would siphon off funds badly needed in the missions for the maintenance of "sumptuous offices and costly advertising." Additionally, Lynck remarked on the exclusion of the laity from any visible role in the Congress. Lynck concluded by saying

> There was much outward 'show' and brilliant ceremony but no decision
> of practical value...Evidently, the time is not yet come for the holding
> of a *real* missionary congress...[48]

The *Review*'s criticism of the Congress provoked rebuttals, two of which Preuss published.[49] Although Lynck and Preuss realized that the latter's criticism of the Congress had been provocative, neither man anticipated the recriminations that followed. On February 14, 1914, Father Francis Markert, S.V.D., who supervised the printing of the *Review*, wrote to Preuss with distressing news. Markert reported that the day before, the provincial superior of the Divine Word house at Techny, Father James A. Burgmer, S.V.D., had met with the Archbishop of Chicago, James Quigley. At that meeting, Quigley informed Burgmer of his displeasure with various articles in the *Review* that the Divine Word Fathers had published. Archbishop Quigley's complaints centered on remarks Preuss had made regarding Governor James Dunne of Illinois, and the piece critical of the Mission Congress. Archbishop Quigley, who also happened to be the chancellor of the Church Extension Society, told the Divine Word superior that his fellow bishops were convinced that the article on the Mission Congress had been written by a member of the Society. Therefore, Quigley demanded to know the identity of the author of the article. According to Father Markert, the archbishop also demanded that every issue of the *Review* be submitted to the diocesan censor for approval. Otherwise, the Society of the Divine Word at Techny must cease to publish Preuss's journal.[50] Preuss responded immediately to Market on this latest imposition.

> I have no doubt that this action is unjust. I have spent a lifetime as a Catholic editor suffering under such persecution. However, the Lord has always upheld me. He will certainly help me again. To be subject to the censorship of the Archbishop would, as you rightly note, mean hari-kari for the *Fortnightly Review*.

Preuss stated that he "would go to St. Louis this afternoon to get advice on the matter from Herr Kenkel, Herr Gummersbach and other kindred spirits."[51] The next day Preuss wrote to Markert that his friends had advised him to "forget Archbishop Quigley and bring the *F.R.* back to St. Louis...Archbishop Glennon himself will protect you from unnecessary trouble." Preuss also told Markert that he expected his friend, Abbot Charles Mohr of St. Leo's Abbey, to be named the next bishop of St. Augustine, Florida. "In this case, I would move the *Review* and myself under his aegis."[52]

By this time, Preuss was corresponding directly with the superior of the Divine Word Fathers at Techny, Father Burgmer. As Preuss related to Markert, he had little respect for the latter's superior who, out of fear of Archbishop Quigley, was trying to break the contract to publish the *Review* without honoring the three-month grace period originally agreed upon. Still, though the Society was giving into episcopal pressure and severing its ties with him, in a letter to Father Markert, Preuss expressed his gratitude to the priests at Techny for the nine years they had worked together.

> This is not the first time that I have had to get myself out of a difficult situation...nor will it be the last. It is sad though that the Church in

America is governed with so little wisdom. This spiritual tyranny will some day bring the most bitter revenge...I am grateful to the Society of the Divine Word as a whole and especially to you. Working with you has been a blessing and a comfort. God Bless you! I take this as so many early trials, patiently, and as part of the persecution of the true word of the Saviour that is given to those who love Him, and who fearlessly serve truth and justice.[53]

Preuss's expressions of gratitude were not mere formalities. He had developed genuine friendships with some of the priests at Techny such as Hermann Richarz, Father Lynck and especially, Father Markert. Preuss had been to Techny several times for retreats and some of the priests from there had been overnight guests in his home. So Archbishop Quigley's action to end the partnership between Preuss and the S.V.D. priests at Techny was as much an emotional hardship as a professional one for those involved.[54]

Later Preuss reported to Markert that he had learned that copies of the offending article had been sent to church officials in Rome and Quigley had been embarrassed by the unfavorable references Lynck had made to the Church Extension Society. Vowing that "it is not as easy as Quigley thinks to destroy a Catholic paper in America," Preuss was not above exacting a little revenge of his own.[55] On May 1, 1914, Preuss published a short article aimed at Quigley's friend, Governor Dunne. Under the title "A Catholic Governor's Bad Example," Preuss took Dunne to task for sending all of his children to public schools in defiance of the decrees of the Third Plenary Council of Baltimore. And, in a swipe at Archbishop Quigley, Preuss concluded by saying of such Catholic politicians:

...is the bad example they give, and the culpability they incur, in any way offset or diminished by the fact that, for reasons easy enough to divine, they sometimes leave a few of the minor offices at their disposal to be filled by Bishop X or Father Y....?[56]

Although the *Review* survived its expulsion from the Archdiocese of Chicago, the whole affair took a heavy toll on Preuss's health. Just before learning of Archbishop Quigley's actions against him, Arthur Preuss had been instructed by his doctor to stop working altogether for two or three months in order to recover from nervous exhaustion.[57] The crisis cut his break short and by June his health had deteriorated to such an extent that he could not even use a typewriter. Gradually, after a long rest in Colorado, Preuss regained his strength and returned to his normal pace.[58]

Rest, however, could do nothing to ease the *Review*'s financial difficulties. Subscriptions continued to drop off and the termination of his contract with the Society of the Divine Word had increased the *Review*'s production costs. By December of 1914, Preuss was considering making the *Review* a monthly in order to reduce expenses. Added to these professional troubles was Preuss's share in the general, German-American concern over the war in Europe, his personal grief over the death of his infant son, Francis Joseph, in February, 1915, and the death of his only sister, Marie Peoples, at the age of thirty-seven, in June of that year.[59] These were hard years indeed for Arthur Preuss.

The seriousness of Preuss's financial predicament can perhaps be measured by the fact that as soon as he learned that Archbishop Quigley was terminally ill in July 1915, he asked Father Markert to inquire into the possibility of resuming the Society's previous arrangement to publish the *Review*. The Divine Word Fathers eventually agreed to Preuss's proposal, although Preuss now had the *Review* mailed to subscribers from St. Louis in order not to draw attention to Techny.[60]

Preuss did not know what to expect from the new Archbishop of Chicago, George Mundelein. Though Mundelein was of German extraction, he was "a confirmed, though cautious Americanizer."[61] The German-Catholic "Deutschtum" was not an idea to which Mundelein gave much support. Preuss soon learned not to expect much support for the Catholic press from Mundelein either. On March 21, 1916 Preuss wrote to Markert that in the course of going through his files he discovered Mundelein's name among the "dead beats" who never paid for their subscriptions. "This is indicative of how the Catholic press in this country is treated by both high and low."[62]

Although Preuss put his delinquent subscriber on the *Review*'s "gratis" mailing list, it did not deter Mundelein from moving against the journal. Without any provocation on Preuss's part, Archbishop Mundelein told the provincial superior at Techny to cancel the S.V.D.'s contract with Preuss in May 1916. Preuss was not surprised. Coming at a time when he was still very concerned about both his declining subscriptions and his deteriorating health, the news of Mundelein's action appeared simply as another portion of his cross in life.

> ...one cannot publicly fight for truth and right for twenty-five years in this land of humbug and spinelessness and not make a million enemies. But I serve the truth and His will and therefore I have an inner freedom.
>
> ...I am accustomed to being treated as a criminal by Catholic bishops and so I have not gotten overly excited by this latest instance.[63]

The reaction of Preuss's friends to his latest setback was much stronger. Frederick Kenkel, on learning of Mundelein's action, wrote to Preuss that he was "embittered and disturbed."[64] For his part, Father Markert took it upon himself to ask Mundelein to reconsider his decision. In a letter to the archbishop, Markert conceded that at times the *Review* spoke "sharply." But Markert asked Mundelein to consider Preuss's devout Catholicism, his unstinting service to the Church, and his many accomplishments. Markert also told the archbishop that if the S.V.D.'s were once again forced to cease publishing Preuss's *Review* it would result in financial hardship for his family.[65]

Apparently, as a result of Markert's letter, Archbishop Mundelein relented and the Fathers at Techny were allowed to continue publishing the *Review*. However, the reprieve did nothing to shake Preuss's disillusionment with the American hierarchy over their lack of support for the Catholic press. From Preuss's perspective, his years of promoting the cornerstones of Catholic culture in America, family, parish, schools, and newspapers seemed to bring him the same results; "the days continue as they always have. Instead of support, one gets hostility...." Preuss was especially discouraged that "among the episcopate spiritual values were so lacking." He found it "difficult to hope that conditions will improve if Rome does not provide better bishops."[66]

One might be tempted to conclude from these remarks that Arthur Preuss was an incurable pessimist. He was labelled as such by one of his journalistic colleagues who referred to him as "the ever angry Herr Preuss." But such a characterization does not do justice to the man or correspond to the testimony of his friends and family as to his good cheer and gentleness. After reading an account of her father's role in the Americanist crisis Arthur Preuss's daughter, Alma Preuss Dilschneider, remarked to the author, "More and more...I find that Arthur Preuss was two people, and I have no memory of, and did not know the man you found...If he ever showed anger and hostility in his writings, he never showed it to us."[67]

Preuss himself remarked on occasion of the perplexity some of his long time readers experienced when they finally met him in person. The slight man with the kindly demeanor they encountered was not the image of Arthur Preuss that they had formed from reading his *Review*. Preuss provided an explanation of this paradox as he articulated his understanding of his vocation as a Catholic journalist in 1902.

> ...though it may seem paradoxical to many who have watched my career as a 'fighting editor,' the journalistic profession is irksome to me, and grows more irksome from year to year. Much against my own inclination I am compelled to spend a considerable portion of my none too exuberant energy in criticizing other people —a life of antagonism

> that is not naturally congenial to me. 'We might have much peace' says the saintly a Kempis, 'if we would not busy ourselves with the sayings and doings of others'...How I long for such peace! Frail health may bring it quicker than I expect. Meanwhile, I mean to do what I conscientiously and prayerfully conceive to be my duty as a twentieth-century Catholic editor, harshly though it may clash at times with my natural inclinations; if I fail to do it to the full extent of my bodily and

spiritual powers, the good God Who has given me this difficult and, from a worldly viewpoint, ungrateful mission, may show me the way to a humbler and more congenial sphere, where I have a better chance to attend to the 'unum necessarium'...[68]

Arthur Preuss's apparent "pessimism" then was professional, an occupational hazard of a man with a prophetic "mission." It did not carry over into his personal relations or ever dim his faith in a "good God."

Edward F.R. Preuss (1834-1904), father of Arthur and
editor of the Catholic newspaper, *Die Amerika*.
(Photo courtesy of the Preuss family)

Arthur and Pauline Preuss on their
wedding day, October 13, 1900.
(Photo courtesy of the Preuss family)

Arthur Preuss and family c.1910
(Photograph courtesy of the Preuss family)

Rev. John E. Rothensteiner, friend and collaborator.
(Central Bureau of the Catholic Central Union)

Monsignor Joseph Schroeder
(Archives of the Catholc University of America)

Rev. Joseph Pohle
Arthur Preuss's adaptation into English of Pohle's
theological volumes, the Pohle-Preuss series,
were used in seminaries for fifty years.
(Archives of the Catholic University of America)

Frederick P. Kenkel (1863-1952)
Preuss's chosen successor as editor of *Amerika*.
Kenkel later became the director of the
Central Bureau of the Central Verein.
(Central Bureau of the Catholic Cenral Union)

Patrick H. Callahan
Prominent in the Democratic Party
and the Knights of Columbus, Callahan was a financial
benefactor of Preuss's *Review* in the 1920s.
(Louisville *Courier-Journal*)

Arthur Preuss
shortly before his death in 1934.
(Photo courtesy of the Preuss family)

VII The Great War

One of the trials of Arthur Preuss's life, a trial that he shared with his fellow German Americans, was that of being a member of a suspect minority both before and during America's war with Germany. Most studies of the German-American experience in these years make a distinction between what German Americans were saying and doing during the period of American neutrality, and the way that they responded once war was declared on April 6, 1917.[1] However, in studying Arthur Preuss's attitudes toward the war it is clear that for him, and perhaps most German Americans, there were actually three distinct phases in his response to the crisis.

The first phase occurred between August, 1914, and April, 1917, when America was officially neutral. The second phase began on April 6, 1917, when the United States declared war on Germany and concluded in November, 1918, with the cessation of hostilities. The final phase was the period in which German Americans came to terms with the outcome of the war. This last stage is important because German Americans had to acclimate themselves to the accelerated process of Americanization the war had forced on them. It is also important for the fact that it was only when the shooting had stopped, and civil liberties had been restored, that German Americans like Arthur Preuss were free to express themselves on issues related to the war.

"Sincerely Neutral"

During the thirty-one months of American neutrality, Arthur Preuss strove to keep that same neutrality in the pages of his *Review*. Dean Esslinger, who conducted a study of "American German and Irish Attitudes Toward Neutrality, 1914–1917," and concluded that the majority of Catholic publications "were of pro-German sentiment in tone if not in outright policy," found that Preuss's *Review* to be an exception to this pattern.[2] Edward Cuddy conducted a similar study of pro-Germanism among American Catholics and differed from Esslinger in concluding that "Catholic journalism, marked by a wide diversity of opinion, generally occupied the middle ground of neutrality." Cuddy also differs from Esslinger in his assessment that "American Catholicism, in the main, remained faithful to the official policy of American neutrality." Cuddy, however, did agree with Esslinger's evaluation of Preuss's journal by classifying the *Review* as neutral but with "muted sympathy for Germany." According to Cuddy "its editor slipped at times, in his profound desire to remain neutral," but "its German-American editor, Arthur Preuss, exercised remarkable restraint and was justly complimented for his deep sense of impartiality." Of the Catholic publications that Cuddy evaluated, Preuss's *Review* was the only organ associated with German Americans to maintain such objectivity on the war in Europe.[3] Preuss's restraint is especially remarkable when one remembers that *Die Amerika*, under the editorship of his friend, Frederick Kenkel, and published by Preuss's employer at the B. Herder Company, Joseph Gummersbach, was avidly pro-German.

The boundaries of neutrality that Arthur Preuss observed were circumscribed for him, as were most things, by his duties as a Catholic. Other German Americans, including many of Preuss's associates, were actively involved in debating the merits of the German cause, its employment of submarine warfare, American loans to the Allied powers, an embargo of arms sales to the belligerents, and the candidate to back in the presidential election of 1916.[4] Arthur Preuss concerned himself primarily with how the war related to the Christian faith, the truthfulness of the war's partisans, the role of the papacy in establishing peace, and the effectiveness of the Wilson administration in observing true neutrality.

In his first reference to the conflict, found in the August 15, 1914, issue of the *Review*, Preuss noted that while it was "too early to comment on the causes of the war" and "useless to speculate on its possible outcome...so much, unfortunately seems certain: with all Europe aflame, religion is sure to suffer."[5] A month later, in what was Preuss strongest apologetic for the German cause, he stated

It is charged that the Germans are conducting an inhuman war. But so are all the others...no war ever was that did not drag down women and children...We would, of course, not palliate needless cruelties or wanton destruction. But if certain Belgians, certain Russians, Austrians, and Germans have not kept their passions in check, if they have murdered innocent non-combatants...why it is the system, not the men who are at fault. Such things will be so long as Christianity is unable to banish from the earth the wickedness and folly which is war.[6]

The next two issues of the *Review* brought out for the first time the other three themes in Preuss's war coverage during the years of American neutrality. In an article entitled "The Father of All the Faithful," Preuss took issue with insinuations that Pope Benedict XV secretly favored the Central Powers. Preuss offered his opinion on the press accounts of the first few weeks of the war in the October 15 issue of the *Review* where he facetiously recommended "a handy little war guide called "500 Lies, Classified, Summarized and Arranged According to Nationality." This number of the *Review* also took notice of Woodrow Wilson's pledge not to make partisan political speeches prior to the upcoming congressional elections. Preuss praised the president for his neutrality on the war and for acting "prudently in refraining from doing anything that might cause political controversy to rage divisively around him."[7]

Having established the themes of his commentary on the war, Preuss would return to them regularly over the course of the next two years. However, he did not simply repeat them. Instead, different aspects of each topic were explored. For example, the relationship of religion and the war included Preuss's concurrence with the Church's constant teaching that the scourge of war was directly related to man's infidelity to God. Greed and "the conceit of human progress" he saw as contributing causes of the calamity. The *Review* also discussed whether the war qualified as being "just" according to the criteria of Catholic moral theology.[8] Anthony Beck, of the *Dubuque American Tribune*, contributed two articles to the *Review* with the controversial thesis that the war could be a "blessing in disguise" by proving that "it is absurd to babble about universal peace as long as human nature remains the same." Beck pointed to the popular support in Europe that accompanied the declarations of war and contended that it will always be so "until the generality of men become practical followers of the Prince of Peace." Beck went on to assail the hypocrisy of decrying the evils of war while ignoring "peace horrors." According to Beck, the "divorce evil" was destroying homes as effectively as the war. Sixty thousand American women were victims of the "social evil," demon alcohol and homicide took the lives of many and preventable industrial accidents and diseases caused fifty thousand deaths a year. Beck, closed his protest by saying "the silent systematic butchery of thousands of women and children, as well as men, by 'peaceful evils,' troubles only the reformers and some few leaders."[9]

Preuss himself discovered some disguised blessings in moving accounts of acts of mercy and compassion that transcended national hostilities. Preuss published these stories under the heading, "The Fine Things of the War." On the disheartening side, Preuss commented with sadness on the divisions within Catholicism being created by the war as evidenced by the willingness of French and German-Catholic leaders to issue manifestos claiming religious sanction for their national causes.[10]

Preuss's approach to the pro-British bias in much of the American press went further than simply pointing out its manifestations, although he did this on one occasion. Rather, Preuss focused his criticism on the unreliability of war news as mediated by the British censors. Because of such censorship Preuss maintained that "we shall have to wait a number of years for a dispassionate and sane discussion of the ultimate and contributing causes of this unfortunate war."[11] As for the role of the papacy during the conflict, Preuss suffered no uncertainties. The Pope was neutral because he had to be. And because he remained above partisanship, the belligerents should heed his calls to end the fighting. They should also recognize that any peace conference that excluded the pope, the only truly disinterested party, "was already foredestined to tragic failure."[12]

Preuss's treatment of President Wilson follows the same general pattern as that of German-American publications with the important difference that Preuss was, for the most part, silent on specific policies. In the fall of 1914, Preuss praised Wilson's strong support of neutrality. However, when a year later, Wilson joined Theodore Roosevelt in a "full scale assault on hyphenism" in order to block Roosevelt's use of the issue for a political comeback, Arthur Preuss shared in the German-American community's dismay. As Wilson and Roosevelt "rode the crest of intolerance" directed at German-American supporters of the Central powers, even the "sincerely neutral" Preuss was compelled to strike back.[13]

Of the various administration policies opposed by German Americans such as the sale of arms to the belligerents, and loans to the Allies, the only policy the *Review* concerned itself with was the proposal for an American arms build up. "Preparedness" in this manner Preuss opposed and he was sympathetic to the views expressed on this issue by American pacifists by asking "Is not our Holy Father Benedict XV himself a pacifist?" Arthur Preuss's own desire for peace was so strong that even after Wilson's "unwarranted attack" on the loyalty of German Americans, he optimistically reported the president's efforts to mediate a peace agreement at the end of 1916.[14]

In addition to Preuss's published views regarding the war in Europe while America was at peace, his extant private correspondence offers additional insight into his thinking.[15] The correspondence available from this period are letters written by Preuss to Francis Markert, S.V.D. who preserved them. Preuss's references to the war in these letters for the most part take the same tone as what Preuss published for public consumption. However, his sympathy for Germany is a bit more noticeable. But so is his desire for peace.

> Wilson's initiative, which I noted in the first December issue, fills me with such hope for peace. I wish that the Holy Father would also use

all of his influence now...Then the British might finally come to reason.[16]

It is possible that Preuss's anti-British tone in this letter was accentuated by the fact that his reader, Father Markert had already lost his brother to the fighting in France and his family in Germany was destitute on account of the war. Two months later, in the midst of the diplomatic crisis brought about by Germany's resumption of unrestricted submarine warfare, Preuss wrote to Markert, "I hope and pray that Germany and the United States do not come to war. It would be so tragic!"[17] The tragedy that Arthur Preuss and his fellow German Americans feared did come, and with it a change in their relationship to American society.

Belligerence

Arthur Preuss's belief that American entry into the war in Europe would be a tragedy was a conviction that only deepened when his forebodings became reality in April, 1917. Based on his adherence to the Catholic belief that war is most often a divinely permitted scourge for the punishment of sin, Preuss deeply regretted that the United States had now placed itself under the lash. By doing so America had exposed herself to all the societal evils that accompany the violence of war. The worst of these evils, as Preuss experienced them, were government repression of constitutional freedoms, and the intensification of ethnic and religious bigotry in American society. These evils would be the focus of the *Review*'s war coverage during the period of declared hostilities with Germany, as well as in the immediate post-war years.

One of the most notable aspects of American participation in the First World War was the rapidity with which the previously neutral nation was mobilized to meet the exigencies of modern, total warfare. Equally striking, and distressingly so, was the willingness of American government at all levels to suppress the basic civil rights of American citizens in order to enforce adherence to its policies. Through the use of modern methods of thought control, the United States government, under the direction of the Wilson administration, succeeded in establishing almost universal support for a war that many thoughtful citizens, at least privately, found objectionable. To establish this widespread conformity, the government legitimated traditionally abhorrent "vigilance committees," severely restricted the freedom of the press, and participated in the harassment of its own citizens who happened to be of German descent.

This campaign to enforce conformity began even before war was declared. In late March, 1917, in preparation for hostilities with Germany, Thomas Gregory, Attorney General of the United States, obtained President Wilson's approval to use volunteers to gather information on "suspected aliens and disloyal citizens."[18] These volunteers were to report their findings to the Justice Department which would then oversee follow-up investigations. What was particularly disturbing about this employment of vigilantes was that in the process the government specifically designated a "superpatriotic" organization, the American Protective League, as a semi-official auxiliary of the Justice Department's Bureau of Investigation. Based in Chicago, the American Protective League had been formed in March, 1917 by a private businessman. Its membership quickly swelled to over 200,000 members. These zealous, but untrained "detectives" immersed themselves in hundreds of thousands of investigations. Armed with badges issued by the League, these APL "agents" began by spying on suspect aliens but soon included their fellow citizens suspected of disloyalty. Foreign born applicants for government positions had their private lives investigated by League members. Persons with German names or accents, regardless of their citizenship, were targets of suspicion. Predictably, since the American Protective League was a nativist organization founded to fight foreign subversion, they routinely raised fears of sedition although they failed to discover a single German spy.[19]

Another mechanism authorized by the Wilson administration to galvanize support for the war effort was the Committee on Public

Information. This federal agency, which Wilson created by executive order in April, 1917, sought to capture "the minds of men, for the conquest of their convictions."[20] As chairman of the Committee on Public Information, Wilson appointed his young protege and former journalist, George Creel. Once appointed, Creel so dominated the activities of the organization that it came to be known popularly as the "Creel committee." Employing all the techniques of modern advertising at a time when such techniques were still new, the Creel committee effectively mobilized public opinion in support of "Wilsonian idealism and wartime notions of patriotism."[21]

Rather than simply censoring the traditional channels of public opinion, the Creel committee inundated them with its own messages. Under George Creel's direction, the Wilson administration created public opinion. The Committee on Public Information employed thousands of artists, journalists, and advertising agents "in a vast patriotic campaign that thundered on the consciousness of every person in America who could read or understand a picture."[22] Creel's artists produced thousands of posters promoting enlistments, the draft and the Liberty Loan campaign that was financing America's war effort. These evocative illustrations appeared on billboards and in periodicals. A corps of volunteers from the academic world, including several noted historians, produced hundreds of popular pamphlets that advanced American war aims and "Wilson's notions regarding the peace settlement."[23] The German-American community was given particular attention by the Creel committee. German-language newspapers were monitored by the committee for the purpose of co-opting their pages for government propaganda. Patriotic tracts produced by Creel's stable of scholars were translated into German and fed into the German-speaking community. Among these tracts was one entitled "American Loyalty" written by "Citizens of German Descent." A million copies of this pamphlet, more than half of them in German, were published.[24]

In addition to dominating the print media, the Creel committee put 75,000 volunteer orators in the field who, as "Four Minute Men," appeared at every type of social gathering. Delivering standardized speeches prepared by the Creel committee on "Why We Are Fighting," and "The Meaning of America," the Four Minute Men appeared at churches and lodge meetings, schools, and theaters. In the age before the widespread use of radio, the use of the Four Minute Men represented an imaginative means for dominating public discourse.[25]

For the most part, the message conveyed by Creel's artists and orators was a positive one. Instead of hectoring the populace, especially the various ethnic groups, into supporting the war, the Creel committee used the approach of positive reinforcement. Through the control of communication, the entire population was enticed to join the patriotic parade whose cacophony was silenced only when the war was over. In a war of longer duration, a similar propaganda campaign based on emotionalism would have worn thin. However, over the course of America's twenty-month war against Germany, Creel's tactics were most effective in selling America and Woodrow Wilson to the world.[26]

Still, though the Committee on Public Information took a positive approach in its propaganda efforts, "It contributed immeasurably to the climate of intolerance." The program of the Creel committee effectively defined patriotism as conformity of thought. Those who dissented from the Wilson administration's definition of patriotism were labelled as disloyal. The Creel committee also accentuated the popular hostility directed at all things German by feeding fears of German subversion. In the vision of the Creel committee, Americanization meant Anglicization as the characteristics of English culture became the definition of culture itself.[27]

The activities of the Justice Department and the Creel committee spawned similar programs on the state level. The so called "Councils of Defense" established in many states at the request of President Wilson were in many instances a menace to civil liberties and vehicles for ethnic hatred. In some states these councils were merely panels of prominent citizens who acted as advisors on issues related to the war effort. However, in the Midwestern states, where suspicion of German

Americans ran deep, the state councils of defense were frequently given wide powers to combat perceived threats to national unity. In some states the councils of defense actively persecuted allegedly disloyal German-American citizens. Using vigilante methods in their pursuit of 'slackers' and 'Kaiserism;' they subjected thousands of Americans to accusation by secret informers, the restriction of free speech, terrorism, and violence.[28]

It was in this heated atmosphere of narrow patriotism, coerced conformity, and hatred for things German that Arthur Preuss labored on his *Review* during period of America's involvement in the Great War. The articles that he published in these months reflect his experience of the war as a Catholic American of German descent. In the early months of the war, before the government began cracking down on public dissenters, Preuss still felt free to question the wisdom of Wilson's decision for war. As his first published comments on America's entry into the conflict, Preuss simply reproduced the *L' Osservatore Romano*'s criticism of Wilson's policies.

> The man who last December championed peace, today champions wider war, and is leading the New World to participation in the horrors of the greatest human butchery ever witnessed by the Old World.[29]

On May 15, 1917, Preuss brought his reader's attention to the fact that from the American Revolution to the War with Spain, Americans

> have never yet entered upon a war with a unanimity of mind, or given it united support.[Therefore] it were foolish to deny that a large percentage of the people are opposed to the present war. Calm patriots are reserving their judgement until certain facts which seem to have been divulged to Congress, but not to the people, are made generally known. It is possible...that these facts will put an altogether different face upon the matter and justify the conduct of the Administration.[30]

Preuss sounded a similar dissonent note in the August 15th issue of the *Review* where, in response to claims that American entry into the war to safeguard democracy was a noble inspiration to the world, he stated that

America wielding her mighty influence to secure liberty and peace without oceans of blood, and halting instead of hastening the destruction of the world, would be a far nobler and more inspiring example.[31]

This would be the last time that Preuss questioned American involvement in the war before the Armistice. Events of the summer of 1917 made it increasingly dangerous to voice open opposition to the war. German Americans in particular had need to be cautious as their perceived lack of enthusiasm for the cause was coming under attack from the president on down. On June 17, 1917, Flag Day, President Wilson had lent his office to identifying German Americans as a suspect group.

The military masters of Germany filled our unsuspecting communities with vicious spies and conspirators and have sought to corrupt the opinion of our people [they have] spread sedition among us and sought to draw our citizens from their allegiance.[32]

George Creel's Committee on Public Information distributed seven million copies of Wilson's speech in the midst of a concurrent rise in anti-German feeling. Up until this time much of the German-language press had continued to express its reservations regarding U. S. policies. Now the backlash set in. In July and August 1917 the popular magazines *Atlantic Monthly* and *Outlook* featured articles entitled "The Disloyalty of the German-American Press," and "The Menace of the German-American Press." In September, the magazine *Current Opinion* carried an essay detailing the growing demand for the suppression of the German-American press. These articles represented and stimulated the increasing distrust directed at German Americans.

While such badgering may have caused the German-language press to reconsider their views concerning American involvement in the war, government restrictions quickly silenced all dissent. The Espionage Act passed by Congress in June 1917 authorized local postal inspectors to revoke second class mail permits for publications they deemed seditious.

The German-language press was specifically targeted in October 1917 when a new law required their publishers to provide postal inspectors with English translations of any articles they published which referred to the government or the war. The burden of these restrictions forced the German-language press to avoid controversial topics or to take on the expense of providing translations. Consequently, the content of the papers deteriorated. Furthermore, since simply reading German papers was considered offensive to some Americans, the circulations of such papers declined dramatically. Many of the smaller German-language papers were put out of business.[33]

The *Review*, as an English language publication, escaped the repressive measures aimed at the German-language press. But the press in general had been put on notice as to the limits of the government's tolerance of free discussion. Some Socialist papers had been shut down for their criticism of U.S. policy and one Irish-American paper was also suppressed for its hostility to Britain. Preuss was also well aware that *Die Amerika* was suffering from the effects of government restrictions and the anti-German campaign. In fact, in order to provide work for the technical staff of *Amerika*, Preuss eventually brought the production of the *Review* back to St. Louis thus ending his business relationship with the Divine Word Fathers at Techny, Illinois. The circulation of the *Review* also declined as a result of the war as Preuss lost over a hundred foreign subscriptions. This loss was partially offset by the contribution of a benefactor that enabled Preuss to send two copies of the *Review* to twenty-five army camps.[34]

Preuss did not give up trying to maintain journalistic freedom despite the oppressive atmosphere created by the government's repressive measures. His way of indirectly criticizing official policies was to cite historical precedents for dissenting points of view. This was exemplified in articles like "Washington's Warning" which recounted the first president's admonition against American participation in "European wars of supremacy."[35] Preuss addressed the question of the free press in similar fashion with his article "The Liberty of the Press in Wartime."

Recounting the Lincoln administration's suppression of the *Freeman's Journal* and the incarceration of its editor, James McMaster, Preuss concluded that because of such measures "Many an ardent patriot lost all faith and hope in the cause of Democracy."[36] The inference was obvious. In these and other articles Preuss suggested that the repressive policies being imposed by the Wilson administration posed a real threat to democracy. Throughout 1917 the *Review* joined the protests against loyalty oaths, the "reckless" preferment of treason charges, and the "conscription of free thought." Preuss also spoke out against the campaign to bar the use of the German language in American society, particularly in schools.[37]

The growth in anti-Catholicism that accompanied the popular xenophobia was also indicted in the pages of the *Review*. Preuss castigated the religious bigotry that led federal officials to search German-Catholic churches in Milwaukee for weapons. This particular "insult to every Catholic" was simply the most blatant example of the anti-Catholic sentiment that was cropping up as a result of the war.[38] By December 1917, a discouraged Preuss wrote to his friend Father Markert,

> How we suffer, we who are not even German born, but third generation Americans. Who would have thought it possible...in the 'free land' of America? One can hardly open one's mouth...without being afraid that it will bring trouble. The speculation that the congressional elections for 1918 will be suppressed doesn't surprise me. Anything is possible in this land of 'mobocracy.' Therefore, please burn this letter. It would be better if I could speak to you personally for a few hours...Hopefully, the time will soon come when we can again speak and write freely...[39]

With the new year, themes that Preuss had sounded in the days of American neutrality continued to find space in the *Review*. Preuss never stopped advocating a papal role in the peace talks. The theme of war as a divine scourge was also replayed, even while Preuss hoped for a peace settlement without recriminations. A surprisingly new note was Preuss's praise for the Knights of Columbus for their work in providing for the spiritual needs of Catholic soldiers.[40]

As the first anniversary of the American declaration of war neared with no end to the conflict in sight, public hostility towards Germans and German Americans intensified. A two-month-long Senate investigation of the National German-American Alliance begun in February 1918 heightened the rage against "Teutonism" by perpetuating the myth of German-American disloyalty. Acts of discrimination and violence against German Americans continued on the upsurge. German Americans were denied promotions and hounded for their supposed lack of support for the Liberty Loan drive. Throughout the Midwest, mobs forced individual German Americans into humiliating displays of "patriotism" by demanding that they kiss the flag or denounce the Kaiser.[41]

By this time agitation against the use of the German language had reached a fever pitch. Numerous articles appeared in national publications calling for a complete ban on the use of German in America. The American Defense Society, which claimed Theodore Roosevelt as its honorary president, made the outlawing of German a priority and led the campaign to eliminate German place names. One of its pamphlets asserted that "any language which produces a people of ruthless conquestadors such as now exists in Germany, is not a fit language to teach clean and pure American boys and girls."[42] Several states began to legislate against the use of German in both private and public schools as an obstacle to "100% Americanization" of immigrants. (These restrictions were eventually banned by the Supreme Court in 1923.)[43] Preuss's home state of Missouri established an "honor roll" for churches, schools, and associations that eliminated the use of German. German books were burned in "patriotic rituals" across the country, while in South Dakota and Iowa the state governments banned the use of German over the telephone or in gatherings of three or more people. Even the use of music written by German composers was banned in places.[44] In the midst of all this anti-German hostility the *Review* continued to take a calm tone despite the personal anguish its editor was undoubtedly experiencing. Arthur Preuss's most direct response to the hysteria was published in the *Review* of March 15, 1918.

> In these days of hysteria and chauvinism it is well to realize what patriotism really is and what it is not. Patriotism is the love of one's country and loyalty to its institutions and authorities. It is not mere sentiment, but an obligation. It is not chauvinism, which glorifies love of country into a religion and puts the flag where the cross ought to be. It is not jingoism, inspired by racial hatred. It is not nationalism, which holds that we have a divine mission to bring the world to our way of thinking. It is not internationalism, in the current sense of the term, which asserts that all national aspirations...must be destroyed to make way for universal socialism. Patriotism, in its purest form, is inculcated by the Catholic Church, who adapts herself with divine adequacy to every nation.[45]

One of the ironies of this hostility directed at all things German was that "church Germans," the German Americans who associated German culture with their religious practice, but not with their politics, suffered most. Those German-American organizations that had proudly associated themselves with German national interests in the period of American neutrality had by this time made an about face and had readily dissociated themselves from the German language. "Church Germans" on the other hand, because they had never associated themselves with German war aims, saw no need to be apologetic about their continued use of the German language, and so became the targets of the anti-German backlash. German-speaking Mennonites and Hutterites were especially abused because of their pacifism. Two Hutterites died in federal custody after four months in solitary confinement, where they were required to stand all day with their hands chained above their heads. German Lutheran congregations also suffered from the terrorism. Their churches were burned and some pastors were assaulted.[46] German Catholics were generally more fortunate. The "superpatriots" considered them to be foreign, but more Roman than German. Also, the public pronouncements of Catholic bishops supporting the war effort enhanced the patriotic image of the Catholic Church. This however did not prevent the harassment of individual priests like the Rev. J. D. Metzler, pastor of St. Boniface in Edwardsville, Illinois. Threatened with tar and feathering in April 1918 after allegedly making pro-German remarks, Father Meztler took a leave from his pastorate of twenty years.[47]

This terror campaign against German ethnicity culminated in the lynching of a German laborer by a mob on April 5, 1918 in Collinsville, Illinois, ten miles northeast of Preuss's home in St. Louis. The murder of Richard Prager was greeted in many places with outrage. However, a jury refused to convict the admitted perpetrators and in the surrounding communities of Illinois and Missouri the crime was followed by several more acts of violence against German Americans.[48] Although Preuss did not publicize accounts of specific acts of anti-German bigotry, he did write to Father Markert of his own experience of this hostility.

> A few days ago someone nailed up a placard near us on the corner of Hamilton Avenue which said 'Warning! Alien Enemies'. It was the first time I realized that we lived in a forbidden zone. Now many of our old friends no longer visit us. Isn't it wonderful to live in the land of freedom and brotherhood?[49]

As the movement against the German language continued through the summer and into the fall of 1918, Preuss expressed growing concern for the anti-Catholic animus of the "patriotic" campaign. Nativist campaigns in the United States have always viewed Catholicism as "un-American," and German-Catholic parish schools were seen as obstacles to Americanism. In the spring of 1918 a law to ban all parochial elementary schools was being proposed in Michigan. By July, a Canadian contributor to the *Review*, reflecting on the rising anti-Catholicism, warned of "the coming Kulturkampf." In September 1918, Archbishop Glennon, alarmed at "the rising state absolutism in America," spoke out against the attempts to regulate parochial education.[50]

Given the intolerance that then permeated American society, the sad experience of German Americans during the war, and his own distrust of liberal ideology, it is not surprising that Arthur Preuss was among those who believed that America was "on the eve of a serious Kulturkampf."[51] The repressive laws and popular hostility that had so recently been visited upon German Americans, now appeared to be gathering for an attack on Catholic schools. Thus, this issue became a major topic in the *Review* in the last months of 1918. As "the American Kulturkampf was clearly in sight," Preuss reiterated his perennial appeals for a strong Catholic press and a social movement built on "Catholic Solidarism."[52]

The question of postwar reconstruction had been treated periodically in the *Review*. Preuss shared the opinion of many on the left that the greed engendered by the capitalist system had fueled the flames of war while big business profited from the destruction. He also believed that if substantive social reforms were not undertaken, the propaganda of Bolshevism would win over America's down-trodden working class.[53] Together with the problem of anti-Catholicism, the social question was one of the principal concerns of the *Review* at war's end.

Aftermath

Following the armistice on November 11, 1918, the *Review*, now free from wartime restrictions on free speech, returned to its criticism of American involvement in the war. As the nation entered a period of disillusionment in the postwar period, especially with the idealism of Woodrow Wilson, Arthur Preuss, like other German Americans, believed that his anti-war stance had been vindicated.

The tone of Preuss's postwar reflections on the conflict was set in the first issue of the *Review* published following the commencement of hostilities. This essay also expressed the anger that Preuss had suppressed during the months that dissent was being stifled by government regulations and the anti-German hysteria. Commenting on the sweeping victory of the Republican party in the recent congressional elections, Preuss attributed it to the restrictive policies pursued by the Wilson administration.

Almost from the beginning of the war a rigid censorship prevented the circulation...of facts which the American public had a right to know... Newspapers and reviews whose editorial policy, in the opinion of the post-office department, tended to interfere with the plans of the government, were suppressed or threatened with suppression...Taking their cue from the conduct of the administration, the courts sentenced men and women to prison for ten or twenty years... for expressing opinions which did not suit the autocrats. The utmost social pressure was brought to bear on every citizen to devote all his energies to the prosecution of the war, whether he approved of it or not...The administration expressly or tacitly, sanctioned the use of all available methods of persuasion or coercion which would reinforce the appearance of national unity, forgetful of the fundamental democratic principle that national unity is worth nothing if it has to be purchased by the suppression of honest convictions. Need we wonder that the people in their wrath spurned the President's appeal and elected a Republican congress? The wonder is that they did not elect a Socialist Congress.[54]

For the next few years Preuss would return often to the topic of the war, the peace negotiations and Woodrow Wilson's involvement in them. In this period, as new information came to light, Preuss would say what he previously only suspected, or had been prevented from saying by the wartime atmosphere of repression. He printed articles on the propaganda efforts that had duped Americans from the beginning of the war as to the true nature of its causes and on Wilson's insincere neutrality. The issue of government repression of free speech and the press was re-explored. And the failure of Wilson to live up to the Armistice agreement when negotiating the Versailles treaty was condemned.[55] That Preuss's bitterness over the Wilson administration's repression of free speech and exploitation of ethnic hostilities was enduring is attested to by the remarks he published just prior to the 1920 presidential election. The vehemence of his remarks is particularly striking when one remembers that Preuss, as a matter of principle, had never before involved in the *Review* in partisan politics.

...the people should not forget that the Democratic administration systematically exploited war intolerance..sponsored more laws inimical to American liberty than ever proposed in America... [signed a peace treaty that] rests upon a dishonorable repudiation of the pledges on which the armistice was based... [and that] the League of Nations is essentially an alliance of conquerors to safeguard the spoils.[56]

A year after the war ended, Arthur Preuss's comments on the conflict and its aftermath gained an additional venue when he was asked to become the corresponding editor of the *Echo*. The *Echo* was a Catholic weekly paper established in 1915 in Buffalo, New York. Published by the German Catholic Orphanage of that city, under the directorship of Francis X. Schifferli, the *Echo* was the English language sister publication of *Die Aurora*, which was printed in German.[57] As an independent paper, edited and published by German-American Catholics, it recorded their distinctive perspective on the issues of the day, which tended to be much more radical than the many "official" Catholic organs then in publication.

From November 1919 until his death in December 1934, the editorial pages of the *Echo* were "conducted" by Arthur Preuss, who had been recruited by Francis Schifferli to assist Schifferli's son, Joseph, in the publication of the paper.[58] Of course, the readers of the *Echo* were already used to seeing sentiments expressing German-American reaction to the wartime attacks on them printed in its pages. Preuss's predecessor as editor had written regularly about the campaign against the use of the German language, repressive government measures, war profiteering by big business, the manipulation of popular opinion through propaganda, and Wilson's "betrayal" of a just peace at Versailles.[59]

In one of his first editorials for the *Echo*, "True Causes of the War," Preuss reiterated the themes expounded by his predecessor. Preuss asserted that the war was the natural product of a "bankrupt civilization." The capitalism, nationalism, and general immorality of modern society had brought about the calamity, and all the participating nations, not just Germany, should share the blame.[60] The idealism of Americans in entering the war was naive at best considering the secret treaties and imperialistic motives of her erstwhile "allies," particularly "perfidious Albion."

> Had we minded our own business and stayed out of the bloody conflict between the two imperialistic rivals in Europe, we should not now be staggering under a debt of thirty billion dollars and trembling on the verge of a fearful social upheaval.[61]

American social life was further compromised by the repressive measures the Wilson Administration employed to suppress dissent against its war policy.

> The brutal infliction of grievances on thousands and thousands of good citizens, during the war and after, often in the name of 'law and order,' has made conditions ripe for a Socialist upheaval.[62]

American government officials and the press were also taken to task by Preuss and the *Echo* for deliberately spreading "atrocity hoaxes" about the conduct of the German army that led to the "terror of patriotism" in America. As for the peace settlement at Versailles, "it no more settles the problem of Europe than the compromise of 1820 settled the problem of American slavery."[63]

According to the *Echo* the treaty ending the war was fundamentally unjust as it was predicated on the false notion that the Central powers alone were responsible for the war. In a clear betrayal of Wilson's "Fourteen Points," and of American sentiment, the Allied governments had imposed a humiliating "peace of victory" on their defeated opponents. The United States, by its support of Britain and France in imposing indemnities on the Central powers was aiding the French objective of the complete "economic destruction of Germany." Likewise, the Allies' dismemberment of Austria, had led to widespread economic hardship and starvation. According to the *Echo*, "reparation that exacts the lives of innocent women and children is un-Christian, inhuman, and worthy only of barbarians."[64]

Reflecting the views of the German-American community, the *Echo* held Woodrow Wilson largely responsible for dragging America into a war it did not want, and for aligning her with the vindictive policies of her allies. President Wilson and the American government were castigated further for not allowing Pope Benedict XV to be involved in the peace process.[65] Preuss believed that papal involvement in the deliberations could have insured a just settlement. However, with Pope Benedict not allowed to exercise his influence, the victors succeeded in forcing hard terms on the vanquished making another war inevitable.

> Men will undoubtedly soon go to war again over the issues left unsettled, or settled wrongly, by the Treaty of Versailles, unless indeed the victorious nations will listen to the voice of the Great White Shepherd of Christendom and revise the iniquitous Treaty in conformity with the laws of justice, charity and true democracy.[66]

Consistent with its criticisms of the Treaty of Versailles, the *Echo* rejected American involvement in the League of Nations. Preuss was not an isolationist. He supported the idea of a council of nations, but he believed that as constituted, "the League was no true League at all but an aggregation of robber bands which have scorched and looted Europe." Its purpose was vague and its exclusion of the Holy See was another strike against it.[67]

The *Echo*'s rejection of the Treaty of Versailles and pessimism regarding the League of Nations found positive expression in active support for the disarmament movement that emerged in the early twenties. Arthur Preuss's editorials on the issue sounded two distinctive notes. First, disarmament was imperative if the world powers were to resist being lured into another war by the imperialism of nationalists and the machinations of the munitions profiteers. Second, Catholics were failing to fulfill their special duty to promote disarmament and resist nationalism and militarism.[68]

That the war with Germany was a traumatic experience for the German-American community there can be no doubt. Apart from the tragedy of making war on their ancestral homeland, the trial of being considered disloyal for no other reason than their ethnic culture and preservation of the German language was a bitter one. For German Catholics like Arthur Preuss, the tragedy of the war had further alienated them from American society, a society which they had found hostile in many ways even before American participation in the conflict.

Many German Americans responded to the crisis by making feverish attempts to be accepted as "100% American" through the repudiation of their heritage. The twenty months of official hostilities thus greatly accelerated the inevitable process of assimilation.[69] Though Arthur Preuss was not one of those who sought protection from the anti-German hysteria by distancing himself from his German heritage, his published remarks suggest that he too was "Americanized" by the experience. That is, for the first time in his public life Arthur Preuss became a champion of two of the basic principles of American democracy, representative government and the freedom of the press.

That American society had failed to live up to these principles, even while President Wilson was claiming the cause of democracy as the reason for American involvement in the war, simply confirmed what Preuss had always suspected. American idealism was just that, and would be quickly jettisoned whenever it conflicted with the real driving force of American society, the pursuit of wealth and power. Thus, liberalism, the basis of American democracy, was not only inimical to Catholicism, by turning to intolerance and "autocracy" in order to pursue a questionable war, it had proven itself unfaithful to its own high-sounding principles. During the years of national and international turmoil that followed the war, German-Catholic opinion, as manifested in the pages of the *Review* and the *Echo*, and in particular, the editorials of Arthur Preuss, readily found indication for having opposed American involvement in the First World War. In the end, the experience of the Great War had confirmed Arthur Preuss in his distrust of liberal ideology and encouraged him in his conviction that only in Catholicism could one the find principles on which to base a truly just civil order.

VIII Into the Twenties

"A Journal of Protest"

Although Arthur Preuss had made a conscious decision as a young man to pursue his vocation as a Catholic journalist from within the ranks of the English-language press, he was not unaffected by the vicissitudes of the war that devastated German-language newspapers. Subscriptions to the *Review* fell off during the war years and new subscribers were hard to come by. Attempts to get current subscribers to enlist their friends as supporters of the *Review* had little success. Eventually, responding to the initiative of a priest subscriber who sent him a hundred dollars for a "lifetime" subscription, Preuss was able to sell twenty-five such subscriptions at fifty dollars or more, in honor of the *Review*'s silver anniversary. The funds raised in this fashion enabled Preuss to pay off his debt to the Divine Word Fathers at Techny and to put aside some money for his children's education.[1]

The generosity of his benefactors greatly eased Preuss's concern regarding the support of his family and the continuance of the *Review*. However, the other publication associated with the Preuss family name, *Die Amerika*, was in desperate straits at the end of the war. Even though Preuss had not been actively involved in the daily operations of the paper since 1905, when he recruited Frederick Kenkel to succeed him as editor, Preuss still took an active interest in the paper. For one thing, he still owned his father's shares in the paper's parent company, the German Literary Society of St. Louis. Additionally, his employer at the B. Herder Company, Joseph Gummersbach, who ran the business operations of *Die Amerika*, regularly consulted Preuss its affairs.

As a German-language paper, *Amerika* had experienced an enormous drop in subscriptions and advertising once hostilities with Germany began. Undoubtedly, the avidly pro-German editorial policy pursued by Kenkel during the period of American neutrality contributed to the *Amerika*'s sudden misfortunes, as many former readers trying to demonstrate their loyalty, dropped the paper. The paper also suffered from the anti-German hysteria of the general public and at one point it was denied a mail permit for not being sufficiently loyal to the war effort. Then too, the inevitable Americanization of German immigrants had been gradually dissolving the readership of the German-language press even before the war began.[2]

Sensing the need that *Die Amerika* adapt or die, Preuss had been suggesting privately for years that the paper make the conversion to English-language usage. As early as 1903, Preuss had responded to Archbishop Glennon's inquiry about establishing an English Catholic daily paper in St. Louis with the suggestion that *Die Amerika* be adapted for this purpose.[3] For whatever reason, his advice was not taken. In June 1918 Preuss suggested in pages of the *Review* that changing *Amerika* to the English language would not only save the publication but would also expand its influence as a Catholic daily paper.[4] Again, however, Preuss's suggestion was ignored and the paper limped along in the postwar years with a falling readership and rising debts.

Die Amerika's difficulties came to a head in the fall of 1920 when Frederick Kenkel resigned as editor ostensibly so that he could devote himself full time to his duties as the Secretary of the Central Bureau of the Central Verein. Actually, the circumstances of Kenkel's resignation were, as Arthur Preuss explained to Father Markert, a bit more complex.

> Herr Kenkel has resigned the editorship of *Amerika* to devote himself entirely to Central Bureau of the D.R.K.C.V. It is a fortunate solution to a knotty problem; for I must tell you in *strictest confidence*, that if he had not resigned, we should have been compelled to dismiss him. With all his good qualities he has a most unfortunate temperament and in the course of time had alienated the sympathy and good will of practically all of his co-workers...they threatened to walk out as a body if he remained.[5]

Understandably, Preuss was concerned that his role in Kenkel's ouster would bring an end to their friendship. Fortunately for both men, it did not, and in Preuss's last years the friendship of the two men appears to have reached a greater degree of intimacy.[6]

Apart from Kenkel's feelings, Preuss had another immediate problem.

As of November 1, 1920, he was once again editor of *Die Amerika*. Preuss had given up this position in 1905 as his six years of running the paper, first in his father's name and then in his own, had convinced him that he was not cut out to meet the demands of directing a large daily paper. Even as a young man Preuss had found the burden too taxing and a restriction on his literary pursuits. So it was with reluctance that Preuss gave into Joseph Gummersbach's request, and perhaps his sense of duty to the memory of his father, and once again assumed the editorship of the now fading *Amerika*.

Arthur Preuss experienced his second stint as editor of *Amerika* as a tremendous burden. In addition to the financial worries, he had to restore harmony to a staff that had grown fractious under Kenkel. He complained to his friend Markert that these problems kept him from doing much actual writing.[7] There was also the frustration of being unable to convince the board of directors to change the paper to an English-language publication. Even before taking over as editor, Preuss had told Father Markert that "with all my love of the German language and German ideas, I think that it is a terrible mistake to attempt to perpetuate the language in spite of conditions that militate against it." However, even with the difficulties, Preuss had resolved to stay with the paper long enough to retire its debt of $12,000.[8] It was not to be.

Preuss's second editorship lasted only a year and ended in profound discouragement. On October 29, 1921, Preuss wrote to his friend Father Peter Guilday

> Some of the principal stockholders of the *Amerika* have just sold out to a capitalist promoter who has promised to continue the daily edition in the same spirit. This sale came about very much against my will, as we have no guarantee that the new owners will not change the character of the paper and make it a mere instrument for earning dividends, which they probably hope to do by making it as colorless as possible. I should have preferred to see the paper stop honorably. But I was outvoted. Of course I promptly resigned the editorship of the paper as soon as the 'deal' was consummated... [9]

The sale of *Die Amerika* to a "capitalist promoter" dealt a tremendous blow to Preuss's dream of a strong Catholic daily newspaper. Just months before the sale Preuss had conducted intense negotiations with Nicholas Gonner, publisher of the *Daily American Tribune*, in Dubuque, Iowa, over the possible merger of the two papers as an English Catholic daily published in St. Louis. Those negotiations broke down due to the inability of the two men to agree to terms.[10] Preuss later discovered that, contrary to Gonner's claims, the *Tribune* was as strapped financially as *Amerika*. Still, until the sale of *Amerika*, he held out hope that it could be a strong Catholic daily paper. In writing to Father Markert of the sale, Preuss gave full vent to his anger and disappointment that ideals always lost out to money in "this crass land of materialism."

> I have seen almost all my dreams fall into ruins, the latest being *Amerika*, and I have become truly pessimistic. Catholic journalism in this country has no future and we are fading away. However, we cannot throw in the towel but must continue to struggle until the end.[11]

When it became known that *Die Amerika* had been sold, Preuss's friends sent him their condolences. The funereal tones they employed were well chosen for after a nearly fifty-year association of the Preuss family name with *Amerika*, the sale of the paper, to business interests no less, was like a death in the family.[12]

For all his sadness, the end of his association with *Amerika* must have brought Arthur Preuss a sense of relief as well. He was no longer burdened with editing the paper or worrying about its financial predicament. He still had more than enough work, and not just on the *Review*. Preuss's recruitment by a former member of the *Amerika* staff, Francis X. Schifferli, to become the "chief editorial writer" for the *Echo* of Buffalo kept him busy writing weekly editorials on topics of the day. Preuss wrote editorials and provided copy for the *Echo* on a weekly basis for the next fifteen years. As his work was unsigned, it is difficult to say with certainty how much of what the *Echo* published can be ascribed to him. However, in publishing Preuss's obituary and acknowledging publicly for the first time his association with the paper, the publisher stated that "For fifteen years Preuss conducted the editorial pages of the *Echo*."[13] In any case, the *Echo* provided Preuss another forum, and one with a much larger circulation, (19,500 per week in 1930),[14] from which to address the issues of the day and it seems he rather enjoyed the anonymity of his work with the paper. In effect, Preuss's work with the *Echo* enabled him to amplify the views he published in the *Review* without too many people knowing that he was in fact responsible for both.[15]

In addition to his editorial work for the *Echo*, Preuss also wrote editorials for the *Mt. Angel Magazine* from 1920 through 1927. Published monthly by the Benedictine monks of Mt. Angel, Oregon as a family journal, the *Mt. Angel Magazine* was not an intellectual publication, but it did have an enormous readership reaching 40,000 subscribers in 1927.[16] Another editorial assignment Preuss accepted was that of part-time editor of the Belleville diocesan paper, the *Messenger*, from June 1920 until March 1922.[17] While accepting these additional commitments strained Preuss's already frail health, he appears to have valued them as opportunities to expand his readership.

This same motivation, to broaden his audience, led Arthur Preuss to consider the most unlikely of partnerships, the publication of the *Review* by the Catholic University of America. On December 18, 1919, Preuss wrote to Francis Markert of this possibility.

'Sub rosa' there are negotiations underway between Catholic University and yours truly. The gentlemen there would like to buy the *F.R.* from me, and take it and myself to Washington where it would be published, under my editorship as a weekly magazine in the manner of the *Nation*. The proposal is enticing, however I am cautious about it and have conveyed to Dr. Shahan that if it is the will of providence that I should be associated with C.U., the loving God will have to bring considerable means to bear in order to pry me away from my present sphere of activity and give me the necessary patience and humility to surrender my sole control of the *F.R.* to the direction of the faculty or a committee of the same. This is all in confidence. It may be that I am already too old to adapt to such an entirely new situation...[18]

This offer was conveyed to Preuss by Father Peter Guilday. The two men had corresponded for several years and Preuss was an enthusiastic supporter of the fledgling *Catholic Historical Review* and the American Catholic Historical Association, both founded by Guilday. The proposal was, of course, never carried through and it remains unclear whether it was actually authorized by the administration of the Catholic University or simply a trial balloon sent up by Guilday on his own.[19] That Guilday, and not the administration of the University, had authored the proposal is suggested by Preuss's letter to Guilday on May 14, 1920.

> I trust that you have done nothing more in the matter of getting me to come to the University. The more I think it over, the greater grows my disinclination to sacrifice my freedom of utterance for any, even the highest paid position the C.U. could possibly offer or provide.[20]

By this time, Guilday appears to have been distancing himself from the proposition by cutting off its discussion, "...the University project has died down. Don't ask me to talk about it. I am a bit disappointed."[21]

Later it was suggested to Preuss by Father Heinrich Schumacher, a Scripture instructor at the Catholic University whose book on the New Testament was edited by Preuss for the B. Herder Company, that the idea of the University sponsoring the *Review* was just an elaborate attempt to buy Preuss's silence.[22] However, Preuss discounted this possibility, refusing to believe that Guilday would have betrayed their friendship by being party to such a plot.[23] Given Guilday's own stormy relationship with the administration of the University as recounted in his letters to Preuss, he would have had little motivation for participating in a plan to co-opt the *Review*. What is more probable is that the proposal was never anything more than wishful thinking on Guilday's part. That Preuss even considered the notion of selling the *Review* to Catholic University is an indication of the dilemma he was in as an independent Catholic publisher. The sponsorship of Church institutions offered financial stability to struggling Catholic publications, but at what cost? Preuss himself concluded that, no matter how enticing financial security might be, and it could be very enticing to the father of ten children, after twenty-five years as an independent Catholic journal, the *Review* and its editor were too old to be domesticated now.

As for Preuss's friendship with Guilday, it remained unaffected by this incident. Preuss continued to promote the *Catholic Historical Review*, though he declined Guilday's request that he present a paper at the first annual meeting of the American Catholic Historical Society held in the fall of 1920.[24] According to Guilday, his association with Preuss did nothing to endear him to his colleagues at the Catholic University.[25] However, this did not inhibit Guilday from asking Preuss to edit his book, *An Introduction to Church History*, which was published in 1925 by the B. Herder Company with an appreciative note for Preuss's assistance.[26] Surprisingly, Guilday would confide in Preuss that despite his success, he did not particularly enjoy writing historical biographies. Guilday also told Preuss that his proposal that the Catholic University should eliminate its undergraduate departments and dedicate itself exclusively to graduate studies, was regarded as "too German" and eliminated him from being considered as a rector for the University.[27]

Arthur Preuss's relationship with Peter Guilday is just one illustration of how this basically retiring editor was able to form friendships with other Catholic intellectuals. Clerics and laymen who were familiar with Preuss through his writings would make a point of calling on him as they passed through St. Louis. In June 1919 he wrote to Father Markert

Yesterday, Dr. Ryan from the Catholic University was here with Father Engelen, S.J. and Father Thomas Oesterreich, O.S.B. of Belmont Abbey, N.C., all interesting gentlemen. Today came several more, among them two bishops. In this way, though a semi-invalid, I stay in touch with the outside world. I am only sorry that we do not have a proper guest room in which to make visitors comfortable. Unfortunately, that is not possible with numerous children.[28]

Among the priests who became Preuss's friends, importance must be given to another Church historian, Father Francis Borgia Steck, O.F.M.

As a member of the Franciscan community that operated Quincy College, Steck knew Preuss not only as the College's most illustrious alumnus, but also as the father of several sons who were enrolled at Quincy in the 1920s Preuss began publishing articles by Steck in the early twenties. These articles usually addressed aspects of Catholic history, but occasionally Steck wrote articles related to current Franciscan affairs.[29] Preuss facilitated Steck's introduction to Father Peter Guilday under whom the latter studied for his doctoral degree in history at the Catholic University in the mid-twenties.[30] When Steck published his dissertation, "The Joliet-Marquette Expedition; 1673," the *Review* became the forum from which he defended the work against attacks by various Jesuits who resented Steck's assertion that Marquette was not the discoverer of the Mississippi.[31] Preuss's support for Steck apparently alienated many in the Society of Jesus and perhaps explains the belittling obituary that *America* published at the time of Preuss's death. In that notice Wilfrid Parsons, S.J. went so far as to challenge Preuss's stature as a journalist.[32]

Father Steck appreciated the loyalty of his benefactor. Recognizing Steck's loyalty to Preuss, when the "eminent editor" died, Father Markert suggested to Frederick Kenkel that Steck be enlisted to write Preuss's biography.[33] It is to be regretted that this did not happen as Steck and Preuss both believed strongly that historians should not be afraid to publish the unvarnished truth. Preuss shared some of his thoughts on historical writing when he wrote to Steck, asking him to write a review of James Walsh's popular book, *The Thirteenth, Greatest of Centuries*.

> ...in spite of my friendship with Dr. Walsh, it seems to me that from the trained historian's point of view the book is very unsatisfactory indeed. A German Catholic historian of note, to whom I submitted the work years ago for review refused to touch it saying that it was so amateurish as to be unworthy of notice by a professional historian. What do *you* think of Dr. Walsh's methods? I am afraid that they are injuring the Catholic cause in the eyes of non-Catholics and some

historian ought to arise amongst us to declare that not all of us believe
in this sort of pseudo-apologetics...I always feel humiliated when my
non-Catholic friends in secular universities point out to me the lack of
the true historical spirit and the woeful ignorance of scientific historical
methods among so many of our soi-disant Catholic historians.[34]

Another friendship that Arthur Preuss formed at this time was with
Horace A. Frommelt. Although a lesser-known figure than Guilday and
Steck, Frommelt became an important contributor to the *Review* and the
Echo. Trained as an engineer, Frommelt had spent seven years in the
Society of Jesus with Preuss's younger brother James, before leaving due
to ill health in 1920. Shortly after his departure from the Society,
Frommelt wrote to Preuss seeking literary work.[35] For Preuss,
Frommelt's appearance was a God-send. At the time, Preuss had just
taken over the editorship of *Die Amerika* and, in addition to publishing
the *Review* and writing editorials for the *Echo*, was struggling to
complete his adaptation of Anton Koch's *Moral Theologie*. As Frommelt
was fluent in German, Preuss immediately enlisted his help on translating
Koch's four-volume work. Soon Frommelt was also contributing articles
to the *Review*.

Frommelt's first contribution to the *Review* was an article on the
"futility" of Catholic higher education. Entitled, "Ignored Problems in
Catholic Education," Frommelt's article voiced some of the same
criticisms of Catholic higher education that gained John Tracy Ellis
widespread notice some thirty years later.[36] Frommelt anticipated Ellis'
criticism of the poor support Catholic colleges received from hierarchy
and laity alike. He also anticipated Ellis' criticism of the short-sighted
policies of the various religious orders that led to the proliferation of
Catholic colleges with little concern shown for their quality. Frommelt
castigated "the erection of so-called universities which are in reality
nothing but poorly equipped professional schools." While Frommelt
diagnosed some of the same symptoms of anemia at Catholic institutions
of higher learning as Ellis would identify later, the two men differed on

what they saw as the gravest threat to the patient. For Ellis, writing in the fifties, it was the intellectual isolation of Catholics that prevented a dialogue with the prevailing culture. For Frommelt, thirty years earlier, the greatest threat to Catholic higher education in America was the pernicious influence of capitalism, which was co-opting the Catholic challenge to American society. According to Frommelt, Catholic colleges had become so dependent on capitalists for their funding that "it has become absolutely impossible to teach the least bit of doctrine subversive to its [capitalism's] unholy nature." Frommelt concluded his article by asserting that "our university education has been secularized and dominated by the established order to such an extent that it has become almost useless."[37]

Though Frommelt's critique of Catholic higher education had nowhere near the impact that Ellis' would in the fifties, it apparently annoyed some people. Preuss reported to Frommelt that the article had so angered some of his Jesuit readers that the *Review* lost some of its subscribers including Georgetown University.[38] But Arthur Preuss was impressed with Frommelt's work. Since he had now reached the age of fifty and was in declining health, perhaps Frommelt's essays reminded Preuss of the zeal of his own youth. Preuss considered having Frommelt installed as the editor of *Amerika*. Preuss even discussed with Frommelt the possibility of being his successor as the editor of the *Review*. This never happened, probably because by the late twenties Frommelt decided to stick with engineering rather than pursuing Catholic journalism as his life's work. In January 1929 Frommelt became the head of the Department of Engineering at Marquette University.[39] Still, Frommelt continued to write provocative essays for the *Review* as long as the journal was published.

One other friend of Arthur Preuss in this period should be mentioned at this point: Father John E. Rothensteiner.[40] Like Preuss, Rothensteiner was a prominent member of the German Catholic community in St. Louis and the two men had been friends since at least 1890. As Rothensteiner later explained, "After his return from College my personal acquaintance, which soon ripened into friendship, began. Arthur was the younger man by eleven years. But reminiscences were along the same line: SS. Peter & Paul's Rectory, and its pastor, Father Goller."[41] Rothensteiner was also an editor, piloting the German-language *Pastoralblatt* in its last years. Best remembered today for his history of the Archdiocese of St. Louis, Rothensteiner had contributed essays on history as well as poems to the *Review* for a number of years. After Preuss recruited him to write for *Amerika*, Rothensteiner also began to write essays on social issues for the *Review*.[42]

The contributions that Steck, Frommelt, and Rothensteiner, along with Preuss's longtime associate, Albert Muntsch, S.J., professor of Anthropology at St. Louis University, made to the *Review* were important to its continued vitality. Sharing Preuss's German Catholic background and, at least in Frommelt's case, his belief in a "subversive" role for Catholic thought in American society, they helped to maintain the intellectual standards and the conservative outlook of the *Review* during the decade of the twenties.

"The Catholic Radical"

While German-Americans had good reason for believing themselves particular victims of wartime developments, the Great War had a tremendous impact on all of American society. The outbreak of war in Europe had initiated an economic boom in America that lasted from 1915 until 1920.[43] Concerned first with "preparedness" for war and then its prosecution, the federal government very quickly established itself as the regulator of the American economy. Evaluated from the perspective of efficiency, such regulatory bodies as the War Industries Board and the National War Labor Board rendered America's "first experiment in a planned economy" a success.[44] Many progressives hoped that these wartime successes would lead to the acceptance of a planned economy in peacetime as well in order to address economic issues related to the "social question." However, government regulation of the economy was a complete break with the traditional American ideal of laissez-faire capitalism. Woodrow Wilson, the last of the Progressive Era presidents and author of the wartime economic regulation, realized this and, perhaps hoping to soften Republican opposition to his peace plans, moved swiftly to end it. In fact, the Wilson administration dismantled the various wartime agencies so rapidly that it further exacerbated the economic problems associated with demobilization.[45]

The clamor for a return to laissez-faire capitalism was in marked contrast to the general public's seeming support for the government's restriction of civil liberties. During the first eighteen months that immediately followed the end of the war the government and people of the United States manifested an even greater level of intolerance for aliens and dissenters than had been seen during the period of hostilities. The government promoted hysteria that had been aimed at "the Huns," now targeted "the Reds." Alarmed by the triumph of the Bolshevik revolution in Russia and similar uprisings in Germany and Hungary, the United States was plunged into a state of acute fear of revolution.[46]

The hysteria of the "Red Scare" had its origins in the xenophobic "one hundred per-cent American" campaign sponsored by the government during the war. Additionally, 1919 and 1920 were years of social unrest in America. While big business was well rewarded for its wartime partnership with the government, organized labor had gained few long-term benefits and little sympathy when it was severed from the system of a planned economy. With rising unemployment and inflation, organized labor confronted implacable owners over wages, hours, and benefits. In the course of 1919, four million workers were on strike at one time or another in attempts to wrest some concessions away from business.[47]

Unfortunately for organized labor, and the nation as a whole, there *were* a few real-life revolutionaries at large in America at this time. In February 1919 a general strike in Seattle organized by the Industrial Workers of the World with its accompanying violence grabbed national headlines. Two months later, in April 1919, a parcel bomb campaign targeted at politicians and businessmen further inflamed the national

"Red" hysteria. Assisted by newspaper sensationalism, the American people passed the year petrified by "phantom invaders" and disturbed by "groundless fears."[48]

The national state of paranoia induced the popular rejection of the legitimate demands of labor in the steel and coal industries and inspired the Wilson administration to new extremes in the suppression of civil liberties. The height of the government campaign against "the Reds" was reached in January 1920 when the Attorney General, A. Mitchell Palmer ordered the arrest of more than four thousand radicals. Of those arrested, one third were released for lack of evidence, 556 aliens were expelled from the country, and the remainder prosecuted under state syndicalism laws.[49]

However, the "Palmer Raids" seem to have had a cathartic effect on the nation. Within months the "Red Scare," exhausted by its own excesses, abated. Prominent Americans began to speak out against the government's violations of constitutional liberties. When national elections were held in November 1920 many former members of the "Wilson coalition" voted against the Democratic presidential and congressional candidates in retaliation for the administration's betrayal of progressive ideals.[50]

In both the *Review* and the *Echo* Arthur Preuss gave voice to the profound disillusionment with Wilson's presidency, that many Americans, particularly German-Americans, had experienced. A piece Preuss wrote for the *Echo* on the administration's last military budget captured these sentiments. Preuss castigated the Wilson Administration for its "riot of folly and extravagance of the last four years." He held the outgoing government responsible for manipulating public opinion, creating "moral havoc," and leaving the nation in a condition in "which it has never found itself before." William G. Harding's pledge to return the nation to "normalcy" had gained him a landslide victory at the polls of historic proportions. But Preuss found little to cheer about in the Republican's electoral victory. After all, though they had campaigned using "get Wilson" tactics, the Republicans were just as "fanatic" during the war and just as "eager to suppress all contrary opinions." As for Harding's "back to normalcy," the *Echo* interpreted it as the call for the nation "to advance backwards as rapidly as possible." Subsequent events proved that there was something backwards about "normalcy" as "the postwar era bequeathed to the 1920s a heritage of hatred and hysteria that permeated and disturbed every aspect of life and thought."[51]

Arthur Preuss's remarks regarding the election of 1920 are indicative of the seemingly paradoxical attitude he took toward American politics. On the one hand he believed that Catholics in America should work to further the reconstruction of American society through the exercise of their political strength in the electoral process. On the other hand, he was deeply skeptical that any true reform could "be ground out by the existing political machinery." Throughout his life Preuss regarded the American political system as essentially corrupt, for "the people have no real voice."[52] Surprisingly, given his antipathy for Britain, Preuss's preferred system of government would be based on proportional representation, ideally under a "constitutional monarchy which St. Thomas Aquinas declares to be the best because modeled upon the celestial hierarchy and that of the Catholic Church."[53] For the present, Preuss used his columns in the *Review* and the *Echo* to educate his readers in regard to the iniquities of American politics and on the shallowness of certain politicians. Preuss also advised them to be especially wary of Catholic politicians as

> ...almost without exception, the Catholic politicians that rise to fame and influence in this country are unworthy of the confidence of their fellow Catholics and are anything but a credit to their religion.[54]

Not all American politicians fell under Preuss's censure. Senator Robert M. LaFollette often received praise in the pages of the *Echo*, and his Progressive party candidacy for the presidency in 1924 was all but endorsed by the paper.[55] The praise that Preuss and the *Echo* showered on the Wisconsin Senator was no doubt due in part to LaFollette's opposition to the war against Germany and reparations. However, a large measure of LaFollete's appeal for Preuss lay in the fact that he alone among prominent American political figures appeared to recognize the seriousness of America's economic and political problems.

Still, in Preuss's view, for American Catholics to place their hopes in politicians, even Catholic ones, or third-party movements, was naive. This was because the problems in American society were systemic and rooted in capitalist economics. They could not be overcome without the complete reconstruction of economic life.

> ...we should not place the least good hope even in a Catholic party, or one whose tendencies were distinctly Christian. We can see no permanent good that might come from any political party as long as the modern State remains intact and the present Capitalist regime continues to function. That is why we have so little use for the present schools of social reform in this country. They are placing their hopes in methods that take for granted the present governmental and political polity. Our only hope lies in educating the people as to the diseased condition of society and the essential requirements of a moral Christian order...[56]

While such statements occasionally issued from the pen of Arthur Preuss in the prewar era, the experience of the First World War had transformed conservative German Catholics like Preuss into self-described "radicals."[57] Having always distrusted the idealistic claims for American democratic institutions, the war years confirmed Preuss's skepticism when those institutions jettisoned their idealism in pursuit of supposed "domestic enemies" and victory in an unjust war. The intolerance and "autocracy" in the United States during the war and immediately afterward had revealed for all who had eyes to see that the real force driving American society was not the adherence to democratic principles, but unbounded capitalism.

In the aftermath of the war the issue of the day for Arthur Preuss and others was that of the social reconstruction that was needed in American society. For Preuss, of course, the issue was framed by his Catholic identity. Thus, an immediate concern in Preuss's columns in the *Review* and the *Echo* was the freedom of the Catholic Church to pursue its reforming mission in an increasingly repressive and anti-Catholic atmosphere.[58] Preuss was not surprised by these developments. As a German-American, the war had already taught him much about the "new nativism."

> That Nativism would derive an immense impetus from the war was to be expected. That it will show its anti-Catholic fangs after a while need not surprise anyone. The saddest feature of the case is that so many Catholics have helped to nurse this horrible monster by joining in the hue and cry against the Germans.[59]

Not only did American Catholics have reason for remorse for their wartime acquiescence to intolerance, "when the much dreaded Kulturkampf comes, as come it will," they would be ill-prepared to meet the challenge as they lacked a strong press to promote Catholic solidarity and to defend the Church against attack.[60] Since they were in such a vulnerable position themselves, as a matter of both prudence and justice, Catholics in America should make common cause with other imperiled minorities. This included not only Preuss's predictable rejection of coerced "Americanization" of immigrants. But Preuss also felt a bond of solidarity with persecuted radicals. Writing in February 1919 on the election of a Milwaukee Socialist, Victor Berger, to Congress despite efforts to intimidate his supporters, Preuss warned

> No minority that has not the wealth of the country behind it, and is willing to use its wealth without scruple, can henceforth feel safe in America. Least of all the most despised and hated of all minorities in this traditionally anti-papal land, —the children of the Catholic Church. Our coreligionists are blind if they do not see the danger, and neglect to join forces with other imperiled minorities in a concerted effort to make 'government by busybodies,' and 'mob rule by the rich,'...forever impossible in the land of the free and the home of the brave.[61]

That Arthur Preuss would call upon "the children of the Catholic Church" to resist the rising tide of intolerance in America was to be expected and it would be repeated. The increased hostility to Catholicism in America was readily apparent in nativist agitation and in the legislative initiatives in several states that threatened the parochial schools. It was equally apparent that, in "the coming Kulturkampf," the number of defections from the Catholic Church in America would be "appalling" since "the faith of most of our people, even those who practice their religion, is merely an outward veneer and not a matter of conviction based upon a truly Catholic world-view."[62] The new wrinkle in Preuss's statements at this time was his professed willingness to make common cause with other "imperilled minorities."

Arthur Preuss remained unstinting in his criticism of socialism as atheistic and a threat to the right to private property. However, as "under the existing order, a great part of the working class is unable to live decently," the real force behind socialism was the iniquitous nature of American capitalist society. Unless the existing social evils were justly remedied the workers would quite naturally give their support to radicals.[63] Further, Preuss argued that the government's unjust campaign against "the Reds" threatened the freedom of all Americans. The deportation of "foreign agitators" raised the threat of "denaturalization en mass, with all that this means for America."[64] Writing in the January 13, 1921, issue of the *Echo*, Preuss maintained that at least some Americans resented

...a wrong done to a stranger within our gates as keenly as if it were done to a native American. Every true American ought to be interested in preserving the liberties which our fathers won.[65]

Commenting on the refusal of the New York State Assembly to seat five duly elected Socialist members, Preuss warned that tolerating such repression would mean that "no minority is secure in the future against excommunication on the ground that it is 'inimical' to the public interests."[66] Later, in praising John Ryan's public letter of support for the barred Assemblymen, Preuss reproved "our misguided co-religionists" who supported the repression of the Socialists. He called upon "every Catholic in the land" to protest these attacks on liberty and democracy because if "liberty is destroyed in America, no body of citizens will be made to suffer so quickly and so sharply as the members of the Catholic Church."[67]

Preuss's support for the persecuted Socialists was based not only on his empathy for them as another despised minority, but also on his basic agreement with them regarding the evils of the capitalist system.

> There is much truth and justice in the claims of Socialism. There is at least a kernel of justification for the tenets of Communism. A radical social reform is desperately needed...[68]

As Preuss believed that the teachings of the Church necessitated that Catholics work for a radical reconstruction of American society, the advocacy of which led to the suppression of the Socialists, it was not hard for him to imagine that Catholics could also be vilified for championing such a cause. The American bishops themselves, in a historic departure from their traditional silence on such matters, issued their own plan for social reconstruction in February 1919 through the Administrative Committee of the National Catholic War Council.[69] Given such widespread support for a radical reconstruction of American society, Preuss found it easy to speak well of other "radicals." Preuss said of the leading Socialist of the day, perennial presidential candidate Eugene Debs, that he "stands high as a citizen and a humane, honest, and charitable man, beloved by all who know him."[70] The Milwaukee socialist, Victor Berger, was

> admire[d] for his fearlessness and pluck even though we cannot agree with some of his Socialistic tenets. Would that we had a few Catholics with his intellectual capability and moral caliber in Congress.[71]

Arthur Preuss, as has been noted, had campaigned for the reconstruction of American society since the turn of the century. However, the general social turmoil that followed the end of the world war brought a new urgency to the matter of reform. Additionally, the bitter experiences of German-Americans during the war brought a new radicalism to Preuss's advocacy of social reconstruction. In the prewar years, while Preuss and his associates in the German Catholic community were critical of capitalism, their primary motive in advocating social reform appears to have been the fear that the working classes would be lost to the Church and won for socialism if their legitimate grievances were not addressed. This fear of socialism, and its radical offshoot, "Bolshevism", persisted into the postwar years. But now it was no longer the main theme of the *Review*'s treatment of the social question. Reflecting the increased alienation from the American society that had turned on them during the war, German-Catholic intellectuals like Arthur Preuss and his friend Frederick Kenkel, and their respective associates, Horace Frommelt and William Engelen, S.J., engaged in unrelenting attacks on the evils of American capitalism.[72]

Marking this change in emphasis, on April 1, 1919, Preuss seconded the notion that "it is capitalism rather than socialism which lies at the root of the social question." Proof of this point was found in the fact that Leo XIII's encyclical *Rerum Novarum* was issued in order to show the injustice of the present social order under capitalism, while the Pope's criticism of socialism was only secondary. Modern capitalism was driven by the pursuit of unlimited acquisition. It was not in conformity with Catholic ideals and therefore "must be condemned as incompatible with the principles of absolute justice."[73] Catholics needed to recognize the "prior evil of capitalism" and make the Church's condemnation of it well known.[74] Two weeks later, Preuss quoted from an editorial that Frederick Kenkel had written for *Die Amerika* that stated that capitalism and socialism are symptoms of the same malignant disease."[75] Preuss reprinted other calls for radical reconstruction, including those culled from European journals such as the Irish publication, *Studies*, and the English Jesuit's organ, *The Month*.

From his wide reading in American and European publications Preuss concluded that "the war has taught the workers in almost every land to assert their human claims" and they were no longer going to accept "an economic system devoted primarily to the making of profit."[76] Since the grievances of the laboring man were just, Catholics must take seriously the Church's social teaching by ending their acquiescence to the status quo and working for the replacement of the capitalist system.[77] Preuss's attack on capitalism was also carried out in the pages of the *Echo* where one of his editorials proclaimed "Capitalism Must Go!"[78] Preuss's campaign against capitalism in both the *Review* and the *Echo* included the promotion of efforts that would mitigate the effects of its worst abuses. One such effort that received favorable notice from Preuss was the employee profit sharing plan practiced by Colonel Patrick H. Callahan at his Louisville Varnish Company. The work of John Ryan continued to receive favorable notices in the *Review* and the *Echo*, though the Social Action Department of the NCWC, which Ryan directed, was subject to mounting criticism. The model of "labor guilds" was also discussed.[79]

The hostility of both the *Review* and the *Echo* toward capitalism, naturally enough, led these journals to take the side of organized labor in its struggle for better wages and conditions during the immediate postwar years. Yet, while Preuss championed the cause of workers against the corporations and the anti-union movement, he maintained a critical attitude toward the leadership of the unions. An editorial that Preuss wrote on the efforts of the corporations to crush the collective bargaining power of unions through the "open shop" drive demonstrates this point. Speaking of the motives of the capitalists, Preuss wrote that if they succeeded, the laborers would be forced to resume "their places as industrial slaves."

> ...Of course Unionism is not without blame. The selfish opportunism of the labor organization dictated throughout by a highly individualistic outlook on life has brought down on their heads the ill will of large sections of society.[80]

Preuss and his contributors found union leaders like Samuel Gompers of the American Federation of Labor lacking in vision and called on the labor movement to choose new leaders. In its present state, the labor movement in America was moribund. It offered no constructive policy, while its tactics maximized conflict at the expense of cooperation. Most important of all from a Catholic perspective, organized labor was fueled by "class antagonism," which, said Preuss, "is just as immoral a form of injustice as any other."[81]

The indifference of most American Catholics to the need for social justice in the United States did not escape Preuss's notice. In surveying the Catholic press, Preuss wondered if its dependence on its advertisers was behind its overall silence on the evils of capitalism, while Catholic papers regularly excoriated socialism.[82] The *Review* also found the clergy strangely silent about the unjust status quo. American bishops and priests had no difficulty speaking out about the injustices in Ireland, an activity that Preuss also engaged in. But when it came to the unjust economic system under which so many suffered at home, the clergy declined to involve themselves in "worldly affairs." Preuss would not let the clergy, which included the vast majority of his readers, off so easily.

> Capitalism is industrial and economic injustice. In its derivative phases it directly influences morals, as witness 'birth control.' Until the great body of the clergy in the United States recognize this serious matter...the Catholic Church will not only not conquer the world...[she] will remain without vital influence even among her children.[83]

An essay Preuss wrote for the *Echo* in 1924 went even further by scoring the American clergy for opposing the evil of artificial birth control while they said little about its economic causes.

> We Catholics do not fulfill our duty by denouncing a state of affairs which places before Catholic parents the choice of heroic conjugal abstinence and the mortal sin of neo-Malthusian birth control. We must work to change the conditions which make it heroic virtue to avoid sin.[84]

Preuss's campaign to make his readers "more critical" reached a new intensity with a series of articles published in the *Review* in June 1921 authored by a "Catholic Laboringman." The first of these four essays, "The Church and the Laboringman," set the tone for the series by levelling severe criticism at the Church and its leaders. Speaking on behalf of his fellow workers, the "Catholic Laboringman" states that the Catholic laborers he knew were increasingly alienated from the Church. To begin with, they found most of the clergy indifferent to their problems. As for the efforts of those priests who were addressing labor problems, their work was seen as "fruitless." Countless articles about wages, hours, and conditions were missing the real problem of the alienation experienced by workers. As a consequence of these factors, Catholic workers were convinced that the Church in America represented "all that is known by the disliked and even hated word, 'Privilege'."[85]

Rebutting the responses to his criticism formed the basis of the "Laboringman's" second article. One critic stated that the "Laboringman's" criticism was "overdrawn." His critic cited the work of John Ryan as an example of the Church's solicitude for workers. The "Laboringman" responded by saying that ninety per cent of Catholic workers had never heard of Ryan and his ideas. Besides, even if Ryan were known to them, what difference would it make? A thousand Ryan's were needed as well as parish based workingmen's organizations to go with them if the Church was going to seriously address the problems of labor. The cause of social reconstruction lacked "intelligent, whole-hearted ecclesiastical action." There were not enough teachers and organizers of Catholic workers. Further, the Catholic press was entirely too complacent in its "smug contentment with existing conditions and an intellectual sloth...To read them one would think we were living in the millennium without a single trouble..."[86]

A third article, "The N.C.W.C. and the Demands of Our Catholic Laboringmen," contended that the Church in America had been co-opted by the capitalist system. According to the "Laboringman," American Catholicism was so dependent on "the established order" that it was unwilling to risk its economic survival by supporting Solidarism as an alternative to capitalism. He wondered whether "Catholic laborers are sensing the true Catholic tradition when they demand that something more than the present liberal political methods be applied."

As for Father John A. Ryan of the Social Action Department of the N.C.W.C., since he had become a representative of the American bishops, he was now "hampered by their views and opinions" from fully stating his own beliefs. Ryan's earlier zeal for true social reconstruction had been reduced to the promotion of superficial reforms. "The author of *Distributive Justice* is of a different sociological mind than the director of the Social Action Department of the NCWC. For the former I have nothing but the highest respect."[87] Six months prior to this article, Preuss had blasted the NCWC in the *Echo* for resting on its laurels. Preuss asserted that the Council "continues to live on the reputation of an overrated reconstruction programme which is decidedly incomplete and never had breathed into its dry bones even one life giving breath."[88]

The next article in the *Review* ascribed to the "Catholic Laboringman" challenged the reputation of another of the American Church's "labor priests," Father Joseph Husslein, S.J. A member of the staff of the Jesuit weekly, *America*, Husslein enjoyed a reputation as an American Catholic social thinker that was second only to Ryan's. In reviewing a recent book by Husslein, *Work, Wealth, and Wages*, the "Catholic Laboringman" indicated that he had little use for his ideas. He condemned Husslein's book as a compendium of "palliatives and cheap nostrums" that were no different from "those offered by non-Catholic liberal economists." The "Laboringman" ridiculed the very notion of "reform by legislation programmes" and stated that the faith that would-be reformers placed in politics was "unwarranted." The "Laboringman" even blasted the *Central Blatt and Social Justice*, edited by Frederick Kenkel, for the favorable notice it had given to Husslein's "Catholicized Liberalism." He closed his essay by calling on the *Review* to "keep the insurrection alive" by promoting "Catholic radicalism."

> It is time that the Catholic Radical come to the front, uncover himself, and stand square to all comers. The Liberal rather than the Radical will bring the bloody revolution...a break must come in the ranks of our Catholic social reformers and the sooner it comes, the better. [89]

Within a short time, the "Catholic Laboringman" who penned these lines would "uncover himself" and produce his fiery sermons in the *Review* under his own name, Horace A. Frommelt. Some might question the validity of his "nom de guerre," but when Frommelt wrote the "Laboringman" articles he was in fact a worker in a factory, albeit a very well educated one. As for the significance of the articles as an accurate reflection of the opinions of Catholic workers, it can certainly be argued that they are not representative. The cause the articles promoted was probably too intellectual for the average worker. However, Frommelt's essays are significant for representing the radicalism of Preuss's *Review* and his columns in the *Echo*. In rejecting the "Catholicizing Liberalism" of Ryan and Husslein, the *Review* was maintaining its editorial stance that there was a basic contradiction between the Catholic world view and the American way of life.[90]

As an alternative to both capitalistic exploitation and the class antagonism fostered by the labor movement, Preuss joined other German Catholic commentators in Europe and America in promoting a solution based on Catholic social teaching. This was the economic and political philosophy of "Christian Solidarism," which was also being promoted by the Central Bureau of the Central Verein under the leadership of Frederick Kenkel.[91] Preuss offered a summary of Pesch's Solidarism in the *Echo* on November 27, 1924.

> The solidarity demanded by Pesch's system is threefold:
> (a) the solidarity of the entire human race, which involves the abolition of both Capitalism and Socialism, the elimination of class hatred and war, and equal rights for all men and all nations. (b) The solidarity of all the citizens of each state. The State is more than the sum total of its members: it is a moral and organic unity, which has for its ultimate

object the welfare of all its members. To this general purpose all special or particular purposes must be subordinated. The citizens of the State are morally obliged to aid in attaining this object, positively by their labors, negatively, by abstaining from interference with the rights of others or doing anything that may hinder the general welfare. Thus political economy provides the citizens with whatever they need up to their standard of culture.

(c) The solidarity of the members of each trade or profession.

These are the organs of the social body, by means of which it lives and breathes and has its being. To serve its purpose as an organ of the social body, each profession must perform its own function properly, but in due subordination to the general interests of society. The workingman, for instance, is subject to his employer as a helper or an assistant, but not as a mere instrument of production. Labor is not a commodity. Things have their price, but labor has dignity. The members of each vocational group should organize and manage its own affairs independently, but with due regard to the affairs of all others. The unifying consciousness of belonging to the same group and profession must overcome the class struggle. Thus Christian Solidarism stands opposed to Capitalism on the one side and Socialism on the other. Both these systems are extremes, certain to lead to the destruction of society if allowed to develop. Solidarism alone gives to the individual what belongs to the individual and to the State what belongs to the State. The economic processes must not be left to the arbitrary fiat of any individual or group, but must be regulated by the needs of society as a whole and of its individual members. The supply must be made to correspond to the demand. The just price must be enforced by law and production as well as distribution and consumption must be regulated for the best interests of all.

To carry out the ideal social order that Father Pesch has delineated...men must be imbued with Christian principles of justice and charity. If we do not succeed in reconstructing the Christian conscience, he says in a famous passage of his work, all social reform measures will be in vain.[92]

In their advocacy of Christian Solidarism, men like Preuss and Kenkel have been characterized as "alienated utopians."[93] Preuss himself conceded that even some of his contemporaries regarded his support of Solidarism as impractical.

Every now and then someone with a flair for the practical demands of us a social programme which will bring the new era nearer...[But this would be] a useless task comparable to informing a man of a route, the beginning and termination of which he knew not. What does it avail the world to know the means by which it may go from Capitalism to Solidarism...when men for the most part do not yet realize that Capitalism is the cause of so much of their misery...?[94]

Thus Preuss contended that it was the task of Catholic publications like the *Review* and the *Echo* to "make every one of its readers an intellectual factor in the shaping of present day ideas, a force that counts because he or she thinks right and more or less influences the thoughts of others."[95] By doing so they only claimed for themselves the role that a later age would call "consciousness raising." Arthur Preuss believed that if the Church in America would only distance itself from the corrupt capitalist system and devote its energies to the education of workers and farmers in "the Catholic ideals of social justice and statecraft...our liberal friends will come to see that much of our salvation lies right there."[96]

By staking out such a position, Preuss and his allies were not simply rejecting capitalism. They were also resisting the general movement of the Catholic Church in the United States which emerged from the experience of the First World War "with a real sense of belonging to America and a real commitment to American ideals."[97] While most of the intellectual leadership of the Church in America approached the need for social reconstruction with "a new confidence in the congruence of American and Catholic traditions," Preuss remained unconvinced. Preuss maintained that the meliorist position of Catholic liberals was actually creating obstacles to true social reform.

The Catholic Liberal is the real culprit. And unfortunately, he is having his day just now. Wherever we meet him, in the so-called reconstruction programmes, in current literature, or in the field of action, we find him believing in the modern State and pinning his hopes to its destructive methods. Let us take an honest inventory. Let us realize that the modern State must go along with capitalist form of industry, and that to call in the doctrine of State interference in time of necessity will, in the present crisis, lead us into inextricable difficulties. The Catholic Liberals who are directing our present economic thought will some day be recognized as blind leaders.[98]

The fact that the majority of American Catholics did not perceive the fundamentally corrosive nature of capitalism simply confirmed Preuss in the belief that the supposed "congruence" of American and Catholic traditions was really a matter of the former dissolving the latter. William Halsey has written that Catholics were immune to the general American disillusionment with progressive ideals which followed the First World War.[99] Ironically, Arthur Preuss, the arch anti-Americanist, was, at least on this point, more at one with the mind of America than the most of his co-religionists when he rejected their "unwarranted" confidence in progressivism.

IX The Salt of Conservative Progress

"The Latest Outcropping of Americanism"

In his book on the foundation of the National Catholic Welfare Conference, Douglas Slawson has described the movement to establish this organization as "the second phase of Americanism."[1] This is a characterization of the NCWC that Arthur Preuss had made at its outset. Of course, publicly identifying the connection between the Americanist agenda and the thought behind the NCWC was not an academic observation. Within the Church of the twenties, "Americanism" remained an accusation that was not hurled lightly. For this reason, the word does not appear often in either Preuss's private or public comments on the NCWC. However, that he saw similarities between the world views of Americanists and the supporters of the NCWC, there is no doubt.

The two phases of Americanism that Slawson describes, that of the 1890s associated with Hecker, Ireland, Keane, and O'Connell and the later stage, which led to the establishment of the NCWC, can, he says, be distinguished by the "assimilationist" impulse of the former, and the "separatist style" of the latter.[2] This is a distinction that would have been lost on Arthur Preuss. Preuss saw only what Slawson describes as the convergence of the two "phases" around the beliefs that "Catholics made the best Americans and that American Catholics were the best the church had to offer" and that "the principles underlying democratic government were identical with those cherished by the church."[3] While Preuss would certainly agree that "Catholics made the best Americans," he continued to reject its corollary, muted by Slawson, that "Americans made the best Catholics." Preuss could find nothing in American society, past or present, that validated the notion that it was inherently more hospitable to the Catholic world view than any other society. In fact, he found many reasons for arguing the contrary and principal among these was American capitalism. Preuss's campaign against the Americanism of the 1890s indicated his criticism of American society was not directed at its democratic institutions, but at its materialism that made these institutions irrelevant. By the 1920s his critique of America had developed into a complete rejection of its capitalist system. In Preuss's understanding, and that of his associates like Frederick Kenkel, it was capitalism which drove America, not democracy. The repressive measures and ethnic hostility promoted by the government during the war had proven that. Thus the attempt to meld the Catholic world view with that of America, which the Americanists proposed, could only lead to the detriment of the faith. This was the thinking that formed the basis of his opposition to the attempts of the NCWC to take up the cause of American liberal progressivism.

Judged by his few references to it in the *Review*, Preuss's initial reaction to the forerunner of the NCWC, the National Catholic War Council, was one of indifference. Preuss, as has been shown, hated the war and American involvement in it. It is not surprising then that he expended little effort commenting on its prosecution. However, as an ardent Catholic, he was concerned about the care of Catholic servicemen and from time to time praised the work being done for them by the Knights of Columbus and the Central Verein. From his perspective, while the war was being waged, the NCWC was little more than the American bishops' mouthpiece for pro-ally propaganda. Since he was not free to challenge its message, he evidently chose not to speak of it at all.[4]

Preuss apparently had no objection to the continuance of the NCWC after the end of hostilities. His own plea that either the American Federation of Catholic Societies or the bishops themselves establish a "vigilance committee" in Washington to monitor federal legislation affecting Catholic schools indicates that he saw the need for Catholics to unite to protect their interests in education.[5] Still, he paid little attention to the process of transition through which the National Catholic War Council became the National Catholic Welfare Council. His later philosophical objections to the NCWC began as complaints about its practices, and in particular, its relationship with the Catholic press.

Arthur Preuss, as has been shown, had a very elevated notion of what it meant to be a Catholic journalist. For him it was an apostolate, a calling to proclaim the truth of Catholicism. From the perspective of his German background, he saw Catholic journalism as one of the pillars of the Catholic community, along with the family, parish church, and school. To carry out its mission that Catholic press needed to be devout, intelligent and independent. As models of what it meant to be a Catholic journalist, Preuss held up for himself and his readers the examples of the Frenchman, Louis Veuillot, Orestes Brownson, James McMaster, and also his father, Edward Preuss.

With such an exalted notion of the role of the Catholic journalist, Arthur Preuss was frequently disappointed in his "contemporaries." As a consequence of this, even though many of his friends were members, he refused to join the Catholic Press Association. When the Catholic Press Association entered into a partnership with the newly created Press Department of NCWC for the purpose of operating a wire service Preuss regarded the whole business with disdain.

> I know that lot from the Catholic Press Association only too well. There is almost no trace of idealism among them...The Catholic Press Association was a bastard from the beginning and nothing good can come from it... The whole [N.].C.W.C. movement is absolute humbug, or much worse, an attempt to gag the Catholic press.[6]

Still, when the NCWC and the CPA got into a conflict over access to the Press Department's News Service, Preuss allowed himself to side with the Association.[7]

As Preuss had years before supported the efforts to establish a wire service under Catholic auspices, his hostility to the NCWC's attempts to establish a wire service may appear as simple pique. However, he was already concerned that the offerings of the Catholic Press Association's wire service were undermining the character and independence of Catholic journalism as many papers were simply reproducing the wire stories without analysis or comment. It was bad enough that some Catholic journalists had been doing this on their own, but the systemization of this process under the auspices of the NCWC was making the problem much worse. The true Catholic journalist of the past was being replaced by mere functionaries. And by substituting the wire stories for genuine journalism, Catholic papers in America were surrendering their character and independence to a bureaucracy in Washington that was bringing down the Catholic press to "one dead level of mediocrity."[8]

Preuss's criticism of the NCWC News Service was not limited to its effects. He was also deeply concerned about its management. Given his own notion of what it meant to be a Catholic journalist, he was outraged when the News Service was placed under the direction of journalists who had earned their credentials not in service to Catholic journalism, but in the "yellow journalism" financed by William Randolph Hearst. While Bishop William Russell, chairman of the NCWC's Press Department, would crow that in hiring Justin McGrath away from Hearst's newspaper empire, he had "gotten the biggest Catholic journalist of the country," Preuss seethed.[9] That Justin McGrath, and his associate, Michael Williams, were journalists who happened to be Catholic, did not make them Catholic journalists. Indeed, the fact that they had enlisted their talents to support Heart's money-driven "yellow journalism" indicated at least a latent antipathy toward the ethos of true Catholic journalism that was now manifest in the material they were now producing under the name of the NCWC.[10] Further, that the NCWC had hired McGrath and Williams over men who had sacrificed financial security to dedicate their lives to the apostolate of Catholic journalism, was just one more reminder that the American hierarchy had no appreciation for what truly Catholic newspapers should be about. Once again the bishops, through the NCWC, had made an important decision, hiring "the biggest" journalist, according to the superficial values of American society, instead of on the basis of what would best serve the advancement of Catholic truth. Had Preuss known that it had taken the promise of a $15,000 annual salary,(which was 7.5% of the NCWC's annual budget, and roughly equivalent to $73,000 today) to lure McGrath away from the Hearst chain, he would have been enraged.[11]

Preuss's *Review* was also critical of the NCWC's handling of the social question. Preuss himself always retained the highest regard for John Ryan. However, this did not inhibit him from printing articles that were critical of the Social Action Department of the NCWC, which was under Ryan's direction. Horace Frommelt's assertion in the *Review* that Ryan's association with the NCWC hampered him from really speaking his mind on the ills of American society, allowed the *Review* to be critical of the Social Action Department while still speaking respectfully of Ryan.[12] Thus Ryan could be commended personally for his good intentions and his efforts to mitigate social evils, while "the prevailing school of Catholic social economy," of which he was a leading member, could be criticized for its "sterility."[13] This editorial policy of criticizing some of the initiatives of the Social Action Department while praising Ryan appears inconsistent. However, it reflects both Preuss's willingness to publish articles with which he was not always in full agreement, and his abiding respect for Ryan. John Ryan could evidently accept this reality as he was able to continue to praise Preuss's work.[14]

In addition to its criticism of the NCWC's Press Department and some of the initiatives of its Social Action Department, the *Review* also found fault with its attempts to start lay organizations. Subscribing to Solidarism's theory of "organic development" of organizations which was regularly propounded by the Central Verein, Preuss scored the National Council of Catholic Men for being unrepresentative of laymen as it really only existed on paper. The well-known difficulties the NCWC was having in gaining acceptance for the new organization would only continue as it was being imposed from above rather than being allowed to develop according to the actual aspirations of Catholic men.[15] With all of the *Review*'s criticism of the NCWC's activities, the existence of the organization itself was not questioned until, at the request of a few American bishops the Sacred Congregation of the Consistory in Rome moved to suppress the NCWC in February 1922.[16] Having heard that a decree suppressing the NCWC had been sent to all the American bishops the week before, Joseph Schifferli, managing editor of the *Echo*, related to his corresponding editor, Arthur Preuss, his efforts to find out more about the story.

> Have you heard the startling news that the N.C.W.C. and the annual meetings of the American hierarchy have been suppressed by Rome? The rescript is said to have reached all the American Bishops late last week. We have been unable to secure a copy, but Bishop Turner's letter has been seen by a number of priests here. The Bishop declined to permit us to use the information and upon telegraphic inquiry at Washington we were told 'that no official word has reached us on the matter.'
>
> Upon receipt of our telegram Father John J. Burke seems to have telephoned Bishop Turner urging him to compel the *Echo* to suppress the story. Since we could not obtain positive information we have made no reference to the report in this week's number. Evidently, every effort is being made by the Bishops to suppress the account of Rome's action.[17]

The information that Schifferli related to Preuss was fully accurate. The only particular he got wrong was that Father Burke had telegraphed, not telephoned, his request to Bishop William Turner of Buffalo that the bishop "compel" the *Echo* to kill the story.[18] Although the *Echo* was an independent Catholic weekly, its publishers were reluctant to further antagonize Bishop Turner as he was already angered that they were competing against his official diocesan organ, the *Church Union & Times*. For this reason, the *Echo* did not publish a story on the suppression of the NCWC until the news had been widely carried in the secular press.[19]

When the *Echo* finally did break its silence it was to carry an account of the suppression of the NCWC based on a disingenuous statement that Archbishop Michael Curley of Baltimore had made to the secular press on the matter.[20] While Curley sought to give the impression that the American bishops themselves had "decided to end the NCWC" at their meeting the previous September, his dissimulation did not convince Arthur Preuss. Writing in the April 15 issue of the *Review* under the title, "Roma Locuta Est" Preuss stated:

Those who have perused the criticisms of this organization, especially its social action and press departments, will agree that the disparition of this whole expensive and poorly managed post-war apparatus will be a real blessing. Once again, Rome with its superior wisdom has nipped in the bud a movement which, though well intentioned, was ill advised and even dangerous.[21]

In the next issue of the *Review* Preuss offered "we adduce that quite a number of bishops were opposed to the high-handed proceedings of the N.C.W.C." He also made his first association between the NCWC and Americanism in hoping that the organization's suppression "will put an end altogether to the Americanistic tendencies of the Catholic Church in the United States." This article quoted approvingly John Rothensteiner's remarks published in *Die Amerika* that the NCWC "fell by overreaching itself."

Its leaders were so intent on being thoroughly 'American' that they forgot Orestes Brownson's dictum 'that though Americanism does well in the political realm, it cannot be transferred to the Church without heresy and schism.'[22]

As the fight for the survival of the NCWC was carried out in the secrecy of Roman offices, Preuss had little more to say on the matter in the next few months. He did note that some of the American bishops had requested that the decree be rescinded, but he did not believe that the decree would be altered in its essentials. Preuss reported on the efforts of the NCWC to kill the story of the suppression decree, and he maintained that according to the canonists he had consulted, and contrary to what defenders of the NCWC were saying, the decree was in effect, even though it had not yet appeared in the official *Acta Apostolicae Sedis*.[23]

Preuss was provoked to point out once again the Americanist tendencies of the NCWC when a letter written by one of the organization's defenders appeared in the *Nation* on July 26, 1922.

Written by John Hearley, who until recently had been on the staff of the NCWC's Social Action Department, the letter complained about the autocratic nature of the Roman Curia. According to Hearley, American Catholics generously supported the activities of the universal Church but had no representation among the cardinals who guided the Roman Curia. This amounted to "taxation without representation," especially as the members of the Curia were not only "un-American," but frequently "anti-American."[24] The Apostolic Delegate, Archbishop Giovanni Bonzano, was reportedly furious about Hearley's letter.[25] And to the dismay of the NCWC's defenders, Preuss ensured its circulation within Catholic circles by reprinting its substance and appending his own analysis of it.

> [this] elucubration proves that the Americanism solemnly condemned by Leo XIII is not yet dead in this country…the ideas expressed by Mr. Hearly [sic] are widespread and constitute a grave danger to Catholicity in a country where so many are inclined to put 'patriotism' above religion. Vident consules![26]

When, in mid-August 1922, the NCWC News Service released the new decree issued by the Sacred Consistorial Congregation regarding the official mandate of NCWC, the reaction in the Catholic press was remarkably similar to what had occurred when Leo XIII had issued his letter on Americanism, *Testem Benevolentiae*, twenty-three years before. Both the official and unofficial supporters of the NCWC described the new decree as a vindication of its status. Arthur Preuss, on the other hand, writing in both the *Echo* and the *Review*, took a different view. His first response appeared in the *Echo* where he pointed out that according to the latest decree, the NCWC was only a voluntary association of the bishops that had no official standing and that it was not to be identified with the American hierarchy as a whole. Additionally, the new decree limited its activities to the fields of social action and education and therefore the Press Office of the NCWC had no sanction.[27]

In his own journal Preuss went further in emphasizing the restrictive nature of the decree. Under the heading "Rome's Coup de Grace to the N.C.W.C.," Preuss declared that "this decree practically confirms that of last February." The NCWC was to be "shorn of all pretense of officiality." Its name and character were to be changed, and it was excluded from "the purveying of news to the Catholic press." As for the interpretation being given to the decree by the NCWC's supporters,

> Those Catholic papers that pretend to regard this decree as a 'splendid triumph for the N.C.W.C.' are either unable to understand the tenor of a Roman decree or are endeavoring, for some reason, to throw dust in the eyes of their readers.[28]

As it turned out, the episcopal supporters of the NCWC interpreted the "tenor" of the Roman decree in a very liberal fashion that enabled them to resume "business as usual," albeit with a name change from the "National Catholic Welfare Council" to the "National Catholic Welfare Conference." While Arthur Preuss stood by his "strict construction" of the decree, he also recognized that though Rome had spoken, it had done so ambiguously, and was not enforcing any particular interpretation of its words.[29] Consequently, Preuss dropped his public opposition to the existence of the NCWC and concentrated his fire on its questionable activities. Over the next three years Preuss could only fight a rearguard action against the NCWC's incursions into the independence of the Catholic press.[30] The occasion for a new campaign against the NCWC would not arise until the arrival of new issues and new allies in the spring of 1926.

"We Should Talk up as Well as Down"

In trying to define Arthur Preuss's outlook on the issues of the day, it has been convenient to describe them as being "conservative." This is a term that Preuss regularly applied to himself. However, it should be kept in mind that in describing himself as a conservative, Preuss, as always, was thinking in religious, and specifically Catholic terms. Thus, while his support for radical social reconstruction was in conflict with

American political conservatism, it was fully consistent with his views as a conservative Catholic. Conservative Catholics like Arthur Preuss, believed that western society as a whole had been pursuing an ever more errant course since the Protestant revolt when it had rejected the authority of the one true Church. His notion of a just society was one where Christian principles, as expounded by the Roman Catholic Church, animated the lives of individuals, families, the economy, and government. Philip Gleason, in describing the thought of Frederick Kenkel and the leadership of the Central Verein, has called them "alienated utopians."[31] Arthur Preuss was also one of these, and he saw the social criticism that he engaged in through his *Review* as "the salt of conservative progress."[32] For this reason he was able to form friendships and champion causes that reached beyond the bounds of what is now regarded as conservatism.

Perhaps the most important friendship Preuss established in the twenties was with Patrick H. Callahan.[33] It was an improbable association and perhaps for that reason, not an intimate one. Callahan was one of the most prominent Catholic laymen of his generation. From the time that he became president of the Louisville Varnish Company, Callahan emersed himself in public affairs. In 1912, the governor of Kentucky gave him the honorary title of "Colonel" in appreciation for his service to the state.[34] He first attained national recognition in 1914 when he became the chairman of the "Religious Prejudices Commission of the Knights of Columbus," an organization that was largely his creation.[35] This commission was dedicated to two of Callahan's lifelong concerns –responding to anti-Catholic bigotry and fostering better relations with other religious communities.[36] By the time of the American entry into World War I, Callahan's prominence and associations with leaders of the Democratic Party led President Wilson to offer him the post of chairman of the Federal Trade Commission. However, Callahan had already accepted responsibility for organizing the Knights of Columbus' efforts on behalf of Catholic servicemen. He chose to stay at his post as chairman of the Knights "Committee on War Activities" and so turned down Wilson's offer.[37]

It was Callahan's work with the "Committee on Religious Prejudice" that first brought him to Preuss's notice.[38] Four years later, Preuss commented favorably on Callahan's profit- sharing arrangement with his employees and described Callahan as "one of the more progressive employers."[39] This notice led to correspondence between the two men and Callahan quickly became the *Review*'s most generous supporter. Beginning in 1921, Callahan provided Preuss with a financial subsidy in order that an annual subscription to the *Review* could be provided for every American bishop who was not already on Preuss's mailing list.[40] Eventually, Callahan extended his beneficence to cover the costs of subscriptions for Catholic editors and colleges.[41] Concurrent with Callahan's funding of the *Review*, but evidently not contingent on it, the "Colonel" became a regular contributor to the pages of the journal.[42] Callahan had been promoting his views among his friends and associates on topics of the day through circular letters known as the "Callahan correspondence." Writing to a friend, the Catholic journalist Denis McCarthy, probably in late 1922, Callahan stated that he had "just completed arrangements with the *Fortnightly Review* of St. Louis, by far the best journal of Catholic opinion, to carry articles regularly from me."[43] Starting in 1923 Callahan contributed over forty articles and several letters to the *Review* over the next six years.

The collaboration between Arthur Preuss and Patrick Callahan was of mutual benefit. Through Callahan's subsidy, the *Review* was given greater financial stability and was now finding its way to most of the leaders and thinkers of the Church in America, whether they wanted it or not. For his part, by his partnership with Preuss, Callahan had also gained an established medium and a larger audience for his views. By sending the *Review* to every member of the hierarchy, because Callahan believed "we should talk Up as well as Down," both men hoped to influence the policies of the Church in America.[44] Through Callahan's generosity, Preuss's critiques of American Church policies arrived in the mailboxes of every bishop and most of the Catholic editors in the nation.

Likewise, under Preuss's sponsorship, Callahan's views reached not only the bishops and editors, but also a few thousand priests who had always formed the bulk of the *Review*'s subscribers. Callahan saw to it that the *Review* found its way into non-Catholic circles as well by having Preuss print an additional hundred copies of every issue that contained one of Callahan's essays which the Colonel then sent to his prominent friends and associates. Sometimes Callahan would attach a note to these copies of the *Review*, asking the recipient to subscribe to the journal.[45]

The articles of his that Callahan was so interested in circulating concerned primarily the question of religious prejudice in America. Of the forty-three articles that Callahan wrote for the *Review* between 1923 and 1927, thirty-two of them had this issue as their subject. Based on his experiences with the Commission on Religious Prejudice, the Catholic Laymen's Association of Georgia, and the Catholic Conservation Council of Louisville, Callahan offered the readers of the *Review* a strategy for dealing with anti-Catholicism. The cornerstones of Callahan's program were unified action, under lay control, on a local basis through personal contact with the offending parties.[46] Callahan also wrote a series of articles on how politicians regularly used religious prejudices to advance their own interests based on his observations at the Democratic National Convention of 1924, where religious prejudices were manipulated in such a way that both Callahan's friend, William McAdoo, and the "Catholic candidate," Governor Al Smith, were prevented from receiving the nomination for president.[47]

Callahan's position on anti-Catholicism was much more irenic than that of Arthur Preuss and his other contributors. During the mid-twenties, when the Ku Klux Klan was enjoying a resurgence built largely on anti-Catholic bigotry, voices other than Callahan's continued to sound the alarm in the pages of the *Review*.[48] These contrasting views on how to interpret and respond to anti-Catholic bigotry within the pages of the *Review* certainly increased interest in the journal as a medium of Catholic opinion. Not all of the *Review*'s readers were enamored with Callahan's non-aggressive approach to bigotry, but he was challenging them to rethink their answers to the problem.[49]

The other articles Callahan had published in the *Review* dealt with the social question and the Catholic peace movement in which he played a prominent role.[50] Preuss also published some of his comments on reforming the Knights of Columbus that Callahan requested be published anonymously.[51] Callahan's collaboration with Preuss brought other writers to the *Review*, such as Benedict Elder, editor of the Louisville diocesan paper, Denis McCarthy, the noted Boston journalist, and the retired diplomat, William Franklin Sands. Even before he had become actively involved in the *Review*, Callahan had described Preuss's journal as "the *New Republic* of the Catholic periodical press."[52] Though the *New Republic* was a decidedly liberal journal, Preuss appreciated Callahan's compliment to the intellectual standards of his *Review*. By his own involvement, and through enlisting his friends to write for the *Review*, Patrick Callahan did much to heighten those standards while at the same time broaden its appeal.

What makes the partnership between Arthur Preuss and Patrick Callahan so remarkable is that they approached the question of being Catholic in America from completely contrasting viewpoints. This contrast was manifested in one of the first essays that Callahan contributed to the *Review* in which he wrote of the American character that "any distinctive American note is essentially Catholic." As for relating to non-Catholics, Callahan offered that there is "much difference between asserting the Catholic note and insisting that it is American, and asserting the American note and showing that it is Catholic."[53] Callahan held this position because he believed, in contrast to Preuss, that anti-Catholicism was out of keeping with the true American mind-set, and if exposed to the American people for what it was, would be repudiated.[54]

These were Americanist views that, when uttered by others, had often earned a rebuke from Preuss. However, Callahan was such a good and generous man that Preuss not only tolerated his Americanist views, but even published them. Callahan, for his part, had a deep appreciation for Preuss's courage in stating his opinions, although he did not always agree with them. In addition to promoting the *Review* with enthusiasm and generosity, Callahan also sought to cultivate Preuss as a personal friend. He invited Preuss to vacation with him, and gently chided the editor for his abstemious diet. Callahan would also visit Preuss and Frederick Kenkel when in St. Louis.[55] Preuss and Callahan amicably differed on a number of the issues of the day. Callahan was a prominent member of the Knights of Columbus, an admirer of Woodrow Wilson, a close friend of William Jennings Bryan and a supporter of William McAdoo at the Democratic convention of 1924. He was also an avid prohibitionist, a supporter of the Child Labor Amendment, hostile to labor unions, and a supporter of the National Catholic Welfare Conference.[56] Preuss took the opposite position on each of these issues and had little use for either Wilson or Bryan, and he regarded McAdoo's defeat as "a deliverance."[57] The two men did have in common their belief in the Church's teaching role and as a defender of human rights. They both opposed laissez-faire capitalism, although Callahan was willing to extend government control over the private sector while Preuss was not.[58] Finally, Callahan was quite opposed to Catholic "separatism," while Preuss supported it in principle, if not always in practice. That Preuss and Callahan were able to work together despite their differences is simply a testimony to their mutual devotion to Catholicism and their willingness to recognize what was best and noblest in each other.

"The Negro Belongs to Us"

A cause not normally associated with a conservative mind-set that Arthur Preuss continued to promote in the twenties was that of African-Americans. Preuss had long spoken out against the violence committed against "Negroes," and he had encouraged the Church in America to be active on their behalf. These protests became more insistent in the twenties when the nation as a whole was becoming more sensitive to racial justice. Preuss's awareness of the problem, and in particular the poor record of American Catholics in this regard, was undoubtedly heightened by his friendly association with numerous priests of the

Society of the Divine Word. The Society established a seminary for the training of black priests in Mississippi in 1921.[59] Also, Preuss had been an enthusiastic supporter of the Catholic Church Extension Society from its inception and promoted its work among blacks and Indians.[60] Additionally, Preuss received and published materials from the Federation of Colored Catholics and its President, Thomas Wyatt Turner.[61]

In taking up the cause of blacks in America, Preuss had two points of focus. The first centered on the injustices that were regularly imposed on black citizens. Citing the dire poverty of blacks in the South, Preuss remarked that it was clear "that slavery was not done away with by the Civil War."[62] As for the discrimination and violence directed at blacks, Preuss prophesied that "this nation will have to suffer severely someday for the crimes it has committed against the black race." Speaking of the white-supremacy movement, Preuss opined that

> We have never been able to find an heavenly edict making the white race masters of the world. [Further] the white race has mighty little to be taken away from it to the benefit of the taker.[63]

The second feature of Preuss's treatment of the "Negro Question" was his insistence that the Church had much to offer blacks and that their conversion to Catholicism was of the utmost importance.

> Negroes are beginning to realize that the hope of interracial peace does not lie in segregation but in closer unity, greater cultural sympathy, spiritual tolerance and human freedom. That unity, sympathy, tolerance and liberty can be attained...if the colored people of America will embrace the Catholic religion and live up to it. Just now...the field appears ripe for Catholic missionary work among American Negroes.[64]

In the *Review*, Preuss advocated fair treatment in the Church for those blacks who were already Catholics. He did this primarily by letting them and their advocates relate their experiences of injustice in the pages of the *Review*. Sometimes this was done in articles, more often as letters to the editor. In either case, Preuss persisted in allowing just criticism of American Catholic indifference to blacks to be aired. Of primary concern were the efforts of the Society of the Divine Word to establish a seminary for black aspirants to the priesthood; they received continuous support.[65] Preuss also gave notice to the practice of discrimination within the Church. An article by Father D. J. Bustin on the exclusion of black sisters from the Catholic University's summer school program, that originally appeared in *Our Colored Missions* magazine, was carried on November 15, 1921. Through the *Review*, Bustin's criticism of "ostrichlike churchmen," who act in an "uncatholic" manner toward blacks out of fear of white bigots, was mediated to Preuss's clerical subscribers who might not have ever seen it otherwise.[66]

Likewise, when Thomas Wyatt Turner wrote of the "Experiences of Colored Catholics," in April 1926, through Preuss's "conservative progressivism," and Patrick Callahan's largess, the story reached all the American bishops, a couple thousand priests, numerous Catholic editors and colleges, and most certainly some of the authorities in Rome. Then there were the plaintive letters of priests and laymen who decried the discrimination that was driving black Catholics out of the Church by barring them from its colleges. One black Catholic college student wrote to Arthur Preuss to thank him for his "sympathy for my race," as it relates to its education."[67]

Preuss's motivation in prodding the Church to do right by black Catholics and for blacks in general was, as in all his work, the belief that Catholics were duty-bound to extend the benefits of the faith that they had received. Preuss's friend and longtime contributor, Albert Muntsch, S.J., summed up well the progressive attitude that the *Review* had taken toward blacks from the time of the journal's inception.

The Negro belongs to us. Too long have we neglected him. We needlessly imagined that it was the proper thing to admire what some people call the Negro's wit and comedy, but there was little attempt made to look upon him as a desirable member of the true Church of Christ. Fortunately, this unjustifiable attitude in undergoing a change…The Catholic Church has as large and urgent duty towards our brethren of the Colored race right here among us as it has toward the people of China and Japan.[68]

"It's the Mass That Matters"

Arthur Preuss's participation in the movement to promote more frequent reception of Communion was discussed in a previous chapter. The focus on more frequent reception of the Eucharist gradually developed into reflection about the importance of the Mass as a whole, which in turn was connected to the study of the historical development of the liturgy.[69] As an avid reader of both European and American journals, Arthur Preuss was well aware of the reawakening of the liturgical sense in Catholic life. Commenting on an article in an American Catholic paper that stated that attendance at the Forty Hour's devotion was the best test of a parish's spiritual fervor, Preuss published the following rejoinder, beginning his reply by quoting a Canadian bishop.

'It's the Mass that matters', and no better test can be made of the religious fervor of any parish than by inquiring into the attendance of the people at Mass, especially in that full sense in which it was understood in the olden time, when all partook of the Sacrament of the Holy Eucharist as often as they attended the offering of the Sacrifice.[70]

In the early twenties various articles in the *Review* began to call for a change in the approach to the Mass. A two-part article published in the fall of 1922 asked, "Why is Frequent Communion Declining?" The article, citing a German Jesuit, Joseph Kramp, S.J., suggested that "the exaggerated and unnatural devotions" associated with the Eucharist were to blame for the decline.

Is it possible to bring poor, weak, human nature daily, or even frequently to the heights of intense spiritual enthusiasm and at the same instant to a groveling sense of its unworthiness and complete degradation? Are communion devotions as used by the faithful, suited as means to an end?…Are the prevailing communion devotions of the faithful psychologically possible?[71]

Kramp then went on to relate the history of Eucharistic practices in the Church beginning with their Scriptural basis. This account relates the now well known tale of how both the people and the reception of Communion became separated from the liturgy through the course of the centuries. The author concluded by stating,

> The difficulties that arise in frequently communicating will entirely disappear if Communion is made as an integral part of the Mass; if it is looked upon as nourishing our spiritual lives, rather than as a reverencing of the Eucharistic Christ; if the mind of the Church is followed as regards the 'devotions' of the Mass and Communion.[72]

The publication of this article led to a renewed discussion of the question why the Eucharistic fast was being "allowed to stand for so long a time between the needy soul and the source of Grace?"[73] Preuss also noted the new books being published on the liturgy by the German priests Odo Casel, O.S.B. and Romano Guardini, and hoped "that the movement will be transplanted to English-speaking countries." An experiment in reading from the Gospels in the vernacular also received a positive report.[74]

On October 15, 1923, Preuss published a front-page article entitled "The Liturgical Movement," noting its progress in Europe and calling it a "providential phenomenon." The goal of the liturgical movement was described as bringing "the faithful back to the liturgy of the Church as the source of their private devotion...to rouse their interest and to induce them to take an intelligent and active part in it." Invoking the authority of Pius X's decrees, the article charges the *Review*'s priest readers to recognize that the pope's reforms

> ...are a forcible appeal to our conscience to effect through the Liturgy a living union of the people with Christ. The Liturgy creates a true Christianity...Therefore, we must restore union with Christ by opening

to our people the treasures of the Sacred Liturgy.[75]

These articles show a noticeable progression in thinking about the role of the Eucharist in the lives of Catholics. The previous description of the Eucharist in almost exclusively medicinal terms was being broadened to include other more positive themes. A Scripturally based approach was being used to stress that the Eucharist is intended to bring about the recipients' communion with the person of Christ and as nourishment for the spiritual life. As for the liturgy, the preoccupation with private devotion was giving way to the communal aspect of the Eucharistic sacrifice. Additionally, these articles radiate an enthusiasm for the potential power of the liturgy to transform the world.

> Who does not see the glorious possibilities of the Liturgical Movement? There are those who fondly believe that this movement will eventually effect the redemption of the world from its present day multiform and most lamentable degradation. Fiat, fiat![76]

Subsequent articles suggested that true reverence for the Eucharist would be protected by distributing Communion within the context of the rite and by involving all the participants in the liturgy in "praying the Mass." There were articles on how the "Missa Recitata" was to be conducted and where to obtain the books for congregational use.[77] Frequently these articles would carry spirited testimonials to the power of the new liturgical expression. In an article published on November 15, 1923, Arthur Preuss published a third-person account of attending a "Missa Recitata" in a convent.

> The loving enthusiasm and devout understanding with which Sisters, novices and candidates followed the sacred action at the altar contrasted favorably with the irrelevant devotions and hymns in vogue elsewhere. There vividly came to him the realization of our poverty in spite of infinite riches. His soul was gripped with an intense yearning that at least our seminary and college directors might comply with the wish of the saintly Pius X. In our zeal for holy Communion, blessed as it is

forever, let us not lose sight of the Eternal Sacrifice, of which Communion is but a part and the reward.[78]

Additional articles would return to the notion of Mass and Communion as union with Christ. "[Christ] wishes that we eat [His] disposition into our being...and thus become living images of Himself so that our lives appear more and more a visible revelation of Christ on earth."[79]

Many of the articles that Preuss published on the liturgy were taken from essays originally written in German and adapted by Father John B. Kessel for circulation in the *Review*.[80] When the liturgical movement began to spread to the United States, American authors started to produce their own essays on the liturgy for the *Review*. In 1926, while in the process of founding the journal, Orate Fratres, an activity Preuss warmly supported, Virgil Michel, O.S.B. contributed book reviews and articles on the liturgy, as well as on Thomistic philosophy, to the *Review*.[81] Martin Hellriegel, a friend and fellow German Catholic from St. Louis, proclaimed in the *Review* that the new focus on the liturgy was an apostolate that sought "to lead the faithful to active participation in the liturgy...a most potent instrument in the hands of the Church for the renewal and perfection of Christian piety...."[82]

There are many other examples that demonstrate that Arthur Preuss was enthusiastic in his support of the liturgical movement.[83] That he would give the liturgical movement such support is really no surprise. First of all, it appealed to his appreciation for the importance of beauty in Catholic life and worship. Ever since Pius X's decree on the reform of liturgical music the pages of the *Review* had sung the praises of Gregorian chant and had endorsed congregational singing at Mass.[84] Second, the liturgical movement appealed to his own religious sensibilities by promoting a return to a Christocentric spirituality, unencumbered by the accretions of exaggerated popular devotions.[85] Third, the liturgical reforms were being promoted by the Catholic elite, priest-professors, and lay intellectuals, partially in response to the new emphasis on the liturgy being promoted by the Holy See. These were men and women of learning and imagination, far different from the blustering brick-and-mortar prelates Preuss often contended with.[86] Some of the leaders of the movement, like Virgil Michel and Martin Hellriegel, had come to be his friends.[87] Then too, on a deeper level, the liturgical movement, by making the connections between worship, work, and social justice, encouraged an integrated Catholic world view, a cause to which Preuss had long been devoted. Finally, the liturgical movement was unabashedly Catholic and shared with Preuss the insight that only the Church was capable of transforming the "lamentable degradation" of the modern world.

X   "There Are a *Few* Good Men"

"An Unholy Arrangement"

At the end of the First World War, when the American bishops were pondering the future status of the National Catholic War Council, a principal factor in their determination to continue its operations was their belief that Catholics in the United States needed a collective voice to speak for them on issues related to education. Also, when the NCWC was threatened with dissolution in 1922, its defenders predicated its continued necessity largely on its role as the collective voice of American Catholics against threats to their parochial school system.[1] Such an organization was needed as American society as a whole had been forced to reevaluate its system of education as a result of its glaring weaknesses which became painfully apparent at the time when the nation mobilized for war.[2] Additionally, there was a concern on the part of many that the nation's inefficient system of education was not sufficiently "Americanizing" immigrants.

With a large, independent school system of their own, American Catholics quite naturally observed the discussion of educational reform with some apprehension. Arthur Preuss was one of those, along with the German Catholic community in general, the Catholic Educational Association, and the Society of Jesus, who perceived early on the incipient dangers for the Church in America lurking on the fringes of the educational reform movement.[3] The anxiety of those like Preuss who regarded the education reform movement with alarm was threefold. First, the movement for improving education had embraced the agitation to eliminate foreign-language instruction, particularly German, from American schools, both public and private. In doing so, the education reform movement was pursuing a policy of aggressive Americanization of immigrants, which was something conservative Catholics had always opposed. Second, the advocates of educational reform desired a strong role for the federal government in implementing the proposed reforms through the establishment of a Department of Education in Washington. The "federalization" of education was seen as a triple danger. On the philosophical level, it raised the specter of further government infringement on the rights and responsibilities of parents for the education of their children. Practically speaking, it would also mean that more of the tax money of American Catholics would be allocated for the support of the public school system, that many of them rejected. And on the level of perception, at least for German-Americans, federal involvement in education raised many concerns. German-Americans held the federal government largely responsible for encouraging the ethnic hatred that had led to their persecution during the war. A final reason why there was strong opposition to the education reform movement among some American Catholics was the fact that the strongest proponents of the movement, the National Education Association, the Scottish Rite Masons, and assorted nativist groups, made no secret of their hostility toward Catholic schools.[4]

It is no surprise then that Arthur Preuss was quick to sound the alarm when the forces promoting educational reform coalesced around the proposal to create a federal Department of Education. Preuss published three articles in the last half of 1918 opposing a heightened role for the federal government in education. The last of these three articles, "A Plot Against Our Schools," which was republished in at least two other papers, called on either the American bishops or the American Federation of Catholic Societies to establish a "vigilance committee" in Washington to protect Catholic interests from intrusive federal legislation.[5] The "vigilance committee" that was eventually established by the American bishops was the Department of Education of the National Catholic Welfare Council. In 1926, after what he regarded as the failure of the NCWC's Department of Education to represent Catholic interests on education, Arthur Preuss perhaps regretted that he had ever suggested the need for such an organization.

Prior to this time, while Preuss regularly criticized the NCWC's News Service and Social Action Department, and its sponsorship of the National Council of Catholic Men, its efforts in the field of education had received occasional commendations in the pages of the *Review*.[6] The

NCWC's Department of Education had some success as it had not only led the legal challenge against an Oregon law that was detrimental to Catholic schools, it had also helped to block congressional legislation that would have established a federal Department of Education.[7] However, Catholic opposition to increased federal involvement in education was not monolithic. A number of bishops and other Catholic leaders were concerned that an across-the-board condemnation of such measures might fuel the flames of the anti-Catholicism that was already on the rise in the early twenties. Additionally, as Arthur Preuss and other Catholic conservatives would soon discover, their philosophical opposition to federal in involvement education was not shared by the staff of the NCWC or their sponsors among the American episcopate.

For Arthur Preuss, the Central Verein, and other conservative Catholics, their opinions regarding relations between Church and state, as well as their experience of federal excesses, precluded them from having a positive attitude toward any increased involvement of the federal government in education. But for liberal Catholics in America, those who supported a strong role for the government in social reform, the prospect of the "federalization" of government was not all bad. As early as 1919, Father Edward Pace, vice-rector of the Catholic University of America and the first executive secretary of the NCWC's Department of Education, advised Cardinal James Gibbons that a more active federal role in education might actually be a benefit to Catholic schools. Pace made this recommendation because he believed that the results of federally sponsored standardization of testing might actually demonstrate the superiority of Catholic schools. Further, observing attempts in Michigan, Nebraska, and Oregon to legislate compulsory public education, Pace maintained that the establishment of greater federal control over education "might be the only salvation for the Catholic schools."[8] The decision of the United States Supreme Court of June 1, 1925, overturning the Oregon school law eliminated the need for the Catholic school system to seek its "salvation" through "federalization." Still, even with the Court's decision, not all of those who were active in opposing the Oregon law were convinced that the principle of state supervision of the Catholic schools had been rejected. The Rev. John J. Burke, general secretary of the Administrative Committee of the NCWC, for one was of this opinion. Thus, opposition to increased federal involvement in education remained "soft" at the NCWC and among the American bishops.[9]

Reflecting the ambivalence of the NCWC toward increased federal involvement in education, its Administrative Committee in September 1925 decided to recommend to the American bishops that they remain neutral on the latest legislative effort of the National Education Association to establish a federal Department of Education as well as on a proposal by President Coolidge to strengthen the already existing federal Bureau of Education. The members of the Administrative Committee, under the chairmanship of Archbishop Edward Hanna, took this position on the NEA bill because it did not include provisions for federal funding of education with its consequent supervision of local schools. They also believed that the research activities of the proposed department would be beneficial to both Catholic and public schools alike. The Administrative Committee's benign interpretation of the NEA measure is somewhat surprising considering that Father James H. Ryan, the current executive secretary of the NCWC's own Department of Education, had reported to the Committee that in sponsoring the bill, "The NEA was in reality conceding nothing as it planned to seek federal subsidies once it had succeeded in establishing a Department of Education." Indeed, "the aim of the legislation remained the same: federal control of education."[10]

This position of neutrality that the Administrative Committee of the NCWC recommended was eventually adopted by the fifty-six bishops who gathered at the hierarchy's annual meeting in September 1925. The fact that only half of the American bishops attended this meeting contributed to the ensuing confusion regarding the actual position of the Church in America on the proposed NEA bill. The bishops who were present at the annual meeting had instructed Father Burke, as the General

Secretary of the Administrative Committee of the NCWC, that in regard to both the NEA bill and the President's proposal, they wanted them opposed informally, but with "no propaganda against the measures."[11]

The subsequent inactivity of the NCWC against the proposed measures, and the silence of its Department of Education, gave rise to criticism that the General Secretary was not carrying out the bishops' wishes on the matter. The real problem, however, lay with the instructions Burke had received. The bishops choice of only informal opposition to the proposed measures had resulted in the publicly perceived inactivity of the Church against the bills. Furthermore, the bishops had ensured that a controversy would erupt as "neither Congress, the Catholic press, especially *America* magazine, nor Archbishop Curley, who missed the [bishop's] convention, knew that the hierarchy had muted, not abandoned, its opposition to federalization."[12]

The Jesuit weekly *America* was the first Catholic press organ to catch wind of the bishops' new policy of "muted opposition," that it interpreted as the acquiescence of the NCWC to the federalization of education. Under the leader, "An Alarm and a Warning," published on January 2, 1926, the editors of *America* reported an "ugly rumor" that a "political deal" had been struck to secure passage of the NEA sponsored Curtis-Reed bill to establish a federal department of education.[13] Some readers inferred that the editorial's query, "Are the guardians of our interests now betraying them?" was a reference to failure of the NCWC to oppose the measure. Cardinal O'Connell and Archbishop Curley also began to draw unfavorable conclusions from the silence of the NCWC on the bill. However, it was only when Burke himself concluded that the policy of not opposing the NEA proposal publicly was being interpreted in Congress as a sign of Catholic support for the measure, that the NCWC began to actively oppose the Curtis-Reed Bill.[14]

When the congressional hearings on the Curtis-Reed Bill opened on February 24, 1926, the NCWC was ready to join the public opposition to the bill. Father Burke himself had recruited forty-five educators, both

Catholics and non-Catholics, to testify against the Bill. Among those who testified against the bill were two representatives from the NCWC, William Montavon from the Conference's Legal Department and Charles Dolle of the National Council of Catholic Men. In addition to mounting formidable opposition to the Curtis-Reed bill, the Department of Education of the NCWC, at the urging of Edward Pace, decided it was also advisable to offer an alternative proposal. This decision was based on the belief that a sound alternative measure would not only ensure the defeat of the Curtis-Reed proposal but also gain for the Catholic schools the benefits of a stronger U.S. Bureau of Education.[15] This alternative measure would enable the federal government to offer the same services as proposed in the Curtis-Reed Bill without establishing a department of education and with a much smaller appropriation. Ghost-written by William Montavon, and carrying the NCWC's promise of support, this alternative bill was introduced into Congress by Senator Lawrence Phipps on March 11, 1926. The NCWC issued a prepared statement over the signature Archbishop Austin Dowling, chairman of the Conference's Department of Education, on March 15, 1926, that praised the new "Phipps Bill" as "a forward looking document" and "statesmanlike." Making good on its promise of support, the NCWC, under Burke's direction actively promoted the Phipps Bill and, utilizing Senator Phipps's franking privileges, sent copies of the bill to every bishop, the entire Catholic press, and several hundred Catholic educators.[16] This two-pronged strategy effectively side-tracked the Curtis-Reed bill. However, the testimony of the two witnesses chosen by the NCWC to testify against the Curtis-Reed bill, and its support for the Phipps measure, opened the Conference to charges that it misrepresented its competence to speak for American Catholics and that it was either ignorant of, or indifferent to, their opinions.

Through the *Review*'s many "exchanges," including that with *America*, Arthur Preuss was undoubtedly aware of the controversy surrounding the NCWC's handling of the Curtis-Reed bill. Further, as the corresponding editor of the *Echo*, he would have been familiar with the NCWC's reporting of the matter as the Buffalo weekly subscribed to the Conference's News Service. Still, for all of that, Preuss published only one passing reference to the Curtis-Reed bill in the *Review* prior to May 15, 1926.[17] Perhaps he was only saving up his ammunition. In any case, as soon as Preuss took up the controversy his charges landed like a "bombshell" on the NCWC.

Under the title, "By What Authority?" Preuss found William Montavon statement at the Curtis-Reed hearings that he represented American Catholics cause enough to reopen the question of the NCWC's status as the voice of Catholics in the United States. Preuss was incensed that while Montavon was unknown to ninety-nine per cent of American Catholics, he testified before the congressional hearing that he was appearing as the spokesmen on the Curtis-Reed bill for all Catholic citizens in the country.

> Need we insist on the gravely damaging nature of these statements made before a joint committee of the Senate and the House of Representatives by a man who has no more right to speak for you and me than has the ex-Hearst journalist who perpetrates the N.C.W.C. weekly news sheet or the Rev. John J. Burke, C.S.P., who writes dictatorial letters to Catholic editors and their contributors 'in the name of the episcopal chairman of this board.' The Holy Office was correctly informed when it condemned the whole idea of the N.C.W.C., and we shall probably live to rue the fact that its original decree was not put into effect.

Quoting the decree on the NCWC issued by the Consistorial Congregation in July 1922 that "all should know that this organization is not to be identified with the hierarchy of the United States," Preuss closed his attack with a devastating question.

> If it is not to be identified with the hierarchy, and is not elected by the laity, as Mr. Montavon admits, just for whom or for what does it stand, and what right has Mr. Montavon or any other member of that executive board of his to appear before official bodies like a joint congressional committee and make statements which gravely compromise the Catholic cause?[18]

Preuss's criticism of Montavon's testimony struck a responsive chord. Even Catholics who had no quarrel with the NCWC were concerned that Montavon's claim to be the hierarchy's chosen representative of all American Catholics lent weight to the arguments of anti-Catholics who insisted that the Catholic people were slavishly subject to their bishops even in public matters. That Preuss's criticism of Montavon's posturing as *the* Catholic lay spokesman was shared by others is indicated by a letter that John Cochran, assistant to Congressman Harry Hawes of Missouri, wrote to Frederick Kenkel:

> Mr. Preuss puts it admirably, "By What Authority?" I have no objection to legitimately formed organizations whatever their lawful purpose. But 'paper' bodies or bodies that speak without actual authority, however laudable their purposes, get us all in trouble sooner or later. I have no quarrel with either the N.C.W.C. or the N.C. of C.M. If they actually represent us then we should be given a voice in their deliberations, or certainly in the selection of those who consider these important matters. In my opinion both of these organizations have lost strength recently by their actions on various subjects.[19]

Arthur Preuss also wrote to Kenkel concerning the response to his essay:

> From a priest who visits the N.C.W.C. offices at Washington frequently I hear that the 'By What Authority?' article 'fell like a bombshell into their camp' and 'may have far reaching consequences.' I wonder what these will be? If I had my way about it, I would clear out this whole nest of ignoramuses and hypocrites (of course there are a *few* good men like Dr. John A. Ryan among them, but they seem to be powerless).[20]

Preuss's letter to Kenkel was occasioned by a letter Preuss himself had received from a lawyer in Washington named James R. Ryan, who had been on the legal staff of the NCWC for five years until his resignation in January 1926.[21] Ryan had written to Preuss to commend him on his article and to request twenty-five copies of the piece "to place in the hands of persons much interested" in the matter. Ryan also volunteered the information that the NCWC, "or rather Father Burke had decided to remain neutral" on the Curtis-Reed bill. "I suspect, but cannot prove that there was a 'deal' between certain officials of the N.C.W.C. and some of the proponents of this character of legislation."[22]

According to Ryan, the NCWC was driven into its "perfunctory opposition" to the Curtis-Reed bill only when the editors of *America* had written on the betrayal of Catholic interests by the NCWC in its January 2, 1926, issue. Ryan suggested that part of the alleged 'deal' included the deliberate absence of both Father Burke, as General Secretary of the NCWC, and Father James H. Ryan, executive secretary of its Department of Education, at the congressional hearing on the Curtis-Reed bill. Instead, Montavon, "who has demonstrated his incompetency to handle this matter," was sent as the principal representative of the NCWC. Ryan contended that Montavon was unqualified both to represent the NCWC or even to hold his present position on its staff. Ryan pointed out that Montavon had been hired by Burke to direct the NCWC's Department of Laws and Legislation, even though he was not even a lawyer. Further, as Montavon had spent most of the previous ten years in South America as a representative of "oil interests" he could not justly claim to be knowledgeable of "the Catholic viewpoint in this country." In Ryan's view, the NCWC's handling of the Curtis-Reed Bill had been devised in order to lay the foundation of the Conference's subsequent endorsement of the Phipps bill. Ryan advised Preuss to oppose the Phipps bill as it was "every bit a dangerous" to Catholic interests as the Curtis-Reed bill. The Phipps proposal was "only the vestibule to create the Department of Education" that was openly advocated in the Curtis-Reed bill. Ryan closed his letter to Preuss by expressing his admiration and by stating, "if I can be of service to you at any time, you have but to call me."[23]

Preuss's immediate response to Ryan's letter was to send it Kenkel to inquire if the latter knew this former staffer of the NCWC and whether he thought Ryan was reliable. Preuss also asked Kenkel his opinion of the Phipps bill and whether "we ought to fight it?"[24] While Kenkel could not vouch for Ryan's reliability, he did concur with the opinion that the

Phipps bill should be opposed.[25] This Preuss set out to do and in mounting the *Review*'s opposition to NCWC-sponsored Phipps bill, he received the invaluable service of the Conference's disgruntled former lawyer, James R. Ryan. Together, the two men would launch a full-scale challenge to the authority of the NCWC to represent Catholics in America.

James Ryan's first letter to Arthur Preuss would be followed by forty-five others over the course of the next eighteen months. Together they comprise a fascinating record of the two men's collaboration in their systematic attacks on the NCWC. With the information contained in Ryan's first letter, Preuss wrote his own article critical of the NCWC's activities.[26] Soon, however, Ryan was writing articles on the NCWC himself. Preuss would edit Ryan's submissions if necessary and then publish them without attribution or under a pen name. The motive for concealing his authorship of the articles was that Ryan wanted to protect a friend in the NCWC Press Office, Grattan Kerans, who was providing him with inside information. Ryan did not even disclose to Preuss the identity of the "mole" inside the NCWC until it became necessary in order deflect suspicion away from Kerans. This was done by publishing a biting attack on Kerans in the *Review* that had been written by Ryan with the former's approval.[27] When Ryan had to leave Washington to take a job with the U.S. Bureau of Customs in New York, Kerans began to communicate with Preuss directly.

Well before this time, the triumvirate of Preuss, Ryan, and Kerans had broadened their attack on the NCWC to include its involvement in the Mexican crisis, its monitoring of the movie industry, and some of its organizational initiatives.[28] Their criticisms of the Conference's policies in these areas were simply the extension of the basic objections to the NCWC's activities that Preuss had outlined in his article, "By What Authority?" The first of these objections was that the NCWC claimed for itself an authority that it did not have by pretending to represent the American hierarchy and American Catholics.[29] The second objection that Preuss and his collaborators lodged against the NCWC was that not only did the Conference lack the official authority to speak for American Catholics, but its operatives were incompetent and indifferent to the true sentiments of the nation's Catholics. Representatives of the NCWC often gave their support to programs that many Catholics opposed. Further, the organizations that the NCWC sponsored had no support among the Catholic populace and really existed only on paper.[30] The third basic criticism of the NCWC voiced in this series of articles was that the Conference was completely dominated by its General Secretary, John Burke.[31] Douglas Slawson has suggested that James Ryan's attacks on the NCWC may have been due to his resentment at having been passed over for the job of heading the Conference's legal department in favor of Montavon.[32] For his part, Arthur Preuss resented what he regarded as Burke's high-handed treatment of the Catholic press "by sending dictatorial letters to Catholic editors and their contributors" and claiming episcopal authorization to do so.[33]

However, apart from any personal resentment for Burke that Ryan and Preuss may have had, the belief that Burke alone was responsible for the policies and activities of the NCWC was widespread, and even held by many bishops. A month before Preuss's attack on the NCWC in May 1926, Burke had appealed to the seven bishops on the Administrative Committee to make it known that the operations of the Conference were under their "immediate care, attention and direction."[34] Clearly, Father Burke was in an unenviable position. As General Secretary of the Administrative Committee of the NCWC, he was the most visible officer of the Conference and came under fire whenever its decisions were criticized. Still, Burke was far from being the pliant instrument of the hierarchy's collective will.

Even if the bishops on the Administrative Committee were responsible for giving Burke his instructions as the general secretary, the organizational schema of the NCWC ignored one fact. Burke was not only the one to execute the directives of the Administrative Committee, but was also its most important advisor. Thus, Burke and his staff were not just carrying out the bishop's policies they were creating them. A case in point would be the NCWC's decision to offer an alternative to the Curtis-Reed Bill. A member of the NCWC's Department of Education, Edward Pace, responding to Burke's call for action on the Curtis-Reed measure, suggested that the conference offer alternative legislation. The Department of Education, under the chairmanship of Archbishop Austin Dowling, endorsed the idea, and then Burke had Montavon write up the new "Phipps Bill." In the whole process there is no evidence of any episcopal initiative. The bishops involved, Dowling and Archbishop Hanna, chairman of the Administrative Committee, simply gave their blessing to a proposal that originated among the NCWC's staff. Therefore, Burke's characterization of himself as simply the obedient servant of the American bishops was disingenuous. That both outside observers, like Preuss, as well as current and former members of the NCWC staff, like Ryan and Kerans, came to see the Conference as "the play thing of Father Burke," suggests that there was at least a grain of truth in their charges.[35]

Viewing Burke in such a negative light, Ryan and Kerans wrote, and Preuss published their articles on the NCWC with the shared goal of forcing the general secretary's resignation. Ryan had developed a passionate dislike for Burke and believed that the general secretary's leadership of the Conference was placing Catholic interests at risk. Ryan told Preuss that Burke's "vanity, his greed for power, his resentment of counsel, and complete lack of discretion make him a dangerous occupant of his place of power."[36] According to Ryan, during his tenure at the NCWC, the reports of the various departments had "either been prepared or edited by Father Burke...and then signed and read as their own. In many instances important facts have been suppressed." And the American bishops were being presented "a wholly unreliable picture."[37] As an example of this Ryan asserted that Archbishop Dowling had been "decoyed" by Burke into approving the NCWC's "inertia on the Curtis-Reed Bill" and "the espousal of the Phipps Bill."[38]

Ryan was so intent on ousting Burke as the general secretary of the NCWC that he urged Preuss to enlist his episcopal friends to challenge

Burke on the operations of the Conference. Ryan also arranged for an unnamed bishop to carry copies of the *Review* articles on the NCWC to curial officials in Rome.[39] Provocative articles were timed to appear in the *Review* just before gatherings of the American bishops and the National Council of Catholic Men. Ryan concocted letters to the editor of the *Review* that appeared over the pen name "Ignotus." These letters were written in such a way as to give the appearance that they came from a member of the American hierarchy.[40] Ryan even endeavored to capitalize on the grievances that some Mexican exiles had against Burke for the way that the NCWC had involved itself in the Mexican Church's affairs.[41]

Preuss's own position on events in Mexico, where the Church was under attack from the revolutionary government, was no different from that being pursued by the NCWC. For instance, in both the *Review* and the *Echo*, Preuss opposed the position of Catholic militants like Archbishop Curley and the Knights of Columbus who were demanding American intervention. Preuss even suggested on more than one occasion that "sympathy is wasted on a group of co-religionists who have chiefly themselves to blame for the persecution to which they are subjected." Nevertheless, Preuss believed that by getting involved in the Mexican crisis the NCWC was overstepping its competence and compromising the efforts of Church authorities in Rome to come to an agreement with the Mexican government.[42]

James Ryan was distressed early in the campaign against Burke when the Holy See issued an affirmation of the NCWC in August 1926. Though Ryan was tempted "to wash my hands of all Catholic activity," Preuss's admonition that it was Ryan's "duty" to continue his interest in Catholic public questions, persuaded him to carry on.[43] Success seemed possible in early 1927 when Grattan Kerans reported to Preuss that Burke's removal appeared imminent. Kerans was off the mark. However, the criticism of Burke and the NCWC was not without effect both within the NCWC and among the American bishops. In June 1926, Burke felt compelled to try enlist Bishop Joseph Schrembs to refute Preuss's charge that the National Council of Catholic Men really only existed on paper.[44] Then in September 1926, Ryan wrote to Preuss that "the articles in the *F.R.* have brought about a panic at the N.C.W.C. headquarters. Officials of high rank have been scurrying around the country endeavoring to line up bishops in support of the administration." Ryan told Preuss that the decision of the American hierarchy to have a committee of bishops, instead of the staff of the NCWC, write a pastoral letter on the Mexican situation was due in part to the negative impression of the NCWC among members of the hierarchy created by the articles in the *Review*.[45] The critical articles in the *Review* also became an occasion of comment among the staff members of the NCWC and its affiliated organizations. Commenting on the October 1926 convention of the National Council of Catholic Women, Ryan told Preuss that it was "a perfect sewing circle of gab and gossip about the articles in your *Review*."[46]

Father Burke of course survived these efforts to oust him as general secretary of the NCWC and the triumvirate was frustrated in attempting to secure his dismissal. The press office of the NCWC even succeeded in landing a blow on Preuss when one of its former staffers, William C. Murphy, labelled the *Review* as "the enfant terrible" and the "Jersey mosquito of current Catholic journalism" in an article on the Catholic press that appeared in H. L. Mencken's *American Mercury* in December 1926.[47] By January 1928, the collaborative effort of Arthur Preuss, James Ryan and Grattan Kerans dissolved, perhaps a casualty of Kerans' severe illness and Ryan's distance from events in Washington. However, their eighteen-month campaign "for reform in the personnel, policies and procedures of the N.C.W.C." had succeeded in undermining the claims of Conference's staffers to speak for the American bishops and American Catholics in general. Perhaps their efforts had instilled in the Conference's officials a stronger sense of circumspection in regard to their role as functionaries of the American bishops.

In his study of the first decade of the NCWC, Douglas Slawson has likened the Preuss-Ryan-Kerans campaign against the Conference to the opposition it received from Cardinal William O'Connell. Slawson makes this connection based on the supposition that all four men were opposed to the new brand of Americanism that the Conference embodied.[48] However, it seems more accurate to say that the four shared basic misgivings about how the NCWC exercised its authority in the name of the Church and American Catholics. Cardinal O'Connell's aspirations to succeed Cardinal Gibbons as the de facto "primate" of the American church, and his hostility toward the NCWC for frustrating these designs have been dealt with elsewhere.[49] Yet, it should be mentioned, that Arthur Preuss had no use for O'Connell's pretensions and had as early as 1912 questioned the Boston Archbishop's character and criticized his "delusions of grandeur."[50] If, as Slawson suggests, O'Connell saw himself as the successor to Archbishop Michael Corrigan in the fight against Americanism, it was a vision not shared by the late Archbishop's loyal apologist, Arthur Preuss. Given O'Connell's frustrated ambition, his labelling of the NCWC with the error of "Americanism" was perhaps only a useful epithet, which when applied effectively to ecclesiastical rivals could discredit them in the eyes of Rome. This is not to deny that O'Connell had sincere difficulties with the ecclesiology that was being advanced by the NCWC's supporters. But one doubts that O'Connell would have ever raised the issue of the Americanist tendencies of the NCWC if he had succeeded in his goal of controlling the Conference himself.

As for James Ryan and Grattan Kerans, their attacks on the NCWC were quite clearly motivated by their belief that "the Conference had become the play thing of Father Burke." To ascribe philosophical or theological motivations to their actions is to give them a complexity that they did not have. That such larger issues as Americanism did not motivate Ryan and Kerans is indicated by the fact that they employed the word only once in their attacks on the Conference.[51] Additionally, when the campaign against Burke failed, both Ryan and Kerans ceased to write for the pages of the *Review* and their shadowy figures disappeared from record of American Catholicism altogether.

Arthur Preuss was the only one of the four who had no personal motivation for criticizing the NCWC. And it is worth noting that Preuss was most circumspect in raising the issue of Americanism in connection with the NCWC in the years 1926 and '27. The reason for this is related to Preuss's conception of what constituted the real error of Americanism and in his loyal acceptance of decisions made in Rome. It is true that in his first challenge to the NCWC, Preuss had accused the Conference of Americanist tendencies. When the Holy See had apparently dissolved the NCWC in 1922, the efforts by the Conference's supporters to halt the implementation of the decree smacked of Americanism to Arthur Preuss. Later that year, when one of the Conference's defenders and former employees had had the audacity to suggest that the universal Church needed to incorporate into its own workings the principles of American representative government, Preuss penned his only article that explicitly linked the NCWC to Americanism. [52]

Preuss clearly took issue with what he regarded as the NCWC's overly optimistic appraisal of American society, an error that was also characteristic of the Americanist movement of the eighteen-nineties. This caused him to differ sharply with the NCWC's promotion of the Phipps Bill and other measures that, to his mind, exhibited a dangerous naiveté in regard to anti-Catholic biases of American government and society. He also believed that the ambiguous relationship between the NCWC and the American hierarchy was an "unholy arrangement" that often led the Conference's staff, particularly John Burke, to overstep the parameters established for the NCWC by the decree of the Sacred Consistorial Congregation issued in June 1922.[53] However, he accepted, albeit sadly, that by this decree, Rome had approved the existence of the NCWC while seeking to limit its authority. Subsequently, as long as the Conference's supporters refrained from remarks which dissented from Roman policies or asserted a providential view of America and the superiority of American Catholicism, principles that animated the Americanist movement, Preuss's would not subject them to the charge of Americanism. That the NCWC was incompetent as the voice of Catholics in America was reason enough for Arthur Preuss to find fault with it.

"Do We Want a Catholic President?"

The campaign of Governor Al Smith of New York in 1928 for the presidency occasioned the last important controversy of Arthur Preuss's career as a Catholic journalist. As with his previous involvement in the Americanist crisis, the American Federation of Catholic Societies, the First World War, the Social Question, and the founding of the National Catholic Welfare Conference, Preuss again found himself challenging the tendency of his co-religionists to compromise Catholic principles in order to gain acceptance in America.

Al Smith's presidential aspirations and their relation to Catholicism in America had been thoroughly discussed in the *Review* by Patrick Callahan in his series of articles on the 1924 Democratic National convention. Callahan, who had opposed Smith in the Governor's first campaign for the presidency, had cautioned the *Review*'s readers in 1924 to resist being manipulated by devious politicians who deliberately stirred up religious animosities simply to win elections. In October 1926, as Smith's supporters were preparing for the next presidential campaign, Preuss repeated Callahan's earlier warning by stating that "to a careful observer it seems that a good deal of the anti-Smith feeling is being shrewdly manipulated by Gov. Smith's friends."[54] Preuss's point, that Catholics should not be goaded into supporting Smith simply on the basis of his religion would be the *Review*'s constant refrain through the course of the campaign. Preuss questioned whether Smith's election was something American Catholics should hope for. Preuss himself certainly did not think so.

...there is absolutely no need of having a Catholic president in the White House; ...the nomination of a Catholic for the office would unleash all the forces of bigotry and fanaticism in this country, much to our discomfort...If a Catholic is nominated for the presidency –which is improbable– we may expect a campaign which for heat and bitterness will throw all previous campaigns into the shade and may prove the severest test of patience that Catholic Americans have ever been called upon to face.[55]

Preuss lamented the fact that Governor Smith had been cast into the role of being a national representative of the Catholic faith and was playing the part very poorly. Smith's deficiencies on this score were brought to light through his public exchange with Charles Marshall. Marshall, a New York attorney had an open letter published in the *Atlantic Monthly* in April 1927 which contended that as a Catholic Smith could have difficulty in upholding American laws. Marshall challenged Smith as to whether

as a Roman Catholic, you accept as authoritative the teaching of the Roman Catholic Church that in case of contradiction, making it impossible for the jurisdiction of the Church and the jurisdiction of the State to agree, the jurisdiction of the Church shall prevail; whether, as a statesman you accept the teaching of the Supreme Court of the United States that, in matters of religious practices which in the opinion of the State are inconsistent with its peace and safety, the jurisdiction of the State shall prevail; and if you accept both teachings, how do you reconcile them?[56]

When Marshall's letter was published in April 1927, Arthur Preuss was among those who opined that since "Gov. Smith is not a canonist or theologian, but a plain, blunt layman, who knows nothing about the controversies his opponents are trying to entice him into," he should not attempt to answer the challenge but rather, simply stand on his record. Preuss believed that the defense of the Church's teaching on the relationship between Church and State should be left to canonists and apologists.[57] Smith did in fact let "one schooled in the Church law" provide him with a response to the theological aspects of Marshall's challenge. Smith chose as his advisor Father Francis P. Duffy, the decorated war hero and chaplain, "whose patriotism neither you [Marshall] nor any other man will question."[58]

After reading Smith's reply, Arthur Preuss and other educated

Catholics questioned Duffy's explanation of the relationship between the Church's teaching and the conscience of the individual Catholic. Preuss was especially concerned as Smith's reply, which the Governor called "my creed as an American Catholic," was being interpreted as valid for all Catholics in America. The most questionable passages of Smith's "creed" concerned the hypothetical issue of a conflict between Church teachings and the nation's laws.

> ...in the wildest dreams of your imagination you cannot conjure up a possible conflict between religious principle and political duty in the United States, except the unthinkable hypothesis that some law were to be passed which violated the common morality of all God fearing men. And if you can conjure up such a conflict, how would a Protestant resolve it? Obviously by the dictates of his conscience. That is exactly what a Catholic would do. There is no ecclesiastical tribunal which would have the slightest claim upon the obedience of Catholic communicants in the resolution of such a conflict.[59]

Given the seriousness of the question being addressed, it is surprising how poorly formulated Smith's response was, particularly the last sentence. While Smith's reply elicited favorable comments around the country, among Catholics and non-Catholics alike, not all of the Governor's coreligionists were satisfied with his presentation of the Church's teaching. Preuss composed a criticism of Smith's reply that he wanted printed in a late April edition of the *Echo*. However, Joseph Schifferli, managing editor of the paper, felt "reluctantly compelled" to return it to Preuss unpublished. Schifferli explained that while he personally agreed with the substance of Preuss's criticism of Smith's "liberalism," he had been advised by his friends not to publish Preuss's editorial as "the sentiment for Smith is so strong among Catholics here in the East, that it would have done the *Echo* irreparable harm to sound a discordant note at this time."[60]

There is no record of Preuss's response to Schifferli, but he must have been disappointed by the latter's refusal to publish his remarks. By not publishing Preuss's criticism of Smith's reply, even though he professed to agree with it, Schifferli and the *Echo* had fallen sway to the movement that was seeking to make a Catholic cause out of Smith's candidacy. Preuss kept pressing Schifferli to publish some criticism of Smith's reply, which he did in the issue of June 9, 1927, by quoting *America*'s critique of the Governor's response.[61]

For a time, Preuss delayed his attack on Smith's reply in his own *Review*, while reiterating his belief that there were no benefits but only liabilities for Catholics in Smith's candidacy for the office of president.[62] Finally, in remarks appended to a *Catholic World* article on Smith, Preuss stated that Smith's

> reply to Charles C. Marshall has shown Smith to be a dangerous liberal in religion...A fair minded Protestant as president would be infinitely preferable to a Catholic politician saturated with the liberalism so strongly condemned by Pius IX and Leo XIII.[63]

Conservative Catholics like Arthur Preuss were not the only ones who detected an apparent deviation from Catholic orthodoxy in Smith's reply. On September 1, 1927, Preuss quoted a Masonic journal as stating that Smith had "virtually repudiated the papal doctrine of the superiority of the Church over the State...amid the applause of almost the entire nation."[64] Preuss lamented the general acceptance of Smith's position on Church-and-State relations among Catholics, and continued to point out that not all Catholics were behind Smith.[65] The *Review* also carried an essay by William F. Sands that criticized the simplistic nature of Marshall's original challenge.[66]

Smith's "religious liberalism" was again the target of a Preuss editorial published on October 15, 1927. Under the title, "The Liberalism of Gov. Smith," Preuss reprinted an essay by the well-known journalist, Walter Lippmann, that had appeared originally in the magazine *Vanity Fair*. In his preface to the Lippmann essay Preuss explained why he was republishing it.

The real significance of Governor Alfred E. Smith's reply to Charles C. Marshall...seems to have escaped many Catholics. It is that Gov. Smith is a 'Liberal' whose attitude is essentially Protestant.

Preuss then quoted Lippmann as confirming the same point. Lippmann said of Smith that

one would be tempted to say that he has avowed the essential Protestant doctrine of the right of private judgement in all matters where secular matters are involved. [And since Smith's reply had been endorsed by bishops and priests Lippmann concludes that]...for American Catholics there is absolutely no distinction between their attitude and the attitude of Protestants. The ultimate authority is conscience. He makes no qualifications. He does not say conscience as guided by the authority of the Pope. The Catholicism of Gov. Smith is the typical modern, post-Reformation, nationalistic religious loyalty in which the Church occupies a distinct and closely compartmentalized section of an otherwise secular life.[67]

Preuss must have been pleased to have this confirmation of his views coming from such a reputable secular journalist. Lippmann had hit the nail on the head. As Preuss saw it, the compartmentalized Catholicism of Al Smith was the inevitable result of the liberal, Americanist tendencies of so many Catholics in America. They were surrendering a Catholic world view for an American one that had very little room for the teachings of the Church.

Preuss must have been even more gratified by a letter he received that confirmed his view of Smith's error. This letter, sent to Preuss in December 1927 by Father Elliot Ross, C.S.P., is remarkable for a number of reasons and because of this it is reproduced almost in its entirety. Ross wrote

Dear Mr. Preuss,

In view of the comments you have made on Governor Smith's reply to Mr. Marshall, I thought that you might be interested in this inside history. It is not for publication, however, and since it concerns others besides myself, I must ask you to keep this letter confidential.

As soon as I learned that Governor Smith would reply to Marshall, I got in touch with the Governor and the *Atlantic Monthly* and asked permission to reprint his answer as a Paulist Press pamphlet. Arrangements had been made to do this, and I was anticipating an enormous sale.

But when the reply came out, I was decidedly disappointed. It seemed to me, as it has seemed to you, too loosely worded from a theological standpoint. In fact, I do not see how Fr. Duffy could sanction some of the statements you have called attention to. So I immediately recommended that we should not handle any reprint.

This answer may get by now in the excitement of a political contest. But when the dust settles, I think there will be a different attitude on the part of the Catholic public. And if the Paulists had reprinted it, that would have been another proof in the eyes of a great many that we are really tainted with the 'Americanism' with which some have charged us.

While writing, may I express my appreciation for the work you are doing. You are an institution in the Catholic Church in America, and I wish there were more like you. Of course, I do not always agree with you, but that makes no difference. One thing we Catholics in this country need to learn is how to differ with other people in a courteous, gentlemanly way...

Assuring you of my personal esteem...

Elliot Ross, C.S.P.[68]

Ross's letter to Preuss is of interest for three reasons. First of all, Ross not only agreed with Preuss's criticism of Smith's reply but canceled the Paulists' plans to publicize it. Second, he agreed that the tenor of Smith's reply was reminiscent of Americanism. Third, despite their acknowledged differences, Ross expressed his admiration for Preuss as an "institution in the Catholic Church in America." That Elliot Ross, a Paulist Father and follower of the spirituality of Isaac Hecker, could extend such fulsome praise to Arthur Preuss, the bane of Americanism, is a testimony not only to Ross's fair-mindedness, but also to the stature that Preuss had attained as a Catholic commentator in America.

Over the course of the election year of 1928, Preuss addressed the issue of Smith's campaign eight more times in the *Review* and a dozen more times in his editorials for the *Echo*. Interestingly, the *Review's* political expert, Patrick Callahan did not have any articles on the campaign published in the journal during this period. This was probably due to the fact that Callahan publicly opposed Smith for his "wet" position on Prohibition and had become a prominent member of the "Democrats for Hoover." In the twenty notices Preuss wrote on the campaign further references to Smith's reply appear in only three places and then only briefly.[69] Most of the other pieces Preuss wrote concerned themselves with the issue of anti-Catholic prejudice. And of these, the predominant theme is that Catholics should not allow themselves to be manipulated by religious bigotry to support one candidate or another.[70]

Two of the more interesting essays that appeared, one by a contributor to the *Review* and the other an editorial by Preuss in the *Echo*, reflect well the attitude of conservative Catholics toward Smith's candidacy. The first of these, entitled "Catholics and the Presidency," was written by Father Francis J. Martin, a parish priest in Kentucky, and published anonymously at his request in the January 1, 1928 issue of the *Review*.[71] Six pages in length, Martin's piece was the longest essay to ever appear in a single issue of the *Review*. The basic point of the essay was that while Al Smith was personally qualified to be president, bigotry was still so strong in America, that neither Protestants nor Catholics were ready to deal constructively with the issue of Smith's religion. Martin was particularly concerned that Catholics would be goaded into making a political cause out of what should remain a political campaign.

> Judging success as God measures success, it will be far more profitable for us to expend in saving souls the energy that so many of us appear ready to put forth for the vain glory of a political triumph. Souls for Heaven, not a Catholic president, should be the summum bonum at which we aim...So far as the Church is concerned, the game is not worth the candle.[72]

A month before the general election, Preuss cautioned the readers of the *Echo* not to interpret the potential failure of the Smith campaign as being due solely to religious prejudice. Plenty of people were opposed to Smith on other grounds, and so his defeat should not be seen as a "crisis" for Catholics in America. Also, Preuss rejected the suggestion that had surfaced that Catholics should form their own party in the wake of Smith's defeat. Such a move would only "inject religion into politics" which was precisely the problem with the current campaign. This rejection of a Catholic party marks a clear reversal from the position that Preuss had held in the days when the American Federation of Catholic Societies was being formed. Preuss's change of heart on this matter was related to his pessimism regarding the ability of the American political system to bring about any real social change. By 1921 he had arrived at the conclusion that even a "Catholic party" could achieve little within the reigning liberal capitalist social order.[73]

Many American Catholics, including such notables as John A. Ryan and Peter Guilday, were depressed by Smith's resounding defeat in the presidential campaign of the 1928. They were particularly embittered by the manifestations of anti-Catholicism that Smith's candidacy engendered.[74] *America* magazine went so far as to publish a letter by Leonard J. Feeney, "The Brown Derby Letter," that compared Smith to the crucified Christ.[75] That Preuss could accept Smith's defeat with comparative equanimity was no doubt due in part to his wizened years. Years of advice from Patrick H. Callahan regarding the manipulation of religious bigotry by politicians probably influenced Preuss's calm demeanor as well.[76] But the biggest factor in Preuss's placid response to the anti-Catholic bigotry that had arisen against the Smith campaign and his subsequent defeat was Preuss's philosophical detachment from what Smith stood for. Preuss found the campaigns of both contestants devoid of any intellectual substance. There were no great issues at stake, certainly none that Preuss thought of importance.[77] Both candidates subscribed to the same bankrupt policies of liberal capitalism. And there was certainly nothing Catholic about Smith's platform. It was simply a matter of politics as usual, and apart from Smith's misrepresentation of Catholic beliefs, there was little else to be surprised about.

XI "So Long Thy Power Has Blest Me"

Although Al Smith's campaign for the presidency in 1928 marked the last heated controversy that Arthur Preuss engaged in with his American co-religionists, the debate over being Catholic in America was not finished. The "terrible blight of Americanism which is slowly destroying the vitality of the Catholic faith in the midst of seeming prosperity" continued to a be a concern.[1] However, new developments in 1929, both personal and global, started to dominate Preuss's thoughts. In late February of that year, a severe attack of rheumatoid arthritis broke his health and permanently affected both his professional work and private life. The stock market crash on "Black Tuesday" in October 1929, delivered a similarly devastating blow to the world economy. The impact of these two events formed the context of Arthur Preuss's activities throughout the remaining five years of his life.

The crippling attack of arthritis that Arthur Preuss experienced in the winter of 1929 had been preceded by a gradual decline of his fragile health over a number of years. Every year the coming of winter in St. Louis was for Preuss the onset of several months of recurring bouts of extreme and unrelieved pain due to his rheumatic condition. Since 1910 or so he had sought relief from this condition by spending a few weeks each winter in warmer climes, particularly Florida, where Preuss had established a strong friendship with Abbot Charles Mohr and the monks of St. Leo's Abbey. By 1929, these trips to Florida, usually alone, had become an annual ritual for Preuss. He sought relief there in the salt water baths at various spas, but in the end, only the warm sunshine really helped. Still, despite these annual respites, as Preuss aged, the cold of St. Louis became harder for him to bear, and each winter brought more frequent and serious attacks of arthritic paralysis. Finally, in February 1929, Preuss was completely incapacitated by an arthritic attack that left him bedridden for six weeks. Though Preuss gradually regained the use of his painfully gnarled hands and feet, his doctors warned him that he must reduce his work load and leave St. Louis permanently if he wished to avoid permanent paralysis. In the face of this ultimatum,

Preuss informed the subscribers to the *Review* that he could only continue to publish the journal on a monthly basis. Preuss regretted the change but offered that "perhaps the oldest Catholic journalist…continuously engaged in the profession, [has] earned the right to 'otium cum dignitate'" and the right to spend his last years "in the manner of a human being, and not as an abject slave to his profession, noble though that profession be."[2] The one remaining task that Preuss committed himself to was the completion of his adaptation into English of Johannes Brunsman's *Lehrbuch der Apologetik*, which was published by B. Herder in the years 1928 to 1932.

The disclosure of his condition brought Preuss many expressions of sympathy. These admirers encouraged Preuss to continue the publication of the *Review*, and expressed their willingness to continue its support, even though it would now appear less often. Perhaps the most telling of these words of condolence were those printed by an old adversary from the Americanist controversy, the *Catholic Citizen* of Milwaukee.

> …even those who, in the past, were nettled by his [Preuss's] sharp comments, now agree that this sort of freedom is a good and perhaps a necessary thing in the Catholic field. In Brother Preuss's case there was, besides, scholarship and accuracy.[3]

As for leaving St. Louis, Preuss considered moving to southern California, or San Antonio, Texas where the large German Catholic community and his friend, Archbishop Arthur Drossaerts, would have provided a warm welcome. Eventually, in October 1929, Preuss determined to move his "Lares and Penates" to Jacksonville, Florida, although he was uncertain if his wife Pauline could bear the strain of leaving family and friends behind in St. Louis. His ability to continue publishing the *Review* also remained a concern for Preuss. In fact, his fractured health, and the financial demands of moving his family to Florida, forced Preuss to seriously consider selling the *Review* "to some one who can and will continue it in the traditional spirit" if, after another year at the helm, he found the burden too much.[4]

A contributing factor to the precarious financial situation of the *Review* in 1929 had been Patrick H. Callahan's decision a year before to withdraw his patronage from the journal. Callahan made his decision to end his subsidy of the *Review* in the fall of 1928 because of financial difficulties at his Louisville Varnish Company. Despite Callahan's explanation, Preuss could not help wondering if "my failure to champion his favorite cause, Prohibition, made him lose interest in the *Review*." An awkward silence descended over the two men's friendship. After a hiatus of three years, Preuss and Callahan resumed a friendly correspondence but their collaboration was never renewed.[5] Preuss's financial situation was further exacerbated as the B. Herder Company, hard hit by the Depression, had less and less demand for his editorial work on new books.[6]

Perhaps, if Preuss had succeeded in transplanting his family to Florida, he would have been forced to sell the *Review* for establishing a new publishing operation in Jacksonville did not appear feasible. In the event, Preuss's family was unable to make the transition. His older sons, unable to find jobs in Florida as the Depression worsened, returned to St. Louis to look for work. As Preuss related to Frederick Kenkel,

> After the boys left on account of not being able to find employment, she [Preuss's wife, Pauline] became more and more depressed, and I simply had to let her go back home, as she could not bear the idea of seeing the family split up. So I am alone again and must carry on as best I can, for it would be suicidal for me to return to St. Louis until warmer weather has set in permanently. I surely will not spend another winter there if I can help it.[7]

With this development, the pattern of Arthur Preuss's remaining years had been set. From this point on, he would spend as much of the winter season as possible in Florida, though not happily. These lengthy separations from his family were difficult for all of them. Then too, Preuss was never sure if he would have the financial wherewithal to embark on these lonely sojourns.[8] Continually racked by pain, and concerned about his continued ability to provide for his family, these must have rather gloomy years in Preuss's life.

Fortunately for Preuss, both his health and financial situation gradually improved. In early 1930, unbeknownst to him, one of Preuss's old friends at St. Leo's Abbey, Father Jerome Wisniewski, solicited contributions from Preuss's friends in order to provide a "purse" for him.[9] Additionally, Preuss's editorial writing for the *Echo*, and the recently launched English-language version of the *Wanderer*, continued to provide him with badly needed income. Then too, his progress in completing his English adaptation of Brunsmann's *Apologetik* gave him encouragement.[10]

By the summer of 1932, Preuss had more than enough work again, though the income he was earning had to be stretched to support not only his wife and younger children, but also some of his adult children and their families who were out of work. There were numerous privations imposed by the Depression, but Preuss remained grateful that he at least was still able to earn a living and provide for his family.[11] Many others at this time, of course, were not as fortunate. And grappling with the national and international ramifications of the Depression became the focus of Preuss's editorial writing. Now that the *Review* was being published only monthly, and its pages increasingly given over to the work of his contributors, Preuss's weekly editorials for the *Echo* contained his most vital and interesting journalistic efforts.

Following the worldwide crises of the early 1930s through the editorials that Arthur Preuss wrote at the time is a fascinating exercise in a form of historical omniscience. Rather than seeking to uncover hitherto obscure facts regarding his life and his commentary on the Church in America, the researcher must focus instead on giving an account of Arthur Preuss's understanding of the well known but profound historical events that were unfolding before the whole world.

Like most other people at the time, nothing in Arthur Preuss's previous experience enabled him to perceive the full ramifications of the stock market crash when it happened. His initial response was one of concerned bewilderment. As banks and businesses folded, Preuss became certain that government leaders and business spokesmen were trying to hide the magnitude of the crisis behind optimistic public statements.[12] Increasing unemployment and reductions in wages were giving the lie to the myth of prosperity, and if not remedied, could soon lead to worse evils. All the Catholic press could do was

> ...to preach a return to sound principles of political economy, the practical application of the laws of social justice and charity and pray that the suffering of millions of victims of economic Liberalism...will lead to effective reform measures before the country falls a victim to Bolshevism.[13]

In the meantime, Preuss cautioned his readers to question "pollyanna" statements that sought to obscure the true gravity of the economic situation, as well as the "scare tactics" of "silly conservatives" who were casting the nation's unemployed workers in the role of "red agitators." As for short-term solutions to the growing problems of economic hardship, Preuss saw positive aspects in the proposals of the "progressive" program of Senator Robert LaFollette of Wisconsin. LaFollette was the lone prominent elected official who was calling for the major restructuring of American economic and political life. Preuss believed that LaFollette's proposals for public ownership of natural resources, the elimination of excessive profits, and the curtailment of bank centralization, "may bring us closer to Christian Solidarism."[14] Still, even the proposals of LaFollette were not radical enough to eradicate the greed that permeated American industry and finance. This could come only with the end of the capitalist system and the reconstruction of society in accord with the social encyclicals of Pope Leo XIII, *Rerum Novarum*, and Pope Pius XI, *Quadragesimo Anno*, issued in 1931.[15]

From the indications that he observed around him, Preuss concluded that western civilization was entering a new era. This new era was being ushered in by "utter chaos in morals, religion, economics and statesmanship."[16] The only stable and viable force for positive change that remained was the Catholic Church. If American Catholics would simply educate themselves in the Church's social teachings and apply them to their own lives, the potential for the establishment of a truly just society over the wreckage of capitalism might be realized. Pius XI himself had specifically called on the Catholic laity to recognize their rightful role in the Church and to transform society through Catholic Action. Preuss had always promoted a stronger role for the laity in the life of the Church, and inspired by the Pope's support for the Catholic Action movement, the *Review* and the *Echo* became more insistent in their calls for lay leadership.[17]

An article by Robert Hull published by the *Review* in October 1929, citing the teaching of Pius XI on "the royal priesthood of believers," proclaimed that a "turning point" had come in the life of the Church as "the laity have come into their own."

> Thus, at length, the layman realizes his true dignity and lays hold of the fullness of his Catholic inheritance. Having already heard the invitation to 'participate actively' in the Holy Sacrifice of the Mass –the call of the new liturgical movement, –he begins to 'participate actively' in the Christian apostolate. Best of all, in all probability, he remains a layman without becoming a 'sacristan.'[18]

Horace Frommelt, the voice of much of the "Catholic radicalism" that appeared in the *Review* after 1920, was an ardent champion of lay leadership in the Church.

> ...the clergy and the hierarchy should treat the laity as an intelligent factor in American Catholic life, rather than as a mere cash register that can be punched at will. We need sympathetic and intelligent leadership to accomplish great things for the Church in America...we lack downright vigorous intellectuality; but there is sufficient average ability and loyalty and common sense in evidence among Catholic laymen to set this world of Columbus and his faithful missionaries on fire as Christ explicitly declared.[19]

A few months after this essay appeared, Frommelt would ask if American Catholics were "priest-ridden" as their detractors claimed.

> When a Catholic educational system is conducted and administered solely by clerics, except for the financing, then the people living under such a system may rightly be characterized as 'priest-ridden;' when the social action programme of the same group is dominated by clerics, that group is 'priest-ridden;' when the Catholic press of 20,000,000 people is primarily considered to be a function of the hierarchy, then that people may be justly called 'priest-ridden.'[20]

Yet, to the dismay of Arthur Preuss and his contributors, the American Catholic laity were failing to take their necessary role in the reconstruction of society. This was due to the fact that American Catholics in general, and laity in particular, remained largely ignorant of the Church's social teachings. American Catholics had been educated to be mere "sacramentalists." That is, like the socially impotent Catholics of France, American Catholics, though quite concerned about frequent reception of the sacraments, exerted little effort in "the cultivation of the virtues the sacraments ought to nourish."[21] Their "sacramentalist" spirituality and their secular world view left American Catholics tragically unprepared to promote real solutions to the current crisis. Writing for the *Review* in 1933, Horace Frommelt criticized his American co-religionists for their nescience of their own philosophical heritage that could provide "the antidote for the ills of capitalism." In the same article, Frommelt echoed some of the aspirations of the liturgical movement to establish a relationship between "liturgy and life."

> Catholic philosophy, if it were a national heritage among 15,000,000 Americans, would save this critical day in which we live; it would help gradually to change and alter the capitalistic system from its present pagan form into a Christian one. The more devout American Catholics

> have largely become 'Sacramentalists,' they have been educated to support a parish church and a parochial grade school, but beyond that

> Catholicism has not yet penetrated their lives and thought. This has never been so evident as in the present crisis, when American Catholics, though a minority, could institute a far reaching programme of Christian social reform if they constituted a well informed and homogeneous class.[22]

Because the ignorance and apathy of American Catholics prevented them from offering a plan of social reconstruction based on the principles of Christian Solidarism, Preuss and some of his contributors to the *Review* were apprehensive that the United States, like Russia, Italy, and Germany, would fall for the only other alternative, state absolutism.[23]

The election of Franklin D. Roosevelt as president and the inauguration of his "New Deal" in 1933 presented Preuss's powers of discernment with a new challenge. Roosevelt had been elected to office on a platform that promoted a strong role for the government on promoting social welfare that sounded similar to principles laid down by the popes in their social encyclicals. Yet, Preuss remained skeptical of Roosevelt's true motivations and his ability to bring about significant change. As he confided in Abbot Francis of St. Leo's,

> I doubt whether the 'new deal' which the Democratic party promised the American people will amount to anything more than a change in exploiters, but as things can hardly be any worse under Democratic (sic) than they were let's hope for best.[24]

Hoping for the best soon blossomed into actual enthusiasm for Roosevelt's New Deal. In two editorials commenting on Roosevelt's first days in the White House, Preuss praised the new president and suggested "The President's official acts justify the opinion that a new era of social justice is dawning."[25] After three years of unrelieved economic and social depression, Arthur Preuss, like so many of his fellow countrymen, could not help but be moved by Roosevelt's message of hope and courage and the way that message was raising the morale of the nation.

> Whatever one may think of his ideas and suggestions for reform, one cannot help being impressed by the sincerity of Mr. Roosevelt, by his obvious desire to right an economic situation which has gone sadly awry, by his precise and lucid literary style, and his love for the common people.[26]

Preuss recognized that the New Deal was not Christian Solidarism, but he believed that Roosevelt's initiatives had the potential to lead American society in that direction. Because Roosevelt spoke in terms of social justice, Preuss thought that the reform programs that the president was proposing could be the bridge to something even better.[27] While the *Review* published the more guarded opinions of Frederick Kenkel and others concerning the New Deal legislation, the general tone of the journal and of Preuss's editorials in the *Echo* was one of support for Roosevelt.[28] Preuss's contributor, Horace Frommelt, while conceding that the philosophy of the New Deal was not entirely Catholic, it was "sufficiently close to it to be adequately radical for the times in which we live."[29]

The level of Preuss's support for the New Deal corresponded to the degree that Roosevelt's programs were likely to challenge the political and economic status quo. Even Senator Huey Long of Louisiana received muted praise from Preuss, who saw in the "Kingfish" "real qualities of leadership." The other populist hero of the early thirties, Father Charles Coughlin, was not treated so sympathetically. The *Review* chastised Coughlin for distorting both Scripture and history in his speeches, and Preuss believed that, as a priest, Coughlin should stay out of politics.[30]

In evaluating the developments in American society, Arthur Preuss was much influenced not only by papal social teaching, but also by events in Europe. There too, Catholics were trying to make sense out of the chaos brought on by the Depression. To Preuss it appeared that many Europeans were abandoning doomed liberal capitalism in favor of state absolutism, in either its communist or fascist variety, while at least some Catholics were working for the establishment of Christian Solidarism. Preuss believed that this same choice would inevitably confront

Americans. Therefore, Americans should be taking a lesson from events in Europe.

In formulating his opinions on European political developments, Preuss probably felt himself to be on steadier ground as a Catholic journalist than when he dealt with American politics, as the Holy See took an active interest in the political affairs of a number of European nations and regularly publicized the Church's position on such matters. Unfortunately, relying on the guidance of the Holy See in the formulation of his commentary on events in Italy left Preuss reversing himself as he tried to follow the Church's efforts to arrive at a modus vivendi with Mussolini's Fascist regime. In the mid-twenties, following "Il Duce's" rise to power, he cautioned the Catholic papers in America, some of which had praised Mussolini, that they would do well to adopt the Vatican's policy of "watchful waiting" in regard to "Fascismo."[31] Later, Preuss was consistently critical of the Italian dictator, whom he called a "political lunatic."[32] But then, when Mussolini and the Holy See agreed on the Lateran Pacts in 1929, Preuss accepted the superior wisdom of the Roman authorities that a compromise was possible with the Italian Fascist movement.[33] Also, following the lead of the hierarchy, Preuss allowed that Mussolini's Fascist movement might even be "the providential antidote for Bolshevism."[34] As with the New Deal, there were elements of the fascist program that appeared to be in conformity with the social encyclicals.[35] And even if Mussolini exercised a "despotic control" over Italy, the menace of Fascism was a lesser evil for the Church than the militantly atheistic program of communism.[36]

The response of Church authorities in Germany to the rise of Adolf Hitler's National Socialist party, played a similar role in forming Preuss's evaluation of nazism. Discerning the enormous evil that Hitler would eventually visit on the world was not an easy task in 1933 and '34. As in Italy, the Nazis appeared to be the only alternative to a communist take-over in Germany. Besides, reports coming out of Germany following Hitler's appointment to the office of chancellor were conflicting. For Arthur Preuss, who relied on Catholic sources of information, the task of discernment was further complicated by the fact that both the German episcopate and the Holy See were trying to make the best of the bad situation in Germany. As a result, they initially promoted a policy of conciliation with Hitler, repeatedly acquiescing to his demands in the hopes of staving off an open persecution of the Church in Germany.[37]

Arthur Preuss perceived that "the elevation of Hitler spells something of a persecution of Catholicism" in Germany and that "Catholic ideas and ideals have been put to heel."[38] However, like the German bishops, Preuss had no conception of just how far Hitler was willing to go. He could not conceive the depth of Hitler's hatred for the Jews, and so in the first months of the Nazi regime he dismissed the accounts of atrocities against them as exaggerated.[39] In 1933 at least, Preuss was willing to believe his German sources which reported that there was a real difference between Hitler and some of his fanatical followers like Alfred Rosenberg and Joseph Goebbels.[40] The Vatican also seemed to subscribe to this line of thinking in agreeing to a concordat with the Nazi regime in July 1933 out of a concern to protect the interests of the Church in Germany, particularly her schools and organizations. In effect, the Concordat became one of the first of many failed attempts to appease Hitler and gave him and his henchmen international credibility.[41] The concordat between the Vatican and Hitler's government created a "true state of euphoria" among German Catholics as they no longer had to stand aloof from the enthusiasm for Hitler that animated the rest of their countrymen. Citing one of his long trusted sources, the Jesuit journal, *Stimmen der Zeit*, Preuss informed the readers of the *Echo* in July 1933, that

> ...the best and most conservative Catholic leaders in Germany are advising the people to recognize existing conditions and co-operate with Hitler and his followers for the welfare of the Fatherland, so far as self-respect will permit.[42]

By the end of 1933 a writer for the *Stimmen der Zeit*, in speaking of the relationship between Nazism and Christianity, would say of the swastika and the cross that "the symbol of nature only finds its consummation in the symbol of grace."[43]

With "the best and most conservative Catholics" in Germany offering such advice, and the Vatican itself pursuing rapprochement with Hitler, Preuss was ill prepared to offer an objection to conciliation with the Nazis. Besides, the situation between the Church and Hitler's regime remained so fluid. Some of the headlines published by the *Echo* in early 1934 graphically illustrate this point. On January 18, 1934, the front-page headline in the *Echo* read "Catholics Urged to Support Hitler." The attached story related how Germany's vice-chancellor and leader of the Catholic Centre Party, Franz von Pappen, had issued this encouragement. Just a month later, another front-page headline declared "Kulturkampf Appears Imminent in Germany," and the attached story told how the Church was being persecuted by the Nazis. With such contradictory messages being sent out by Catholics in Germany, it is no wonder that observers in America were confused about the actual situation.[44]

As the events of 1934 unfolded, Preuss took an increasingly more critical stance toward the Nazi regime.[45] Whatever misconceptions he may have had about Hitler appear to have been dispelled by reading the 1933 Advent sermons of Cardinal Michael von Faulhaber, which were published outside of Germany in the spring of 1934. Having read them, Preuss concluded that there "can be no doubt, in light of these addresses, that Nazism is essentially a pagan reaction to Christianity."[46] The last few essays Preuss lived to write about Hitler's Germany took an increasingly harder line on the regime.[47]

If Preuss can be faulted at all in his evaluation of the fascist movements of Benito Mussolini and Adolf Hitler, it would be for the "failure" of thinking too much with the mind of the Church. Following the lead of the Pope, the bishops and other Catholic leaders, Preuss allowed himself to be deluded about the true nature of fascism. With the Church, he overlooked the intention of the fascists, particularly the

Nazis, to destroy Christianity as a viable force in the life of European society. His initial failure to be more discerning of the true aims of fascism resulted from his neglect of one of his own rules of thumb. Through out his life, Arthur Preuss had maintained that in order to evaluate properly the various intellectual currents and movements that percolated through modern society, one must examine their philosophical roots and compare them with the tenets of Catholicism. "Going to the roots," he declared in 1903, was the source of his own Catholic "radicalism." It was his justification for rejecting Americanism, the Modernist impulse in the Catholic Church, and liberal capitalism. Perhaps if Preuss had been less willing to follow the leadership of the Church in regard to the fascist movements, and had relied instead on his own radical critique, he would have condemned them consistently from the outset. But then, Arthur Preuss had never claimed to be more Catholic than the Pope.

Conclusion   "The Flower of Chivalry"

Arthur Preuss died at the age of sixty-three, on December 16, 1934, in Jacksonville, Florida, three weeks after suffering a heart attack there at the beginning of his annual winter visit. His exile was over.[1]

Solemn Requiem Mass was offered for him at St. Rose's parish church in St. Louis on December 21, 1934 by his brother Joseph, with his brothers James and Francis assisting. A letter of condolence from the Apostolic Delegate, Archbishop Amleto Cicognani, to Preuss's wife Pauline, was read at the Mass. It had been signed by nine American archbishops. Albert Muntsch, S.J., Preuss's long-time friend and contributor to the *Review*, delivered the eulogy. Muntsch's remarks centered on Arthur Preuss's literary and journalistic achievements on behalf of the Catholic Faith, his outspokenness on issues of social justice, and his commitment to Catholic education. Citing the legends that surrounded Preuss's namesake, Muntsch dubbed the deceased editor, "Flos Regum Arthurus," which he freely translated as "Arthur, the Flower of Chivalry."[2]

The *Review* followed its founder to the grave a month later. Although the Preuss family had hoped to find someone to continue the journal, their attempts failed. The last number of the *Review* appeared in January 1935 and was dedicated to the memory of Arthur Preuss. With tributes from some of Preuss's closest friends, Frederick Kenkel, Francis Borgia Steck, John Rothensteiner and Joseph Matt, the issue closed with one last essay on social justice by Horace A. Frommelt. The *Review*, which for over forty years had been a remarkable voice of independent, conservative Catholicism in America, ceased publication.

Any conclusions regarding the ultimate significance of Arthur Preuss's life must, of course, be left up to the Master whom he endeavored to serve. However, the historian might safely hazard a few remarks concerning Preuss's contribution to the Church in the land of his sojourn. First, Arthur Preuss was not only an important commentator on Catholicism in America in the first decades of this century, but also a thoughtful one. The one-dimensional caricature of Preuss that has often appeared in American Catholic historiography has not done justice to the intelligence and complexity of the man. In his day, Arthur Preuss was well respected, even by his adversaries, as an articulate spokesman of authentic Catholic conservatism. Secondly, Preuss's conservatism was broad enough to embrace such "progressive" positions as the need for a strong, independent Catholic press in the United States, the rightful role of lay leadership in the Church, the end of racism in both the Church and society, and a committed Catholic effort to transform American economic and political institutions in the interests of social justice. As all of these issues still confront American Catholics, Preuss's views on these subjects in principle are still pertinent, if not inspiring. Indeed, even in some of his specific arguments, for example his difficulties regarding the authority and administration of the national bishops' conference, Arthur Preuss can be seen as a precursor of some elements of contemporary thought.

Finally, the position that Arthur Preuss took on *the* question of American Catholicism, that is, "how are we to be both Catholic and American," is as germane today as it was in his lifetime. Preuss believed that Catholicism must work to counter the skepticism, materialism, and excessive individualism of American society, and that this requires that one's loyalty to America not stifle the "subversive" character of Christianity.

To be successful in such a struggle Preuss believed that the Catholic Church in America had to survive as a distinctive community and to do this it must propagate a "Catholic world view" or culture. This world view could only be sustained if Catholics of the twentieth century, like their immigrant ancestors, continued to look to the Church as the central locus of their daily lives. Thus, as we have seen, Preuss was a strong supporter of Catholic educational institutions, the Catholic press, the propagation of the Church's social teaching and informed participation in the Church's liturgy. And though at times he despaired at the quality of American bishops, Preuss was unwavering in his loyalty to the Holy See that appointed them. Unquestioning fidelity to papal leadership was crucial to Preuss's notion of a Catholic world view. It was only by maintaining this transnational loyalty that Catholics in America would elude the double-edged threat of Americanism; this included the myth of American providentialism of the Americanists and the notion of American Catholic "particularism" within the universal Church which Preuss believed the National Catholic Welfare Council was promoting. Through the maintenance of their distinctive identity the Catholics of the United States could make a positive contribution to American society by being a "sign of contradiction" to the prevailing culture and a viable alternative to it.

Unfortunately, in the view of Preuss's Americanist opponents, such a world view offered no practical means for Catholics in America to transcend the confines of their "ghetto" and thus actively transform the wider society. For them, Catholic "separatism" was not only not a desirable long-term option, it was also unrealistic. Ironically, while Arthur Preuss sooner than most German-Catholics correctly perceived that through Americanization the immigrant ghettos based on language would inevitably disappear, throughout his life he hoped against hope and all the signs of the times that indicated that the prospect of maintaining a distinctive Catholic identity in America was also doomed. But then, the Americanists never could have envisioned what a one-sided conversation their dialogue with modernity and American culture would become.

No doubt Preuss would have been pleased that the old debate over "Americanism," albeit a marginal one, has been reopened in recent years.[3] Nor would the renewal of the debate some sixty years after his death have surprised him. For Arthur Preuss, the tension that exists in being both Catholic and American, in adhering to an ancient faith tradition while living in a modern world, is to be expected. It is the analogue to being both "in the world" but "not of it." Undoubtedly Preuss would be saddened that so few of his American co-religionists now understand the dilemma. But then the controversy over Americanism never engaged a wide audience even in his own day.

For himself, given the choice between ancient verities and hoping in the zeitgeist, Preuss clearly cast his lot with the past, believing as he did that, this side of the Second Coming, the Church's most important day was its first. In taking such a position, Arthur Preuss stands in the radical tradition of the Augustinian philosophy of history that has rejected the empire worship of every "modern" age. At a time when many conservative Catholics in the United States have embraced American providentialism it is well to remember that true Catholic conservatism is much more profound, and if nothing else, Arthur Preuss's life demonstrated that.

Notes

Abbreviations

APP   Arthur Preuss Papers
ACB   Archives of the Central Bureau, Catholic Central Union
AQC   Archives of Quincy College
AUND   Archives of the University of Notre Dame

Introduction

1. Philip Gleason. *The Conservative Reformers: German-American Catholics and the Social Order* (Notre Dame: University of Notre Dame Press, 1968), 7. Gleason goes on to point out that German American Catholics would continue to feel alienated from their fellow Catholics and their fellow Americans into the 1930s.

2. The most exhaustive treatment of this topic is to be found in Colman J. Barry, 0.S. B., *The Catholic Church and German Americans* (Milwaukee: Bruce Publishing Co., 1952). Other sources are Thomas McAvoy, *The Great Crisis in American Catholic History, 1895-1900* (Chicago: Henry Regnery Co.,1957) and of course the previously mentioned *The Conservative Reformers* by Philip Gleason.

3. Jonathan Sperber, *Popular Catholicism in Nineteenth-Century* Germany (Princeton,NJ:PrincetonUniversityPress, 1984), 10-38. Thomas F. O'Meara, *Church and Culture:German Catholic Theology,1860-1914 (Notre* Dame, IN: University of Notre Dame Press, 1991),19-24.

4. The bulk of German Catholic immigration to the United States occurred during or after the period of unification and the Kulturkampf with nearly 1.7 million such immigrants arriving between 1880 and 1895. John S. Kulas, *Der Wanderer of St. Paul; The First Decade, 1867-1877* (New York: Peter Lang Publishing Inc., 1996), 33-34, 36-37. Jay P. Dolan, *The American Catholic Experience: A History from Colonial Times to the Present* (Garden City, NY: Doubleday & Company, Inc., 1985), 129-130.

5. Sperber, 11, 51-52, 91-98. Rudolf Lill, "The Kulturkampf," *The History of the Church* IX ed. Hubert Jedin (New York:Crossroad Publishing Company, 1981), 26-45 and 55-75. David J. O'Brien, *Public Catholicism* (NewYork: Macmillan Publishing Co., 1989), 55-61, 77-81.

6. Sperber, 97-98, 185-186.

7. Oskar Koehler, "The Development of Catholicism in Modem Society," *The History of the Church* IX ed. Hubert Jedin. ibid, 25 1. Rudolf Morsey, "Die deutschen Katholiken und der Nationalstaat zwischen Kulturkampf und Ersten Weltkrieg," *Historisches Jahrbuch* 90 (1970):31-64. Lill, 73-75. O'Meara, 21.

8. On the early history of *Der Wahrheitsfreund* see Paul J. Foik, C. S. C, *Pioneer Catholic Journalism* (New York: The United States Catholic Historical Society, 1930), 181–187. On John Martin Henni see Sr. M. Mileta Ludwig, F.S.P.A., *Right-Hand Glove Uplifted* (New York: Pageant Press, 1968), 130 ff., 384 ff. Henni (d. 1881) was named the first bishop (1843) and archbishop of Milwaukee (1875).

9. Estimate based on figures from Barry, 5–7 and Gleason, 46–47.

10. Gleason, 48–49.

11. The only attempt to classify the most important German Catholic papers of this period found by this researcher was a list composed by Joseph Matt, editor of *Der Wanderer,* in his memorial essay for Arthur Preuss. In his essay Matt cited nine German Catholic editors who were active at the time that Preuss began his publishing career. Of the ten journalists, nine have been identified. Joseph Matt, "Arthur Preuss," *Review* XCII (January 1935):5–6.

12. *Waisenfreund* not only served as a strong voice for German Catholics during the ethnicity struggles of the era, it was also a vehicle for Jessing to promote funding for the orphanage he ran and the seminary he founded, the Pontifical Collegium Josephinum, which opened in 1892. By the 1890s the *Waisenfreund* had a nationwide circulation of 55,000. It was succeeded by an English-language publication during the First World War. The *Volksfreund* of Buffalo was established in 1868 and continued in various forms until 1966. Wilhelm Keilmann had a long association with the paper and was its editor from 1893 until 1899. Joseph Matt began his career in journalism with this paper in 1885. The circulation of the *Volksfreund* during the 1890s ranged from three to four thousand copies. *Die Stimme der Wahrheit* was founded in Detroit in 1875. J. B. Mueller, its editor, was an experienced newspaperman in his native Germany. Its circulation in the 1890s ranged from five to seven thousand copies. The *Herold des Glaubens* was established as a weekly paper in St. Louis in the 1870s. Father Johann N. Enzelberger, who was active in the Priesterverein movement and an active opponent of Americanization, was editor of the paper from 1895 to 1902. The circlation of the paper reached 33,000 in 1895. Father Anton Heiter had a long association with the *Christliche Woche* which was established in Buffalo in 1875. During the 1890s its circulation ranged from three to four thousand copies. Nicholas Gonner, Sr. founded the *Luxemburger Gazette* in 1871 in Dubuque. Gonner was also editor of the German-language *Iowa* which under his son and namesake became *Katholisches Westen* in 1892. These papers had a circulation of a few thousand copies during the 1890s. *Der Wanderer* of St. Paul, Minnesota was founded in 1867. Hugo Klapproth became the paper's editor in 1883 and its owner in 1899. Joseph Matt became his assistant from 1897 and was also Klapproth's son-in-law. In 1895 *Der Wanderer* had a circulation of 11,500 copies per week. The career of Edward Preuss, editor of *Die Amerika* will be covered within the text.

Information on these newspapers is taken from the pertinent state-by-state volumes of Eugene P. Willging and Herta Hatzfeld, *Catholic Serials of the Nineteenth Century in the United States* (Washington, D.C.: The Catholic University Press of America, 1965-1968). See also Apollinaris W. Baumgartner, *Catholic Journalism: A Study of Its Development in the United States,* 1789-1930. (New York: Columbia University Press, 1931).

13. The *Pastoralblatt,* (1866-1925) was established by Father Michael Heiss and Father Henry Muelsiepen. The journal published articles on the practice of pastoral care, official documents and historical sketches. Heiss became the first editor. Heiss went on to become the bishop of LaCrosse and the second archbishop of Milwaukee. Muelsiepen was vicar general for the Germans in the Archdiocese of St. Louis.

14. Other important Catholic English-language periodicals at the time included the *Catholic Telegraph* of Cincinnati (est. 183 1. circulation in 1895:7800.), the *Pilot* of Boston (est. 1837. circulation in 1890s:70,000), the *New York Freeman's Journal* (est. 1840. circulation in 1895:12,500), The Baltimore *Catholic Mirror* (est. 1849. circulation in 1896:16,500), *the Monitor* of San Francisco (est. 1858), The *Western Watchman* of St. Louis (est. 1865), the Milwaukee *Catholic Citizen* (est. 1870. circulation in 1900: 10,000), the Buffalo *Catholic Union & Times* (est. 1872. circulation in 1890s: from 10,000 to 15,000), *the Northwestern Chronicle* of St. Paul, Minnesota (est. 1874. circulation in 1890s: from 4000 to 6000), the *Church Progress* of St. Louis (est. 1878. circulation in 1892:22,500), *the Catholic News* of New York (est. 1886), the *New World* of Chicago (est. 1892. circulation in 1892:17,500), the *Globe* of New York, (est. 1889 circulation in 1905 :5000) and the *Catholic Standard and Times* of Philadelphia (est. 1895). Of these newspapers, only the *Church Progress,* under the editorship of Condé Pallen, and the *Globe,* edited by William Thome took the "conservative" position during the years surrounding the Americanist crisis. For information regarding the editors and circulations of these papers see the Willging and Hatzfeld series, ibid. There were five prominent Catholic journals at the time. The *Catholic World* was founded in New York by Isaac Hecker, C.S.P in 1864 and was published by the Paulist Fathers (Estimates of its circulation range from 2500 to 55,000!) *Ave Maria* was established at Notre Dame by the Holy Cross Fathers in 1865. The *Messenger of the Sacred Heart* was established at Woodstock, Maryland by the Jesuits in 1866 (circulation in 1897:20,000). The *American Catholic Quarterly Review* was established in 1876 by the Archbishop of Philadelphia, Patrick J. Ryan (circulation in 1897:4500). In 1889 the *American Ecclesiastical Review* was established as an independent journal by Rev. Herman Heuser (circulation in 1896:650). (For an introduction to the important work of Heuser see Joseph Hubbert, C.M. "'Less Brains and More Heart ': Father Herman J. Heuser, Founder of the American Ecclesiastical Review," *U. S. Catholic Historian* 13

(Winter 1995):95–122. According to McAvoy, all of these journals shied away from controversy during the Americanist crisis, although the *Catholic World and Ave Maria* were sympathetic to the Americanist faction.   For information regarding the most important English-language periodicals of the day, and their perspectives on contemporary controversies see McAvoy, 81–82 and Samuel J. Thomas, "The American Periodical Press and the Apostolic Letter *Testem Benevolentiae,*" *Catholic Historical Review* 62 (July 1976):408–423 and "The American Press and the Encyclical Longinqua Oceani," *Journal of Church and State* 22 (Autumn 1980):474–485.

I Beginnings

1. Ludwig E. Fuerbringer, *Eighty Eventful Years.* (St.   Louis: Concordia Publishing House, 1944) Chapter 25. Cited in "In Commemoration of Dr. Edward Friederick Reinhold Preuss" edited by Austin F. and M.M. Preuss. 1984 Unpublished.

2. Edward F.R. Preuss. *Zum Lobe der Unblefleckten Empfdngnis der Allerseligsten Jungfrau* (St. Louis: Herder, 1879) translated and quoted in the *Review* in fifteen installments from August 25 through December 8, 1904.

3. This book was later printed in Scotland under the title *The Romish Doctrine of the Immaculate Conception Traced From Its Source.* (Edinburgh: T&T Clark, 1867) Translated by George Gladstone.

4. Edward Preuss, "The Story of a Conversion," *Review* XI 34 (September 8, 1904):535–536. (September 15, 1904):533–534.

5. Ibid., *Review* XI 36 (September 22, 1904):567–570.

6. Ibid., *Review* XI 36 (September 22, 1904):567–570. 44 (November 17, 1904):613.

7. "A Plea for Converts," *Review* XIII 6 (March 15, 1906):163.

8. Interviews. Alma Preuss Dilschneider and Charles Arthur Preuss, August 2, 1992.

9. "Annual Catalogue of St. Francis Solanus College 1887–1888 " "Testimony for the Collegian Arthur Preuss, 1889–90," Archives of Quincy College.

10. John E. Rothensteiner, "Reminiscences of Dr. Arthur Preuss," *Review* XCII (January 1935):2

11. Edward Preuss to Arthur Preuss, September 20, 1887.   Arthur Preuss Papers, Reel 13. Arthur Preuss's papers are now held on fourteeen microfilm reels by the Central Bureau of the Catholic Central Union (Verein) of America, in St. Louis, Missouri. Subsequent references will be listed as A.P.P. with the reel number.

12. Arthur Preuss to Edward Preuss, June 18, 1889. A.P.P. Reel 13.

13. Edward Preuss to Arthur Preuss, February 1, 1888. A.P.P. Reel 13.

14. Edward Preuss to Arthur Preuss, October 11, 1887. A.P.P. Reel 13. Father

Francis Goller was pastor of the German parish of SS. Peter and Paul in St. Louis and an active promoter of the " Priesterverein, " an association of German priests in America. See Barry, 98, 113, 172–175. Claire Marie Bachhuber, "The German-Catholic Elite: Contributions of a Catholic Intellectual and Cultural Elite of German-American Background in Early Twentieth Century Saint Louis," (Ph. D. diss., Saint Louis University, 1984), 54–55.

15. Edward Preuss to Arthur Preuss, November 8, 1888. A.P.P. Reel 13.

16. Edward Preuss to Arthur Preuss, May 2, 1890. Translated and quoted in Preuss Family History. Unpublished.

17. Edward Preuss to Arthur Preuss, April 18, 1888. A.P.P. Reel 13. John Henry Newman, "The Pillar and the Cloud," *in Prayers, Verses and Devotions*. (San Francisco: Ignatius Press, 1989).

18. Interview. Alma Preuss Dilschneider and Charles Arthur Preuss, August 2, 1992.

19. Interview. Alma Preuss Dilschneider and Charles Arthur Preuss, August 2, 1992.

20. "The Ultramontanes, " *Review* IX 48 (November 28, 1902):755–756.

21. Interview. Alma Preuss Dilschneider and Charles Arthur Preuss, August 2, 1992. "Notice to Our Subscribers," *Review* XXII 2 (January 15, 1915):34. XXVIII 2 (January 15, 1921):20. XXXVI 7(April 1, 1929):140. Arthur Preuss to Fr. Francis Markert, S.V.D. October 10, 1912, October 17, 1919 and May 9, 1928. A.P.P. Reel 13. The Divine Word Fathers at Techny, Illinois published Preuss's *Review* for a number of years, 1906–1918. Fr. Markert handled the project and the two men became close friends through their regular correspondence.

22. "Flotsam & Jetsam," Review XVIII 6 (June 15, 1911):378 & XXVII 20 (October 15, 1920):307.

23. Eugene P. Willging and Herta Hatzfield, *Catholic Serials of the Nineteenth Century in the United States: A Descriptive Bibliography and Union List* (Washington, DC: Catholic University Press, 1965) Second Series, Part Nine "Missouri," 22.

24. John E. Rothensteiner, "A Sketch of Catholic Journalism in St. Louis," *PastoralBlatt* 58 (June 1924):81–93.

25. Carl Wittke, *The German Language Press in America* (Frankfort: University of Kentucky Press, 1957),178.

26. Willging and Hatzfeld,"Missouri," 20.

27. Georg Timpe, *Katholisches Deutschtum in den Vereinigten Staaten von Amerika* (Frieburg: Herder & Co.,1937), 10–11. Willging and Hatzfeld, 21.

28."In Commemoration of Edward Preuss," Unpublished. Preuss Family Papers. The selection of Edward Preuss as the 1887 recipient of its Laetare Medal was not made public by the University of Notre Dame until 1916.

29. For a detailed account of the Abbelen Memorial and the Cahensly affair see Barry, 44–182.

30. Edward Preuss to Arthur Preuss, October 11, 1887 and February 29, 1888. A.P.P. Reel 13.

31. Joseph Matt, "Arthur Preuss, " *Review* XCII (January 1935):4.

32. Edward Preuss to Arthur Preuss, September 20 and October 5, 1887. A.P.P. Reel 13.

33. Edward Preuss to Arthur Preuss, May 21, 1889. A.P.P. Reel 13.

34. "A Catholic Daily," *Review* XXIII 7(April 1, 1916):130.

35. "The Catholic Press," *Review* XVIII (September 15, 1919):279.

36. Arthur Preuss to Father Francis Markert, S.V.D. September 28, 1912. A.P.P. Reel 14.

37. Diary. May 30, 1906. Arthur Preuss started a diary in 1906. Unfortunately, he was unable to keep it up for more than a few months so it does not amount to more than a dozen pages. A. P. P. Reel 2.

38. *Church Progress*, February 20, 1892 and March 12, 1892. Clippings in A.P.P. Reel 1.

39. See Barry, 196–236 and Gerald P. Fogarty, S.J. *The Vatican and the American Hierarchy 1870–1965*, (Stuttgart, Germany: Anton Hiersemann, 1982 and 1985) (Wilmington, DE: Michael Glazier, 1985) 69–85, 93–130.

40. Edward Preuss to Arthur Preuss, September 4, 1893. A. P. P. Reel # 1 3. Otto Zardetti to Arthur Preuss, October 8, 1893. A.P.P. Reel 1.

41. Willging, ibid, Second Series Part 3, "Illinois," 101. See also Karl J. Arndt and May E. Olson, *German-American Newspapers and Periodicals, 1732–1955: History & Bibliography* (Heidelberg: Quelle and Meyer, 1961).

42. Walter Smitts to Arthur Preuss, November 24, and December 10, 1892, January 1, and October 9, 1893. A.P.P. Reel 1.

43. Edward Preuss to Arthur Preuss, February 15, 1894. Charles Jaegler, publisher of the *Pittsburger Beobachter* had written to Arthur Preuss on November 20, 1893 about a position with his paper. A.P.P. Reel 13.

44. Edward Preuss to Arthur Preuss, March 15, 1894. A.P.P. Reel 13.

II The Birth of the *Review* and Americanism

1. Thomas T. McAvoy, C.S.C. *The Great Crisis in American Catholic History 1895–1900*, Ibid.

2. Preuss's *Review* was originally called the *Chicago Review*. However, as another publication had already obtained postal privileges under this title, Preuss was forced to change the name of his journal to the *Review*. I 2 (May 1, 1894):1 There would be two more name changes in the course of its history. It became the *Catholic Fortnightly Review* in 1905 and then in 1912, the name was

shortened to the *Fortnightly Review*. In the fourth issue of the *Review* Preuss stated that he was inspired to publish a "German paper in English dress" by the example of the *Christian Friend* of Oregon. Edited by Father Sommer, the *Christian Friend* lasted less than a year (1893–94), but Preuss stated that it was the "prototype" for his own journal. *Review* I 4 (July 1, 1894):8.

3. During the first six months of the *Review*'s existence William Kuhlmann, Preuss's employer at the *Katholisches Sonntagsblatt*, was also listed as the publisher of the former journal. The *Review* regularly carried advertisements for Kuhlmann's shipping business. Presumably, the profits from this enterprise financed both publishing ventures.

4. For a discussion of the meaning of "Deuschtum" among nineteenth-century German Catholics see Philip Gleason, *The Conservative Reformers*, 14–50.

5. For a thorough account of these controversies see Barry, *The Catholic Church and German Americans*, ibid.

6. *Review* I 2 (May 1, 1894): 1.

7. The American Protective Association was a nativist organization founded in 1887 by Henry Blowers of Clinton, Iowa. The stated purpose of the A.P.A. was to combat the "threat" that Catholicism posed to American public life especially in the areas of politics and education. The A.P.A. was particularly strong in the Midwest where its candidates won a number of local elections in the early 1890s. As an organization its influence peaked in 1894 when it claimed several hundred thousand members. However, internal disputes undermined the organization and it soon went into rapid decline. Donald L. Kinzer, *An Episode in Anti-Catholicism: The American Protective Association* (New York, 1964).

8. "The Language Question," *Review* I 27(September 26, 1894):4.

9. "Nationalization," *Review* I 2 (May 1, 1894):2.

10. Preuss's allegations in this regard were not farfetched. Ireland and Msgr. Denis O'Connell actively sought to manipulate public opinion on this and other issues. See Thomas E. Wangler, "American Catholic Expansionism: 1886–1894," *Harvard Theological Review*, 75 (1982):369–93. Gerald P. Fogarty, S.J., *The Vatican and the Americanist Crisis: Denis J. O'Connell, American Agent in Rome, 1885–1903* (Rome: Gregorian University Press, 1974), 94–95, 253–254, 287–289.

11. "The Cahensly Bugaboo In Rome," *Review* I 33 (November 7, 1894):4.

12. Moore, 67.

13. "Emile Zola on Archbishop Ireland, " *Review* II 43 (January 16, 1896):7. The Frenchman had described Ireland as the potential leader of an American church and "the apostle of a new religion."

14. R. Scott Appleby, *"Church and Age Unite!": The Modernist Impulse in American Catholicism* (Notre Dame: University of Notre Dame Press, 1992),

86 on Ireland's support for the modernist Alfred Loisy and the former's realization "with horror that he had helped spur a heretical movement."

15. The exact role of the third leading member of the Americanist faction in promoting the movement, Msgr. Denis O'Connell, was not fully comprehended by Preuss until the latter's Fribourg address on Isaac Hecker in August 1897. Preuss and the *Review* did have some suspicions as to O'Connell's role as the Roman agent for the liberals and as the source of reports favorable to the Americanists that appeared frequently in the press. "Who Is 'Innominato'? " *Review* III 21 (August 13, 1896):1.

16. "The Catholic University At Washington," *Review* I (April 1, 1894): 1.

17. "The Catholic University," *Review* I 28 (October 3, 1894):4. Thomas Bouquillon, a Belgian moralist and Thomas O'Gorman, a professor of ecclesiastical history, were members of the University's faculty who had earned the animosity of German Catholics by their agitation on behalf of their Americanist mentors during the school controversy. On Bouquillon and his role in the school controversy, see Daniel F. Reilly, O.P. *The School Controversy (1891-1893)* (Washington: The Catholic University of America Press, 1943). Also, C. Joseph Nuesse, "Thomas Joseph Bouquillon (1840-1902), Moral Theologian and Precursor of the Social Sciences in the Catholic University of America," *The Catholic Historical Review*, LXXII 4 (October, 1986):601-619.

18. "The Catholic University Bulletin," *Review* I 44 (January 23, 1895):4. Reports of the factionalism at the University made it into the secular press at this time over Schroeder's and Périès' complaints that they were being denied publication in the Bulletin of the University. For this and the stormy tenure of Périès at the University see Patrick H. Ahem, *The Life of John J. Keane Educator and Archbishop 1839-1918*. (Milwaukee: Bruce Publishing Co, 1955), 162-164 ,172-174.

19. "The Catholic University of America," *Review* II 50 (March 5, 1896): 1. Barry, 236 n.93. Unfortunately, these letters are not part of the collection that was microfilmed for the Central Bureau at the University of Notre Dame in the 1960s. The only letter from Schroeder to Preuss in the collection as it now exists is a letter of condolence written in 1900 on the death of Preuss's wife.

20. "With Our Exchanges, " *Review* III 8 (May 14, 1896):4. "An Appeal For the Establishment of a German Chair in the Catholic University," III 13 (June 18, 1896):5. "Cardinal Satolli on a German Chair at the Catholic University," III 14 (June 25, 1896):3.

21. "Editorial Paragraphs, " *Review* I 28 (October 3, 1894):4.

22. "The Catholic University Bulletin," *Review 1* 44 (January 23, 1895):4.

23. "Father Brandi and 'Neo-Pelagianism'," *Review* III 7 (May 7, 1896):1 and III 8 (May 14, 1896): 1. Salvatore Brandi, S.J. was editor of the Jesuits' Roman journal, *La Civilta Cattolica*. Having spent some years in the United States, in Rome he was considered to speak authoritatively on American matters. He

actively opposed the liberal tendencies of Ireland, Keane and O'Connell. John L. Ciani, "Across a Wide Ocean: Salvatore Maria Brandi, S.J. and the *Civilta Cattolica*, from Americanism to Modernism, 1891-1914," Ph. D. diss., The University of Virginia, 1992. Gerald P. Fogarty, S.J. *The Vatican and the Americanist Crisis,* 94-95, 253-254, 287-289.

24. "Mgr. Satolli and the Apostolic Delegation," *Review* I 29 (October 10, 1894):4.

25. "The Pope's Letter," *Review* I 42 (January 9, 1894):4.

26. For Satolli's Pottsville speech and its significance see Barry, 223-234.

27. "The Causes of the Leakage," *Review* II 44 (January 23, 1896):4.

28. "To Christianize the Public Schools," *Review* I 6 (August 1, 1894):3.

29. Arthur Preuss to Rev. Peter A. Baart, December 17, 1898. Peter A. Baart Papers, Box #2, The Archives of the University of Notre Dame. Father Baart was a pastor in Marshall, Michigan, an authority on canon law, and occasional contributor to the Review. Priests with grievances against their bishops frequently sought his advice as did Preuss on this occasion. Preuss asked Baart to "watch the *Review* with an ever critical if friendly optic" and to warn Preuss should anything appear in the *Review* for which he could be liable. Preuss to Baart, January 5, 1899. Baart Papers, CBAA Box 2, AUND.

30. "An Explanation," *Review* III 24 (September 3. 1896):4.

31. "The Death Throes of Liberalism," *Review* III 30 (October 15, 1896):7.

32. O'Connell, 317-347. Gerald P. Fogarty, S.J. *The Vatican and the American Hierarchy from 1870 to 1965*, 69-80.

33. "A Midland Reviewer's Superfluous Suggestion," *Review* III 34 (November 12, 1896):7.

34. "Exchange Comment," *Review* III 31 October 22, 1896):3. The Rochester paper was perhaps giving voice to the views of its ordinary, Bishop McQuaid, on this matter.

35. "True Import of the Late Anti-Liberal Press Campaign," *Review* III 39 (December 17, 1896):1.

36. "Can A Liberal Catholic Be A Good Catholic?" *Review* III 52 (March 18, 1897):5.

37. Fogarty, *The Vatican and the Americanist Crisis,* 258-261. O'Connell, 436-439. "Refractaires" as a term of opprobrium had first been applied to the French Conservative opponents of Pope Leo's attempts to reconcile French Catholics with the Third Republic.

38. "Refractaires?" *Review* IV 3 (April 8, 1897):1-2.

39. Tilly, "The Church and Modern Progress," *Review* IV 10 (May 27, 1897): 1. This essayist stated that since the modern world had fallen away from Catholicism there could be no reconciliation between the Church and the age. Such a unification would mark the descent from Catholic doctrine into

Such a unification would mark the descent from Catholic doctrine into "modernism."

40. For Schroeder's removal from the faculty of Catholic University see Barry, 230–236. O'Connell 432–435. Fogarty, *The Vatican and the Americanist Crisis*, 272–275. Peter E. Hogan, SSJ, *The Catholic University of America, 1896–1903: The Rectorship of Thomas J. Conaty* (Washington, DC: The Catholic University Press, 1949), 149–156.

41. Hogan, 172.

42. "Monsignor Schroeder and His Enemies," *Review* IV 33 (November 4, 1897):5. In his history of the Catholic University in these years, Father Peter Hogan stated that it was through an unknown source that the stories of Msgr. Schroeder's drinking in Washington taverns were leaked to the press. Hogan, 154. O'Connell, 435. However, a contemporary account of the affair in the *New York Freeman's Journal* and reprinted in the *Review* of November 11, 1897 states that the private detective hired to gather incriminating evidence against Schroeder was present at the Catholic University during the Board of Trustees deliberations on Schroeder's fate. "The Schroeder Case," *Review* IV 34 (November 11, 1897):1–2.

43. "The Schroeder Case," *Review* IV 36 (November 25, 1897):6. "A Purse For Monsignor Schroeder," IV 36 (January 6, 1898):4.

44. Schroeder's "Case" also brought his former colleague at the Catholic University, Dr. Joseph Pohle, to Preuss's attention. In February and March the *Review* reprinted from various German papers Pohle's defense of Schroeder against attacks mounted in Germany by Schroeder's old adversary and Americanist fellow traveller, F.X. Kraus. Preuss also published Pohle's account of his own resignation from the Catholic University. "The Schroeder Case in Germany," *Review* IV 48 (February 17, 1898):6–7. J.F. Meifuss, "Frustrated!" *Review IV* 51 (March 10, 1898):4.

45. "A Casus Belli?" *Review* IV 49 (February 24, 1898):1.

46. "The Patriotism of Catholic Citizens," *Review* V 3 (April 7, 1898):1–2.

47. "Monsignor Ireland, the Vatican, and the Spanish-American Conflict," *Review* V 5 (April 21, 1898):5. For an account of Ireland's efforts as a mediator see O'Connell, 441–454. John T. Farrell, "Archbishop Ireland and Manifest Destiny," *Catholic Historical Review* XXXIII (October, 1947):269–301. John Offner, "Washington Mission: Archbishop Ireland on the Eve of the Spanish-American War," *Catholic Historical Review* LXXIII 4 (October, 1987):562–575.

48. "Can War Be Justified?" *Review* V 8 (May 12, 1898):8.

49. "The Church-Monarchy, Aristocracy and Democracy," *Review* V 2 (March 31, 1898):1.

50. On the myth of Americanism see, Thomas E. Wangler, "American Catholic Expansionism: 1886–1894,"*Harvard Theological Review* 75:3 (1982) 369–93

and "Americanist Beliefs and Papal Orthodoxy: 1884–1899," *U.S. Catholic Historian* XI 3 (Summer, 1993):37–52.

51. "Americanism," *Review* 33 (October 7, 1897):3.

52. "True and False Americanism," *Review* IV 30 (October 14, 1897):4–5.

53. "A True View of the Life of Fr. Hecker," *Review* IV 31 (October 21, 1897):1–2.

54. "Monsignor Keane's 'American'" *Review* V 2 (March 31, 1898):6–7. "Monsignor Keane's 'American' and the Parliament of Religions," V 3 (April 7, 1898):7. and "Monsignor Keane's 'American'and Modem Civilization," V 4 (April 14, 1898):6.

55. "Bishop Neumann and Isaac Hecker," *Review* V 9 (May 19, 1898):1–2.

56. "Two Missionaries," *Review* V 14 (June 23, 1898):7–8.

57. "Father Hecker–His Illness," *Review* V 19 (July 28, 1898):6.

58. Ibid., Thomas Wangler echoes Meifuss' charge that it was the Americanists and their French Liberal allies who had distorted Hecker's image. "The zealous Hecker ended up the used Hecker." Thomas Wangler, "Americanist Beliefs and Papal Orthodoxy: 1884–1899," *U.S. Catholic Historian* XI 3 (Summer 1993):51.

59. Marvin O'Connell reports that Ireland was heavily involved in real estate speculation and, apparently, not very successful at it. O'Connell, 375–385.

60. "True and False Liberalism," *Review* V 12 (June 9, 1898):3.

61. "Father Hecker, Is He a Saint?" *Review* V 15 (June 30, 1898): 1. For a biographical sketch of Charles Maignen (1858–1937), see Emile Poulat, *Intégrisme et Catholisme Intégral Un réseau secret international antimodemiste: La "Sapinière" (1909–1921),* (Casterman, 1969), 273–275.

62. For details on the promotion campaign which surrounded the publication of Elliot's *Life of Father Hecker* in France see McAvoy, 163–173. Fogarty, *The Vatican and the Americanist Crisis*, 261–272. John Tracy Ellis, *The Life of James Cardinal Gibbons* (Milwaukee: Bruce Publishing Co., 1952) Volume II, 50–54.

63. See Fogarty, *The Vatican and the Americanist Crisis*, 281–282 and McAvoy, 210 for confirmation of this. Ellis, 56.

64. "Liberalism Staggering Under a Terrific Blow," *Review* V 16 (July 7, 1898):3.

65. Synchronos, "Roman Letter," *Review* V 16 (July 7, 1898):2.

66. Wangler, "American Catholic Expansionism." Eugene Boeglin worked with O'Connell in Rome with promoting the Americanist agenda through use of the press until his expulsion from Italy in 1894. After this date he continued this work from Paris as the bi-weekly correspondent for the *New York Sun*, as well as other papers, using the pen name "Innominato." By 1897 Preuss was aware of "No name"'s true identity *Review* IV 27(September 23, 1897):3.

67. Franz X. Kraus and Herman Schell were liberal German theologians as well as friends and collaborators with the Americanists, O'Connell and Ireland. Fogarty, *The Vatican and the Americanist Crisis*, 260, 269–272. David F. Sweeney, O.F.M., "Herman Schell, 1850–1906: A German Dimension to the Americanist Controversy," *Catholic Historical Review* LXXVI 1 (January 1990):44–70. Robert C. Ayers, "The Americanist Attack on Europe in 1897 and 1898 " in *Rising from History* ed. Robert Daly (Lanham,MD: University Press of America, 1987) 81–92.

68. A. J. DeLattre was a Belgian Jesuit and his critique of Americanism appeared in Europe on June 16, 1898. McAvoy, 225–226.

69. "Americanism in a French Light," *Review* V 20 (August 4, 1898):7.

70. "The Movement Against Americanism–An Italian View," *Review* V 21 (August 11, 1898):I-2. McAvoy attributed this pamphlet to Salvatore Brandi, S.J., editor of *La Civilta Cattolica*. McAvoy 229 & 233.

71. "The Abbe Maignen and His Book," *Review* V 22 (August 18, 1898):4.

72. "Monsignor O'Connell's Disavowal of Americanism," *Review* V 22 (August 18, 1898):8.

73. "Father Hecker, A Bone of Contention," *Review* V 23 (August 25, 1898):6.

74. "Americanism," *Review* V 24 (September 1, 1898):5-6. McAvoy, 229–233.

75. McAvoy, 261–262.

76. "The Elements of Americanism," *Review* V 33 (November 3, 1898):3.

77. "Dr. Maignen's Book and the Benzinger Brothers," *Review* V 28 (September 29, 1898):3.

78. Preuss's suggestion of Archbishop Keane's direct involvement in this affair was not repeated in the *Review* or in any of the standard works on Americanism.

79. "An Unwelcome Production," *Review* V 31 (October 20, 1898):2.

80. "Maignen's Book on Hecker, " *Review* V 31 (December 1, 1898): 1.

81. Arthur Preuss to Peter Baart, December 17, 1898 Baart Papers, CBAA Box 2, AUND.

82. Fogarty, *The Vatican and the Americanist Crisis*, 286–288. O'Connell, 457. McAvoy, 264 & 272.

83. "Status of the Hecker Controversy," *Review* V 35 (November 17, 1898):4.

84. Synchronos, *Review* V 38 (December 8,1898):2. & 41 (December 29, 1898):1

85. Ibid.,

86. J. F. Meifuss, "The Reason Why?" *Review* V 42 (January 5, 1899):3.

87. "A Badge of Misrepresentations," *Review* V 42 (January 5, 1899):2.

88. J. F. Meifuss, "A Rotten Plank Held Out to Save Americanism," *Review* V 43 (January 12, 1899):5.

89. "Americanism Condemned," *Review* V 50 (March 2, 1899):1-2.

L'Osservatore Romano published the letter on February 21. An English translation was published in Baltimore on February 23. Preuss was not pleased with the English translation of Leo's letter provided to the press by Cardinal Gibbons. Saying that it was made "probably under the supervision of Father Magnien, S. S.", it was "poorly wrought." Preuss was not alone in his criticism and the Jesuits soon provided an alternate translation. McAvoy, 275 n27.

90. On Catholic press reaction in America, McAvoy, 297–300.

91. J. F. Meifuss, "The Liberals Trying to Make Dr. Périès Their Scapegoat," *Review* VI 17 (July 13, 1899):13 1. "The Americanists in Desperate Straits," VI 18 (July 20, 1899):139. Périès dismissal from Catholic University was used to publicly undermine him. McAvoy, 327–330. Archbishop Ireland "leaked" documents held by the University's Board of Trustees to the press in the effort to undermine Périès as the "Real Author of Americanism", see Hogan, 165–167.

92. As the responses from the various groups of American bishops to *Testem Benevolentiae* were made public, Preuss published them in the *Review*. On the "submissions" and the responses of the American bishops see McAvoy, 281–287, 290–297.

93. "The Voice of McQuaid," *Review* VI 17 (July 13,1899):129. On McQuaid's sermon see Robert F. McNamara, "Bernard J. McQuaid's Sermon on Theological 'Americanism,'" *Records of the American Catholic Historical Society of Philadelphia*, 90 (1979):33–52. Glen Jamus, "Bishop Bernard McQuaid: On 'True' and 'False' Americanism," *U.S. Catholic Historian* Vol. 11 n.3 (Summer 1993):53–76. McQuaid cited as instances of Americanism participation in the Parliament of Religions, John Keane's speech in a Harvard chapel, the support for Catholic use of public schools, and the toleration of Catholic membership in secret societies.

94. "That Unpublished Index Decree," *Review* VI 3 (April 6, 1899):20. "Retraction Wanted From Father Elliott," VI 5 (April 20, 1899):37. "Dr. Zahm Withdraws *Evolution and Dogma*," VI 16 (July 6, 1899):12 1.

95. "Charbonnel and Cardinal Gibbons," *Review VI* I (March 23, 1899):4. "Cardinal Gibbons and M. Charbonnel: A Denial," VI 6 (April 27, 1899):47. Victor Charbonnel was a young priest and writer who actively promoted a the "equality" of all religions. Charbonnel left the Church in 1896 after Pope Leo XIII prohibited Catholic participation in a Parliament of Religions to be held in 1900 at the World's Exposition. Much to the embarrassment of the Americanists, Charbonnel continued to profess that he was merely a follower of their group. McAvoy, 123, 127 & 152.

96. Archbishop John Kain to Alphonse Magnien, April 8, 1899. Quoted in William B. Faherty, *Dream By the River* (St. Louis: Piraeus Publishers, 1973), 133.

97. For a concise treatment of this stage in the controversy over Jansenism see Louis Cognet, "Ecclesiastical Life in France," in *The History of the Church* VI ed. Hubert Jedin, ibid., 24–56.

98. "A Roman Interpretation of the Pope's Brief on Americanism, " *Review* VI 3 (April 6, 1899):21.

99. "Our Heckerites and Their Jansenistic Methods," *Review* 8 (May 11, 1899):57. The *Catholic Citizen* of Milwaukee was edited by Humphrey Desmond who was a supporter of Archbishop John Ireland.

100. See McAvoy, 296–297 for text of the bishops' letter,

101. McAvoy, 297 n46 & 331. O'Connell, 583 n1O6. Although the *Northwestern Chronicle* was not the official Catholic paper for the Archdiocese of St. Paul, Archbishop Ireland frequently wrote editorials for the paper. McAvoy, 81, 134–135.

102. Charles Maignen, "A Little Syllabus," *Review* VI 3 (April 6, 1899):17. See McAvoy, 301–302 on Maignen's "Little Syllabus."

103. J. F.Meifuss, "Throwing Volumes of Divinity at a Donkey," *Review* VI 29 (October 5, 1899):228.

104. "Important Notice," *Review* VI 48 (February 15, 1900):1.

105. "Diligentibus Deum Onmia Cooperantur in Bonum, " *Review* VI 50 (March 1, 1900):1.

106. Interview Austin Preuss, November 13, 1993.

107. Coincidently, all three of these priests wrote their letters on March 5, 1900. These letters are found on Reel 13 A. P. P.

108. Abbot Charles Mohr to Arthur Preuss, March 3, 1900. Reel 13 A.P.P. Abbot Charles and Arthur Preuss maintained a regular correspondence from 1907 until the Abbot's death in 1931. Unfortunately, Preuss's half of the correspondence is no longer extant.

109. Michael Corrigan to Arthur Preuss. February 24, 1899 Reel 13, A.P.P.

110. Arthur Preuss to Michael Corrigan, March 1, 1900. Archives of the Archdiocese of New York, G–21 (copy).

111. J. F. Meifuss, "Archbishop Corrigan and Dr. McGlynn," *Review* VI 48 (February 15,1900):2. For an account of the long conflict between Archbishop Corrigan and Father Edward McGlynn over the latter's political activities see Robert Emmett Curran, S.J. *Michael Augustine Corrigan and the Shaping of Conservative Catholicism in America, 1878–1902* (New York: Arno Press, 1978).

112. "Archbishop Corrigan," *Review* IX 19 (May 15, 1902):293.

113. "How Archbishop Corrigan Became a Cardinal," *Review* IX 24 (June 19, 1902):380. "Notebook," IX 28 (July 17, 1902):447. Dr. James F. Corrigan to Arthur Preuss, June 29, 1902, July 22, 1902 and August 5, 1902. Reel # 1, A.P.P. Neither Ellis' *Life of Cardinal Gibbons*, or Curran's, *Michael Augustine*

Corrigan address James Corrigan's claims in regard to his bother.

114. "Archbishop Ireland and the Cardinalate," *Review* VII 47 (February 14, 1901):373.

115. See *Review* issues for March 22, April 5, April 26, July 29,& August 16,1900.

116. "Topics of the Day," *Review* VII 29 (October II, 1900):229.

117. "Outcroppings of Americanism," *Review* VI 43 (January 4, 1900):339.

118. "Is Heckerism Really Condemned?" *Review* VI 9 (May 18, 1899):65.

119. "The End of Americanism in France," *Review* VII 2 (March 29, 1900):10. VII 3 (April 5, 1900):19. and VII 4(April 12, 1900):26.

120. "The End of Americanism in France," *Review* VII 4 (April 12, 1900):26.

121. Wangler, "Etheridge," 90.

122. "The Americanism Which Pope Leo Condemned," *Review* VIII 17 (July 10, 1901):129.

123. On the Vatican influence on the English pastoral see David G. Schultenover, S.J., *A View From Rome: On the Eve of the Modernist Crisis* (New York: Fordham University Press, 1993), 65–130.

124. Sarda y Salvany's book, *El liberalismo es pecado*, caused much controversy in Spain when it was first published. It has been called the "vademecum of the Integrists." The English version has recently been reprinted under the title, *Liberalism Is a Sin*. John N. Schumacher, "Integrism: A Study in Nineteenth-Century Spanish Politico-Religious Thought," *Catholic Historical Review* XLVIII 3 (October, 1962):343–364.

125. "Liberalism," *Review* VI 34 (November 9, 1899):265–266.

126. *Review* VI 38 (December 7, 1899):297.

127. "Sacred Articles From the Philippines in American Junk Shops," *Review* VI 37 (November 30, 1899):293.

128. O'Connell, 455. Wangler, "American Catholic Expansionism,"

129. J. F. Meifuss, "Vision and Reality," *Review* VI 14 (June 22, 1899):109.

130. "The Catholic Federation," *Review* VII 38 (December 13, 1900):297.

131. "Again the Heathen at Home," *Review* VI 40 (December 21, 1899):313.

132. "Paganism in Our 'Christian' Country," VI 38 (December 7, 1899):297.

133. *Review* VIII 6 (May 2, 1901):81–83.

134. "Our Sixth Year," *Review* VI 1 (March 23, 1899):1.

135. The notice that Keane, Elliot and Klein gave to the *Review* has already been noted. In 1903, Archbishop Ireland wrote to Denis O'Connell remarking on Preuss's incredulity that O'Connell had been named rector of the Catholic University. Fogarty, 289.

136. Curran, 510–511.

III Militant Catholicism for the Twentieth Century

1. David Thompson, *Europe Since Napoleon*, (London:Longmanns,1986), 390-391. David Shannon, *Twentieth Century America* Vol. I "The Progressive Era" (Chicago:Rand McNally & 1969), 3-4. Arthur S. Link and William B Catton, *American Epoch: A History of the United States Since the 1890s* (New York: Alfred Knopf, 1967),17.

2. "A French View of Religion in America," *Review*, X 19(May 14, 1903):289-292.

3. "The Fifth Commandment of the Church," *Review* X 35 (September 17, 1903):545-547. "On the Needless Multiplication of Catholic Societies," XII 16 (August 15, 1905):452-453. "The Catholic Church and the American Negro," XII 13 (July 1, 1905): 379-380. "Marginalia," XIII 14 (July 15, 1906):459. "Prominent Catholics in Public Life," XIV 3 (February 1, 1907):76. "Flotsam & Jetsam," XVI 7 (July 1, 1909):218.

4. "The Historic Groundwork of the Legend of the Holy House of Loretto," *Review* IX 2 (January 16, 1902):22-23. "The Holy House of Loretto and Critical Catholic Scholarship," XIV 3 (February 1, 1907):67-69. "A Learned Jesuit on the Legend of Loretto," XVII 24 (December 15, 1910):756.

5. "Objectionable Devotions," *Review* XIV (April 15, 1907):240-241. "Concerning Pious Practices," XII 10 (May 15, 1905):294-296. "Alleged Relics of the Precious Blood," XVI 10 (May 15, 1909):295-298. "The History of a Curious Relic," XIII (November 15, 1906):714-717.

6. "Regarding Lourdes," *Review* XII 24 (November 1, 1905):718-720. "A Letter from the Bishop of Tarbes on Lourdes," XIII 4 (February 15, 1906):102-105. "Another Letter from the Bishop of Tarbes," XIII 10 (May 15, 1906):329-330. "The Secret of La Salette," XIV 20 (October 15, 1907):613-615.

7. "Devotional Practices and Criticism," *Review* XIII 7 (April 1, 1906):219-220. Herbert Thurston, "Messina's Buried Palladium," XVI 19 (October 1, 1909):554-558. "Iconoclastic Criticism," XVIII 9 (May 1, 1911):268-271. Hermann Grisar,"Ultra-Conservatism in Catholic Historical Criticism," VIII 9 (May 23, 1900):129-135. H. Delehaye, "Legends of the Saints," XV 9 (May 1, 1908):258-261.

8. Oskar Koehler, "Forms of Piety", *History of the Church* IX, ed. Hubert Jedin (New York: Crossroad Publishing Company, 1981), 260-262. For an account of American Catholic devotion to the Eucharist see Chinnici, 146-156.

9. "Conservative versus Liberal Catholics," *Review* VIII 31 (July 15, 1902):481.

10. "How Can Religion Be Brought to Bear on the Lives of Our College

Students?" *Review* XIII 2   (January 15, 1906):34. Arthur Preuss to Francis Markert, S. V. D. October 26, 1912.   Francis Market to Archbishop George Mundelein June 9, 1916 (copy) Reel 14. A.P.P.

11. Arthur Preuss's papers contain many letters from Bede Maler. A.P.P.

12. J.A.K. "The Difficulty of Spiritual Communion," *Review* XVI 20 (October 15, 1909):579.

13. "Confession versus Communion," *Review* XIX 12 (June 15,1912):363. L. F. Schlathoelter, "Confession and Daily Communion," XIX 13 (July 1, 1912):419. XIX 21(November 1,1912):595. XXII 17 (September 1, 1915):559.

14. Sarah C. Burnett, "A Plea for the Modification of the Eucharistic Fast," *Review* XIX 7 (April 1, 1912):208. "Concerning the Modification of the Eucharistic Fast," XIX 14 (July 15, 1912):487.   "The Modification of the Eucharistic Fast," XIX 15 (August 1, 1912):582. XX 8 (April 15, 1913):233. "For The Mitigation of the Eucharistic Fast," XX I (January 1, 1913):1.

15. "Interpreting the Pope's Decree on First Communion," *Review* XVIII 3 (February 1. 1911):65. "Three Objections Against the New First Communion Practice," XVIII 7(April 1, 1911):209.

16. Erwin Iserloh, "Movements within the Church and Their Spirituality," *History of the Church* X ed. Hubert Jedin, 312–313.

17. "Church Music," *Review* I 14 (November 21, 1894):4. "Pius X On the Reform of Church Music," XI 4 (January 28):54–56. 5 (February 4, 1904):73–76. 6 (February 11, 1904):83–85.

18. "Joseph Otten," *Review* XXXIII 24 (December 15, 1926):555.   Otten's wife, Susan Tracy Otten, "an extraordinarily gifted woman," also wrote numerous articles and reviews on literature for Preuss over a period of twenty-five years. "Susan Tracy Otten R.I. P." XXXIII 9 (May 1, 1926):195. Joseph Otten, "Our Status in Church Music," XI 18 (May 5, 1904):284–285. "Church Music," XIV 14(July 15, 1907):432–435. "As To Congregational Singing," XVI 19 (October 1, 1909):563–564. "Why Protestant Hymns Should Not Be Sung In Catholic Churches," XVIII 18 (September 15, 1911):567.

19. "Mixed Marriage as a Principal Cause of Catholic Defection," *Review* XI 5 (February 4, 1904):77 "Against Mixed Marriages," XV 21 (November 1, 1908):644–648. "How to Check the Mixed Marriage Evil," XVIII 19 (October 1, 1910):587–589.

20. "Concerning Mixed Marriages," *Echo* October 12, 1922.

21. "Our Hierarchy and Mixed Marriages," *Review* X 15 (April 16, 1903):230–232.

22. "A Grave Public Scandal," *Review* XVIII 14 (July 15, 1911):411–413.

23. "Longinqua oceani," in *Documents of American Catholic History* Vol. II ed. John Tracy Ellis (Wilmington, DE: Michael Glazier, 1987), 499–513.

24. "The Church and Divorce," *Review* XV 17 (September 1, 1908):522–524.

25. Bernard Otten, S.J.,"Protestantism and Divorce," *Review* XIII 20 (October 15, 1906):654. Comte E. D'Amoux, "The Root of the Divorce Evil," XVII 3 (February 1, 1910):47–48.

26. "Race Suicide and How to Combat It," *Review* XVI 23 (December 1, 1909):680–683. Also "The Race Suicide Problem," XVII 7 (April 1, 1910):205–207.

27. "The Catholic Physician," *Review* XI 42 (November 3, 1904):657–662. "Ante-Natal Infanticide," XII I (January 1, 1905):10–12. "Race Suicide in the United States," XIV 19 (October 1, 1907):581–582.

28. "A Protestant Layman on the Decadence of Protestantism," *Review* X (January 8, 1903):6–9.

29. Dr. Ferdinand J. Schmidt, "The Decline of Protestantism," *Review* XI 20 (May 19, 1904) 312–313. Also "The Failure of Protestantism," XV 14 (July 15, 1908):418–42 1.

30. "The Bankruptcy of Protestant Theology," *Review* XIII 5 (March 1, 1906):152–153.

31. "Protestantism's Dilemma," *Review* XIV 4 (February 15, 1907):104–106.

32. "The Late Mr. Moody," *Review* VI 42 (January 4, 1900):332. Washington Gladden, "Mr. Sheldon's Daily Christian Newspaper," VII 5 (April 19, 1900):35.

33. "The Vagaries of Liberal Theology," *Review* XVI 1 1 (June 1, 1909):331–334. "Protestantism's Real Peril," XIX 20 (October 15, 1912):556–557.

34. Martin E. Marty, *Righteous Empire: The Protestant Experience in America* (New York: The Dial Press, 1970),181.

35. "The Duty of the Hour," *Review* IX 2 (January 6, 1902):17–18.

36. Alfred J. Ede, *The Lay Crusade for a Christian America: A Study of the American Federation of Catholic Societies, 1900–1919* (New York: Garland Publishing,Inc, 1988), 57.

37. Francis P. Prucha, S.J., *The Churches and the Indian Schools 1888–1912* (Lincoln:University of Nebraska Press, 1949), 27–40.

38. "Our Catholic Indian Schools," *Review* VII 52 (March 8, 1900):412. "In the Interests of the Catholic Indian Bureau and Its Charges," XI 33 (January 9,1904):524–525.

39. Frank T. Reuter, *Catholic Influence on American Colonial Policies* (Austin: University of Texas, 1967), 98.

40. "The Responsibility for the Spanish War," *Review* IX 8 (February 27, 1902):113–114. "The Preventable War with Spain," IX 10 (March 13, 1902):145–147. "American Tyranny in the Philippines" IX 5 (February 6, 1902):83. "Catholic Grievances in the Philippines," XIII 14 (July 15, 1906):444–446. "The Protestantization of the Philippines," IX 20 (May 22,

1902):308–311. "Morality in the Philippines," X 34 (September 10, 1903) 537–539. "American Blessings For Catholic Filipinos," XIV 14 (July 15, 1907):430–432. "Grabbing the Friar Lands in the Philippines," XVII 7 (April 1, 1910):209.

41. Reuter, 31, 68–69, 85–87.

42. Ede, 59–62.

43. "American Catholic Centre Party for the U.S.," *Review* V 33 (November 3, 1898):4

44. "The Growing Need for an American Catholic Centre Party," *Review* VI 3 (November 3, 1898):4. Ludwig Windthorst (1812–1891) was the founder of the Centre Party in Germany in 1871. The Centre Party was established to protect and advance Catholic interests in that country.

45. "Catholic Political Parties, " *Review* VI 47 (February 1, 1900):364.

46. Ede, 45–47. Gleason, 76–77.

47. "Shall Our Catholic Societies Unite?" *Review* VII 50 (March 1, 1900):396.

48. "Exchange Comment," *Review* VII I (March 22, 1900):4–5.

49. "Bishop McFaul in Favor of a Centre Party for the U.S.," *Review* VII I 1 (May 31, 1900):60.

50. "How Are We to Make Our Rights Respected?" *Review* VII 14 (June 21, 1900):108. Congressman John F. Fitzgerald of Boston was regarded as the only "effectual" Catholic member of Congress and he "became something of a hero to the Catholic press." Reuter, 31. He was also the grandfather of the only Catholic elected president of the United States.

51. "Exchange Comment," *Review* I 10 (June 21, 1900):110.

52. "Is Catholicity a Bar to Public Office?" *Review* VII 19 (July 26, 1900):148.

53. Most Rev. Sebastian Messmer, "The Duty of Catholic Laymen in Our Age," *Review* VII 21 (August 16,1900):163–164. 170–171.

54. Ede, 64–65. "A Program for Catholic Federation," *Review* VII 34 (November 15, 1900):265–266.

55. Ede, 65–66, 70–72, 78. Ellis, 375–378.

56. "Catholic Federation Movement," *Review* VII 38 (December 13, 1900):292.

57. "Catholic Federation Movement," *Review* VII 40 (December 27, 1900):316. "Catholic Federation Movement," VII 41 (January 3, 1901):324–325.

58. "Catholic Federation Movement," *Review* VII 46 (February 7, 1901):365.

59. Ede, 71–73.

60. "Catholic Federation Movement," *Review* VIII 5 (April 25, 1901):74.

61. "Bishop O'Connell's Advice," *Review* VIII 19, August 8, 1901):301.

62. "An Opposing Federation," *Review* VIII 28 (October 10, 1901):447.

63. "Catholic Federation, Its Objects," *Review* VIII 27 (October 3, 1901):426.

64. "The Germans and the Cincinnati Congress," *Review* VIII 33 (November 14, 1901): 524. "The Catholic Federation," 34 (November 21, 1901):543.

"The Catholic Federation," 35 (November 28, 1901):554.

65. Ireland to McFaul, March 26, 1901 cited in Ede, 71-72.

66. "The Catholic Federation," *Review* VIII 35 (December 5, 1901):553.

67. "Editorial Notes," *Catholic World* LXXIV (November 1901):274.

68. "A Dissenting Voice," *Review* VIII 34 (November 21, 1901):543.

69. "The Archbishops and Federation," *Review* VIII 34 (November 21, 1901):542."The Archbishops and Federation," 35 (November 28, 1901): 553-554. *Catholic Telegraph* (Cincinnati) 48 1901 cited in "Opposers of Federation," *Review* VIII 37 (December 12, 1901):586.

70. Gleason, 63-65.

71. "The Cincinnati Convention and Catholic Federation," *Review* IX I (January 9, 1902):3-6.

72. "The Catholic Federation," *Review* IX 10 (March 13, 1902):154-155.

73. "Note Book," *Review* IX 10 (March 13, 1902):159. Coincidentally, the Protestant minister who invited Minahan was Washington Gladden, who had been praised previously by Preuss. See n.49.

74. "The Catholic Federation," *Review* IX II (March 20, 1900):170-171.

75. "The President of the Catholic Federation and the *Review*," *Review* IX 13 (April 3, 1902):196-203.

76. "Catholic Federation," *Review* IX 17 (May 1, 1902):264. "The Catholic Federation," *Review* IX 19 (May 15, 1902):282.

77. Ede, 92-97.

78. "The Federation Movement, Archbishop Ireland, and the German Element," *Review* IX 44 (November 13, 1902):699.

79. Cited in Frederick J. Zwierlein, *Theodore Roosevelt and Catholics, 1882-1919* (Rochester, N.Y.: Art Print Shop, 1956),55.

80. Ede, 92-93.

81. "Archbishop Ireland vs Archbishop Ireland," *Review* IX 36 (September 18, 1902):562-563.

82. "Irelandism Exit," *Review* IX 36 (September 18, 1902):562-563.

83. "The Catholic Federation and Politics," *Review* X 5 (February 5, 1903):65-66.

84. "The Fundamental Error of Modern Democracy," *Review* IX 31 (August 7, 1902):486-489. Preuss never stated how "the better sort" and those of lesser talents were to be distinguished within the political system.

85. "The Catholic Federation and Politics," *Review* XI 2 (January 14, 1904):2. "A Catholic Party for Australia," XI 43 (November 10, 1904):681. "The Catholic Federation and Politics," XVI 12 (June 15, 1909):378.

86. "Shall We Demand a Share in the Public School Fund?" *Review* XIV 12 (June 15, 1907):357-359. ibid, 16 (August 15, 1907):505.

87. "The Catholic Federation and the Stage," *Review* XIII 2 (January 15,

1906):51. "The Catholic Federation and the Divorce Laws," XIV 2 (January 15, 1907):47.

IV The Fallacy of Socialism and Masonic Tomfoolery

1. Arthur S. Link and William B. Catton, *American Epoch: A History of the United States Since the 1890's*, 17, 36.

2. On the "Social Gospel" movement see Jean Miller Schmidt, *Souls or the Social Order: The Two Party System American Protestantism* (New York: Carlson Publishing, Inc., 1991). Martin Marty, ed. *Modernism and Its World: Historical Articles on Protestantism in American Religious Life* v. 6 "Protestantism and Social Christianity" (New York: K.G. Saur, 1992). Shannon, 5–7. Link and Catton, 13–14, & 37.

3. Link and Catton, 58–63.

4. Arthur Preuss, *The Fundamental Fallacy of Socialism* (St. Louis: Herder, 1908). Aaron J. Abell, *American Catholicism and Social Action: A Search for Social Justice 1865–1950* (Garden City, NY: Doubleday & Co., 1960), 140–141.

5. Abell, 61. Arthur Nichols Young, *The Single Tax Movement in the United States* (Princeton: Princeton University Press, 1916), 66–67, 75–78. Link and Catton, 14.

6. For perspectives on the "McGlynn Case" see Robert Emmett Curran, *Michael Augustine Corrigan the Shaping of Conservative Catholicism in America, 1878–1902*, ibid. Gerald P. Fogarty, *The Vatican and the American Hierarchy from 1870 to 1965*, ibid, 93–114.

7. Review II (April 1, 1894):4. II 28 (October 3, 1895) Because of what he regarded as Satolli's inept handling of the McGlynn case, Preuss never did place much trust in the Archbishop even after Satolli joined the conservative assault on his former allies, Ireland, Keane and O'Connell. "The Death of Cardinal Satolli," *Review* XVIII 3 (February 1, 1910):90.

8. Young, 141–217.

9. "On the Single Tax," *Review* XI 15 (April 14, 1904):225–228. 16 (April 21, 1904):250–252. 17 (April 28, 1904):260–263. 18 (May 5, 1904):277–282. 19 (May 12, 1904):292–296. 21 (May 26, 1904):324–329. 22 (June 2, 1904):329–334. 23 (June 9, 1904):356–360. 38 (September 22, 1904):593–600. 40 (October 6, 1904):630–636. 41 (October 13, 1904):645–649. 44 (November 3, 1904):693–696 45 (November 17, 1904):712–716. XII 9 (May 1, 1905):241–243. 10 (May 15,1905):286–290. 11 (June 1, 1905):313–315. 12 (June 15, 1905):341–343.

10. Arthur Preuss, *The Fundamental Fallacy of Socialism*, 154.

11. "An Appeal to the Readers of the Catholic Fortnightly Review," *Review*, XII (June 1, 1905):336. Gleason, 100. Arthur Preuss formally succeeded his father Edward as editor of *Die Amerika* in 1902 although he had in fact been the acting editor in the last few years of his father's illness. Upon the elder Preuss's death in July, 1904, Arthur Preuss began to look for a successor. In letters to both Kenkel and the directors of *Die Amerika* Arthur Preuss indicated that the burden of being the editor of a daily newspaper was too much for his physical health, nor did it suit his temperament. Arthur Preuss to Frederick Kenkel, March 9, 1905. Kenkel Papers CKNA.AUND

12. Gleason, 92–100.

13. Arthur Preuss's Diary, October 12, 1906. Reel 2 A.P.P. Preuss sold his home to Kenkel for $4000 though he believed he could have received $5,500 for it. Kenkel put $500. down and was to pay the remainder over the next three years.

14. Gleason recorded that Kenkel had a "rather autocratic tendency" and "found it difficult to accommodate himself to direction by others." Gleason, 101.

15. Gleason, 102. "The Social Question in America," *Review* XVI 15 (August 1, 1909):433–436.

16. For a summary of Catholic social thought in the early twentieth century see David J. O'Brien, *American Catholics and Social Reform: The New Deal Years* (New York: Oxford University Press, 1968), 3–46.

17. "Editorial Paragraphs," *Review* I 2 (May 1, 1894):16. "Our Atheistic Republic," VIII 6 (March 15, 1906):187.

18. "For A Catholic Social Movement," *Review* IX 11(March 20, 1902):167–169. "The Cost of Cheapness," XII (September 1, 1905):496–499.

19. Link and Catton, 64. Abell, 141.

20. "Catholic Labor Unions," *Review* IX 21 (May 29, 1902):330–331. "Labor Unions Once More," IX 27 (July 10,1902):417–420.

21. "For A Catholic Social Movement," *Review* IX 11 (March 20, 1902):167–169.

22. A sampling of these *Review* articles follows. On Socialism: "Socialism in the United States," X 5 (February 5, 1903):74. "Why Socialists Clamor For 'Free Love'," XIV 12 (June 15, 1907):359–361. "The Socialist Storm Cloud," XV 14 (July 15, 1908):421–423. "Insidious Socialism," XVIII 8 (September 15, 1911):519–520. On Catholic Response: "How Are We to Combat Socialism?" XI 8 (February 25, 1904):113–115. "Catholic Social Reform in Belgium," XI 27 (July 7, 1904):417–420. "The Clergy and Social Reform," XVI 20 (October 15, 1909):596. "Catholic Social Work," XVIII 8 (April 15, 1911):238–239. On Capitalism: "The Steel Trusts Profit Sharing Plan," X 16 (April 23, 1903):248–251. "How Cheaply Life is Held by Some of the Great Corporations," XII 14 (July 15, 1905):405–406. "The Moral Aspects of

Socialism," XVI 18 (September 15, 1909):534. "A Priest's Debate With A Socialist," XVIII 17 (September 1, 1911):488-490.

24. "How Not To Combat Socialism," *Review* XVIII 5 (March 1, 1911):138-139.

25. On Father John A. Ryan see Francis L. Broderick, *Right Reverend New Dealer: John A. Ryan* (New York: The Macmillan Co, 1963) Patrick W. Carey, *American Catholic Religious Thought* (New York: Paulist Press, 1987), 242-252. John Ryan visited Preuss at his home in St. Louis on at least one occasion and for a number of years they remained friendly collaborators. Though they would always have kind words for each other, they parted ways over the establishment of the National Catholic Welfare Council which Preuss opposed. Arthur Preuss to Fr. Francis Markert, June 26, 1919. Reel 14 A.P.P.

26. Mark C. Carnes, *Secret Ritual and Manhood in Victorian America* (Yale University Press: New Haven, 1989), 22.

Lynn Dumenil, *Freemasonry and American Culture 1880-1930* (Princeton University Press: Princeton, 1984),1.

27. Arthur Preuss, *Studies in American Freemasonry* (B. Herder: St. Louis, 1908). iii.

28. "Humanum Genus," *The Papal Encyclicals 1878-1903* ed. Claudia Carlson (Raliegh,NC: McGrath Publishing Co., 1981).

29. Hermann Gruber, "Masonry", *The Catholic Encyclopedia*, 1913 edition.

30. "Humanum Genus," Carlson.

31. For the relationship between Masonry and the Enlightenment see Margaret C. Jacob, *Living the Enlightenment: Freemasonry and Politics in Eighteenth Century Europe* (Oxford University Press, New York, 1991).

32. "The Vaughn Controversy," *Review* III 31 (October 22, 1896):2.

"The Taxil-Bataile-Vaughn Swindle," III 37 (December 3, 1896): 1.

For a brief account of the "Vaughn Affair" see Oskar Kohler, *History of the Church* IX ed. Hubert Jedin, 217-218.

"Editor Preuss and His *Review*." *Review* III 41 (December 31, 1896):3.

33. "Rome's Final Answer," *Review* II 25 (September 12, 1895):1.

L Fouquet, "The Origin of Modern English Cosmopolitan Freemasonry," II 39, 40, 41 & 42 (December 19, 1895, December 26, 1895, January 2, 1896, January 9, 1896). "Satanism in Freemasonry," III 2 (April 2, 1896):3.

34. Writing to Frederick Kenkel in 1926, Preuss said of his *Study in Freemasonry*, "The 'Study,' by the way, went into its fourth edition in 1920, though, of course, as you say, the sale has not been what might have been expected... It may interest you to know that I never received one cent of royalty on this book, having assigned my royalty rights in it to the Society of Jesus in compensation for the aid Fr. Riordan, S.J. gave me in its compilation." Preuss's *Study of American Freemasonry* was also published in a French edition.

35. H.L. Hayward and James E. Craig, *A History of Freemasonry* (John Day Co.,: New York, 1927), 6–7. Carnes, 35, 133–139.

36. Carnes, 9.

37. "Studies in American Freemasonry," *Review* X 21(May 25, 1903):321–325 "Esoteric and Exoteric,"XI 15 (April 14, 1904):231–232. Albert Mackey, *Masonic Lexicon* quoted in "Esoteric and Exoteric Masonry," *Review* XI 15 (April 14, 1904):231.

38. "American Freemasonry is a Religion," *Review* X 22 (June 4, 1903):338–342. "Masonry's Own Admission It Is A Religion," X 26 (July 2, 1903):405–408. "The Religion of American Freemasonry is the Religion of the Pagan Mysteries," X 39 (October 903):620–624. "The Pagan Origins of Freemasonry," X 41 (October 29. 1903):649–652. "Another Masonic Perversion of Scripture," XI 22 (June 2, 1904):344–345. "Phallic Worship in American Freemasonry," X 47 (December 10, 1903):745–748. "How Freemasonry Rejects Jesus Christ As the Cornerstone of Its Moral and Religious System," XI 20 (May 19, 1904):307–309.

39. "American Freemasonry Is In A Special Manner Anti-Catholic," *Review* XI (March 17, 1904):161–162.

40. Carnes, 35.

41. Carnes, 62–63.

42. Carnes, 60–61.

43. "The Knights of Columbus," *Review* VII I (March 22, 1900): 1. "That the Order of the Knights of Columbus is a Stepping Stone to Freemasonry," XI 24 (June 16, 1904):379–380.

44. "An Extract From the Ritual of the Catholic Elks," *Review* VIII 36 (December 5, 1901):562 "The Knights of the Columbus and the *Review*," VIII 39 (December 26, 1901):609–614.

45. Christopher J. Kauffman, *Faith and Fraternalism: The History of the Knights of Columbus 1882–1982* (New York: Harper & Row, 1982),93, 154, 158–159.

V The Modernist Crisis

1. For an account of the Modernist crisis see Marvin R. O'Connell, *Critics On Trial An Introduction to the Catholic Modernist Crisis* (Washington,DC: The Catholic University of America Press, 1994). On the seeming lack of impact of the anti-Modernist decrees on the Church in America see Michael Gannon, "Before and After Modernism: The Intellectual Isolation of the American Priest," in *The Catholic Priest in the United States* ed. by John Tracy Ellis (Collegeville, St. John's University Press, 1971), 337–338.

2. "Conservative vs. Liberal Catholics," *Review* IX (August 7, 1902):481–482.

3. "The Ultramontanes," *Review* IX (December 11, 1902):755–756.

4. Schultenover, *A View From Rome*,131–151.

5. On the contemporaneous discussion of evolution see John Richard Betts, "Darwinism, Evolution and American Catholic Thought, 1860–1900," *Catholic Historical Review* XLV 2 (July, 1959):161–184.

6. Appleby, *Church and Age Unite!,* 13.

7. "Dr. Zahm," *Review* III (April 23, 1896):3. III (February 11, 1897): 4. "Darwin's Unprovable Theory," (September 29, 1898):3. V (January 5, 1899):3. VI (December 28, 1899):2. "Evolution and Dogma," IX (May 8, 1902):278–281.

8. "A Disgruntled Catholic Scientist on Evolution," *Review* IX 23 (June 12, 1902):359–362. "Poisoning the Wells," IX 27 (July 10, 1902):421–423.

9. "A New Theory of Evolution Applied to Man," *Review* XIII 5 (March 1, 1906):137–142. "The Attitude of Catholics Toward Darwinism and Evolution," XIII 8 (April 15, 1906):233–236."Modern Biology and the Theory of Evolution," XIV 7 (April 1, 1907):206–208. "The Humanizing of the Brute," XIV 16 (August 15, 1907):495–500.

10. Philip E. Johnson,"Evolution As Dogma," *First Things* (October 1990). "Creator or Blind Watchmaker?" *First Things* (January, 1993). Howard J. Van Till & Philip E. Johnson, "God and Evolution: An Exchange," *First Things* (June/July 1993). Phillip E. Johnson, "The Unraveling of Scientific Materialism," *First Things* (November 1997).

11. Appleby, 48–50. Gerald P. Fogarty, *American Catholic Biblical Scholarship: A History from the Early Republic to Vatican II* (New York: Harper & Row, 1989), 58–60.

12. For the diversity of views in biblical scholarship see Gerald P. Fogarty, *American Catholic Biblical Scholarship*, 35–170.

13. John F. Meifuss, "New Fangled vs. Approved Exegetical Methods," *Review* VI 1 (April 18, 1899):2. "The Case of Dr. Mivart," VI (February 1, 1900):3. On John Hogan's *Clerical Studies* see Kauffman, *Tradition and Transformation: The Priests of Saint Sulpice in the United States from 1791 to the Present* (New York:Macmillan Publishing Co., 1988), 168–172 and Fogarty, *American Biblical Scholarship*, 72–77.

14."Progress and Tradition in Exegetics," *Review* X 20 (May 21, 1903):317–318.

15. "Historical Science and the Bible," *Review* XII 13 (July 1, 1905):375–377.

16. "The Church and the Bible," *Review* XII 21 (November 1, 1905):609–612.

17."The Church and Biblical Criticism," *Review* XII 23 (December 1, 1905):677–679. "The Bible and Modern Textual Criticism," XII 24 (December 15, 1905):720–722.

18. "A New Professor for the Catholic University of America," *Review* XI 13 (March 31, 1904):205.

19. On the Poels case and the machinations leading to his dismissal from the Catholic University of America see Fogarty, *American Catholic Biblical Scholarship*, 96–119.

20. "The Biblical Commission and the Pentateuch," *Review* XIV 6 (March 15, 1907):167–170. There have been numerous studies of Von Hugel's work. For a helpful overview see Lawrence Barmann, "Friedrich von Hugel as Modernist and More than Modernist," *Catholic Historical Review* LXXV 2 (April, 1989):211–232.

21. *Review* XII 6 (March 15, 1905):158–159.

22. "Neo-Scholasticism," *Review* XIII 13 (July 1, 1906):405–407

23. Kauffman, *Tradition and Transformation*,176. "A Queer Submission," *Review* VI 2 (March 30, 1899): 1. "Father Hogan's 'Clerical Studies' In French," *Review* IX 1 1 (March 20. 1902); 172–173. Anton Koch-Arthur Preuss, *A Handbook of Moral Theology* Volume I (St. Louis,:B. Herder Co., 1919), 3, 6–7, 39–40 & 121.

24. George E. Griener, "Herman Schell and the Reform of the Catholic Church in Germany," *Theological Studies* LIV 3 (September 1993):427–454. On "reform Catholicism" in Germany see Thomas M. Loome, *Liberal Catholicism, Reform Catholicism, Modernism* (Mainz: Mathias Grunewald Verlag, 1979). Roger Aubert in *History of the Church* volume IX, "The Church in the Industrial Age," ibid, 425.

25. Preuss on Schell *Review* (March 16, 1899) and (April 6, 1899). On Shell as an Americanist, David F.Sweeney,O.F.M., "Herman Schell, 1850–1906: A German Dimension to the Americanist Controversy," *Catholic Historical Review* LXXVI 1 (January, 1990):45–70.

26. "The Late Dr. Schell and the Index," *Review* XIII 16 (August 15, 1906):500–501.

27. "A Plea For Caution in the Use of the Term 'Modernism,'" *Review* XVII 19 (October 1, 1910):594–595. "Recent Manifestations of Modernism in Germany," *Review* XIV 17 (September 1, 1907):521–523.

28. "The Abbe Loisy and the Paulists," *Review* X 37 (October 1, 1903):581–583.

29. "The Great Apostasy Today," *Review* XIII 3 (February 1, 1906):68–70.

30. "Flotsam and Jetsam," *Review* XVI 15 (August 1, 1909):453.

31. "True and False Liberalism," *Review* V 12 (June 9, 1898):3–4. On the original essay by Tyrrell see Nicholas Sagovsky, *"On God's Side": A Life of George Tyrrell*, (Oxford:Clarendon Press, 1990),59. Other recent works on Tyrrell include Ellen Leonard, *George Tyrrell and The Catholic Tradition*, (New York:Paulist Press, 1982) and David G. Schultenover, S.J. *George Tyrrell, In Search of Catholicism* (Shepardstown:Patmos Press, 1981).

32. "The Case of Father Tyrrell," *Review* XIII 9 (May 1, 1906):284–285.

33. "The Case of Father Tyrrell," *Review* XIV 3 (February 1, 1907):84–85. "The Case of Father Tyrrell," XIV 8 (April 15, 1907):251. "Elements of the Christian Ideal of Manhood in Nietzsche's Superman," XIV 10 (May 15, 1907):295. "Marginalia," XIV 13 (July 1, 1907):411.

34. "Recent Manifestations of 'Modernism' in Germany," *Review* XIV 17 (September 1, 1907):521–523.

35. Schultenover, *A View from Rome*, 39.

36. "Modernism in America," *Review* XIV 20 (October 15, 1907):611–612. John Slattery, first superior of the Josephite Fathers, and an Americanist, left the priesthood and the Church in 1906. William L.Portier, "Modernism in the United States: The Case of John R. Slattery (1851–1926)" Unpublished. Stephen J. Ochs, *Desegregating the Altar: The Josephites and the Struggle for Black Priests 1871–1960* (Baton Rouge: Louisiana State University, 1990).

37. "On the Juridical Import of the So-called 'New Syllabus'" *Review* XIV 20 (October 15, 1907):617–619.

38. *Catholic Advance*, (July 31, 1909) Clipping in Preuss's personal papers. Reel 2. A.P.P.

39. Rev. F. G. Holweck, "The Assumption of the Blessed Virgin Mary and a Charge of Modernism," *Review* XV 22 (November 15, 1908):674–678.

40. The "Sodalitum Pianem," or "La Sapiniere" was founded in 1909 by Benigni, an undersecretary in the press office of the Vatican Secretariate of State, as "a kind of ecclesiastical secret police." The goal of the "Sodalitium" was to publicly expose Modernists through a network of newspapers and journals affiliated with Benigni's own paper *La Correspondance di Roma* which he had established in 1907. Ciani, 337–338. Emile Poulat, *Intégrisme et catholicisme intégral: Un reseau secret international antimodemiste: La "Sapiniere"*(1909–1921). (Casterman, 1969), 69. "Outre-Atlantique, Benigni avait certainement DDS relations avec la *Fortnightly Review* d'Arthur Preuss (dont les archives sont closes), aux Etats-Unis..." Poulat's assertion that Preuss's archives "sont closes" is undocumented and does not conform with the known facts regarding the accessibility of Preuss's papers.

41. "A Semi-Official View of the Religious Situation in this Country," *Review* XVIII 5 (March 1, 1911):136.

42. Charles Maignen to Arthur Preuss, October 24, 191 1. Reel I A. P. P.

43. The priests characterized by Appleby as being moved by the "modemist impulse" were John Zahm, C.S.C.(1851–1921), John Hogan, S.S. (1829–1900), Henry Poels (1868–1948), John Slattery, S.S.J.,(1851–1926) Edward Hanna (1860–1944),two ex-Sulpicians, James F. Driscoll (1859–1922), Francis Gigot(1859–1920), Francis P. Duffy(1871–1932), and, the only self-proclaimed American Modernist, William Sullivan, C.S.P.(1872–1935).

44. By contrast, Poels's dismissal from the University because of his progressive

views was never addressed in the *Review*.

45. On Hanna's 1907 unsuccessful nomination as coadjutor Archbishop of San Francisco see James P. Gaffey, *Citizen of No Mean City: Archbishop Patrick Riordan of San Francisco 1841–1914* (San Francisco: Consortium, 1976), 282–304. Fogarty, *American Biblical Scholarship*, 132–139.

46. "Rev. Dr. Hanna and Modernism," *Review* XV 3 (February 1, 1908):82. As a strong supporter of the *Catholic Encyclopedia* project, Preuss remarked later "that the Hanna incident has been used by some evil minded people to create distrust" about the publication. "Flotsam & Jetsam," *Review* XV 13 (July 1, 1908):413.

47. Appleby, 117.

48. "Change in the Rectorship at Dunwoodie," *Review* XVI 17 (September 1, 1909):499–500. For accounts of this complicated affair see Kaufffman, *Tradition and Transformation*, 99–224 and Appleby, 91–116.

49. "The Dunwoodie Seminary Matter," *Review* XVI 20 (October 15, 1909):581–584.

50. "Modernism in America," *Review* XVII 23 (December 1, 1910):705.

51. For a discussion of the changing historiography in regard to the relationship between Americanism and Modernism see Philip Gleason, "The New Americanism in Catholic Historiography," *U.S. Catholic Historian* (Summer, 1993):1–18.

52. Appleby, 2.

VI Lay Theologian and Catholic Journalist

1. "Proelia Domini," *Review* XIII 21 (July 1, 1906):666–667.

2. Nuesse, *The Catholic University of America,* 57–58.

3. Nuesse, 94 n.113. The date of the original letter was March 26, 1894. "Dr. Pohle's Letter," *Review* IV 39 (December 16, 1897):1–2.

4. "Book Reviews," *Review* X 48 (December 17, 1903):765. "Book Reviews," X 48 (December 17, 1903):765.

5. "Pesch's Dogmatic Theology," *Review* VI 25 (September 28, 1899):8.

6. A review of the first volume of Pohle-Preuss series published in the *Review* stated that Pohle had asked Preuss to take on the translation of his Lehrbuch. Joseph Pohle to Arthur Preuss, March 7, 1910. A.P.P. Reel #12.

7. Joseph Pohle to Arthur Preuss, February 21, 1908. A.P.P. Reel 12.

8. Arthur Preuss to Frederick Kenkel, January 21, 1928. Kenkel Papers, CKNA Box 3, AUND. Wolfgarten was the theologian who had the original agreement to translate Pohle's Lehrbuch. He also assisted Preuss on the proof sheets for the Koch-Preuss series.

9. Joseph Pohle to Arthur Preuss, November 30, 1909. A.P.P. Reel 12

10. Arthur Preuss to Francis Markert, October 27, 1910. A.P.P. Reel 14.

11. "Dr. Pohle On Justification and An Important Announcement," *Review* XVII 19 (October 10, 1910):577–579. Albert Reinhart, 0. P. *Rosary Magazine* (July 1911) quoted in the *Review* XVIII 15 (August 1, 1911):435–436.

12. *Ecclesiastical Review* XLV 1 (July 1911) cited in "A Standard Work of Reference for Catholic Apologists," *Review* XVIII 16 (August 15, 1911):467–469.

13. James Hennesey, S.J. *American Catholics: A History of the Roman Catholic Community in the United States* (New York: Oxford University Press, 1981), 180.

14. Royalty Statements, B. Herder Book Company to Mrs Arthur Preuss, November 23, 1954. April 23, 1955 an January 23, 1959. Royalty agreement between Arthur Preuss and the B. Herder Company, August 3, 1910. Files of the B. Herder Company. TAN Publishing Company, Rockford, Illinois. The files of the B. Herder Company are now in the possession of Tan Books of Rockford, Illinois which bought out the St. Louis firm in the early 1970's.

15. Arthur Preuss to Francis Markert, S.V.D. October 17, 1919. A.P.P. Arthur Preuss to Frederick Kenkel, November 22, 1926. Kenkel Papers, CKNA, Box 4, AUND.

16. There are dozens of letters from Heck and Frommelt to Preuss in Preuss's files for the years 1920–29.

17. Arthur Preuss to Francis Markert, January 14, 1912. A.P.P. Reel 14.

18. Link and Catton, 39–40.

19. ibid, 40.

20. Joseph H. Meier to Arthur Preuss, August 8, 191 1. Arthur Preuss Papers AUND.

21. Joseph Meier to Arthur Preuss, October 17 and November 4, 1911. Arthur Preuss Papers. AUND. "The Catholic Directory and the French-Canadian Press," *Review* XVIII 18 (September 15, 1911):530–531.

22. For examples of representative articles on this topic see "Our Archbishops and the Prospect of a Catholic Daily," *Review* IX 41 (October 23, 1902):641–643. "The Question of a Catholic Daily," X 42 (November 5, 1903):660–662. "A Catholic Daily Newspaper in Prospect," XI 10 (March 10, 1904):148–151. "The Need of a Catholic Daily Press," XVII 14 (July 15, 1910):437. "The Need of a Catholic Daily Press," XVIII 5 (April 11, 1911):143.

23. "'A Catholic Daily' in New York," *Review* XI (November 10, 1904):673–676.

24. "The Question of a Catholic Daily," *Review* X 33 (September 3, 1903):513–519.

25. "A Catholic Daily Newspaper in Prospect," *Review* XI 1 1 (March 17, 1904):163 –167. "In Favor of a Catholic Daily," XI 45 (November 24,

1904):716–717. "The Catholic Press," XIII 4 (February 15, 1906):121. "Melancholy Reflections on American Catholic Journalism, " XIV 7 (April 1, 1907):200–202. "The Catholic Press," XXXIII 7 (April 1, 1916):130. Archbishop Michael Corrigan to Arthur Preuss, April 15, 1901. G-16 Archives of the Archdiocese of New York.

26. Among Preuss's episcopal supporters at this time were Cornelius Van der Ven, bishop of Alexandria, John Janssen, bishop of Belleville, Sebastian Messmer, Archbishop of Milwaukee, James Blenk, Archbishop of New Orleans, Francis Beckman, auxiliary bishop of Indianapolis and Vincent Wehrle, O.S.B, bishop of Bismarck.

27. F.M. Lynck, S.V.D., "The Catholic Press Convention," *Review* XVIII 18 (September 15, 1911):516–517.

28. Archbishop William O'Connell gained control of the venerable *Pilot* in September 1908 turning the independent paper into an "official organ" under the editorship of Father Toomey. James M. O'Toole, *Militant and Triumphant: William Henry O'Connell and the Catholic Church in Boston,* 1859–1944 (Notre Dame: University of Notre Dame Press, 1992), 83–84.

29. "Shall the Catholic Press be Toomeyized?" *Review* XVIII 18 (September 15. 1911):518–519.

30. Francis Markert, S. V. D. to Arthur Preuss, September 29, 1911. Reel 14, A.P.P.

31. Arthur Preuss to Francis Markert, S.V.D., October 3, 1911. Reel 14, A.P.P. On the unsavory character of Toomey and his sordid career, see O'Toole, 183–187.

32. Arthur Preuss to Francis Markert, S.V.D., December 23, 1910. Reel 14, A.P.P.

33. It was also about this time that Preuss lengthened the title of his journal to the *Catholic Fortnightly Review*. "The Catholic Fortnightly Review," *Review* XII I (January 1, 1905):1–2. The *Review*'s circulation in 1911 remained the same (about 1800 copies) as it was when publication at Techny began in 1905. Arthur Preuss to Hermann Richarz, S.V.D., June 10, 1905. Reel 14, A.P.P.

34. Although he had nothing against beer, Preuss declined to carry advertisements for Anheuser-Busch in the *Review* as he thought them unbecoming in a Catholic publication. Arthur Preuss to Francis Markert, S.V. D., March 10, 1912.

35. Arthur Preuss to Francis Markert, July 22, 1911. Reel 14, A. P. P.

36. "A Hopeful Sign of the Times," *Review* XIX 6 (March 15, 1912):161.

37. John Cardinal Farley to Archbishop John J. Glennon, March 19, 1912. 1–15, Archives of the Archdiocese of New York.

38. John Cardinal Farley to Very Rev, Msgr. B. Cerretti, Regent Apostolic Delegate, March 19, 1912. I-15 Archives of the Archdiocese of New York.

39. Arthur Preuss to Francis Markert, S.V.D., March 25, 1912. Reel 14, A.P.P.

40. Arthur Preuss to Very Rev. B. Cerretti, March 26, 1912. Archives of the Archdiocese of St. Louis.

41. Arthur Preuss to Francis Markert, S.V.D., March 28, 1912. Reel 14, A.P.P.

42. Very Rev. B. Cerretti to Archbishop John J. Glennon, March 30, 1912. Archives of the Archdiocese of St. Louis. By this time, Glennon had extracted himself from the affair and was acting simply as a conduit for Cerretti's messages. Glennon and Preuss continued to maintain a cordial relationship and the Archbishop included Easter greetings to Preuss and his family in a subsequent letter. Archbishop Glennon to Arthur Preuss, April 5, 1912. Archives of the Archdiocese of St. Louis.

43. Abbot Charles Mohr to Arthur Preuss, April 2, 1912. Reel 1 A.P.P.

44. "An Explanation," XIX 8 (April 15, 1912):225.

45. Arthur Preuss to Francis Markert, S.V.D., April 6, 1912. Reel 14 A.P.P.

46. Abbot Charles Mohr to Arthur Preuss, May 13, 1912. Reel 1 A.P.P.

47. "Et Cetera," *Review* XIX 19 (October 1, 1912):547.

48. "The Boston Missionary Congress by a Delegate," *Review* XX 23 (December 1, 1913):673–677.

49. Rt. Rev. Vincent Wehrle, 0. S. B., "The Boston Mission Congress Again," *Review* XXI 1 (January 1,1914):4–6. P. Ambrose Regen, "The Boston Mission Congress," XXI 3 (February 1, 1914):69–70.

50. Francis Markert, S.V.D., to Arthur Preuss, February 14, 1914. Reel 14 A.P.P.

51. Arthur Preuss to Francis Markert, S.V.D. February 16, 1914. Reel 14 A.P.P.

52. Arthur Preuss to Francis Markert, S.V.D., February 17, 1914. Abbot Charles Mohr was not made bishop of St. Augustine —a fact he attributed to his unwillingness to cultivate the influence of Cardinal James Gibbons.
Charles Mohr to Arthur Preuss, March 17, 1914. Reel 3 A.P.P.

52. Arthur Preuss to Francis Markert, March 12, 1914. Reel 14 A.P.P.

53. Preuss never divulged Lynck's authorship of the offending article, not even to Markert.

54. Preuss wrote to Frederick Kenkel that having the *Review* published by a commercial press in St. Louis was going to add an additional $200 to his annual expenditures. "That's a lot of money for a poor devil like me, as you know from experience." Arthur Preuss to Frederick Kenkel, March 12, 1914. Kenkel Papers. AUND

55. Arthur Preuss to Francis Markert, April 1, 1914. Reel 14 A.P.P.

56. "A Catholic Governor's Bad Example, " *Review* XXI 9 (May 1,

1914):262–263.

57. Isabel Preuss to Francis Markert, S.V.D. February 5, 1914. Reel 14, A.P.P. During Preuss's absences from St. Louis, which became more frequent as time passed, his daughters handled his correspondence.

58. Arthur Preuss to Francis Markert, S.V.D. June 15, 1914 and October 10, 1914. Reel 14 A.P.P.

59. Arthur Preuss to Francis Markert, S.V.D. February 7, 1915 and June 22, 1915. Reel 14 A.P.P.

60. Arthur Preuss to Francis Markert, S.V.D. July 3, 1915 and November 20, 1915. Reel 14 A.P.P.

61. Edward R. Kantowicz, *Corporation Sole: Cardinal Mundelein and Chicago Catholicism* (University of Notre Dame Press:Notre Dame, 1983), 72–73.

62. Arthur Preuss to Francis Markert, March 21, 1916. Reel 14 A.P.P.

63. Arthur Preuss to Francis Markert, S.V.D. May 15, 1916 and June 16, 1916. Reel 14 A.P.P.

64. Arthur Preuss to Francis Markert, S.V.D. June 16, 1916.

65. Francis Markert, S.V.D. to Archbishop George Mundelein, June 9, 1916, Copy. Reel 14 A.P.P. As this letter was kept by Markert until Preuss's death, it is unclear whether Preuss ever knew what lengths Markert had gone to on his friend's behalf.

66. Arthur Preuss to Francis Markert, S.V.D. June 16, 1916. Reel 14 A.P.P.

67. Interview, Alma Preuss Dilsehneider January 10, 1993.

68. "Vox Clamantis" *Review* IX 2 (January 8, 1902):17.

VII The Great War

1. On the German-American experience of these years see Frederick C. Luebke, *Bonds of Loyalty:German-Americans and World War I* (DeKalb, Il: Northern Illinois University Press, 1974). Carl Wittke, *The German Language Press in America*, (Frankfort, Ky: University of Kentucky Press, 1957). Philip Gleason, *The Conservative Reformers: German-American Catholics and the Social Order* (Notre Dame:University of Notre Dame Press, 1968). For general background on the period Mark Sullivan, *Our Times: The United States, 1900–1925*, vol. *5 Over Here, 1914–1918* (New York: Scribners, 1933). Arthur S. Link and William B. Catton, *American Epoch: A History of the United States Since the 1890s* (New York: Alfred Knopf, 1967),171–191. David Shannon, *Twentieth Century America* vol. I *The Progressive Era* (Chicago: Rand McNally & Co., 1977), 153–171.

2. Dean R. Esslinger, "American German and Irish Attitudes Toward Neutrality, 1914–1917: A Study of Catholic Minorities," *Catholic Historical Review* LIII 2 (July, 1967):194–216. Esslinger, after commenting on Preuss's

refusal to take sides in the war, then infers that Preuss was disinterested stating that "Preuss seemed to be more concerned with the Menace, the Masons and the Mass (would grape juice be used if prohibition were passed?)." While anti-Catholic bigotry, secret societies and prohibition remained perennial topics in the *Review*, Preuss's journal carried some discussion of the war in almost every issue published during the period of American neutrality. And if there was a subject that vied with the war in Europe for coverage it was the civil war in Mexico.

3. Edward Cuddy, "Pro-Germanism and American Catholicism," *Catholic Historical Review* LIV 3 (October, 1968):427-454. In his 1983 study, Thomas O'Keefe tried to stake out a middle position between Esslinger and Cuddy in regard to the neutrality of some of the leading American Catholic periodicals. Thomas O'Keefe, *"America,* the *Ave Maria* and the *Catholic World* Respond to the First World War," *Records of the American Catholic Historical Society of Philadelphia*, 94 (1983):101-115.

4. Luebke, 129-146. Gleason, 159-170.

5. "The War in Europe," *Review* XXI 16 (August 15, 1914):481.

6. "Inhuman War," *Review* XXI 18 (September 15, 1914):550-551.

7. "Father of All the Faithful," *Review* XXI 19 (October 1, 1914):577. Dragan R. Zivojinovic, *The United States and the Vatican Policies, 1914-1918* (Boulder,CO:Colorado Associated University Press, 1978).
"A Useful War Guide," *Review* XXI 20 (October 15, 1914):610.
"Public Duty Before Party Politics," XXI 20 (October 15, 1914):641.

8. "War in the Sacred Liturgy," *Review* XXI 22 (November 15, 1914):651.
"Mammon and the War," XXIII 4 (February 15, 1916):72. "An Irish Bishop On the War," XXII 12 (June 15, 1915):388. "Christianity and the War," XXI 21 (November 1, 1914):655. "The Laws of War According to SS. Augustine and Thomas," XXII 2 (January 15, 1915):35-36. "Is War Justified By Its Incidental Good Results?" XXII 12 (June 15, 1915):388.

9. "The War and Peace Piffle," *Review* XXI 23 (December 1, 1914):710.
"The War and Peace Piffle," XXI 24 (December 15, 1914):742.

10. "The Fine Things of the War," *Review* XXII 7 (April 1, 1915):20 1. "Some Fine Things In the War," XXII 11 (June 1, 1915):323.
"The German War and Catholicism," XXII 19 (October 1, 1915):538.

11. "Notes and Gleanings," *Review* XXI 23 (December 1, 1914):728. Preuss quoted the *Literary Digest* poll of newspaper editors which reported that while most professed neutrality, a significant number conceded favoring the Allies. "Criticizing the War Censor," XXII I (January 1, 1915):3. "Rules For Reading the War Bulletins," XXII 2 (January 15, 1915):35-36. "The British Press Censorship," XXIII 2 (January 15, 1916):20. "What Happened in Belgium," XXIII 14 (July 15, 1916):209. "The War and Its Censors," XXII

3 (February 1, 1915):69.

12. "Pope Benedict XV and the War," *Review* XXI 24 (December 15, 1914):737–738. Ernest Hull, S.J. "Why the Pope is Neutral," XXII 19 (October 1, 1915):583–586. "Benedict XV to the Peoples Now Fighting," XXII 17 (September 1, 1915):513–514. "Pope Benedict and Peace," XXII 6 (March 15, 1915):167. "The Pope and the Peace Congress,"XXIII 5 (March 1, 1916):65. "Italy Against the Pope at the Peace Conference," XXIII 12 (June 15, 1916):189.

13. Luebke, 140–143. "American Self-Flattery," *Review* XXII 23 (December 1, 1915):720–722. "Notes and Gleanings," XXIII 11 (June 1, 1916):173.

14. "Former President Taft on the Question of National Defense," *Review* XXII 1 (January 1, 1915):10–15. "The Church Peace Movement Against Increased Armament," XXIII 2 (January 15, 1916):20. "Is American Armament A Step Backwards?" XXIII 4 (February 15, 1916):52. "Notes and Gleanings," XXIII 4 (February 15, 1916):57. "President Wilson's Peace Plans," *Review* XXIII 23 (December 1, 1916):358.

15. Unfortunately, although Preuss's papers contain thousands of pages of correspondence, there are virtually no files for the years 1914 through 1919. What makes this particularly exasperating for the researcher is the fact these files apparently existed twenty-five years ago before the collection was microfilmed. Edward Cuddy cited letters written to Preuss in 1916.

16. Arthur Preuss to Francis Markert, S.V.D. Reel 14,. A.P.P.

17. Arthur Preuss to Francis Markert, S.V.D. January 8, 1916, July 14, 1916 and February 17, 1917. Reel 14. A. P. P.

18. Luebke, 211.

19. Luebke, 211–212.

20. Secretary of War, Newton D. Baker cited in Sullivan, 423.

21. Luebke, 212.

22. Sullivan, 429.

23. Sullivan, 433–435.

24. Luebke, 213.

25. Sullivan, 431–432.

26. Sullivan, 439–440.

27. Luebke, 213.

28. Luebke, 214–215.

29. "Notes and Gleanings," *Review* XXIV 8 (April 15, 1917):121.

30. "The United States in War," *Review* XXIV 10 (May 15, 1917):145.

31. "Notes and Gleanings," *Review* XXIV 16 (August 15, 1917):252.

32. Quoted in Luebke, 234.

33. Luebke, 241–242. Wittke, 264–272.

34. Arthur Preuss to Francis Markert, S.V.D. and December 29, 1917.

Reel 14. A.P.P. "Notes and Gleanings," *Review* XXV 1 (January 1, 1918): 11.

35. "Washington's Warning," *Review* XXIV 15 (August 1, 1917):229.

36. "The Liberty of the Press in Wartime," *Review* XXIV 17 (September 1, 1917):258-259.

37. "Notes and Gleanings," *Review* XXIV 8 (April 15, 1917):137. "Notes and Gleanings," XXIV 10 (May 15,1917); 154. "A Protest Against the Conscription of Thought, " XXIV 19 (October 1, 1917):294-295. "Foreign Languages in Our Schools," XXIV 15 (August 1, 1917):230. "German In Our Schools," XXIV 24 (December 15, 1917):370.

38. "Notes and Gleanings,"*Review* XXXIV 1 1 (June 1, 1917):172. "Notes and Gleanings," XXIV 12 (June 15, 1917):186-187. "Notes and Gleanings," XXIV 22 (October 15, 1917):341.

39. Arthur Preuss to Francis Markert, S.V.D. December 20, 1917. Reel 14. A.P.P.

40. "The Exclusion of the Holy See from the Peace Conference," *Review* XXV 2 (January 15, 1918):21. "England and the Pope," XXV 6 (March 15, 1918):84. "The Papal Peace Plan and the Peace Congress," XXV 11 (June 1, 1918):161-162. "The Voice of the Mediator," XXV 15 (August 1, 1918):225. J. Godfrey Raupert, "A Catholic View of the War," XXV 4 (February 15, 1918):50. "The War Ourselves and God," XXV 10 (May 15, 1918):145. "The Main Obstacle to Peace," XXV 8 (April 15, 1918):131. "Notes and Gleanings," XXIV 16 (August 15, 1917):248. "Notes and Gleanings," XXV 10 (May 15, 1918):156.

41. Luebke, 244-245, 273-280.

42. Luebke, 216-217.

43. Henry J. Schmidt, "The Rhetoric of Survival: The Germanist in America from 1900 to 1925," in *America and the Germans: An Assessment of a Three-Hundred Year History* vol. II *The Relationship in the Twentieth Century,* ed. by Frank Trommler and Joseph McVeigh (Philadelphia: University of Pennsylvania Press, 1985), 209-210.

44. Luebke, 248-253.

45. "Notes and Gleanings," *Review* XXV 6 (March 15, 1918):96.

46. Luebke, 15, 257-259, 281.

47. Luebke, 15, 291-292.

48. Luebke, 3-25.

49. Arthur Preuss to Francis Markert, S.V.D. June 26, 1918. Reel 14. A.P.P.

50. "Notes and Gleanings," *Review* XXV 8 (April 15, 1918):139. Timothy Mark Pies, "The Parochial School Campaigns in Michigan, 1920-24; The Lutheran and Catholic Involvement," *Catholic Historical Review* LXXH 2 (April, 1986):222-238. "The Coming Kulturkampf," *Review* XXV 14 (July 15, 1918)219. "The Danger to Our Schools," XXV 18 (September 15, 1918):281.

51. "Notes and Gleanings," *Review* XXV 18 (September 15, 1918):285.
52. "The Politicians and Schools," *Review* XXV 19 (October 1, 1918):290. Joseph Selinger, "Let Us Save Our Schools," XXV 19 (October 1,1918):294. "A Plot Against Our Schools," XXV 20 (October 15, 1918):306. "The Catholic Press," XXV 20 (October 15, 1918):308–310.
53. "How Big Corporations Evade the War Tax," *Review* XXV 12 (June 15, 1918):189–190. "Rough Days Ahead?" XXV 19 (October 1, 1918):294. "Bolsheviki in the U.S.," XXV 6 (March 15, 1918):85. "Preparing for After War Conditions," XXV 21 (November 1, 1918):326. Elliot Ross, C. S. P., "The Right to Work," XXV 22 (November 15, 1918):346–347.
54. "The Election and Its Lessons," *Review* XXV 23 (December 1, 1918):354–355.
55. "British Propaganda in the U.S.," *Review* XXVI 14 (July 15, 1919):23 1. "How Hate Was Manufactured During the War," XXVI 20 (October 15, 1918):309. "How the War Came," XXVI 22 (November 15, 1919):346. "Wilsonian Sincerity," XXVII 5 (March 1, 1920):70–71. "Mr. Creel and His Committee of War Propaganda," XXVII 15 (August 1, 1920):230. "Freedom of Speech," XXVI 2 (January 15, 1919):18. "Mob Rule by the Rich," XXVI 3 (February 1, 1919):34. "Wilson and Free Speech," XXVI 14 (July 15, 1919):197. "A Futile Defense of Wilson," XXVII 19 (October 1, 1920):296. "Finis Austriae," XXVI 14 (July 15, 1919):213. "Wilson the Politician," XXVI 17 (September 1, 1919):267. "The Psychology of Mr. Wilson," XXVI 19 (October 1, 1919):294. "A Monument of Imbecility," XXVI 21 (November 1, 1919):333. "The Two Wilsons," XXVI 23 (December 1, 1919):359. "The Great Failure," XXVII 2 (January 15, 1920):22.
56. "What Voters Should Not Forget," *Review* XXVII 20 (October 15, 1920):319.
57. Eugene P. Wilging and Herta Hatsfeld, *Catholic Serials and Periodicals of the Nineteenth Century in the United States: A Descriptive Bibliography and Union List*. Second Series: Part XIV "New York City and State" (Washington, DC: The Catholic University of America Press, 1965), 43–44.
58. Arthur Preuss to Francis Markert, October 17, 1919. Reel 14. A.P.P. Joseph Schifferli to Arthur Preuss, October 16, 1920. A. P. P. "Arthur Preuss, Eminent Editor and Author, Dead," *Echo* December 20, 1934.
59. "Foreign Languages in the Churches," *Echo* January 2, 1919. "Hysterical Americanism," March 6, 1919. "Unfairness to German-Americans," May 8, 1919. "Repeal the Espionage Law!" February 13, 1919. "We Told You So," May 1, 1919. "Exposing Plutocracy," June 19, 1919. "The War Record of the Press," May 15, 1919. "Foreign Clerical Propagandists," May 22, 1919. "Out of His Own Mouth," May 29, 1919. "Courting World Disaster," June 12, 1919. "An Apple of Discord," June 19, 1919. "A Capitalistic Pluderbund,"

July 3, 1919. "Plunging the World Into Chaos," July 3, 1919.

60. "The True Causes of the War," *Echo* November 20, 1919.

61. "Repudiating British Imperialism," *Echo* December 11, 1919. "Perfidious Albion," April 1, 1920. "Secret Diplomacy and the War," July 1, 1920. "How England Prolonged the War," November 4, 1920. "The War's Real Object," June 23, 1920. "The Causes of the World War," July 28, 1921. "Anglo-American Relations," September 8, 1921. "Why England Entered the War," October 13, 1921. "Freemasonry and the War," January 19, 1922.

62. "The Socialist Menace," *Echo* January 1, 1920.

63. "The Teaching of Hatred," *Echo* November 13, 1919. "The Terror of Patriotism," December 18, 1919. "Atrocity Hoaxes," January 15, 1920. "Lie Factories, " April 1, 1920. "The Problem of the Press, " April 29, 1920. "Atrocities and War Legends," August 26, 1920. "Across the Blockade," January 15, 1920.

64. "Beyond the Indemnity Question," *Echo* May 5, 1921. "Europe on the Verge of Ruin," September 21, 1921. "American Relief for Germany," March 8, 1923. "The Reparations Problem," August 23, 1923. "Germany's Hungry Children," December 27. 1923. "Help For Starving Millions," January 31, 1924. "The Fate of Austria," February 10, 1921.

65. "An American Statesman on Wilson," *Echo* June 24, 1920. "New Light on Wilson's Failure at Paris," February 1, 1923. "Woodrow Wilson and Benedict XV," February 28, 1922. "Benedict XV and Peace," January 29, 1920. "Benedict the Conciliator," February 9, 1922. "Woodrow Wilson and Benedict XV," February 28, 1924.

66. "Our Frustrated War Aims," *Echo* February 12, 1920.

67. "The League of Nations," *Echo* August 11, 1921. "Catholics and the League," March 4, 1920. "The Apostolic League of Nations," September 2, 1920. "The Holy See and the League," October 7, 1920.

68. "Kruppism and World Peace," *Echo* December 4, 1919. "The Stampede of War," April 14, 1921. "The Four Power Treaty," March 2, 1922. "Patriotism vs. Excessive Nationalism," March 16, 1922. "Militarism," March 8, 1923. "After War Hatreds," March 29, 1923. "Seeing Ourselves As Others See Us," May 3, 1923. "Prepare for Peace!" June 21, 1923. "No More War Day," July 26, 1923. "Obstacles to International Peace," February 21, 1924. "A Tremendous Problem," May 29, 1924. "The Need of Christian Brotherhood," July 29, 1920. "Disarmament," March 31, 1921. "Disarmament," September 22, 1921. "The Disarmament Question," October 13, 1921. "Militarism After the Great War," November 2, 1922. "Catholics and International Peace," August 30, 1923. "Militarizing Our Boys," June 12, 1924.

69. La Vern J. Rippley, "Ameliorated Americanization: The Effect of World War I on German-Americans in the 1920s," in *America and the Germans: An*

Assessment of a Three-Hundred Year History vol. II *The Relationship in the Twentieth Century,* ed. by Frank Trommler and Joseph McVeigh (Philadelphia: University of Pennsylvania Press, 1985), 209-210.

VIII Into the Twenties

1. "Notes and Gleanings," *Review* XXV 4 (February 15, 1918):59. "Life Subscriptions and the Permanency of the *Review*,"(November 11 1918):324. Arthur Preuss to Francis Markert, October 9, and December 27, 1918. Reel 14 A.P.P.
2. Wittke, 265-267.
3. Arthur Preuss to Archbishop John Glennon, June 1903 (draft). Reel 13 A.P.P.
4. "The Coming Catholic Daily," *Review* XXV 11 (June 1, 1918):162
5. Arthur Preuss to Francis Markert, October 16, 1920. Reel 14 A.P.P.
6. Arthur Preuss to Francis Markert, November 8, 1920. Reel 14 A.P.P. Arthur Preuss to Frederick Kenkel, January 1, 1930 and February 24, 1934. CKNA AUND.
7. Arthur Preuss, November 8, 1920. Reel 14 A.P.P.
8. Arthur Preuss to Francis Markert, July 13, 1920 and February 5, 1921. Reel 14 A.P.P.
9. Arthur Preuss to Peter Guilday, October 29, 1921. Guilday Papers. Archives of the Catholic University of America (ACUA)
10. Joseph Schifferli to Arthur Preuss, August 20, 1921. Abbot Charles Mohr to Arthur Preuss, August 23, 1921. Reel 5 A. P. P.
11. Arthur Preuss to Francis Markert, November 4, 1921. Reel 14 A.P.P.
12. Peter Guilday to Arthur Preuss, October 25, 1921. Abbot Charles Mohr to Arthur Preuss, November 5, 1921. Joseph Matt to Arthur Preuss, November 28, 1921. Reel 4 A.P.P.
13. "Arthur Preuss, Eminent Editor and Author, Dead," *Echo* December 20, 1934. Preuss himself first acknowledged his editorship of the *Echo* in April 1929. "Important Notice to Our Subscribers," *Review* XXXVI 7 (April 1,1929):121.
14. Baumgartner, 96. Although the *Echo* aspired to be a national Catholic weekly, it is unclear if its readership extended much beyond its base in New York State. Combined with the circulation of the *Review* of some 3000 subscribers and that of the English–language *Wanderer*, which began in 1930 with a circulation of 6600, and to which he contributed on a weekly basis, Preuss's potential readership in the 1930's reached nearly 30,000. Baumgartner, 97. Joseph Matt, "Arthur Preuss," *Review* XCII (January 1935):5-6.
15. Interview with Austin Preuss, November 19, 1993.

16. Br. Celestine Mueller, O.S.B. to Arthur Preuss, July 25, 1923. Reel 5 A.P.P. Br. Celestine Mueller to Arthur Preuss, October 3, 1927. Reel 7 A.P.P. With the death of Brother Celestine in 1927, the Mt. Angel Monthly was subsumed into the *St. Joseph's Mapazine* which became the official organ of the Pious Union of St. Joseph. The editor of this new publication asked Preuss to continue to provide monthly editorials of five hundred words for "the middle and lower classes." Fr. V. Rassner, O.S.B. to Arthur Preuss, December 15, 1927. Reel 8. A.P.P. Willging and Hatzfeld, *Catholic Serials of the Nineteenth Century in the United States* First Series Part II (Washington, D.C.:The Catholic University of America Press,1968),179–180.

17. Arthur Preuss to Francis Markert, June 5, 1920. Reel 14. A.P.P. Joseph Buechle to Arthur Preuss, March 13, 1922. Reel 4 A.P.P.

18. Arthur Preuss to Francis Markert, December 18, 1919. Reel 14 A.P.P.

19. As Preuss's correspondence file for the year 1919 is not extant, the only places where references to this proposal have been found are in Preuss's letters to Fr. Markert and in the correspondence **file** of Father Peter Guilday at the Catholic University of America.

20. Arthur Preuss to Peter Guilday, May 14, 1920. Guilday Papers. ACUA.

21. Peter Guilday to Arthur Preuss, May 19, 1920. (copy) Guilday Papers. ACUA

22. On Heinrich Schumacher see C. Joseph Nuesse, *The Catholic University of America: A Centennial History*, 213–214, 253–254.

23. Arthur Preuss to Francis Markert, June 15, 1921. Reel 14. A.P.P. Preuss also rejected Schumacher's attempt to discredit Guilday on account of the latter's involvement in govemment-sponsored wartime propaganda.

24. Arthur Preuss to Peter Guilday, May 14, 1920. Guilday Papers. ACUA Peter Guilday to Arthur Preuss, October 18, 1920 and December 30, 1920. Reel 3 A.P.P.

25. Peter Guilday to Arthur Preuss, January 15, 1923. Reel 3 A.P.P.

26. Peter Guilday to Arthur Preuss, January 1, March 4, April 17, and April 20, 1925. Reel 5 A.P.P.

27. Peter Guilday to Arthur Preuss, November 17, 1927 and December 1, 1927. Reel 7 A.P.P.

28. Arthur Preuss to Francis Markert, June 26, 1919. Reel 14. A.P.P. Commenting on the frequency of clerical guests in their home, Preuss's son Charles Arthur remarked, "If a man came in the house without a collar on we did not know what to make of him." Interview with Charles Arthur Preuss, July 31, 1992.

29. Arthur Preuss to Francis Borgia Steck, O.F.M. November 23, 1921. Steck Papers. Archives of Quincy College (AQC). Francis Borgia Steck to Arthur Preuss, July 14, 1922. Reel 5 A.P.P.

30. Francis Borgia Steck to Arthur Preuss, November 24, 1929.(copy) Steck Papers. AQC

31. Steck's main Jesuit adversary was Father F.J. Betten, S.J. of John Carroll University and his defense of Marquette was published in *Thought*, a Jesuit journal.

32. *America,* December 27,1934 52:269.

33. Francis Borgia Steck to Charles Arthur Preuss, January 15, 1935.(copy) Steck Papers. AQC Francis Markert to Frederick Kenkel, Reel 14 A.P.P.

34. Arthur Preuss to Francis Borgia Steck, February 9, 1924. Steck Papers. AQC

35. Horace A. Frommelt to Arthur Preuss, November 17, 1920. Reel 3 A.P.P.

36. John Tracy Ellis, "American Catholics and the Intellectual Life," *Thought* (Autumn, 1955)

37. "Ignored Problems of Catholic Higher Education," *Review* XXVIII 21 (November 1, 1921):381–383.

38. Arthur Preuss to Horace A. Frommelt, December 7, 1921. Steck Papers. AQC

39. Arthur Preuss to Francis Markert, February 5, 1921. Reel 14 A.P.P. Horace A. Frommelt to Arthur Preuss, December 14, 1921. Reel 14 A.P.P. Horace A. Frommelt to Arthur Preuss, September 12, 1929. Reel 7 A.P.P.

40. On John Rothensteiner (1860–1936), see Buchhuber, 17–39 and Francis F. Mueller, S.M.,"A Classification and Evaluation of the Journalistic Writings of John E. Rothensteiner," M.A. Dissertation, St. Louis University, 1940.

41. John E. Rothensteiner, "Reminiscences of Dr. Arthur Preuss, " *Review* XCII (January 1935):2. In his memorial to Preuss, Rothensteiner stated that Preuss had received "the title of Doctor Philosophiae H. C. from the University of Notre Dame." However, Rothensteiner's statement is not confirmed by any other source.

42. John Rothensteiner *History of the Archdiocese of St. Louis In its Various Stages of Development from A.D. 1673 to A.D. 1928,* (St. Louis: Blackwell and Weilandy Inc., 1928). J.E.R., "The High Tide of Crime," *Review* XXVIII 1 (January 1, 1921):2. "The Church and the Age," XXVIII 7 (April 1, 1921):106. "The Question of Interest," XXVIII 15 (August 1, 1921):257–259. Rothensteiner continued to write editorials for *Die Amerika* until the paper ceased publication in 1924.

43. Shannon, *Twentieth Century America*, 175, 217.

44. Shannon, 177–178.

45. Burl Noggle, *Into the Twenties:The United States from Armistice to Normalcy* (Chicago: University of Illinois Press, 1974),51–52. Link and Catton, *American Epoch*, 231–232.

46. Noggle, 84–121.

47. Shannon, 198–199.

48. Link and Catton, 238.

49. Link and Catton, 239–240.

50. Link and Catton, 246.

51. "The Administration's Swan Song," *Echo* January 13, 1921. "The Same Old Game," *Echo* June 17, 1920. "Back to Normalcy," *Echo* March 31, 1921. Link and Catton, 240.

52. "The Duty of Voting, " *Echo* February 14, 1924. "The Crisis in the German Centre Party," September 7, 1922. "The Evil of Politics," *Echo* December 8, 1921. "External Machinery," May 4, 1922. "Lobbying At Washington, " *Echo* August 18, 1921.

53. "The Failure of Democracy," *Echo* August 19, 1920. "Proportional Representation," December 20, 1920. "Proportional Representation," February 15, 1923.

54. "A Pseudo-Statesman," *Echo* January 22, 1920. Written about Gov. Calvin Coolidge who Preuss labelled an "autocrat and enemy of labor" whose election to the presidency would bring a "dark day." "The Two Platforms Compared," July 22, 1920. "An Urgent Reform," May 5, 1921. "*Echo*es" March 13, 1924. On Democratic presidential candidate William G. McAdoo, whose defeat "would be a deliverance" since, according to Preuss, he was "smeared all over with oil money." "A Dangerous Tendency," *Echo* February 23, 1922. "What Difference Would It Make?" August 18, 1921. "Can a Catholic Be President?" December 14, 1922.

55. "The New Progressive Movement," *Echo* December 28, 1922. "The Real Problem," May 17, 1923. " LaFollette's Program," August 2, 1923. "The Third Party," April 17, 1924. " LaFollette's Statements Intimate A Third Party," June 5, 1924. "*Echo*es," August 20, 1924. "The Third Party Movement," December 11, 1924.

56. "What We Want," *Echo* June 23, 1921.

57. "Random Topics," *Echo* January 5, 1922.

58. John Higham, *Strangers in the Land*, (New Brunswick, New Jersey, 1955), 265–266. Michael Schwartz, *The Persistent Preiudice: Anti-Catholicism in America* (Huntington, IN: Our Sunday Visitor Press, 1984),80–101. Mark J. Hurley, The Unholv Ghost: Anti-Catholicism in the American Experience (Huntington, IN: Our Sunday Visitor Press, 1992) Edward Cuddy, "The Irish Question and the Revival of Anti-Catholicism in the 1920's," *Catholic Historical Review* LXVII 2 (April 1981):236–255.

59. "The New Know Nothingism," *Echo* March 1, 1920

60. "For A Catholic Daily Press," *Echo* November 17, 1919.

61. "Some Sound Ideas on Americanization," *Review* XXVI 13 (July 1, 1919):193. "A Crying Injustice," XXVI 19 (October 1, 1919):299. "Driving

Out the Devil with Beelzebub," *Echo* March 4, 1920 "Free the Political Prisoners," October 26, 1922. "Mob Rule by the Rich," *Review* XXVI 3 (February 1, 1919):34.

62. "Signs of the Coming 'Kulturkampf'," *Review* XXVI 9 (May 1, 1919):132.

63. "A Socialist's Tragedy," *Echo* January 2, 1919. "Socialism and Catholicism," July 10, 1919. "The Right to Private Property," July 31, 1919. "The Truth About Bolshevism," *Review* XXVI 8 (April 15, 1919):113. "Bolshevism At Home," 11 (June 1, 1919):163. "Bolshevism in America," 13 (July 1, 1919):197. "Producing Bolsheviks," 16 (August 15, 1919):246.

64. "The Real Peril," *Review* XXVII 2 (January 15, 1920):20.

65. "Deporting Aliens," *Echo* January 13, 1921.

66. "A Threat Against Democracy," *Review* XXVII 3 (February 1, 1920):41.

67. "Timely Protests," *Review* XXVII 6 (March 15, 1920):87.

68. "Radical Labor Agitation," *Echo* May 11, 1922.

69. See John Tracy Ellis, *Documents of American Catholic History* Volume II 1866–1966 (Wilmington, DE: Michael Glazier, 1987) "The Bishop's Program of Social Reconstruction," February 12, 1919. On John A. Ryan's authorship of this document, its development and the response it received see Joseph McShane, S.J. "Sufficiently Radical": *Catholicism, Progressivism and the Bishops Program of 1919* (Washington, DC: The Catholic University of America Press, 1986).

70. "A Typical Super-Patriot," *Echo* May 22, 1924.

71. "*Echo*es," *Echo* January 24, 1924.

72. William J. Engelen, S.J. was a regular writer for the Central Verein's publication, "Central Blatt and Social Justice," which was edited by Kenkel. For an analysis of his social thought see Charles E. Curran, *American Catholic Social Ethics: Twentieth Century Approaches* (Notre Dame,In: University of Notre Dame Press, 1982),92–129.

73. "The Catholic in Business," *Echo* July 3, 1919.

74. "Socialism and Capitalism," *Review* XXVI 7 (April 1, 1919):106–107.

75. "Neither Capitalism or Socialism," *Review* XXVI (May 1, 1919):129.

76. "The Church and Economic Reconstruction," *Review* XXVI 9 (May 1, 1919):133–134. "A New Social Order," 11 (June 1, 1919):164. "The Fundamental Cause of Unrest," 22 (November 15, 1919):343.

77. "The Aims of Labor, " *Review* XXVII I (January 1, 1920): 1.

78. "Capitalism Must Go!" *Echo* June 10, 1920. "The First Step," May 26, 1921. "Evils of the Industrial System," September 15, 1921. "What's the Matter with America?" July 6, 1922. "Capitalism," September 20, 1923. "Economic Imperialism," November 15, 1923. "The Cost of Bread," March 6, 1924. "Can A Catholic Be A Capitalist?" January 1, 1925.

79. "Profit Sharing as a Compromise between Capital and Labor," *Review*

XXVII I (January 1, 1920):6–7. While his association with Preuss will be discussed subsequently, it is well to note here that it was Patrick H. Callahan who very aptly dubbed the *Review* "a journal of protest." Patrick H. Callahan to Arthur Preuss, March 31, 1923. Reel 4. A.P.P. "Conditions of Profit Sharing," *Review* XXVII 9 (May 1, 1920):129. "A Queer Reconstruction Pamphlet," *Echo* December 11, 1919. "Catholics and the Guild Movement," *Review* XXVI 23 (December 1, 1919):362. "Democratizing Industry," XXVIII 1 (January 1, 1921):6. "The Labor Movement," 5 (March 1, 1921):74.

80. "The Steel Trusts vs. Labor," *Echo* July 31, 1919. "The Miners Strike," November 6, 1919. "Organized Labor and the Farmers," February 12, 1920. "The Steel Autocracy," February 10, 1921. "Harding's Attitude Toward Labor," August 17, 1922. "The Open Shop Drive," January 20, 1921.

81. "The Policy of Organized Labor," *Echo* February 3, 1921. "The Labor Movement," March 31, 1921. "The American Federation of Labor," July 28, 1921.

82. "The Catholic Press and Capitalism," *Review* XXVII 17 (September 1, 1920):311.

83. "The Priest and Social Reconstruction," *Echo* June 17, 1920. "The Clergy and World Affairs," *Review* XXVIII 13 (July 1, 1921):213. "Birth Control and Economic Conditions," *Echo* December 1, 1921.

84. "Birth Control," *Echo* April 24, 1924.

85. "The Church and the Laboringman," *Review* XXVIII 12 (June 15, 1921):176–178.

86. "The Church and the Laboringman," *Review* XXVIII 14 (July 15, 1921):231.

87. "The N. C.W. C. and the Demands of Our Catholic Laboringmen," *Review* XXVIII 18 (September 15, 1921):321–324.

88. "The Labor Movement," *Echo* March 13, 1921.

89. "A Catholic Laboringman on Father Husslein's Book *Work, Wealth and Wages*," *Review* XXIX 4 (February 15, 1922):68–70. Fromrnelt's criticism of Husslein and a rebuttal were reprinted in the *Echo*. "Father Husslein's Social Teachings," September 7, and 14, 1922.

90. "Denouncing Capitalism," *Review* XXIX I (January 1, 1922):3

91. Gleason, 131–138. On "Solidarism" see Richard E. Mulcahy, *The Economics of Heinrich Pesch* (New York:Henry Holt, 1952). Franz H. Mueller, *The Church and the Social Question* (Washington,DC, American Enterprise Institute, 1984), 100–104. Charles Curran, 92–129.

92. "Father Pesch and Christian Solidarism," *Echo* November 27, 1924. "Father Pesch's Social Programme," September 2, 1920. "Social Reconstruction," September 9. 1920. "A Reconstruction Programme," January 27, 1921. "Our Only Hope," September 29. 1921. "Random Topics," March

29, 1923."The Ownership Problem," May 17, 1923. "Communism in America," January 3, 1924.

93. Gleason, 200. Interestingly, "Solidarism" has found an influential representative in late years in Pope John Paul II. The thought of Heinrich Pesch appears to have had an influence on John Paul II's social encyclicals, *Laborem Exercens* (1981) and *Sollicitudo Rei Socialis* (1987).

94. "The Next Step on the Road to Social Reform," *Review* XXVIII 13 (July 1, 1921):209.

95. "The *Echo* Entering Its Tenth Year," *Echo* February 7, 1924.

96. Ibid.

97. McShane, 83–84.

98. "An Apology for 'Catholic Politicians'," *Echo* May 26, 1921.

99. William M. Halsey, *The Survival of American Innocence: Catholicism in an Era of Disillusionment 1920–1940* (Notre Dame, IN: University of Notre Dame Press, 1980), 1–7.

IX The Salt of Conservative Progress

1. Douglas J. Slawson, *The Foundation and First Decade of the National Catholic Welfare Council* (Washington, D.C.: The Catholic University of America Press, 1992),10. Christopher Kauffman also noted the connection between Americanism and the establishment of the NCWC. *Tradition and Transformation*, 256–261.

2. Slawson, 1–25.

3. Slawson, 22.

4. "Notes and Gleanings," *Review* XXIV 11 (June 1, 1917):184. 15 (August 1, 1917):233 and XXV 1(January 1,1918):11. On the war related work of the NCWC, see Elizabeth McKeown, *War and Welfare: American Catholics and World War I* (New York:Garland Publishing Inc., 1988).

5. "A Plot Against Our Schools," *Review* XXV 20 (October 15, 1918):306.

6. Arthur Preuss to Francis Markert, April 20, 1920. Reel 14 A.P.P.

7. "An Unfair Restriction," *Review* XXVII 10 (May 15, 1920):154–155. Slawson, 75–76, 119–120.

8. "Notes and Gleanings," *Review* XXVII 13 (July 1, 1920):207. XXVIII (June 1, 1921):171. XXIX 3 (February 1, 1922):53. "*Echo*es," *Echo* February 16, 1922.

9. Slawson, 76, 118–119.

10. "Notes and Gleanings," *Review* XXVII 10 (May 15, 1920):154, 12 (June 15, 1920):171. "Random Topics," *Echo* December 8, 1921.

11. Slawson, 76, 310 n. 26.

12. "The NCWC and the Catholic Laboringman," *Review* XXVIII 18 (September 15, 1921):321.

13. "On the Wrong Track," *Review* XXVIII 14 (July 15, 1921):227–228.

14. John Ryan to Arthur Preuss, September 5, 1922. Reel 5. "Points From Letters," *Review* XXXI 9 (May 1, 1924):176. In the English language bibliography that he appended to his adaptation of Anton Koch's *Moral Theologie*, Preuss cited Ryan's work frequently in regard to social justice issues.

15. "Notes and Gleanings," *Review* XXIX 9 (June 1, 1922):206. Slawson, 80–81, 96–100.

16. For an account of the machinations that produced the Roman decree suppressing the NCWC, see Slawson,96–191. Gerald P. Fogarty, *The Vatican and the American Hierarchy*,214–227.

17. Joseph Schifferli to Arthur Preuss, March 31, 1922. Reel 5 A.P.P.

18. Slawson, 139, 324 n. 79.

19. Joseph Schifferli to Arthur Preuss, April 7, 1922. Reel 5 A.P.P.

20. On Curley's subterfuge see Slawson, 140. "Rome Authorities Advise Reorganization of the N. C. W. C.," *Echo* April 14, 1922.

21. "Roma Locuta Est," *Review* XXIX 8 (April 15, 1922):142.

22. "The End of the N.C.W.C.," *Review* XXIX 9 (May 1. 1922):157.

23. "Notes and Gleanings," *Review* XXIX 10 (May 15, 1922):187. "*Echo*es," *Echo* May 18 and June 8, 1922. "The Affair of the N.C.W.C.," XXIX 14 (July 15,1922):265.

24. "Correspondence: 'Taxation Without Representation' In the Catholic Church," *Nation* 115 (July 26, 1922):94–95.

25. Slawson, 180.

26. "The Latest Outcropping of 'Americanism'," *Review* XXIX 17 (September 1, 1922):322.

27. "The New Decree on the N.C.W.C.," *Echo* August 24, 1922.

28. "Rome's Coup de Grace to the N.C.W.C," *Review* XXIX 17 (September 1, 1922):320.

29. Slawson, 186–191. "Notes and Gleanings," *Review* XXIX 19 (October 1, 1922):368. Joseph Schifferli to Arthur Preuss, October 13, 1922. Reel 5 A.P.P.

30. "Notes and Gleanings," *Review* XXXI 19 (October 1, 1924):377. "The N.C.W.C. News Service," 21 (November 1, 1924):425. "Notes and Gleanings," XXXII 20 (October 15, 1925):420. "*Echo*es," *Echo* November 22, 1923.

31. Gleason, *The Conservative Reformers*, 199–203.

32. "Notes and Gleanings," *Review* XXXI 12 (June 15, 1924):251.

33. Edward Cuddy, "Colonel Patrick Henry Callahan, A Proponent of

Cooperative Citizenship," M.A, Dissertation, The Catholic University of America, 1959. Joseph G. Green, Jr., "Patrick Henry Callahan (1866-1940): The Role of an American Catholic Lay Leader," Ph.D. Dissertation, The Catholic University of America, 1963. William E. Ellis," Patrick Henry Callahan, A Kentucky Democrat in National Politics," *The Filson Club History Quarterly*, 51 (January 1977):17-30. "Catholicism and the Southern Ethos: The Role of Patrick Henry Callahan," *Catholic Historical Review* LXIX 1 (January 1983):41-50. A full biography of Callahan's remarkable life has yet to be written.

34. William Ellis, 44.

35. Green, 13-18. William Ellis, 45.

36. Kauffman, *Faith and Fraternalism*, 181-189.

37. ibid., 190-220.

38. "Knights of Columbus Committee on Religious Prejudice," *Review* XXIII 7 (April 1, 1916):104.

39. "Profit Sharing as a Compromise Between Capital and Labor," *Review* XXVII 1 (January 1, 1920):6-7.

40. Patrick H. Callahan to Arthur Preuss, August 3, 1921. Reel 4 A.P.P. There were about one hundred and twenty American bishops at this time. The cost of an annual subscription to the *Review* was three dollars, which would worth be about eighteen dollars today.

41. Patrick H. Callahan to Arthur Preuss, August 1, 1924. Reel 4 A.P.P. Patrick H. Callahan to Frederick Kenkel. March 5, 1925. CKNA AUND

42. Arthur Preuss to Patrick H. Callahan, May 9, 1932. Callahan Papers. ACUA. As Preuss was never able to pay his contributors, having someone of the prominence of Patrick H. Callahan volunteer to provide essays on a regular basis was itself a tremendous benefit.

43. Patrick H. Callahan to Denis McCarthy, undated. (copy) Callahan Papers. ACUA

44. Patrick H. Callahan to Frederick Kenkel, March 5, 1925. CKNA. AUND

45. Patrick H. Callahan to Arthur Preuss, December 26, 1925. Reel 5 A.P.P.

46. Patrick H. Callahan, "A Program for the Conservation of Catholic Truth," *Review* XXX 6 (March 15, 1923):117. "The Louisville Plan for Presenting the Truth to Non-Catholics," XXI 7 (April 1, 1924):121-125.

47. Patrick H. Callahan, "The Politics of Prejudice," *Review* XXXI 16 (August 15, 1924):300-304. "Aftermath of the New York Democratic Convention," 17 (September 1, 1924):321-325. 18 (September 15, 1924):349-351. "Politico-Religious Propaganda," 20 (October 15, 1924) :396-399. "Politics and Prejudice," 21(November 1, 1924):423-424.

48. Ernest Cordeal, "The Re-Awakening of Intolerance," *Review* XXXI 15 (August 1, 1924):281-285.

49. "A Reply to Col. Callahan on the Klan Question, " *Review* XXXI 18 (September 15, 1924):349–351. J. H. Muehlenbeck to Arthur Preuss, June 26, 1927. Reel 7 A.P.P.

50. Patrick H. Callahan,"The Worker and Ownership," *Review* XXX 14 (July 15, 1923):273–274. "The Child Labor Question," XXXII 6 (March 15, 1925):95–98. "The Catholic Peace Movement," XXXIV 5 (March 1, 1927):93–95. "A Catholic Organization for the Preservation of International Peace," XXXIV 11 (June 1, 1927):227–229. "Why War?" XXXIV 23 (December 1, 1927):370–372.

51. "Pelletier and the Knights of Columbus Committee on War Activities," *Review* XXIX I I (June 1, 1922):207. Patrick H. Callahan to Arthur Preuss, November 24, 1926. Reel 7 A.P.P. On Callahan's role as in seeking reform in the Knights of Columbus see Kauffman, *Faith and Fraternalism*, 248–255,

52. Patrick H. Callahan "Notes and Gleanings," *Review* XXIX 10 (May 15, 1922):189.

53. Patrick H. Callahan, "Georgia of Today," *Review* XXX 5 (March 1, 1923):91–96.

54. Patrick H. Callahan, "Anti–Catholic Fanatics in the U.S. Senate," *Review* XXIX 18 (September 15, 1922):343. Green, 144-145.

55. Patrick H. Callahan to Arthur Preuss, February 26, 1927 and July 28, 1928. Reel 7 A.P.P. Arthur Preuss to Frederick Kenkel, March 31. 1924. CKNA AUND

56. Patrick H. Callahan to Arthur Preuss, May 17, 1922. Reel 4 A. P. P. "Notes and Gleanings," XXXII 4 (February 15, 1922):83.

57. "*Echo*es," *Echo* March 13, 1922.

58. Green, 49–54.

59. Cyprian Davis, O.S.B. *The History of Black Catholics in the United States* (New York: Crossroad, 1990),233–245.

60. Preuss served for a period of time on the Board of Governors of the Catholic Church Extension Society. Very Rev. William D. O'Brien to Arthur Preuss, April 22, 1925. Arthur Preuss Papers AUND

61. Thomas Wyatt Turner to Arthur Preuss, October 24, 1926. Reel 6 A.P.P. On Turner see Marilyn W. Nickels, "Thomas Wyatt Turner and the Federated Colored Catholics," *U.S. Catholic Historian* 7 Numbers 2 & 3 (Spring/Summer 1988):215–232.

62. "The Tulsa Race Riots," *Echo* June 30, 1921."The Negro Question," *Echo* March 23, 1922. "Negro Peons of the South," October 26, 1922.

63. "The Negro Point of View," *Echo* October 25, 1923. "Supremacy of the White Race," *Echo* November 17, 1921.

64. "Marcus Garvey," *Echo* August 16, 1923.

65. "Notes and Gleanings," *Review* XXIX 12 (June 15, 1922):231–233. Florian

Haas, S.V.D., "Building a Colored Priesthood," XXXII 2 (January 15, 1925):27–28. "Training a Colored Priesthood," XXXII 17 (September 1, 1925):356. "A Negro Clergy for Negro Catholics," XXXIV 10 (May 15, 1927):218.

66. Rev. D.J. Bustin, "The Catholic Attitude Towards the Negro," *Review* XXVIII 22 (November 15, 1921):405–406.

67. Thomas Wyatt Turner, "Experiences of Colored Catholics," *Review* XXXIII 7 (April 1, 1926):143–145. Rev. Joseph Selinger, "Catholic Colored Students at Lincoln State University of Missouri," XXXII 22 (November 15, 1925):474. "From a Catholic Colored Student at a Non-Catholic Institution of Higher Learning," XXXII 23 (December 1, 1925):494–495.

68. "Converting the Negro," *Review* XXXV 4 (February 15, 1928):81. "Our Colored Brethren," 20 (October 15, 1928):401. Albert Muntsch, S. J., "Catholics and the Race Problem," XXXV 23 (December 1, 1928):406.

69. For accounts of this transition in Eucharistic piety in both its European origins and American development see *History of the Church*, Volume X, ed. by Hubert Jedin, (New York: Crossroad Publishing Company, 1981), 299–315. and Chinnici, 177–185.

70. "The Best Devotion," *Review* XXIII 9 (May 1, 1916):138.

71. *Review* XXIX 20 (October 15, 1922):381.

72. "Why is Frequent Communion Declining?" *Review* XXIX 21 (November 1, 1922):406.

73. Sarah C. Burnett, "Frequent Communion and the Eucharistic Fast," *Review* XXIX 24 (December 15, 1922):486. Correspondence "The Eucharistic Fast," XXX 2 (January 15, 1923):40. Sarah C. Burnett, "The Eucharistic Fast From the Laymen's Point of View," XXX 4 (February 15, 1923):81. "The Eucharistic Fast One More," XXX 8 (April 15, 1923):163–167. "The Eucharistic Fast," XXX 9 (May 1, 1923):186.

74. "Book Reviews," *Review* XXIX 12 (June 15, 1922):233. "The Vernacular in the Liturgy?" *Review* XXX 8 (April 15, 1923):163.

75. "The Liturgical Movement," *Review* XXX 20 (October 15, 1922):3 82.

76. "The Liturgical Movement," *Review* XXX 20 (October 15, 1923):397. "Liturgy and Life," XXXII 16 (August 15, 1925):332–333.

77. "The Safeguard of Communion," *Review* XXXI 3 (February 1, 1924):44–45. "The Canon of the Mass," XXXI 14 (July 15, 1924):265–267. "Lay Participation in the Mass," XXXII 7 (April 1, 1925):145–146. "Notes and Gleanings," XXXI 1(January 1, 1924):18. "Participating in the Mass," XXXII 18 (September 15, 1925):386–387.

78. *Review* XXX 22 (November 15, 1923):433. It is probable that the Mass described took place at the convent of the Sisters of the Most Precious Blood, in O'Fallon, Missouri where Preuss's friend and contributor Father Martin

Hellriegel began his work on liturgical renewal. See note 93.

79. "Liturgical Communion," *Review* XXX 24 (December 15, 1923):477–479.

80. Rev. John B. Kessel to Arthur Preuss, February 23, 1925. Reel 5 A.P.P.

81. Virgil Michel, O.S.B. "The Liturgical Movement," *Review* XXXIII 5 (March 1, 1926):108. "A Popular Liturgical Library," XXXIII 1 1 (June 1, 1926):245. "The Liturgical Sacrifice of the New Law," XXXIII 14 (July 15, 1926):312. "The Intellectual Confusion of Today and the Philosophy Perennis," XXXIII 10 (May 15, 1926):21 1. "Psycho-analysis and the Catholic World-View," XXXIII 17 (August 1, 1926):333–334.

82. Martin Hellriegel, "The Liturgical Apostolate," *Review* XXXIV 1 (January 1, 1927):14. Martin Hellriegel (1890–1981) was born at Heppenheim, Germany and arrived in the United States in 1909 to begin his studies for the priesthood at St. Meinrad's Abbey. After completing his studies at Kenrick Seminary in St. Louis in 1914, Hellriegel was ordained and assigned to St. Peter's parish in St. Charles, Missouri. It is probable that Hellriegel first met the parish's most prominent member, Arthur Preuss, at this time. On Hellriegel and his relationship with Preuss see Buchhuber, 106–123.

83. *Review* 2 (January 15,1924):23. 3 (February 1, 1924):44. 6 (March 15, 1924):107. 14 (July 15, 1924):264. 16 (August 15, 1925):332. 18 (September 15, 1925):386. 15 (August 1, 1927):322. 11 (June 1, 1929):171.

84. Rev. F. Joseph Kelly, "Congregational Singing," *Review* XXVIII 8 (April 15, 1921):121. Rev. F. Joseph Kelly, "Liturgical Congregational Singing," XXVIII 17 (September 1, 1921):306–307.

85. Rev. Bede Maler, O.S.B. "A Dangerous Tendency," *Review* XXXII 21 (November 1, 1925):450. "Thoughts on Popular Devotions," XXXIII 9 (May 1, 1926):199.

86. For example, in regard to the Eucharistic Congress held in Chicago in 1926, Preuss wrote to his friend Fr. Markert, "I will not come to the Eucharistic Congress of Archbishop Mundelein. The prelates' propaganda is loathsome to me." February 16, 1926. "I think a quiet prayer of devotion in the parish church, where the Saviour is also present, would be preferable to Him than attendance at a Congress." June 8, 1926. Reel 14 A. P. P. Preuss's most frequent contributor on the issue of the Eucharistic fast was one Sarah C. Burnett of San Francisco.

87. Preuss's papers contain numerous letters from Michel who frequently wrote book reviews for the *Review*.

X There Are a *Few* Good Men

1. Slawson, 146–147.

2. Douglas J. Slawson, "The Attitudes and Activities of American Catholics

Regarding the Proposals to Establish a Federal Department of Education between World War I and the Great Depression," Ph.D. diss., The Catholic University of America, 1981. Further citations as "Slawson, Education."

3. Slawson, "Education," 68–72.

4. Slawson, "Education," vii, 54–56, 79–82, 266–272. It is worth noting here that Slawson found that the National Education Association is still unwilling to be forthright about its involvement with the anti-Catholic Scottish Rite Masons on this matter.

5. "The Catholic Education Association," *Review* XXV 13 (July 1, 1918):201–202. "Danger to Our Schools," 18 (September 15, 1918):281. "A Plot Against Our Schools," 20 (October 15, 1918):306. Preuss also wrote numerous editorials in the *Echo* on the "schools fight." "A New Peril to Our Schools," August 5, 1920. "The School Controversy in Michigan," August 12, 1920. "The Smith-Towner Bill, " August 19, 1920. "Championing the Private School," November 16, 1922. "The Menace to Catholic Education," December 7, 1922. "The Sterling-Reed Bill," January 24, 1924.

6. "Notes and Gleanings," *Review* XXXI 6 (March 15, 1924):114. "Notes and Gleanings," 21 (November 1, 1924):421.

7. Lloyd P. Jorgenson, "The Oregon School Law of 1922: Passage and Sequel," *Catholic Historical Review* LIV 3 (October 1968):455–466. Thomas J. Shelley, "The Oregon School Case and the National Catholic Welfare Conference," *Catholic Historical Review*, LXXV 3 (July 1989):439–457. Slawson, "Education," 85–88, 191–202.

8. Slawson, "Education," 97–98. Slawson, 82, 101–102.

9. Jorgenson, 461–466. Slawson, "Education," 343–350. Shelley, 454–457.

10. Slawson, 250. Slawson, "Education," 249.

11. Slawson, 250–251.

12. Slawson, 251.

13. "An Alarm and A Warning," *America*, 34 (January 2, 1926):271.

14. Slawson, 251–252.   Slawson,"Education," 418–419.

15. Slawson, "Education," 410–419.

16. "New Education Measure Introduced in U.S. Senate," *Echo* March 18, 1926. Slawson, 253–255.

17. "Notes and Gleanings," *Review* XXXIII 9 (May 1, 1926):197.

18. "By What Authority?" *Review* XXXIII 10 (May 15, 1926):215–217. Slawson, 253–254.

19. John Cochran to Frederick Kenkel, May 24, 1926. CKNA AUND

20. Arthur Preuss to Frederick Kenkel, May 24, 1926. CKNA AUND

21. Slawson, 83, 256.

22. This accusation by Ryan is the same one that America had made in January, 1926. Father Burke had wrangled unsuccessfully with the magazine's Jesuit editors to uncover the source of the charge. It would seem a reasonable hypothesis that it was in fact James Ryan who coincidently left the staff of the NCWC that very month. Slawson, 252.

23. James R. Ryan to Arthur Preuss, May 21, 1926. Reel 6 A.P.P.

24. Arthur Preuss to Frederick Kenkel, May 24, 1926. CKNA AUND

25. Frederick Kenkel to Arthur Preuss, May 26, 1926. Reel 6 A.P.P.

26. "More Light on the Activities of the N.C.W.C.," *Review* XXXIII 12 (June 15, 1926):257–259.

27. James R. Ryan to Arthur Preuss, November 4, 1926. Reel 6 A.P.P. This concocted attack on Kerans occasioned a letter to Preuss from one of Kerans' friends protesting the *Review*'s "attack" on Kerans. Fr. Kirsch to Arthur Preuss, November 19, 1926. Reel 7 A.P.P.

28. On the NCWC's involvement in the Mexican crisis see Slawson,241–248.

29. "The Status of the N.C.W.C.," *Review* XXXIII 12 (June 15, 1926):267. "More N.C.W.C. Meddling and Muddling," 14 (July 15, 1926):307–308. "The N.C.W.C. and Diocesan Autonomy," 16 (August 15, 1926):355356. "The N. C. W. C Motion Picture Bureau," 18 (September 15, 1926):408–409. "Sen. Phipps and the Phipps Bill," 21 (October 1, 1926):433. "The American Hierarchy and the Mexican Kulturkampf," 21 (October 1, 1926):440. "The N.C.W.C. and the Attempts to Federalize Education," 22 (October 15, 1926):455. "The Canonical Status of the N.C.W.C.," XXXIV 2 (January 15, 1927):31–32. "The Hierarchy and the N.C.W.C.," 16 (August 15, 1927):336.

30. "More Light on the Activities of the N.C.W.C.," *Review* XXXIII 12 (June 15, 1926):257–259. "Notes and Gleanings," 16 (August 15, 1926):370. "Archbishop Curley on the National Councils of Catholic Men and Women," 23 (December 1, 1926):523–524. "Unsafe Representatives of the Catholic Cause in the N.C.W.C.," 23 (December 1, 1926):527. "The N.C.W.C. and Birth Control," XXXIV 1 (January 1, 1927):4. "The N.C.W. C. and Legal Advice," 1 (January 1, 1927):10.

31. "A Grave Accusation," *Review* XXXIII 16 (August 15, 1926):359. "The General Secretary's Mistake," 24 (December 15, 1926):552. "The N. C. W. C. News Service as a Promoter of Dangerous Tendencies," XXXIV 7 (April 1, 1927):149–150. "Mysterious Manouvers of the N.C.W.C.," 6 (March 15, 1927):130. "Father Burke's Unsatisfactory Reply to the *Chicago Times*" 17 (September 1, 1927):350–351.

32. Ryan's resentment over this matter surfaced in a letter he wrote to Preuss which suggested that Burke had hired Montavon as a payback. Ryan claimed that Montavon had arranged for his company to pay Burke's way on a junket to

Latin America. James Ryan to Arthur Preuss, August 30, 1926. Reel 6 A. P. P.

33. The incident which provoked this reaction is not mentioned by Preuss nor is it explained in his correspondence. However, as Preuss only used his columns in the *Echo* twice for this second assault on the NCWC, it is possible that something had occurred which made the publishers of the Buffalo paper more intimidated by Burke in 1926 than they were in 1922.

34. Slawson, 255.

35. James Ryan to Arthur Preuss, September 20, 1926. Reel 6 A.P.P.

36. James Ryan to Arthur Preuss, August 30, 1926. Reel 6 A.P.P.

37. James Ryan to Arthur Preuss, September 20, 1926. Reel 6 A.P.P.

38. James Ryan to Arthur Preuss, November 22, 1926. Reel 6 A.P.P.

39. James Ryan to Arthur Preuss, September 23, 1926. September 7, 1927. Reel 7. December 13, 1926. Reel 6 A. P. P.

40. James Ryan to Arthur Preuss, August 23, September 4, October 7, October 11, and November 22, 1926. Reel 6 A. P. P.

41. James Ryan to Arthur Preuss, December 15, 1926. Reel 6. A.P.P.

42. "The Situation in Mexico," *Echo* May 13, 1926.

43. James Ryan to Arthur Preuss, August 19 and 23, 1926. Reel 6 A.P.P.

44. "More Light on the Activities of the N.C.W.C," *Review* XXXIII 12 (June 15, 1926):259–260. Slawson,257–258.

45. James Ryan to Arthur Preuss, September 10, 1926. Reel 6 A.P.P. Bishop Francis C. Kelley of Oklahoma City, a friend of Preuss's since the former's tenure at the Church Extension Society, would later confide in Preuss his role as principal author of the pastoral letter on Mexico. Francis Kelley to Arthur Preuss, December 17, 1926 and January 12, 1927. Reel 6 A.P.P.

46. James Ryan to Arthur Preuss, October 23, 1926. Reel 6 A.P.P.

47. William C. Murphy,Jr., "The Catholic Press," *American Mercury* IX (December 1926):400–408. Preuss's friends enjoyed teasing the editor about this article.

48. Slawson, 275–277.

49. Fogarty, *The Vatican and the American Hierarchy*, 220–228.

50. Arthur Preuss to Francis Markert, March 28, 1912. Reel 13 A.P.P.

51. "The N.C. News Service As A Promoter of Dangerous Tendencies," *Review* XXXIV 7 (April 1, 1927):149–151.

52. "The Latest Outcropping of Americanism," *Review* XXIX 17 (September 1, 1922):322.

53. Arthur Preuss to Frederick Kenkel, June 8, 1926. CKNA AUND.

54. "Notes and Gleanings," *Review* XXXIII 20 (October 15, 1926):468.

55. "Do We Want A Catholic President?" *Review* XXXIV 11 (June 1, 1927):238.

56. Charles C. Marshall, "An Open Letter to the Honorable Alfred E. Smith," *Atlantic Monthly* 139 (April 1927):540–549.

57. "Gov. Smith and the Marshall Letter," *Echo* April 14, 1927.

58. Thomas J. Shelley, "'What the Hell is an Encyclical?': Governor Alfred E. Smith, Charles C. Marshall, Esq., and Father Francis P. Duffey," *U.S. Catholic Historian* vol. 15 n. 2 (Spring 1997):87–107. "Alfred E. Smith, Catholic and Patriot: Governor Smith Replies," *Atlantic Monthly* 139 (May 1927):721–728. "Text of Gov. Smith's Reply to Marshall," *Echo* April 21, 1927. Twenty years prior to this incident Francis Duffy had been a leader of the nascent American Modernist movement at Dunwoodie Seminary in New York. Christopher Kauffman, *Tradition and Transformation in Catholic Culture*, 205-212. Thomas J. Shelley, "John Cardinal Farley and Modernism in New York," *Church History* 61 (September 1992):350–361. Appleby, 111–167.

59. "Text of Gov. Smith's Reply to Marshall," *Echo* April 21, 1927.

60. Joseph Schifferli to Arthur Preuss, April 22, 1927. Reel 7 A.P.P.

61. Joseph Schifferli to Arthur Preuss, April 26, 1927. Reel 7 A.P.P. "The Binding Power of Papal Encyclicals," *Echo* June 9, 1927.

62. "Do We Need A Catholic President?" *Review* XXXIV 11 (June 1, 1927):238 & 240.

63. "The Liberalism of Gov. Smith," *Review* XXXIV 13 (July 1, 1927):276.

64. "A Masonic Journal on the Smith Letter," *Review* XXXIX 17 (September 1, 1927):356.

65. "Notes and Gleanings," *Review* XXXIV 16 (August 15, 1927):339 and 19 (September 15, 1927):374.

66. William F. Sands, "Church and State in America," *Review* XXXIV 19 (October 1, 1927):387–392.

67. "The Liberalism of Gov. Smith," *Review* XXXIV 20 (October 15, 1927):414–415.

68. Elliot Ross to Arthur Preuss, December 20, 1927. Reel 7 A.P.P.

69. "A Priest in Politics," *Echo* February 16, 1928. "Notes and Gleanings," *Review* XXXV 8 (April 15, 1928):164. "Dangerous Half-Truths," 24 (December 15, 1928):470–471.

70. "Catholics and Political Salesmen," *Review* XXXV 3 (February 1, 1928):57. "Catholics and the Presidency," 3 (February 1, 1928):80. "Political Advice," 14 (July 15, 1928):259. "Notes and Gleanings," 15 (August 1, 1928):303. "Anti-Catholic Prejudice," *Echo* May 24, 1928. "The Baptists and Gov. Smith," June 14, 1928. "In the Same Boat," August 9. 1928.

71. Francis J. Martin to Arthur Preuss, November 11 and 29, 1927. Reel 7 A. P. P.

72. (Francis J. Martin) "Catholics and the Presidency," *Review* XXXV I (January 1, 1928):3-9.

73. "What We Need, " *Echo* June 23, 1921.

74. Broderick, *Right Reverend New Dealer,* 183–185.

75. *America*, November 24, 1928. Father Feeney would come under Church censure and incur excommunication for his rigoristic interpretation of the adage "extra ecclesiam nulla salus." Hennesey, 300.

76. Callahan provided the *Review* with an analysis of the campaign which credited Smith's stance on Prohibition and his association with "machine" politics as the primary reasons for his defeat. "Politics and Prejudice, The 1928 Campaign," *Review* XXXVI I (January 1, 1929):5–7. 2 (January 15, 1929):25–26. Historians have been divided in their interpretation of the importance of religious bigotry in Smith's defeat. Some, like Ruth C. Silva, *Rum, Religion, and Votes: 1928 Reexamined* (University Park, PA:University of Pennsylvania Press, 1962) concur with Callahan that Smith's position on the issues, particularly prohibition, led to his defeat. Others, such as Allan J. Lichtman, *Prejudice and the Old Politics: The Presidential Election of 1928* (Chapel Hill, NC: The University of North Carolina Press, 1979) maintain that religious prejudice was *the* issue of the 1928 campaign.

77. "Post-Election Thoughts," *Echo* November 22, 1928.

XI "So Long Thy Power Has Blest Me"

1. "The Unscotched Dragon," *Review* XXXVI 2 (January 15, 1929):21. "A Dissenter and His Defenders," 5 (March 1, 1929):83–84. "While Peter Sleeps," 11 (June 1929):164–166. "Traditionless Catholics," (October 1929):221. "Our Inferiority Complex," (November 1930):285. The publication of an expose of the Church in America, *While Peter Sleeps*, by an apostate Jesuit, E. Boyd Barrett, involved Preuss in another discussion of Americanism in 1929. Against much of the Catholic press, Preuss maintained that Barrett's unfavorable evaluation of the Church in America was in many respects correct.

2. "Important Notice to Our Subscribers," *Review* XXXVI 7 (April 1, 1929):121.

3. "Notes and Gleanings," *Review* XXXVI 9 (June 1929):177. 11 (August 1929):213. "Notice to Our Subscribers," 14 (November 1929):277.

4. Frederick Kenkel to Arthur Preuss, August 13, October 6, and November 24, 1929. Kenkel Papers. CKNA AUND At this point in time, four of Preuss's nine surviving children still made their home with him.

5. Patrick H. Callahan to Arthur Preuss, August 18, and September 13, 1928. Reel 7 A.P.P. Arthur Preuss to Frederick Kenkel, October 24, 1929. Patrick H. Callahan to Frederick Kenkel, Kenkel Papers. March 5, 1930. CKNA AUND. Arthur Preuss to Patrick H. Callahan, May 9, 1932. Callahan Papers.

Patrick H. Callahan to Frederick Kenkel, Kenkel Papers. March 5, 1930. CKNA
Arthur Preuss to Patrick H. Callahan, May 9, 1932. Callahan Papers. ACUA
Arthur Preuss to Frederick Kenkel, May 9, 1933 CKNA AUND. "Notes and
Gleanings," *Review* XXXXI 5 (May 1934):118.
 6. Arthur Preuss to Frederick Kenkel, January 20, 1931. CKNA AUND
 7. Arthur Preuss to Frederick Kenkel, January 9, 1930. CKNA AUND
 8. Arthur Preuss to Frederick Kenkel, January 26, 1931. CKNA AUND Arthur
Preuss to Abbot Francis, June 6, 1931 and January 7, 1934. Archives of St.Leo's
Abbey. Subsequent references "ASLA."
 9. Jerome Wisniewski, O.S.B. to Frederick Kenkel, March 21, 1930. CKNA
AUND. One of Preuss's friends, Virgil Michel, took umbrage at receiving
Father Jerome's solicitation, particularly as it did not have Preuss's sanction, and
as he, Michel, had already been providing book *Reviews* and articles "gratis" to
the *Review* for a number of years. As a point of fact, the *Review* had never been
able to pay its contributors. Jerome Wisniewski, O.S.B. to Virgil Michel,
O.S.B., January 21, 1930. Virgil Michel, O.S.B. to Jerome Wisniewski, O.S.B.
January 28, 1930. Jerome Wisniewski, O.S.B. to Virgil Michel, O.S.B.,
February 2, 1930. Virgil Michel Papers, Archives St. John's Abbey,
Collegeville, Minnesota.
10. Arthur Preuss to Frederick Kenkel, January 26, and July 29, 1931. Kenkel
Papers. CKNA AUND
11. Arthur Preuss to Abbot Francis, O.S.B., July 1, 1932 and February 18, 1933.
ASLA
12. "The Slump in the Stock Market," *Echo*, November 7, 1929.
"The Business Situation," November 21,1929.
"The Business Situation," *Echo*, January 16, 1930.
13. "Unemployment and Low Wages in the Midst of 'Prosperity'," *Review*
XXXVII I (January 1930): 1. On how some other Catholic periodicals responded
to the Depression, see Lawrence B. DeSaulniers, *The Response in the American
Catholic Periodical Press to the Crisis of the Great Depression: 1930–1935*
(Lanham, MD: University Press of America, 1984).
DeSaulniers' study focuses on *Commonweal, America, Catholic World*, and the
Centralblatt and Social Justice.
14. "The Progressives," *Echo*, December 5, 1929. "Only 2,300,000
Unemployed!" September 5, 1930. "Our Effete Party System," October 9, 1930.
15. "A Catholic View of Unemployment," *Review* XXXVII 10 (October
1930):232."What About *Quadragesimo Anno?" Echo*, July 9, 1931. Frederick
Kenkel, *"Quadragesimo Anno," Review* XXXVIII 8 (August 1931):169–170.
16. "Capitalism Cutting Its Own Throat," *Echo* December 31, 1931.
"The Causes of the Current Depression," March 10, 1932. "An Indictment of

Democracy," June 6, 1932."Democracy, Is It a Failure?" *Review* XXXIX
12 (December 1932):366.

17. "The Only Cure," *Echo*, August 13, 1931. "Five Steps Toward Social
Reconstruction," August 18, 1932. "Pius XI on Social Reconstruction,"
Review XXXVIII 9 (September 1931):206. "The Papal Call to Reconstruct
Society," XXXIX 11 (November 1932):249.

"Catholic Action and the Laity," *Echo* April 10, 1930. On the Catholic
Action movement see Konrad Repgen, *History of the Church* vol. X, ed.
Hubert Jedin, 307f.

18.Robert Hull, "The Laity Come Into Their Own," *Review* XXXVI 13 (October
1929):241. Hull was a former Protestant minister and a convert to the Church
who had been on the staff of *Our Sunday Visitor*. Hull left the *Visitor* in
September 1927 because his superiors at the paper found his views "too
Ultramontane." Robert Hull to Arthur Preuss, August 30, 1928. Reel 8 A.P.P.

19. Horace A. Frommelt, "Reckoning With the Laity," *Review* XXXVIII 9
(September 1931):205.

20. Horace A. Frommelt, "Are We Priest Ridden?" *Review* XXXIX I (January
1932):19. In a journal read mostly by clerics, such sharp words did not go
unchallenged and Preuss published letters from priests who castigated the laity for
abdicating their responsibilities. "Are We Priest Ridden? If So Why?" XXXIX
3 (March 1932):62.

21. "A French Criticism of American Catholics," *Review* XXXVIII 3 (March
1931):58. "Notes and Gleanings," 9 (September 1931):204.

22. Horace A. Frommelt, "Catholics and the NRA," *Review* XXXX 10 (October
1933):217.

23. "State Absolutism in America," *Review* XXXVIII 9 (September 1931):204.
"Notes and Gleanings," XXXIX 9(September 1932):229.
"Are We Facing Dictatorship?" *Echo* August 18, 1932.

24. Arthur Preuss to Abbot Francis, O.S.B. November 13, 1932. ASLA
During the campaign, Preuss had interpreted Roosevelt's Masonic affiliations as
a bad sign of what his presidency might bring. "Notes and Gleanings," XXXIX
4 (April 1932):182.

25. "The President's Courageous Action," *Echo* March 23, 1933. "A New Era
of Social Justice," March 30, 1933.

26.This was the highest praise Preuss accorded any American president. "Notes
and Gleanings," *Review* XXXX 6 (June 1933):117.

27. "Are We At The Beginning of a Christian Social Order?" *Echo* June 8, 1933.

28. Frederick Kenkel, "Are We Drifting Into State Socialism?" *Review* XXXX
7 (July 1933):149. "The Philosophy of the New Deal," 9 (September 1933):200.
"On the Way to State Socialism?" 11 (November 1933):273.

29. Horace A. Frommelt, "The Decline of Alfred E. Smith," XXXXI 2

(February 1934):51.

30. "Appraising Huey Long," *Echo* April 13, 1933. "The Louisiana Kingfish," *Review* XXXX 7 (July 1933):146. "Father Coughlin's Radio Discourses 1931–32." XXXX 3 (March 1933):51–52. "A National Union for Social Justice," *Echo* December 6, 1934.

31. "Italian Catholics and Fascismo," *Echo* April 10, 1924.

32. "Fascisti and Freemasonry," *Echo* August 30, 1923. "Italy's Great Menace," *Echo* January 22, 1925. "Fascismo and the Church," March 18, 1926. "Taking Mussolini's Measure," April 1, 1926. "Italy Under Fascismo," October 14, 1926. "After Mussolini What?" November 18, 1926. "Pius XI Against Nationalism," February 3, 1927. "Political Deportations in Italy," February 17, 1927.

33. "The Treaty of the Lateran," *Echo*, March 31, 1929. "The New Mussolini," December 10, 1931.

34. "Talks With Mussolini," *Echo* January 19, 1933.

35. "Fascismo and the Corporate State," *Echo* January 26, 1933.

36. "The Menace of Fascism," *Echo* August 17, 1933.

37. On the various interpretations of the Church's relations with the Nazi regime in these years see Klaus Scholder, *The Churches and the Third Reich* Volume I "Preliminary History and the Time of Illusions 1918–1934" (Frankfurt: Verlag Ullstein, 1977; Philadelphia: Fortress Press, 1988). Ernst Christian Helmreich, *The German Churches under Hitler: Background, Struggle and Epilogue* (Detroit: Wayne State University Press, 1977). J.S. Conway, *The Nazi Persecution of the Churches 1933–1945* (New York: Basic Books, 1968). Guenter Lewy, *The Catholic Church and Nazi Germany* (New York: McGraw-Hill, 1964). Donald J. Dietrich, "Catholic Theologians in Hitler's Reich: Adaptation and Critique," *Journal of Church and State* 23 (1981):1945.

38. "The Crisis in Germany," *Echo* April 6, 1933.

39. "The Situation in Germany," *Review* XXXX 6 (June 1933):134.

40. "Hiitler and the Catholic Church," *Echo* April 27, 1933.

41. Scholder, 381–413. Helmreich, 237–256. Lewy, 57–93.

42. "Nazi Germany," *Echo* July 13, 1933.

43. Ludwig Koch, S.J. "Die Kraft der Symbole," *Stimmen der Zeit* CXXVI (!933–34):272. Cited in Lewy, 112.

44. *Echo*, February 15, 1934.

45. "The Church and Nazi Germany," *Echo* March 22, 1934.

46. "Cardinal Faulhaber's Sermons on Nazism," *Echo* June 21, 1934.

47. "Decay of the Free Press in Germany," *Echo* August 23, 1934. "A Convert's Prophecy," December 6, 1934. "Bellicose Nationalism," *Review* XXXXI 9 (September 1934):193–194.

Conclusion

1. "Arthur Preuss, Eminent Author And Editor, Dead," *Echo* December 20, 1934.

2. "Funeral Services for Arthur Preuss Held in St. Louis," *Echo* December 27, 1934.

3. I refer here to the broadening debate among American Catholics concerning the compatibility of Catholicism and American liberal capitalism which culminated in the fall of 1994 when nine Catholic journals simultaneously issued a manifesto, "Civilization of Love, The Pope's Call to the West." David Schindler, "Is America Bourgeois?" *Communio* XIV 3 (Fall 1987). Richard John Neuhaus, *The Catholic Moment* (Harper & Row: San Francisco, 1987). Glenn Olsen, "The Catholic Moment?" *Communio* XV 4 (Winter 1988): 474–487. Richard John Neuhaus, "In Reply to Glenn W. Olsen and J. Brien Benestad," *Communio* XVI 4 (Winter 1989):552–558. Mark Lowery, George Weigel, and David L. Schindler, "Discussion: Catholicism and American Culture," *Communio* XVIII 3 (Fall 1991):425–472. Michael Novak, "Schindler's Conversion," *Communio* XIX 1 (Spring 1992):145–163. Richard John Neuhaus, *Doing Well and Doing Good: The Challenge to the Christian Capitalist* (Doubleday: New York, 1992). George Weigel, "Catholicism and the American Proposition," *First Things* 23 (May 1992):38–44. Rory T. Conley, "The Triumph of Americanism," *Caelum et Terra* III 3 (Summer 1993):14–18. David L. Schindler, "The Culture of Love," *Catholic World Report* IV 9 (October 1994):42–47. Stratford Caldecott, "In Search of a New Way," *Inside the Vatican* (October 1994):45–55. Daniel Nichols, "A Civilization of Love," *Caelum et Terra* IV 4 (Fall 1994):3–5. Dale Vree "A Civilization of Love," *New Oxford Review* LXI 8 (October 1994). Michael Novak, "The Rediscovery of Our American Catholic Heritage," *Crisis* XII 12 (December 1994):4–7. Michael J. Baxter, C.S.C., "Writing History in a World Without Ends," *Pro Ecclesia* (Fall, 1996). Richard John Neuhaus, "Religion Within the Limits of Morality Alone," *First Things* 72 (April 1997):57–61. Michael J. Baxter, C.S.C. "Well Worth an Argument," *First Things* 75 (August/September 1997):4–5.

SOURCES AND BIBLIOGRAPHY

Sources

The Review Volumes I-XXXXI, 1894-1935
also listed as *"Catholic Fortnightly Review,"* and
the *"Fortnightly Review."*

Echo (Buffalo, New York) Volumes V-XX, 1919-1934

Preuss Family History, unpublished notes compiled by family.

Interviews

Alma Preuss Dilschnieder
Charles Arthur Preuss
Austin F. Preuss

Archives

A.P.P.   Arthur Preuss Papers. Archives of the Catholic Central
          Union (Verein). St. Louis, Missouri.

AANY   Archives of the Archdiocese of New York

ACUA   Archives of the Catholic University of America

AQC   Archives of Quincy College, Quincy, IL

ASVD   Archives of the Society of the Divine Word, Techny, IL

AUND   Archives of the University of Notre Dame

ASLA   Archives of St. Leo's Abbey, St. Leo, FL

ASJA   Archives of St. John's Abbey, Collegeville, MN

Bibliography

Abell, Aaron I. *American Catholicism and Social Action*: *A Search for Social Justice 1865-1950*. Garden City, NY: Doubleday & Company,1960.

Ahern, Patrick H. *The Life of John J. Keane: Educator and Archbishop 1839-1918*. Milwaukee: Bruce Publishing Company, 1955.

Appleby, R. Scott. *"Church and Age Unite!": The Modernist Impulse in American Catholicism*. Notre Dame: University of Notre Dame Press, 1992.

———. "Between Americanism and Modernism: John Zahm and Theistic Evolution," *Church History*, 56 (December, 1987): 474–490.

Arndt, Karl J. and Mary Olson. *German-American Newspapers and Periodicals, 1732-1955*. Heidelberg: Quelle and Meyer, 1961.

Aubert, Roger. "The Modernist Crisis," in *The History of the Church* Vol. IX ed. by Hubert Jedin. New York: Crossroads, 1981.

Ayers, Robert C. "The Americanist Attack on Europe in 1897 and 1898." In *Rising From History* ed. Robert Daly. Lanham, MD: University Press of America, 1987.

Barmann, Lawrence. "Friedrich von Hugel as Modernist and More than Modernist," *Catholic Historical Review* LXXV 2 (April, 1989): 211–232.

Barry, Colman, O.S.B. *The Catholic Church and German Americans*. Milwaukee: Bruce Publishing Company, 1953.

Baumgartner, Apollinaris W. *Catholic Journalism: A Study of Its Development in the United States, 1789-1930.* New York: Columbia University Press, 1931.

Betts, John Richard. "Darwinism, Evolution and American Catholic Thought, 1860-1900," *Catholic Historical Review* XLV 2 (July, 1959):161-184.

Broderick, Francis L. *Right Reverend New Dealer John A. Ryan.* New York:The Macmillan Co, 1963.

Carey, Patrick W. *American Catholic Religious Thought: The Shaping of a Theological and Social Tradition.* New York: Paulist Press, 1987.

Carnes, Mark C. *Secret Ritual and Manhood in Victorian America.* New Haven: Yale University Press, 1989.

Chinnici, Joseph P. *Living Stones: The History and Structure of Catholic Spiritual Life in the United States.* New York: Macmillan Publishing Company, 1989.

Conway, J. S. *The Nazi Persecution of the Churches 1933-1945.* New York: Basic Books, 1968.

Cross, Robert D. *The Emergence of Liberal Catholicism in America.* Cambridge, MA: Harvard University Press, 1958.

Cuddy, Edward."Colonel Patrick Henry Callahan, A Proponent of Cooperative Citizenship," M.A. Dissertation, The Catholic University of America, 1959.

———."Pro-Germanism and American Catholicism." *Catholic*

Historical Review LIV 3 (October, 1968):427–454.

———."The Irish Question and the Revival of Anti-Catholicism in the 1920's." *Catholic Historical Review* LXVII 2 (April 1981):236–255.

Curran, Charles E. *American Catholic Social Ethics Twentieth Century Approaches*. Notre Dame:University of Notre Dame Press, 1982.

Curran, Robert Emmett. *Michael Augustine Corrigan and the Shaping of Conservative Catholicism in America, 1878–1902*. New York: Arno Press, 1978.

Davis, Cyprian. *The History of Black Catholics in the United States*. New York: Crossroad, 1990.

Deedy, John G., Jr. "The Catholic Press," In *The Religious Press in America*. ed. Martin E. Marty. New York: Holt, Rinehart and Winston, 1963.

DeSaulniers, Lawrence B. *The Response in the American Catholic Periodical Press to the Crisis of the Great Depression; 1930–1935*. Lanham, Md.: University Press of America, 1984.

Dolan, Jay P. *The American Catholic Experience: A History from Colonial Times to the Present*. Garden City, NY: Doubleday & Company, 1985.

Dumenil, Lynn. *Freemasonry and American Culture 1880–1930*. Princeton, NJ: Princeton University Press, 1984.

Ede, Alfred J. *The Lay Crusade for a Christian America: A Study of the American Federation of Catholic Societies, 1900–1919*. New

York: Garland Publishing, Inc., 1988.

Ellis, John Tracy. *The Life of James Cardinal Gibbons*. Milwaukee: Bruce Publishing Company, 1952.

———, ed. *Documents of American Catholic History*. 2 vols. Wilmington, DE: Michael Glazier, 1987.

Ellis, William E. "Patrick Henry Callahan, A Kentucky Democrat in National Politics," *The Filson Club History Quarterly*. 51 (January 1977):17–30.

———. "Catholicism and the Southern Ethos: The Role of Patrick Henry Callahan." *Catholic Historical Review* LXIX 1 (January 1983):41–50.

Faherty, William B. *Dream by the River: Two Centuries of St. Louisian Catholicism*. St. Louis: Piraeus Publishers, 1973.

Fenton, Joseph C. "The Teaching of Testem Benevolentiae." *American Ecclesiastical Review* 129 (1953): 124–133.

Fogarty, Gerald P. *The Vatican and the Americanist Crisis: Denis J. O'Connell, American Agent in Rome, 1885–1903*. Rome: Gregorian University Press, 1974.

———. *The Vatican and the American Hierarchy, 1870–1965*. Stuttgart: Anton Hiersemann, 1982. Wilmington, DE: Michael Glazier Press, 1985.

———. *American Catholic Biblical Scholarship: A History From the Early Republic to Vatican II*. New York: Harper & Row, 1989.

Foik, Paul J., C.S.C., *Pioneer Catholic Journalism*. New York: The United Sates Catholic Historical Society, 1930.

Gaffey, James P. *Citizen of No Mean City: Archbishop Patrick Riordan of San Francisco (1841–1914)*. San Francisco: Consortium, 1976.

Gannon, Michael. "Before and After Modernism: The Intellectual Isolation of the American Priest." In *The Catholic Priest in the United States*, ed. by John Tracy Ellis. Collegeville, MN: St. John's University Press, 1971.

Gleason, Philip J. *The Conservative Reformers: German-American Catholics and the Social Order*. Notre Dame: University of Notre Dame Press, 1968.

———. "The New Americanism in Catholic Historiography." *U.S. Catholic Historian* (Summer,1993):1–18.

Green, Joseph G. Jr. "Patrick Henry Callahan (1866–1940): The Role of an American Catholic Lay Leader." Ph.D. Dissertation, The Catholic University of America, 1963.

Griener, George E. "Herman Schell and the Reform of the Catholic Church in Germany." *Theological Studies* LIV 3 (September 1993):427–454.

Halsey, William M. *The Survival of American Innocence: Catholicism in an Era of Disillusionment 1920–1940*. Notre Dame: University of Notre Dame Press, 1980.

Hawley, Ellis Wayne. *The Great War and the Search for a Modern Order: A History of the American People and Their Institutions,*

1917–1933. New York: St. Martin's Press, 1979.

Hayward, H.L. and James E. Craig. *A History of Freemasonry*. New York: John Day Co., 1927.

Helmreich, Ernst Christian. *The German Churches under Hitler: Background, Struggle and Epilogue*. Detroit: Wayne State University Press, 1977.

Higham, John. *Strangers in the Land: Patterns of American Nativism, 1860–1925*. New Brunswick: Rutgers University Press, 1955.

Hogan, Peter E. *The Catholic University of America, 1896–1903: The Rectorship of Thomas J. Conaty*. Washington, DC: The Catholic University Press, 1949.

Holden, Vincent F. C.S.P. "A Myth in 'L'Americanisme'," *Catholic Historical Review*. XXXI (July, 1945):154–170.

Hurley, Mark J. *The Unholy Ghost: Anti-Catholicism in the American Experience*. Huntington, IN: Our Sunday Visitor Press, 1992.

Iserloh, Erwin. "Movements within the Church and Their Spirituality." *History of the Church* Volume X ed. Hubert Jedin. New York: Crossroad Publishing Company, 1981.

Jacob, Margaret C. *Living the Enlightenment: Freemasonry and Politics in Eighteenth Century Europe*. New York: Oxford University Press, 1991.

Jorgenson, Lloyd P. "The Oregon School Law of 1922: Passage and Sequel." *Catholic Historical Review* LIV 3 (October 1968): 455–466.

348

Kantowicz, Edward R. *Corporation Sole: Cardinal Mundelein and Chicago Catholicism*. Notre Dame: University of Notre Dame Press, 1983.

Kauffman, Christopher J. *Faith and Fraternalism, 1882–1982: A History of the Knights of Columbus*. New York: Harper & Row, 1982.

———. *Tradition and Transformation in Catholic Culture: The Priests of Saint Sulpice in the United States from 1791 to the Present*. New York: Macmillan Publishing Co., 1988.

Klein, Felix. *Americanism: A Phantom Heresy*. Atchison, Kan: Aquin Book Shop, 1951.

Koehler, Oskar. "The Development of Catholicism in Modern Society." *History of the Church*. Vol. IX, ed. Hubert Jedin. New York: Crossroad Publishing Company, 1981.

Kurtz, Lester R. *The Politics of Heresy: The Modernist Crisis in Roman Catholicism*. Berkeley: University of California Press, 1986.

Lears, T. J. Jackson. *No Place of Grace: Antimodernism and the Transformation of American Culture 1880–1920*. New York: Pantheon Books, 1981.

Lewy, Guenter. *The Catholic Church and Nazi Germany*. New York: McGraw-Hill, 1964.

Lichtman, Allan J. *Prejudice and the Old Politics: The Presidential Election of 1928*. Chapel Hill: The University of North Carolina Press, 1979.

Lill, Rudolf. "The Kulturkampf." *History of the Church*. Vol. IX . ed.

Hubert Jedin. New York: Crossroad Publishing Company, 1981.

Link, Arthur S. and William B Catton. *American Epoch: A History of the United States Since the 1890's*. New York: Alfred Knopf, 1967.

Loome, Thomas M. *Liberal Catholicism, Reform Catholicism, Modernism*. Mainz: Mathias Grunewald Verlag, 1979.

Luebke, Frederick C. *Bonds of Loyalty: German Americans and World War One*. DeKalb: Northern Illinois University Press, 1974.

Maignen, Charles. *Father Hecker: Is He a Saint?* London: Burns & Oates, 1898.

McAvoy, Thomas T. *The Great Crisis in American Catholic History, 1895-1900*. Chicago: Regnery, 1957.

———. "Americanism and Frontier Catholicism." *Review of Politics* V (July, 1943): 275-301.

———. "Americanism, Fact and Fiction." *Catholic Historical Review* XXXI (July, 1945): 133-153.

———. "Liberalism, Americanism. Modernism." *Records of the American Catholic Historical Society of Philadelphia*, LXIII (1953): 225-231.

McKeown, Elizabeth. *War and Welfare: American Catholics and World War I*. New York: Garland Publishing Inc., 1988.

McNamara, Robert F. "Bernard J. McQuaid's Sermon on Theological

'Americanism.'" *Records of the American Catholic Historical Society of Philadelphia*, 90 (1979): 23–32.

McShane, Joseph. *"Sufficiently Radical": Catholicism, Progressivism, and the Bishop's Program of 1919.* Washington, DC: The Catholic University Press, 1986.

Meng, John. "Growing Pains in the American Catholic Church 1880–1908." *Historical Records and Studies* 26 (1947) 17–67.

Moore, R. Laurence. *Religious Outsiders and the Making of Americans*. New York: Oxford University Press, 1986.

Morsey, Rudolf. "Die deutschen Katholiken an der Nationalstaat zwischen Kulturkampf und Ersten Weltkrieg." *Historisches Jahrbuch* 90 (1970):31–64.

Mueller, Franz H. *The Church and the Social Question*. Washington, DC: American Enterprise Institute, 1984.

Mulcahy, Richard E. *The Economics of Heinrich Pesch*. New York: Henry Holt, 1952.

Nickels, Marilyn W. "Thomas Wyatt Turner and the Federated Colored Catholics." *U.S. Catholic Historian* 7 Numbers 2 & 3 (Spring/Summer 1988):215–232.

Nuesse, C. Joseph. *The Catholic University of America: A Centennial History*. Washington, DC: The Catholic University Press, 1990.

———. "Thomas Joseph Bouquillon (1840–1902) Moral Theologian and Precursor of the Social Sciences in the Catholic University of

America." *Catholic Historical Review* LXXII 4 (October, 1986): 601–619.

O'Brien, David J. *American Catholics and Social Reform: The New Deal Years*. New York: Oxford University Press, 1968.

———. *Public Catholicism*. New York: Macmillan Publishing Company, 1989.

Ochs, Stephen J. *Desegregating the Altar: The Josephites and the Struggle for Black Priests 1871–1960*. Baton Rouge: Louisiana State University, 1990.

O'Connell, Marvin R. *John Ireland and the American Catholic Church*. St. Paul, MN: The Minnesota Historical Society Press, 1988.

———. *Critics on Trial: An Introduction to the Catholic Modernist Crisis*. Washington, D.C.: The Catholic University of America Press, 1994.

Offner, John. "Washington Mission: Archbishop Ireland on the Eve of the Spanish-American War." *Catholic Historical Review* LXXIII 4 (October, 1987):562–575.

O'Meara, Thomas F. *Church and Culture in German Catholic Theology, 1860–1914*. Notre Dame: University of Notre Dame Press, 1991.

O'Toole, James M. *Militant and Triumphant: William Henry O'Connell and the Catholic Church in Boston, 1859–1944*. Notre Dame: University of Notre Dame Press, 1992.

Pallen, Condè B. *What Is Liberalism?* St. Louis: B. Herder, 1899.

Pies, Timothy Mark. "The Parochial School Campaigns in Michigan, 1920–24: The Lutheran and Catholic Involvement." *Catholic Historical Review* LXXII 2 (April,1986): 222–238.

Portier, William L. "The Future of Americanism" and "Two Generations of American Catholic Expansionism in Europe: Isaac Hecker and John J. Keane," In *Rising From History* ed. Robert J. Daly. Lanham, MD: University Press of America, 1987.

–––. "Modernism in the United States: The Case of John R. Slattery (1851–1926)." Unpublished ms.

Poulat, Emile. *Integrisme et Catholicisme Integral: Un reseau secret international antimoderniste: La "Sapiniere"(1909–1921).* Casterman, 1969.

Preuss, Arthur. *The Fundamental Fallacy of Socialism.* St. Louis: B. Herder, 1908.

–––. *Studies in American Freemasonry.* St. Louis: B. Herder, 1908.

Prucha, Francis P. *The Churches and the Indian Schools 1888–1912.* Lincoln, NE: University of Nebraska Press, 1949.

Reher, Margaret Mary. "Pope Leo XIII and 'Americanism'." *Theological Studies* 34 (1973): 679–689.

–––."Americanism and Modernism –Continuity or Discontinuity?" *U.S. Catholic Historian* 1 (1980–81):87–103.

–––."Americanism and the Signs of the Times: A Response to Portier, Wangler and Ayers." in *Rising From History.* ed.

Robert Daly. Lanham,MD: University Press of America, 1987.

———. *Catholic Intellectual Life in America: A Historical Study of Persons and Movements*. New York: Macmillan, 1988.

Reuter, Frank T. *Catholic Influence on American Colonial Policies*. Austin: University of Texas Press, 1967.

Rothensteiner, John E. "A Sketch of Catholic Journalism in St. Louis." *Pastoralblatt* 58 (June 1924): 81–93.

Scholder, Klaus. *The Churches and the Third Reich*. Vol. I *Preliminary History and the Time of Illusions 1918–1934*. Frankfurt: Verlag Ullstein, 1977; Philadelphia: Fortress Press, 1988.

Schultenover, David G. *A View From Rome: On the Eve of the Modernist Crisis*. New York: Fordham University Press, 1993.

Shannon, David A. *Twentieth Century America* Vol. I *The Progressive Era*. Chicago: Rand McNally & Company, 1969.

Shelley, Thomas J. "The Oregon School Case and the National Catholic Welfare Conference." *Catholic Historical Review* LXXV 3 (July 1989):439–457.

———. "John Cardinal Farley and Modernism in New York." *Church History* 61 (September 1992) :350–361.

———. "'What the Hell is an Encyclical?': Governor Alfred E. Smith, Charles C. Marshall, Esq., and Father Francis P. Duffy." *U.S. Catholic Historian* 15 (Spring 1997):87–107.

Silva, Ruth C. *Rum, Religion, and Votes: 1928 Reexamined*. University

Park, PA: Penn State University Press, 1962.

Slawson, Douglas J. "The Attitudes and Activities of American Catholics Regarding the Proposals to Establish a Federal Department of Education between World War I and the Great Depression," Ph.D. diss., The Catholic University of America, 1981.

―――. *The Foundation and First Decade of the National Catholic Welfare Council.* Washington, DC: The Catholic University of Press, 1992.

Sperber, Jonathan. *Popular Catholicism in Nineteenth-Century Germany.* Princeton: Princeton University Press, 1984.

Storch, Neil T. "John Ireland's Americanism After 1899: The Argument from History." *Church History* 51 (December, 1982):434–444.

Sullivan, Mark. *Our Times: The United States, 1900–1925.* 5 vols. New York: Scribners, 1933.

Sweeney, David F. "Hermann Schell, 1850–1906: A German Dimension to the Americanist Controversy." *Catholic Historical Review* LXXVI 1 (January, 1990):44–70.

Taves, Anne. *The Household of Faith: Roman Catholic Devotions in Mid-Nineteenth Century America.* Notre Dame: University of Notre Dame Press, 1986.

Thomas, Samuel J. "The American Periodical Press and the Apostolic Letter Testem Benevolentiae." *Catholic Historical Review* LXII 2 (July, 1976):408–423.

Thompson, David. *Europe Since Napoleon.* London: Longmanns,1986.

Timpe, Georg. *Katholisches Deutschtum in den Vereinigten Staaten von Amerika*. Freiburg: Herder, 1937.

Trommler, Frank and Joseph McVeigh, *America and the Germans: An Assessment of a Three-Hundred Year History* Volume II: *The Relationship in the Twentieth Century*. Philadelphia: University of Pennsylvania Press, 1985.

Wangler, Thomas E. "John Ireland's Emergence as a Liberal Catholic and Americanist, 1875–1887," *Records of the American Catholic Historical Society of Philadelphia* (1970):67–82.

———."The Birth of Americanism:'Westward the Apocalyptic Candlestick'." *Harvard Theological Review* 65 (1972):415–436.

———. "The Emergence of John J. Keane as a Liberal Catholic and Americanist (1878–1887)." *American Ecclesiastical Review* 166 (1972): 457–478.

———. "The Americanism of J. St. Clair Etheridge." *Records of the American Catholic Historical Society of Philadelphia* 86 (1975):88–105.

———. "American Catholic Expansionism." *Harvard Theological Review* 75 (1982):369–393.

———. "Myth, Worldviews and Late Nineteenth Century American Catholic Expansionism." In *Rising From History*. Lanham, MD: University Press of America, 1987.

———. "Americanist Beliefs and Papal Orthodoxy." *U.S. Catholic Historian* XI 3 (Summer, 1993):37–52.

Willging, Eugene P. and Herta Hatzfeld. *Catholic Serials of the Nineteenth Century in the United States*. Washington, DC: The Catholic University Press, 1965.

Wittke, Carl. *The German Language Press in America*. Frankfort, KY: University of Kentucky Press, 1957.

Young, Arthur Nichols. *The Single Tax Movement in the United States*. Princeton: Princeton University Press, 1916.

Zivojinovic, Dragan R. *The United States and the Vatican Policies, 1914–1918*. Boulder: Colorado Associated University Press, 1978.

Zwierlein, Frederick J. *Theodore Roosevelt and Catholics, 1882–1919*. Rochester, NY: Art Print Shop, 1956.

Index

New German-American Studies
Neue Deutsch-Amerikanische Studien

This series features scholarly monographs, published in German or English, that deal with topics in the humanities or social sciences pertaining to the German-American experience.

Original monographs in the following areas are welcome: history, literature, language, politics, philosophy, religion, education, geography, art and architecture, music and musical life, the theater, and contemporary issues of general interest.

All inquiries should be directed to the Editor of the series. Manuscripts should be between two and four hundred pages in length and prepared in accordance with the Chicago Manual of Style.

For additional information, contact the editor:

Dr. Don Heinrich Tolzmann
Langsam Library M.L. 33
University of Cincinnati
Cincinnati, OH 45221